Accommodating Rising Powers

As the world enters the third decade of the twenty-first century, far-reaching changes are likely to occur. China, Russia, India, and Brazil, and perhaps others, are likely to emerge as contenders for global leadership roles. War as a system-changing mechanism is unimaginable, given that it would escalate into nuclear conflict and the destruction of the planet. It is therefore essential that policymakers in established as well as rising states devise strategies to allow transitions without resorting to war, but dominant theories of International Relations contend that major changes in the system are generally possible only through violent conflict. This volume asks whether peaceful accommodation of rising powers is possible in the changed international context, especially against the backdrop of intensified globalization. With the aid of historic cases, it argues that peaceful change is possible through effective long-term strategies on the part of both status quo and rising powers.

T. V. PAUL is James McGill Professor of International Relations in the Department of Political Science at McGill University. He is the author or editor of sixteen books and over sixty scholarly articles and book chapters in the fields of International Relations, International Security, and South Asia, including *International Relations Theory and Regional Transformation* (Cambridge, 2012) and *Asymmetric Conflicts: War Initiation by Weaker Powers* (Cambridge, 1994).

Accommodating Rising Powers

Past, Present, and Future

Edited by

T.V. Paul

McGill University

CAMBRIDGE
UNIVERSITY PRESS

CAMBRIDGE
UNIVERSITY PRESS

University Printing House, Cambridge CB2 8BS, United Kingdom

Cambridge University Press is part of the University of Cambridge.

It furthers the University's mission by disseminating knowledge in the pursuit of education, learning and research at the highest international levels of excellence.

www.cambridge.org
Information on this title: www.cambridge.org/9781107592230

© Cambridge University Press 2016

First published 2016

Printed in the United States of America by Sheridan Books, Inc.

A catalogue record for this publication is available from the British Library

Library of Congress Cataloguing in Publication data
Accommodating rising powers past, present, and future / edited by T.V. Paul, McGill University.
    pages   cm
Includes bibliographical references and index.
ISBN 978-1-107-13404-1 – ISBN 978-1-107-59223-0 (paperback)
1. Middle powers.   2. World politics – 20th century.   3. World politics – 21st century.   4. Middle powers – Case studies.   5. World politics – 20th century – Case studies.   6. World politics – 21st century – Case studies.   I. Paul, T. V.
JC364.A33   2016
327.09172'4 – dc23   2015023772

ISBN 978-1-107-13404-1 Hardback
ISBN 978-1-107-59223-0 Paperback

Contents

Figures

Contributors

MLADA BUKOVANSKI is Professor of Government, Smith College.

MARTIN CLAAR is a PhD student at Northern Illinois University.

NICOLA CONTESSI is a Postdoctoral Research Scholar at the Harriman Institute at Columbia University.

JOHN A. HALL is James McGill Professor of Sociology, McGill University.

KAI HE is Associate Professor, Griffith Asia Institute, Griffith University, Nathan, Australia.

STEVEN E. LOBELL is Professor, Department of Political Science, University of Utah.

LORENZ M. LÜTHI is Associate Professor, History Department, McGill University.

DAVID R. MARES is Professor and Chair of the Americas Chair for Inter-American Affairs, Department of Political Science, University of California, San Diego.

THEODORE MCLAUCHLIN is Assistant Professor, Department of Political Science, Université de Montréal.

T.V. PAUL is James McGill Professor of International Relations, Department of Political Science, McGill University.

KRZYSZTOF J. PELC is William Dawson Scholar and Associate Professor, Department of Political Science, McGill University.

PHILIP B.K. POTTER is Assistant Professor, Department of Politics, University of Michigan.

NORRIN M. RIPSMAN is Professor, Department of Political Science, Concordia University.

ASEEMA SINHA is Wagener Family Associate Professor of Comparative Politics, Claremont McKenna College.

JEFFREY W. TALIAFERRO is Associate Professor, Department of Political Science, Tufts University.

ALI ZEREN is a PhD student in the Department of Sociology, McGill University.

Acknowledgments

This volume resulted from a workshop I organized at McGill University on November 2, 2013 as part of the team project on *Globalization and the Changing National Security State*, with colleagues John A. Hall, Frédéric Mérand, Vincent Pouliot, and Norrin M. Ripsman. The project is funded by *Fonds québécois de recherche sur la société et la culture* (FQRSC). Incisive comments by Mark Brawley, James Der Derian, Miles Kahler, Theodore McLauchlin, and Vincent Pouliot at the workshop, and by Kahler at a subsequent International Studies Association (ISA) annual conference panel in New Orleans in February 2015, helped in revisions of the chapters. Suggestions by the reviewers at Cambridge University Press and remarks gathered at the various universities at which I presented the introductory chapter, in Australia, Canada, Europe, India, and Japan, have helped to sharpen the arguments. Jean-François Bélanger provided able and dedicated research assistance. Thanks also go to John Haslam, editor at Cambridge University Press, for his interest in the project. I also acknowledge my family's support.

Part I

Mechanisms of accommodation

1   The accommodation of rising powers in world politics

T. V. Paul

The year 2014 witnessed a dramatic upsurge of territorial challenges by Russia in Ukraine and by China in the East and South China Seas, bringing back fears of renewed great power conflicts and rivalries after two decades of relative calm. The need to understand the rising power phenomenon has become all the more urgent in today's world, as the potential for violence is high in both these theaters. 2014 also marked the 100th anniversary of the onset of World War I (WWI). The quick rise of China, a resurgent Russia, and potentially an empowered India and Brazil have brought forward the question of peaceful power transitions in the international system, reminding statesmen of the need not to repeat the mistakes of the twentieth century. China especially has been growing rapidly in both economic and military terms and is poised to replace the United States as the number one national economy in the next decade, while India is expected to reach third position in less than two decades, and possibly second by the middle of the century.[1] Even with lower growth rates than projected, these countries will still be leading economies in the decades to come. In the past, the great economic strength of rising powers led to great military strength, which encouraged them to engage in armed contest with established powers. It is yet to be seen if the current era's rising powers will follow this historical pattern. Although they are unlikely to replace the United States as the preponderant military power in the foreseeable future, it is likely that in the twenty-first century different types of power resources may be vital to claiming global leadership roles.[2] Military strength is unlikely to be the only key source of higher status, as different status markers could be

---

[1] National Intelligence Council, *Global Trends 2030: Alternative Worlds*. Available at: www.dni.gov/index.php/about/organization/national-intelligence-council-global-trends. See also *BRICS and Beyond*, Goldman Sachs, 2007, p. 11. Available at: www.goldmansachs.com/our-thinking/archive/archive-pdfs/brics-book/brics-full-book.pdf.

[2] On different forms of power in the twenty-first century, see Joseph S. Nye Jr., *The Future of Power* (New York: Public Affairs, 2011).

used by states to claim leadership positions.[3] Going by this perspective, the accommodation of these rising powers into meaningful international roles may be necessary to obtain a peaceful international order. Even if the rising powers do not challenge the existing order through war, protracted conflicts and crises could occur, as we are already witnessing in East Asia and Ukraine. Disagreements over global governance, as well as spheres of influence, could generate much discord and uncertainty, compromising solutions to collective action problems; consider the inability of the leading states to achieve consensus on a new global free trade agreement or a climate control regime. In fact, countries like China, India, and Brazil have successfully blocked many initiatives in the trade liberalization and climate change areas – initiatives proposed by the United States and other Western countries – while Russia has successfully stopped Washington from launching military action or sanctions against Syria and Iran with UN approval.

This volume is guided by a central concern for major power accommodation and war prevention in the twenty-first century. It seeks to explore, with the aid of historic cases, whether, and when, peaceful accommodation of rising powers works against the conditions that generate intense rivalry and conflict. The central argument is that though structural conditions can lead to conflict, proper synchronization of strategies for peaceful change by established and rising powers can mitigate the possibilities of violent conflict.

What is accommodation?

Accommodation in international relations at the great power level involves mutual adaptation and acceptance by established and rising powers, and the elimination or substantial reduction of hostility between them. The process of accommodation in international politics is exceptionally complicated, as it involves status adjustment, the sharing of leadership roles through the accordance of institutional membership and privileges, and acceptance of spheres of influence: something established powers rarely offer to newcomers. Accommodation is viewed by some as the creation of "sustained peace" or "deep peace" among major power actors, akin to the "warm peace" described by Kenneth Boulding.[4] Others have categorized three types of order: "war, cold peace (stability based on competition and mutual deterrence), or warm peace (stability

---

[3] Deborah Welch Larson, T.V. Paul, and William C. Wohlforth, "Status and World Order," in *Status in World Politics*, eds. T.V. Paul, Deborah Welch Larson and William C. Wohlforth (Cambridge: Cambridge University Press, 2014), chapter 1.

[4] Kenneth E. Boulding, *Stable Peace* (Austin: University of Texas Press, 1978), 43.

based on cooperation and mutual reassurance)."[5] All of them involve some form of accommodation.

Accommodation as conceptualized in this project is more than the achievement of stability or absence of war, as unequal powers could be at peace without their status being adjusted. It is also feasible to consider accommodation among rivals as one great power viewing the other as a legitimate stakeholder and conceding to it a certain amount of global and regional power status, as well as a sphere of influence, even though they might not be close friends or allies. The accommodation of a rising power simply implies that the emerging power is given the status and perks associated with the rank of great power in the international system, which includes in many instances a recognition of its sphere of influence, or the decision not to challenge it militarily. It does not assume deep friendship or lack of competition. If competition leads to intense conflict and war, it is not a peaceful accommodation, as the rising power has not been accommodated peacefully, nor it is willing to play by mutually acceptable norms and rules.

Accommodation at the international level involves the accommodated state obtaining a larger share of global governance rights, and/or spheres of influence, and being contented with it. It is more than simple reconciliation, because temporary reconciliation need not last if the reconciled power becomes unhappy with the order. In the long run, accommodation may involve the replacement of the dominant power by the rising power, or substantial sharing of positional rights and obligations but without war and intense rivalry. In the contemporary world, accommodation has become more complicated, as smaller states are able to resist legally and militarily, in some instances through asymmetric means, the efforts by a rising power or a status quo power to maintain or redraw spheres of influence.

Accommodation of different categories of state can take place at different levels, as only a handful of countries are great power candidates at any given time. *Full accommodation* at the global level involves the recognition of a rising power's position in a leadership role in the conduct of international politics in both security and economic areas, through appropriate status recognition within global institutions and consultative mechanisms where its voice is given substantial weight among its peers. This also implies the rising power gaining acceptance for the affairs of its sphere of influence. A key example is the United Kingdom

---

[5] Charles A. Kupchan, "Introduction: Explaining Peaceful Power Transition," in *Power in Transition: The Peaceful Change of International Order*, eds. Charles A. Kupchan, Emanuel Adler, Jean-Marc Coicaud, and Yuen Foong Khong (Tokyo: United Nations University Press, 2001), 6.

accommodating the United States in the late nineteenth and early twentieth centuries. The rising power here possessed many parameters of global power status and was a potential or actual global challenger to the established order. *Partial or limited accommodation* may be focused on institutional, as opposed to economic or military, reconciliation. For instance, the USSR was institutionally accommodated by the United States and its allies in the postwar era, but not economically. The Soviets adopted the same approach vis-à-vis the United States and its allies. Militarily, both were superpowers, forcing them to accommodate each other by way of their exclusive spheres of influence. But each refused to accommodate the other in economic and ideological terms, and their containment strategies precluded extensive cooperation. United States-created institutions such as the World Bank (WB) and the International Monetary Fund (IMF) had no Soviet membership and the Soviet-sponsored Council for Mutual Economic Assistance (COMECON) had no Western presence. The United States recognizing China in the 1970s and according it UN Security Council membership, as well as opening up its market to Beijing, is also an example of partial accommodation.

Non-accommodation at the global level is when a rising power with most of the material parameters of great power status is largely ignored in the conduct of international governance and is given little or no recognition at international forums or bilateral exchanges. In fact, it might be a target of sanctions, and to some extent ridicule, by the established powers, due to its current or past behavior. Defeated Germany after WWI falls into this category, as does Japan during the interwar period. The People's Republic of China (PRC) until 1972 also represents a case. *Symbolic accommodation* would constitute the giving of some measures of accommodation by an established power to a rising power. The United States' symbolic accommodation of India since 2005 constitutes such an example. Symbolic accommodation may be the precursor to substantive accommodation in the future. *Region-specific accommodation* is also possible, where a rising power is given primacy in a specific region, but not at the global level. In some sense, the rising powers of today – India, Brazil, and South Africa – constitute three examples of regional accommodation, though they would like to accrue more global recognition in key decision-making areas. Some of this may involve specific areas where the rising power has particular interests and strength. Thus, Brazil may be a good candidate for accommodation in the areas that it has most interest in; that is, global financial institutions and other UN forums, such as those dealing with climate change. Not all states have the wherewithal or the resolve to be recognized as great powers, and indeed very few make the cut to obtain the pinnacle of leadership roles. Hence, historic accommodations may not be good examples for today's world, as some of the current aspiring countries (except China, and potentially India) do not have material or other capabilities for obtaining great power status in the next two decades. But in the longer term of three to four decades, this could change, as they make economic, technological, and military advances.

One thing is clear from international history: non-violent accommodation is a rare event, as rising powers are often not peacefully integrated by established powers. As a rising power reaches a certain capability threshold, it is often tempted to search for higher status through wars, or to alter the existing order through military conflicts and crises. However, there can be a time lag involved in a country's achieving economic wealth and expanding its larger political and military interests abroad, due largely to domestic political constraints.[6] In the past, established powers responded to rising powers' demands for status adjustment with policies such as preventive war, containment, bandwagoning, binding, engagement, and distancing/buck-passing.[7]

Theories and accommodation

Historically, wars have been the major propellants of structural change and status accommodation in the international system. Not surprisingly, dominant International Relations (IR) theories contend that major changes in the system are generally possible only through violent conflicts. For example, power transition and hegemonic stability theories contend that war is the principal agent through which systemic changes occur in international politics, whereby one global leader replaces another.[8] Gilpin, in his masterly work, argues that the fundamental nature of international politics has not changed over the millennia. Because of the changing economic and military capabilities of major states, the differential growth of power generates unevenness in the international system. The shifting balance of power weakens the existing order, and the rising powers will find it rational to contest the order militarily through expansion until the marginal costs are greater than the benefits they gain from

---

[6] On the US case, see Fareed Zakaria, *From Wealth to Power: The Unusual Origins of America's World Role* (Princeton: Princeton University Press, 1998).

[7] For these, see Randall L. Schweller, "Managing the Rise of Great Powers: History and Theory," in Alastair Iain Johnston and Robert S. Ross, eds., *Engaging China: The Management of an Emerging Power* (London: Routledge, 1999), chapter 1.

[8] A.F.K. Organski, *World Politics* (New York, Knopf, 1958); Jacek Kugler and Douglas Lemke, eds., *Parity and War* (Ann Arbor: The University of Michigan Press, 1996).

such a policy.[9] Marxist and class-based theories have assigned enormous importance to imperial struggles as the cause for system-wide changes.[10] Similarly, long cycle and world system theorists believe in the necessity of war for major change to occur.[11] While many historical power transitions and accommodations in the modern international system occurred through wars and postwar settlements, which often favored the winners, will history repeat itself or will we have a more peaceful power transition in the emerging international context?

The main reason for structural theories to argue that power transitions and subsequent status accommodations of rising powers occur only through war is the notion of power structure being characterized by persistence and continuity. Changes occur only when violent tumults take place in the system that affect the power distribution among major power actors. Indeed, many transitions in the past occurred through war, as major wars provided the catalyst for new powers to emerge. Yet, war is not the only source of change in world politics, as the end of the Cold War powerfully attests. Additionally, structural theories suffer from determinism, as they do not provide much guidance for policymakers on how to avoid war and obtain peaceful change. Power transition theories also tend to focus on dyadic interactions while ignoring third parties and their role in generating great power conflicts, or preventing them as members of balancing coalitions or war alliances.

All this suggests that IR theory is weak in explaining or predicting peaceful change. Very few of the classic IR texts talk about peaceful transformation. An exception is *The Twenty Years' Crisis* by the pioneering English scholar, E.H. Carr, who argued: "The problem of 'peaceful change in national politics' is how to effect necessary and desirable changes without revolution and, in international politics, how to effect

[9] Robert Gilpin, *War and Change in World Politics* (Princeton: Princeton University Press, 1981). Recently, John J. Mearsheimer picks up the same argument in his book *The Tragedy of Great Power Politics*, updated edn. (New York: W.W. Norton, 2014).

[10] John A. Hobson, *Imperialism: A Study* (London: Allen & Unwin, 1902); Vladimir I. Lenin, *Imperialism: The Highest Stage of Capitalism* (New York: International Publishers, 1939); Joseph A. Schumpeter, *Capitalism, Socialism and Democracy*, (New York: Harper and Brothers, 1947).

[11] Manus I. Midlarsky, *On War: Political Violence in the International System* (New York: The Free Press, 1975); Immanuel Wallerstein, *The Capitalist World-Economy* (Cambridge: Cambridge University Press, 1984); George Modelski, *Long Cycles in World Politics* (London: Macmillan, 1987); Karen A. Rasler and William R. Thompson, *The Great Powers and Global Struggle: 1490–1990* (Lexington: University Press of Kentucky, 1994); Dale C. Copeland, *The Origins of Major War: Hegemonic Rivalry and the Fear of Decline* (Ithaca: Cornell University Press, 2001). For a counter view, see Charles F. Doran, *The Politics of Assimilation: Hegemony and its Aftermath* (Baltimore: Johns Hopkins University Press, 1971).

such changes without war."[12] He exhorted Great Britain and other dominant powers of the time:

The defence of [the] status quo is not a policy which can be lastingly successful. It will end in war as surely as rigid conservatism will end in revolution. "Resistance to aggression," however necessary as a momentary device of national policy, is no solution; for readiness to fight to prevent change is just as unmoral as readiness to fight to enforce it. To establish methods of peaceful change is therefore the fundamental problem of international morality and of international politics.[13]

In recent years, a few theorists have attempted to map out peaceful change and status accommodation. Charles Kupchan lists three conditions that characterize peaceful transition. Firstly, the "hegemon and rising challenger must engage in a sustained process of strategic restraint and mutual accommodation that ultimately enables them to view one another as benign polities." Secondly, "peaceful transition emerges from ideational contestation when hegemon and rising challenger succeed in fashioning agreement on the outlines of a new international order." And finally, "peaceful transition depends not just on the ability of the hegemon and the rising contender to forge agreement on order, but also on their ability to legitimate that order."[14] The problem is that these conditions are rather stringent, and it is unlikely they will meet the emerging dynamics between the United States and China, for instance.

More concretely, Stephen Rock hypothesizes three conditions for the emergence of peace among all categories of states: when states are "heterogeneous in the exercise of national power," "heterogeneous in their economic activities," and "homogenous in their societal attributes." These conditions imply that peace is possible (in our context, among rising and established powers) if state objectives and interests minimally collide, if they produce and export different commodities and services, and if they have somewhat similar political and social cultures, as well as ideological approaches.[15] The big challenge in an era of economic

---

[12] E.H. Carr, *The Twenty Years' Crisis, 1919–1939*, reprint edn. (New York: Harper and Row, 1964), 209. See also E.H. Carr, *International Relations since the Peace Treaties* (London; Macmillan, 1937). Few others during the interwar period wrote about the need for peaceful accommodations. In particular, see Frederick Sherwood Dunn, *Peaceful Change: A Study of International Procedures* (New York: Council on Foreign Relations, 1937); C.A.W. Manning, *Peaceful Change: An International Problem*, new edn. (New York: Garland Publishing, 1972).

[13] Carr, *The Twenty Years' Crisis*, 222.   [14] Kupchan, "Introduction," 8–9.

[15] Stephen R. Rock, *Why Peace Breaks Out: Great Power Rapprochement in Historical Perspective* (Chapel Hill: The University of North Carolina Press, 1989), 12–15. Scholars who work in the area of enduring rivalries also offer ideas for conditions that produce peaceful accommodation. For instance, see Paul F. Diehl and Gary Goertz, *War and Peace in International Rivalry* (Ann Arbor: University of Michigan Press, 2000); Karen

globalization is that state interests in the political and economic realms could collide, and countries and corporations could compete in the same economic domains. Moreover, rapid wealth creation may encourage major powers to disregard the principles of free and fair trade. Great powers are generally ones with global interests, though their regional interests might be different from their global interests, and as such they may not exercise power in a heterogeneous fashion. It is also unlikely that regime compatibility among great powers is achievable, however desirable it might be. The question, then, is how to fashion an international order in which different types of rising powers and dominant actors can co-exist and reduce points of tension while recognizing each other's power and status aspirations.

Despite the occasional foray into peaceful change by a handful of scholars like the ones just listed, mainstream IR theories are yet to focus on peaceful change vigorously or offer the conditions under which a rising power is admitted to the rank of major power, even if it is a rival of the established powers. Hence, their prescriptions for peaceful change seem inadequate. In spite of this general weakness in IR, many relevant ideas for change and accommodation exist, and they can be gleaned from the core positions of these theories on relations among major power actors.

War avoidance strategies in realism

Realist theories rarely talk about peaceful power transitions or the accommodation of rising powers. There is a status quo bias in realism (and, for that matter, in strands of liberalism and constructivism as well), as scholars often unwittingly follow the political calculations of dominant states, especially those of the most powerful Anglo-Saxon countries, Great Britain and the United States, which have been the leading global powers for the past century, or more in the British case. However, the key mechanism in realism for accommodation or containment can be located in the balance of power. To realists, balance of power considerations can lead dominant powers to accommodate a rising power, as the United

Rasler, William R. Thompson, and Sumit Ganguly, *How Rivalries End* (Philadelphia: University of Pennsylvania Press, 2013). Some other pertinent works include: Richard Ned Lebow and Thomas Rise-Kappen, eds., *International Relations Theory and the End of the Cold War* (New York: Columbia University Press, 1995); Jeffrey T. Checkel, *Ideas and International Political Change* (New Haven: Yale University Press, 1997); David A. Welch, *Painful Choices: A Theory of Policy Change* (Princeton: Princeton University Press, 2005), Jeffrey W. Legro, *Rethinking the World: Great Power Strategies and International Order* (Ithaca: Cornell University Press, 2005); Benjamin Miller, *States, Nations, and the Great Powers: The Sources of Regional War and Peace* (Cambridge: Cambridge Uiversity Press, 2007).

States did with China in the 1970s, and Great Britain with the United States in the late nineteenth century. In both these cases, a common enemy or potential rival was needed, against which the interests of the powers could converge. Conversely, balance of power considerations can keep a rising power at bay. For, though realism assumes that material power capabilities change among the leading actors, and that competition for power inevitably leads to conflict among rising and established powers, it has avoided the question of change without war. However, realism offers prescriptions for war avoidance among great powers that are often based on three strategies: balance of power, containment, and deterrence. Status quo states are expected to follow these strategies to prevent the rise of a challenger to the existing international order. If a challenger arises, war or threat of war may become necessary to restore the balance and peace itself. These coercive strategies assume that a threatening state can be dissuaded from starting a war if the costs of war are made higher than the benefits. When balance of power exists, stability is maintained, as no single actor will become so powerful that it engages in aggressive behavior and resorts to system-changing wars.[16]

The containment strategy is predicated on the assumption that a challenger can be restrained through different coercive mechanisms, including economic and political deprivation and military denial.[17] The logic of deterrence is that a challenging state can be prevented from initiating war if the costs of an attack are made higher than the benefits through a threat of retaliatory attack or denial of victory.[18] These strategies are meant to preserve the system and the positions of the status quo powers. They do not address the possibility that the material capacities of the dominant power might decline and that it might not be able to achieve balancing or deterrence continuously to prevent the rising power from emerging as a system-challenging lead actor.

Moreover, the single-minded pursuit of balance of power and containment, as well as deterrence, can produce vicious conflicts in the international system. Implementation of these strategies may be viewed

---

[16] For some very interesting chapters on the failure of balance of power, see Jeffrey W. Taliaferro, Norrin M. Ripsman, and Steven E. Lobell, eds., *The Challenge of Grand Strategy: The Great Powers and the Broken Balance between the World Wars* (Cambridge: Cambridge University Press, 2012).

[17] George F. Kennan, "The Sources of Soviet Conduct," *Foreign Affairs* 65, no. 4 (July 1947), 852–68; John Lewis Gaddis, *Strategies of Containment* (New York: Columbia University Press, 1982).

[18] Glenn H. Snyder, *Deterrence and Defense: Deterrence and Defense Toward a Theory of National Security* (Princeton: Princeton University Press, 1961); Thomas C. Schelling, *Arms and Influence* (New Haven: Yale University Press, 1966); Patrick M. Morgan, *Deterrence: A Conceptual Analysis* (Beverly Hills: Sage, 1983).

as highly threatening by some challengers, forcing them to engage in protracted conflicts, subsystemic wars, or preventive warfare. In fact, balance of power strategies have been blamed for causing major wars in Europe.[19] Deterrence can be perceived as provocative and aggressive by a challenger, and it may resort to a preventive strike, as with the US deterrence strategy toward Japan prior to World War II (WWII), which was seen by the latter as highly threatening.[20] Even if deterrence succeeds initially, when a challenger finds the status quo unbearable war is likely to break out. A single-minded pursuit of deterrence thus does not necessarily guarantee peaceful change, though it could buy time in terms of war avoidance. Moreover, deterrence theorists have largely refrained from discussing change in their analysis. Theories of mutual deterrence thus assume that if capabilities are maintained at sufficient levels, and threats of punishment or denial of victory are credible to opponents, the preservation of the status quo is possible.

In the post-1945 world, nuclear weapons have played a major role in realist understandings of the preservation of the status quo. There is also a belief that mutually assured destruction (MAD) has been robust and will prevent the outbreak of major cataclysmic wars, especially initiated by rising powers. However, it is still possible that rising powers will emerge without fear of being attacked by established powers under conditions of nuclear deterrence. Further, a declining power can give up its dominant status under the protection offered by nuclear weapons, as the Soviet Union did in the 1990s. This logic, however, has some problems, as it assumes that the possession of a particular weapons system can lead to peaceful change. Although it is arguable that nuclear weapons would force adversaries to behave more cautiously, it does not logically follow that nuclear opponents would inevitably settle their conflict. Given its nuclear arsenal, the Soviet Union could have continued the Cold War for much longer if it had wished to do so. In fact, some theorists during the Cold War era believed in the robustness of nuclear deterrence and the continuation of the bipolar system for a long time to come (e.g., Kenneth Waltz).[21] Probably more than nuclear deterrence, it was the fear of losing economic competitiveness that prompted the Soviet leader Mikhail Gorbachev to introduce reforms that eventually undid the USSR. The Cold War era saw high levels of conflict in the developing world, and many crises were hyped up by the superpowers in the name of

---

[19] Hedley Bull, *The Anarchical Society: A Study of Order in World Politics* (New York: Columbia University Press, 1977).

[20] Alexander L. George, *Forceful Persuasion: Coercive Diplomacy as an Alternative to War* (Washington, DC: United States Institute of Peace Press, 1991).

[21] Kenneth N. Waltz, *Theory of International Politics* (New York: Random House, 1979), chapter eight.

bipolar stability. Thus, under conditions of MAD and nuclear umbrellas the international arena can witness much chaos and crisis, with leading states engaging in conflict behavior, especially in the so-called peripheral regions of the world.

Liberal prescriptions

The contending paradigm to realism, *liberalism*, treats peaceful change more effectively. Various perspectives under this school locate the sources of peaceful change in international institutions and regimes, interdependence among major actors, democratic norms, and the creation of a liberal international economic order.[22] John Ikenberry, in particular, has argued that peaceful international orders can be created by a liberal leader like the United States if it is successful in binding other powers in a constitution-like arrangement within the framework of international institutions.[23] Proper institutional mechanisms can provide collective security to states and allow gradual change, thereby averting the need for war. Similarly, great powers interlinked by their democratic political order are unlikely to wage power transition wars against each other. They have democratic norms and institutional mechanisms to settle disputes. Moreover, democracies can develop a cultural affinity toward one another. From this perspective, a democracy and a non-democracy pitted against each other could be the biggest source of power transition conflict. Dominant democracies need not accommodate non-democratic challengers and vice versa. However, the larger context of strategy for change by the leading actors is often given less prominence in these liberal theories. In practice, especially in recent years, liberal states have shown conflicting tendencies to use unlimited force to compel others – especially weaker regional challengers – to follow their lead, or to show excessive restraint, emphasizing non-intervention and moderation; this creates a legitimacy deficit for these states.[24]

---

[22] Richard N. Rosecrance, *The Rise of the Trading State: Commerce and Conquest in the Modern World* (New York: Basic Books, 1986); Robert O. Keohane and Joseph S. Nye Jr., *Power and Interdependence*, 2 edn. (New York: Harper Collins, 1989); Bruce Russett, *Grasping the Democratic Peace: Principles for a Post-Cold War World* (Princeton: Princeton University Press, 1993); John M. Owen, *Liberal Peace, Liberal War: American Politics and International Security* (Ithaca: Cornell University Press, 1997); Bruce Russett and John R. Oneal, *Triangulating Peace: Democracy, Interdependence and International Organizations* (New York: W.W. Norton, 2001).

[23] G. John Ikenberry, *After Victory: Institutions, Strategic Restraint, and the Rebuilding of Order after Major Wars* (Princeton: Princeton University Press, 2001). See also Mark R. Brawley, *Afterglow or Adjustment* (New York: Columbia University Press, 1999).

[24] Georg Sorensen, *A Liberal World Order in Crisis: Choosing Between Imposition and Restraint* (Ithaca: Cornell University Press, 2011).

Ideas, norms, and peaceful change

The third dominant IR paradigm, *constructivism*, is yet to produce a theory on power transitions, though its main focus on ideas and security communities could be applied to the problem at hand. Constructivist ideas on change are useful in understanding peaceful power transitions and the accommodation of rising powers. The emerging literature based on practice theory may also be helpful here.[25] The security communities literature, for example, discusses the change of regions into peaceful communities and the sources of such a change. The evolution of Western Europe as a pluralistic security community in a region where bitter power transition wars were waged for centuries offers hope for change without war.[26] The big challenge for this literature is to show how, and to what extent, these notions of community are translatable to other regions and states, especially to Asia and the rising powers there, such as China and India. How do we obtain peaceful transitions if the leading states are not bound by the idea of a security community, or the community's norms of cooperation and co-existence? What if the rising powers and established powers do not share the same peaceful norms and the former view the norms created by the latter as instruments for the perpetuation of their dominant power status?[27] This is an Achilles' heel for constructivism, as scholars have not elaborately discussed the non-Western norms or non-liberal norms that a rising power might hold.[28] Constructivists may also be unwittingly helping the status quo maintained by Western powers if they do not pay attention to the normative claims of rising powers. Some of them may not be liberal-oriented.

The role of ideas in international change goes beyond constructivism. A number of scholars have used ideational and normative factors to account for change, arguing that war as a mechanism for transformation has become obsolete and that major powers are unlikely to wage wars to obtain power positions. Major wars, according to John Mueller, have

---

[25] For instance, see Vincent Pouliot, *International Security in Practice: The Politics of NATO-Russia Diplomacy* (Cambridge: Cambridge University Press, 2010).

[26] Emanuel Adler and Michael Barnett, eds., *Security Communities* (Cambridge: Cambridge University Press, 1998).

[27] For instance, Chinese conceptions of order are based on the tributary system, which offered centuries of peace and order. See David C. Kang, *China Rising: Peace, Power and Order in East Asia* (New York: Columbia University Press, 2007); David C. Kang, *East Asia Before the West: Five Centuries of Trade and Tribute* (New York: Columbia University Press, 2010).

[28] An exception is Amitav Acharya, *Whose Ideas Matter? Agency and Power in Asian Regionalism* (Ithaca: Cornell University Press, 2009). For another perspective on non-Western norms, see Kishore Mahbubani, *The New Asian Hemisphere: The Irresistible Shift of Global Power to the East* (New York: Public Affairs, 2009).

become obsolescent, just like other social institutions, such as slavery and dueling.[29] John Vasquez argues that Europeans had a peculiar conception of power and that the world wars they fought were largely the product of the practice of power politics among them.[30] Going by these theorists, changes in ideas and norms will make war the least desirable option for great powers and aspiring great powers. The changing norms thus make it possible for rising powers to seek alternative routes and allow established powers to integrate them into normative orders that preclude war.[31]

Grand strategies of peaceful change

Are there grand strategies for peaceful accommodation? This volume assumes that material changes relating to wealth acquisition methods and technological innovations among leading states will produce shifts in power capabilities. The rise of new power centers demands accommodative strategies for obtaining change without war and a peaceful international order. Thus, this volume locates the main source of non-violent change at the systemic level in the grand strategies of the status quo states. It enquires: (1) What strategies adopted by the leading states and the rising powers could avoid war and help a peaceful systemic transformation? (2) Conversely, what strategies would lead to the rise of a revisionist state bent on system change by resorting to war?

The argument of this volume is that peaceful transformation is possible despite structural changes if the dominant status quo powers follow a mixed grand strategy that gives more or less equal weight to gradual accommodation and balance/deterrence against a potential challenger. The challenger must also hold a peaceful rise strategy and seek incremental, as opposed to rapid, change. Accordingly, rising challengers may have to be identified and accommodated into the international order prior

---

[29] John Mueller, *Retreat from Doomsday: The Obsolescence of Major War* (New York: Basic Books, 1989).

[30] John A. Vasquez, *The War Puzzle* (Cambridge: Cambridge University Press, 1993).

[31] Peaceful change at the international level has been discussed from the English school perspective. Hedley Bull, Adam Watson, and Barry Buzan are a few scholars who dwell on international order and international society, though it is unclear what concrete strategies they are offering. The key argument is that a society of states exists in the anarchic international system based on rules and regulations that are applicable to great powers. There is much buried in this literature that could be useful for understanding peaceful power transitions and stable international order, even if they do not offer rigorous explanations for these phenomena. For this literature, see Bull, *The Anarchical Society*; Martin Wight, *Systems of States*, ed. Hedley Bull (Leicester University Press, June 1977); Barry Buzan, *From International to World Society? English School Theory and the Social Structure of Globalisation* (Cambridge: Cambridge University Press, 2004); Andrew Hurrell, *On Global Order: Power, Values, and the Constitution of International Society* (Oxford: Oxford University Press, 2007).

to their becoming militarily hostile to the status quo states. If attempts at accommodation do not succeed at the early stage of systemic challenge, the strategy should focus on coercive approaches such as balance of power, containment, and deterrence, while at the same time providing sufficient opportunities for peaceful accommodation of the revisionist state. A successful accommodation strategy may require an effective political role for the challenger and acceptance of its sphere of influence not only geopolitically, but also in other domains where its interests matter most. Increasing the cost of aggression deters the outbreak of war at least for a period of time. However, even when deterrence and containment are pursued, without a strategy that offers the challenger a role in system management that effectively ingratiates it, a system-wide or region-specific conflict can erupt, especially if military balances and political opportunities suddenly tilt in favor of the rising challenger and if its leaders perceive that their position could deteriorate in the future. This accommodation is also very much in the self-interest of a status quo state, as it may decline in the long-run, and at that time, the new system leader is likely to uphold elements of the previous order only if it has earlier been integrated into the norms of that order.

The rising power must also pursue a strategy of incremental peaceful change, as opposed to violent change. It should be willing to accept institutions as arenas for change and use its position to achieve its goals peacefully. This may require it to develop norms of co-existence even when acquiring more material capabilities. It should not violently alter the order, or especially the territorial status quo in its immediate region. Thus, the greater the synchronization of the strategies of the established power and the rising power, the higher the chances for peaceful accommodation. It is also assumed that status quo powers will decline slowly but surely and will want to adjust to their decline and create some powerful norms and principles that will be in existence even after they lose their prime status. Further, the rising powers will increase their capabilities over a period of decades, not years, allowing them to adjust and integrate slowly and without resorting to violence.

The strategies of accommodation

In this project, the most critical factor in determining whether peaceful accommodation is likely to occur is whether established powers pursue a strategy of gradual accommodation prior to, and at each stage of, a structural competition and whether they succeed in convincing the rising power to join ranks in maintaining a peaceful order. It must be emphasized that accommodation is a slow process and occurs mostly when contending states accept the crucial norms of an existing order as legitimate and valuable. Variations in this strategy can be elaborated. The following propositions summarize the strategies and their expected effects.

Ideological/normative accommodation: Peaceful accommodation takes place when the established powers and the rising powers accept the core ideological and normative frameworks of the international order as legitimate. Under this scenario, a simultaneous process takes place: the challenger recognizes and accepts at least some of the core normative framework offered by the dominant power and vice versa – the dominant power accepts many elements of the normative order offered by the challenger or potential challenger. The possibility of accommodation is higher if both sides are democratic states, as the axioms of democratic peace can work in this relationship. The order they create should be legitimate in the eyes of other key states, especially regional powers. In the contemporary world, this would mean regional states voluntarily accepting power transition as legitimate, unlike in the past, when great powers could obtain legitimacy through coercive means and postwar settlements among themselves.

Territorial accommodation: Peaceful accommodation is feasible when both the rising power and the status quo powers consider the territorial settlements as legitimate, and neither seeks to overthrow the territorial status quo by force. This is not just direct control of territory, but control of spheres of influence as well. The latter is complicated by the rise of notions of sovereign equality, nationalism in smaller states, and norms that forbid territorial expansionism. A further complication is that two rising powers can contest over territory and spheres of influence, as China and India do today in the Indian Ocean and Asia-Pacific regions. Historically, territorial issues and the unwillingness of established powers to concede territorial rights or spheres of influence to rising powers caused major conflicts. In the contemporary world, due to intense nationalism among smaller powers and the prevalence of the territorial integrity norm, such territorial divisions among powerful states are not easy to accomplish. Even when they have been achieved, powers can have spheres of influence, and neither the established nor the rising power should seek territorial revisions to alter forcefully the spheres in the great power near-abroad. Here the established powers may have a greater role to play in making adjustments for joint management of the various oceans of the world in cooperation with influential regional powers. Joint management of global commons like outer space and Arctic/Antarctic territories may also be useful. Expansion of status quo powers' alliances into a rising power's sphere of influence should be avoided.

Economic accommodation: Peaceful power transition can emerge when potential challengers are integrated into the global economic order and the interdependence among the economies is deep and multifaceted. Deepened economic interdependence and resultant societal interactions thus make it difficult for both the challenger and the dominant state to engage in power transition conflicts, as war will be perceived as costly to their survival and prosperity. A problem here is that changing economic fortunes might cause the expectations of the powers to diverge over time.

Institutional accommodation: Peaceful accommodation can take place when challengers and potential challengers are co-opted through international institutions and the norms and principles inherent in them. Smaller actors, who are likely to join the revisionist state in a war, are also integrated through the institutional set up. Accommodation would mean effective participation of emerging major states in system-wide decisions and, thereby, provide them with some key leadership roles. Rising powers should make every effort to peacefully develop their spheres of influence and give a voice to the regional states through institutional mechanisms. It may take leadership in creating new institutions, but meaningful membership of established and rising powers is essential to such institutions not becoming arenas of exclusive privilege and power contestation.

Thus, how the established states distribute economic and political benefits to rising powers matters because dividing systemic benefits is essential for successful accommodation. None of the leading states should take undue advantage of the economic order, as continued grievance could produce military challenge. None of this assumes change will always be smooth and absent of crises. It is the willingness to accept a rising power without war that is the main concern here. Periodic crisis may in fact spur the parties to compromise, out of fear of the consequences of war outpacing the benefits.

Not all rising powers equally seek territorial adjustments or spheres of influence. In the contemporary world, accommodation could be more in the areas of participation in institutions and governance and in economic privileges. Thus, a country like Brazil is not seeking a sphere of influence in Latin America in the classical European sense, but a higher say in international governance. India also seeks such readjustments, though it may not want others upsetting its sphere of influence in South Asia and the Indian Ocean region. The two most active powers today for sphere of influence are Russia and China; the former wants to regain influence over its immediate region, while the latter seeks to gain control over the South China Sea, with all the economic advantages that come with it. The challenge to their ambitions is from smaller states that will be affected by these efforts, and the United States cannot easily accommodate them as previous great powers did at the end of global wars. Institutional accommodation of a rising power may be thwarted by another rising power or by smaller states, as evident in the stalled negotiations for UN Security Council reforms that are supposed to offer countries such as India and Brazil permanent membership.

Strategies of rising powers

The strategies of the rising powers also matter greatly in the process of peaceful accommodation. The most relevant question here is: Does the rising power want to pursue a peaceful rise strategy or does it want to accelerate its search for a leadership role through war and territorial conquest? Rising powers which perceive that the order is malleable and can accommodate their interests may not challenge it violently. Those who believe that the order is unlikely to be changed without violent challenge may resort to conflict if the perceived costs are lower than the perceived benefits. Moreover, whether the rising power is willing to be accommodated at four levels – ideological/normative, territorial/spheres of influence, economic, and institutional – matters considerably in the eventual outcome. This may entail the rising power adjusting its grand strategy to incremental advancement as opposed to a violent overturning of the existing order. The power may also need to have a strategy of peaceful accommodation with other rising powers as well.

A big constraining factor here could be nationalism and the perceived sense of grievance within a rising power. For instance, as the material strength of the rising power increases, powerful internal constituencies and factions could demand a more immediate accommodation, or higher benefits as well as territorial adjustments and spheres of influence from the established powers and regional states. Perceived historical injustices or unjust territorial divisions in the past could be a source of such revanchism. Weak domestic political elites could prop up nationalism to sustain their position. Or, within the rising power, different domestic groups could intensify their competition and more hawkish factions gain control over the state's power. Externalization of internal conflicts thus could become a major source of instability between rising powers and established powers, as well as regional states, which may also have factions that believe in non-compromising positions. These dynamics within the rising power could be met with more strident positions by the established powers. Peaceful change thus depends on the elite's ability to prevent nationalist and hawkish domestic groups from establishing their control over the political order.

One of the key strategic approaches of a rising power could be to wait and gradually seek normative adjustments rather than quick adjustments in status. As newcomers are rarely accepted into privileged clubs, they may still seek incremental adjustments without violence. Much depends on how willing established powers are to accommodate rising powers within a reasonable time frame. If their efforts do not succeed, they can start creating new global or regional institutions and force the established powers to negotiate. China has started this process with the proposal for the creation of the Asian Infrastructure Investment Bank (AIIB) and the BRICS (Brazil, Russia, India, China, and South Africa) Development Bank and the large-scale interest these have received from major states, including several US allies.

Many questions arise from this discussion: How much accommodation is feasible, and how much is enough to satisfy a rising power? Further, does the accommodation have to be tailored to different levels of material advancement of the rising power? If so, what are the markers for each stage? How would one know the rising power is satisfied or dissatisfied with its status accommodation? Is there a point of diminishing utility or returns in terms of status adjustment for the rising power and the established powers? More fundamentally, what if the established power is declining rapidly vis-à-vis the rising power yet controls many levers of power through institutional roles and does not want to give them up?

Case studies

The modern international system offers only a few cases of peaceful accommodation. In fact, there are more cases of non-accommodation or violent challenge by rising powers than of peaceful transition. Hence, it is important to explore those cases of success and failure, even though the global context for power transitions has changed considerably in the twenty-first century. Not all aspiring powers today claim their status on the basis of military power, but do so through other markers such as economic power and even soft power. We should also acknowledge that accommodation in the areas of territory and spheres of influence is extremely complicated in today's decolonized world.

One case that stands out in terms of peaceful accommodation is that of the dominant power Great Britain accepting and integrating the rising United States in the late nineteenth and early twentieth centuries.[32] As Ali Zeren and John Hall argue in Chapter 6, this is also partially a case of a strengthening America gatecrashing the club, which a retreating Great Britain felt compelled to accommodate due to its inability to maintain a viable military presence in the Americas.

A second case is the partial but significant accommodation of China, first by the United States and later by US allies, in the 1970s, when it was offered substantial economic and political concessions such as UN membership and market access in return for a security alliance against the Soviet Union. This is especially interesting given the two states had totally opposite political systems: liberal democracy versus an authoritarian communist system. Moreover, the partial accommodation was sustained even after the end of the Cold War, though fissures are starting to develop in the relationship as the twenty-first century advances and China's economic power capabilities increase and the United States declines in a relative sense. As Lorenz Lüthi reminds us in Chapter 7, this was not a full accommodation among equals, as China's power capabilities were not anywhere near those of a great power. Even then, China's acceptance was viewed as tilting the balance in favor of the US alliance in a major way vis-à-vis the Soviet Union.

The end of the US–Soviet rivalry provides an important case for transition without war. In this case, a leading power accepted its declining material status and adjusted accordingly. Although effort was made to arrest decline, it produced the opposite result. However, it cannot be categorized in the same group as the first two, as one of the dominant powers basically gave up the conflict. The United States did not do much then, or later, to accommodate Moscow, and subsequently Russian unhappiness increased as a result. Today Russia considers itself a resurging power, partially challenging the order whenever it can. The conquest of Crimea and the aggressive military postures in Ukraine's eastern border areas suggest a Russia willing to charge ahead to reclaim its lost geopolitical space and sphere of influence.

Against this backdrop are two cases of abject failure in rapprochement or containment/deterrence vis-à-vis rising powers. They are Germany

---

[32] Charles A. Kupchan, "Benign States and Peaceful Transition," in Kupchan, *Power in Transition*, 21–24.

prior to WWI and WWII and Japan in the 1930s. The latter was an ally of the Allied powers in WWI, yet subsequently chose to challenge the order for a variety of reasons. The British and French strategies prior to the world wars neither effectively contained nor deterred nor co-opted the challenger, though some accommodationist overtures were made toward Berlin. When the challenger armed and rearmed, Britain and its allies could not develop an effective deterrence strategy. Economic difficulties within Britain prevented it from developing the rapid military capabilities essential for effective deterrence.[33] Chapters 2 and 8, by Steven Lobell and by Martin Claar and Norrin Ripsman, powerfully show the failures in British strategy. Germany's aggressive buildup of naval power to match Britain might have tipped the balance against peaceful accommodation.

E.H. Carr, among others, had argued that the crisis that followed WWI was largely due to the fact that "territorial settlement in Europe had been so favorable to the victors and so tough on the vanquished that it could provide security for neither in the long run. The economic impact of the creation of so many new states in Central Europe had also been disruptive, as had the system of reparations."[34] Even if this is not the established wisdom of history, for the purpose of lessons for the future it is worth examining why Germany and Italy became so revisionist and engaged in immense violence to change the system in their favor. Interestingly, defeated France after the Napoleonic Wars was treated differently and was still given the respect of a great power. The credit partially goes to the efforts of French diplomat Charles-Maurice de Talleyrand, who was successful in restoring the French position as a great power in the Concert of Europe. Obviously, the victors made the concessions, and the question is: If a system similar to the Concert existed to integrate defeated Germany in 1919, would world history have been different? The League was not sufficient to do this as it contained powerful retributive elements meant to keep the vanquished powers downtrodden forever.

Similarly, the US strategy vis-à-vis Japan prior to WWII lacked both effective deterrence and accommodation. Japan's search for autarkic economic development through territorial expansion was viewed as dangerous. As Jeffrey Taliaferro argues in Chapter 9, neither the United States nor its Western allies attempted in a major way to integrate Japan into

[33] Richard Rosecrance and Zara Steiner, "British Grand Strategy and the Origins of World War II," in *The Domestic Bases of Grand Strategy*, eds. Richard Rosecrance and Arthur A. Stein (Ithaca: Cornell University Press, 1993), 124–53.

[34] Charles Jones, *E.H. Carr and International Relations: A Duty to Lie* (Cambridge: Cambridge University Press, 1998), 29. Drawn from E.H. Carr, *International Relations Since the Peace Treaties* (London, Macmillan, 1927).

the international system. Did the Allies lose windows of opportunity or was Japan beyond the point of accommodation without major territorial adjustment, which the colonial powers were not prepared to offer? When militarists assumed power in Tokyo, no credible deterrent threat was available either. The internal dynamics within the United States, especially isolationist impulses, prevented the creation of an effective strategy.

The emerging power transition

As the world enters the second and third decades of the twenty-first century, long-term systemic changes are bound to occur, with China, Russia, India, and Brazil emerging as likely contenders for systemic leadership roles, the latter two more on the basis of economic strength and population size, as well as dominant regional attributes rather than relative military power. According to many theories on power transition, war appears to be inevitable. Russia and China have already started asserting themselves militarily in their immediate neighborhoods. However, war as a system-changing mechanism, as in past historical epochs, is unimaginable given that it would escalate into nuclear conflict and the destruction of the planet. It is therefore essential that policymakers in status quo powers and rising states devise strategies to allow changes without resorting to armed conflict. Does the world system today offer a better chance of accommodation than previous eras? Some fundamental changes have taken place at both the material and ideational levels.[35] These changes are:

- Increased economic globalization and deepened interdependence.
- The presence of many institutions that allow strategies such as engagement and soft balancing.
- Norms that proscribe forceful change in territorial boundaries and spheres of influence.
- The dominance of defense and deterrence in military technology, partly caused by the nuclear revolution.
- The absence of intense nationalism and expansionist ideologies among the rising and declining powers.
- The increased nationalism and desire for sovereign equality among non-great powers.

---

[35] Some believe the behavioral patterns of today's rising powers are essentially conservative and driven by domestic stakeholders who support the existing order rather than wanting to overthrow it. For this, see Miles Kahler, "Rising Powers and Global Governance: Negotiating Change in a Resilient Status Quo," *International Affairs* 89, no. 3 (May 2013), 711–29.

Intensified globalization has indeed brought the economies of all rising and established powers to an unprecedented level of interconnectedness. In terms of trade and investment, these economies are linked, and developing an autarkic economy has indeed become very difficult for any rising power. Going by the arguments of the interdependence school, the resulting interdependence should offer a certain level of comfort for peace, as deeply entrenched economies would be reluctant to escalate rivalries to the military level. The fact that all rising powers are benefitting from deepened globalization is a positive feature of the current system.

The second liberal mechanism of peace, the widespread availability of *international institutions* to engage and constrain one another, offers rays of hope for peaceful change and accommodation. Institutions offer a great arena for soft balancing and engagement, two dimensions of the hedging strategy that major powers have used in the current transition phase.[36] While hard balancing relies on traditional military buildup and alignment, soft balancing is used to restrain threatening behavior through limited ententes and institutional and other means, such as economic sanctions, in a sustained fashion. The proliferation of institutions at the global and regional levels suggests that there are different arenas available in which a rising power can assert itself and acquire higher status. China, for instance, is a member of the core institutions of the system, such as the United Nations and its agencies, G20, and financial institutions such as the World Trade Organization (WTO), the WB, and the IMF, though it may want a greater voice within them. The rising powers themselves are creating new institutions, such as BRICS and the Shanghai Cooperation Organization (SCO), suggesting that established institutions are not the only venues they see for status recognition and advancement.

The third factor is the prevalence of *norms of territorial integrity* against forceful change of borders. These norms grew out of the Cold War era and were strengthened by the decolonization process. They offer a certain level of assurance against blatant territorial expansion. The newly emerged states assiduously want to defend their autonomy and sovereignty, as evident from their resistance in many instances to great power aggressions and behavior at the UN and other global forums. If these norms are well entrenched, and the rising powers do not then engage in territorial conquests as they did in previous historical eras, will

---

[36] T.V. Paul, "Introduction: The Enduring Axioms of Balance of Power Theory and Their Contemporary Relevance," in *Balance of Power: Theory and Practice in the 21st Century*, eds. T.V. Paul, James J. Wirtz, and Michel Fortmann (Stanford: Stanford University Press, 2004); T.V. Paul, "Soft Balancing in the Age of US Primacy," *International Security* 30, no. 1 (Summer 2005), 46–71; Robert A. Pape, "Soft Balancing Against the United States," *International Security* 30, no. 1 (Summer 2005), 7–45.

the world see a different kind of transition in the coming decades? Do the norms encompass indirect control of foreign states, or only direct acquisition of territories? Here, China may not be following the norms fully, as made evident by its challenges to the territorial orders in the South and East China Seas and toward India. Its active pursuit of land acquisition and control of oil and natural gas fields in Africa, Central Asia, and Latin America may also generate potential problems for the indirect control issue. Russia's behavior in Ukraine in 2014 also challenges the territorial integrity norm in a significant manner.

The *technological innovations of warfare* are yet another factor that prohibits direct conquest. Nuclear weapons embellish the deterrent aspect, but a whole array of weaponry today supports defense and deterrence, as opposed to offense. The "cult of the offensive" is often credited for war in Europe.[37] This factor is critical in constraining rising powers from adopting offensive military doctrines and strategies. But what if future revolutions in military affairs produce new weapons, especially in cyberspace and outer space, that allow easy offense? Asymmetric strategies can also be used for offensive purposes, as evident from the widespread use of cyber war in different theaters even during peacetime, including those by the rising China.

The nuclear revolution in particular deserves our attention. The uncontestable nature of nuclear weapons is now well established.[38] The advent of nuclear weapons has made large-scale wars of conquest almost impossible, given the chance of mutual annihilation. It has also taken away many short war illusions and the advantages of offensive doctrines. Powers, even if they are unhappy with the order, are constrained by deterrence, though they may attempt to design around it. Future power contests by rising powers are therefore likely to rely on asymmetric means until new weapons systems allow offensive advances and defense and deterrence are whittled down.

Finally, the *absence of intense nationalism* propelled by expansionist ideologies such as fascism, Nazism, and Marxist-Leninism offers a certain amount of comfort that rising powers may not succumb to the temptation to become highly revisionist as previous rising powers did. However,

---

[37] Stephen Van Evera, "The Cult of the Offensive and the Origins of the First World War," *International Security* 9, no. 1, (Summer 1984), 58–107.

[38] On this, see Bernard Brodie, *The Absolute Weapon: Atomic Power and World Order* (New York: Harcourt, Brace, and Company, 1946); Robert Jervis, *The Nuclear Revolution: Statecraft and the Prospect of Armageddon* (Ithaca: Cornell University Press, 1989); Richard J. Harknett, "State Preferences, Systemic Constraints, and the Absolute Weapon," in *The Absolute Weapon Revisited: Nuclear Arms and the Emerging International Order*, eds. T.V. Paul, Richard J. Harknett, and James J. Wirtz (Ann Arbor: University of Michigan Press, 1998), 47–72.

what is noticeable is the suddenness with which expansionist ideologies can successfully emerge and change a population's attitude. Germany and Japan succumbed to fascism even though they previously had quasi-democracies in power. The international climate became intolerable from the militaristic elite's point of view, while the population appears to have bought into the idea through the elite's propaganda. The established powers' attitudes did not help. For instance, the racist immigration policies of the United States might have strengthened the Japanese public's hostility toward the United States.

Are these five factors sufficient for peaceful change? Or are we condemned to see another power transition conflict, for instance between China and the United States? What are the sources of potential rivalry and conflict? Under what conditions will the current era of limited hard balancing and soft balancing lead to intense balance of power competition? What role will changing technologies, especially technologies of warfare – nuclear, conventional, and cyber – play in the challenging of the order by the rising powers? Will territory and spheres of influence play a big role in the emerging order, as they did in previous eras? Will nationalism reemerge as a powerful force among rising and declining powers, propelling them to conflict? Will economic changes encourage smaller states to jump on the bandwagon of the rising powers that offer them security and economic goods?

In the case of China's accommodation, there are many factors that point to a limited but crisis-ridden accommodation and the emergence of a cold peace between Beijing and the United States. China has partially accepted some of the norms, but has a big weakness in terms of democratic governance of its domestic political system. The United States is unlikely to accommodate China fully unless it becomes a democratic state, a prospect that looks remote. China's insertion into the global economic order is a silver lining here. In this sphere, largely due to China's economic strategy, the United States has at least not contested China's emergence as a powerful economic actor. In the institutional arena, China's accommodation is already largely accomplished, though it is still a limited player in global financial institutions: a fact China is trying to rectify itself through the creation of new institutions such as the Asian Infrastructure Development Bank (AIDB).

China's big challenge is its conflictual relations with other leading Asian powers, such as Japan and India, in addition to a majority of the Association of Southeast Asian Nations (ASEAN) member states, including Vietnam. The Chinese territorial claims in the East China and South China Seas and toward India are one reason for this. Further, ideologically, most democratic Asian states do not have much in common with China, despite the increased use of soft power by Beijing to create legitimacy for its dominant status in the region. This is not to deny the limited civilizational influence of China over East and South East Asia, especially through the vestiges of the old tributary system. This suggests that if China asserts itself too much militarily it may provoke a hard balancing coalition among major and minor powers. China's "peaceful development" (formerly "peaceful rise") strategy has somewhat checked the possibility of an intense balance of power conflict. The question, naturally, is for how long this will be sustainable. The United States, China, and other regional states affected by China's rise have pursued soft balancing and engagement strategies under the larger umbrella of hedging, at least during the first two decades of the post-Cold War era, only to now enter into a limited hard balancing competition.[39] China's bargaining strategy, as Kai He argues in Chapter 10, provides some possibilities for peaceful accommodation, though it could go the opposite way if the bargaining ends up in miscalculations on either side.

The Indian accommodation is more likely to happen peacefully. The US–India rapprochement since 2005 is an example of partial accommodation of a rising power, though it is still a work in progress. This case is ongoing, and it will be interesting to see whether it progresses positively, since India and the United States share many goals relating to the ideological/normative, economic, and institutional realms. Yet full convergence is difficult given India is still not materially strong enough to challenge the established powers. It is slowly being inserted into the global economic arena, and its democratic norms are somewhat convergent. However, its leadership role in institutions still remains unfulfilled. If a change occurs in this area, India is likely to be accommodated peacefully.[40] Much depends on India's own internal development, which at times looks questionable. A condition that may accentuate India's accommodation would be balance of power politics. If the US–China balance of power competition heats up, India could become a major third player in tilting the balance either way, as China managed to do with the US–Soviet power equation in the 1970s.

Brazil's accommodation, similar to India's, may also occur peacefully. However, Brazil's weaknesses in military strength may have to be compensated through other means, such as a greater institutional leadership

---

[39] Kai He and Huiyun Feng, "If Not Soft Balancing, Then What? Reconsidering Soft Balancing and US Policy toward China," *Security Studies* 17, no. 2 (2008), 363–95.

[40] On this, see T.V. Paul and Mahesh Shankar, "Status Accommodation through Institutional Means: India's Rise and the Global Order," in *Status in World Politics*, eds. T.V. Paul, Deborah Welch Larson, and William C. Wohlforth (Cambridge: Cambridge University Press, 2014), 165–91.

role. Brazil may be a different player among the rising powers.[41] It could also offer a test case for a large state being accommodated based on non-military attributes. The question, though, is whether the Brazilian elite will be content with low-ranking military status or will seek weapons, including nuclear, to establish its great power credentials.

What is also possible is that in the new order these powers will remain important actors but will not be the only ones playing significant roles. The G20 membership shows that there are other significant states in the world system, and they may also play important parts in the emerging order. Regional states such as Turkey, Nigeria, and Indonesia are unlikely to give up their claim for a role in global governance. As Kupchan has argued, the twenty-first century could witness for the first time no power rules.[42] On specific issue-areas, the leading powers could still frame and reframe the global agenda, and how rising powers as well as dominant powers allow these and other contenders a meaningful role in institutional governance may well determine the emergence of deep peace in the world system. Many states, such as Turkey, Pakistan, and Argentina, are pivotal in their regions and have been able to assert themselves in powerful roles partly by opposing their regional rivals.

In conclusion, this volume seeks to explore when structural and material changes generate demand for changing power positions and status adjustments, and whether or not decision-makers with agency can play a concrete role in generating conditions for peace. Unlike structural theories, which are to a great extent deterministic, many chapters in this volume point out that peaceful change is possible through the pursuit of effective long-term strategies of change by both rising and status quo powers. This volume assumes that, though the international system is characterized by competitive interactions, major states do have maneuverability within the limits of the semi-anarchic structure, and that they can avert cataclysmic wars by devising effective grand strategies of change. Prevention of major war is in the interests of both the status quo states and smaller states in the international system. Often, a systemic war is likely to unseat a status quo state from its top position more rapidly than would occur otherwise, even if it wins. Smaller states are frequently victims of major power war and can even lose their sovereign existence.

---

[41] Andrew Hurrell, "Brazil: What Kind of Rising State in What Kind of Institutional Order?" in *Rising States, Rising Institutions: Challenges for Global Governance*, eds. Alan S. Alexandroff and Andrew F. Cooper (Washington, DC: Brookings, 2010), 128–50.

[42] Charles A. Kupchan, *No One's World: The West, the Rising Rest, and the Coming Global Turn* (New York: Oxford University Press, 2012).

Research questions

I. Is violent conflict among established great powers and aspiring great powers inevitable as a prelude to power transitions?
    A. Do rising powers have to reach full parity in military capability in order to challenge the existing order?
    B. Has international order changed so profoundly that military conflict is unlikely to become the instrument for power transitions?
    C. Do different types of power resources – military, economic, and technological, as well as soft power attributes – matter in determining a rising power's status in international politics today?
II. If war is not a necessary condition for change, what else can bring change to the international order?
    A. What are the principal mechanisms by which a rising power can be accommodated?
    B. Do institutions offer the best arena for accommodation?
    C. How can spheres of influence be adjusted in the decolonized world, where sovereign equality is taken for granted by the international community, especially the smaller states?
    D. What do historical examples of accommodation or non-accommodation tell us about future transitions?
III. Under what conditions do accommodation efforts fail? Under what conditions do established powers accommodate, or not accommodate, rising powers?
    A. When is accommodation not appeasement?
    B. How does a dominant power delicately balance between accommodation and containment of challenger?

The chapters

Chapter 2 deals with dominant accommodation strategies as envisioned in realist theories by Steven Lobell. He contends that dominant realist explanations do not adequately explain peaceful transitions. He proposes a components of power theory which suggests that states assess power capabilities based on specific components of power and whether they threaten vital geostrategic interests, rather than relative power distributions of the hegemonic powers. Shifts in aggregate power are unlikely to provoke counterbalancing, but what matters is whether the state has the appropriate elements of power to pose a major threat. This implies that emerging powers such as Russia and China may only provoke violent response from the United States if they challenge the particular element of power that makes the lead actor dominant (e.g., naval power in the Pacific).

Counter views are presented in a set of chapters based on prescriptions couched in liberal approaches, including economic globalization, interdependence, and international law and institutions, as well as ideational positions discussing normative factors that allow for change without war. Phil Potter contends in Chapter 3 that the interplay between independence and accommodation is context-dependent and is no guarantee of peaceful accommodation, despite beliefs otherwise in many policy circles. In Chapter 4, Krzysztof Pelc offers a new look at E.H. Carr's concerns about international law and international institutions and their limitations in preserving the status quo, especially if they leave insufficient space for the interests of rising powers. Finally, in Chapter 5, Mlada Bukovansky asserts that a refined understanding of the identities of the key states concerned and a specification of the role of ideas and diplomatic practices in the process of accommodation is essential to understanding the phenomenon of great power accommodations.

The first two chapters of Part II present two successful cases of peaceful accommodation – that of the United States by the United Kingdom in the late nineteenth century, and that of China by the United States in the 1970s –in order to see whether any of the factors discussed in Part I played a significant role. These chapters have a different take from other accounts on both the causal factors and the magnitude of the adjustment in these cases. In Chapter 6, Ali Zeren and John Hall do not think the UK accommodation of the United States was a case of full accommodation, but rather was a power transition, as the United States did not buy into British ideas for a long time, as evident in Washington's isolationism from the conflicts in the European theater. It is still worth analyzing why a power transition in the Americas occurred without a major war, unlike in the European theater. To Lorenz Lüthi, in Chapter 7, the US accommodation of China occurred due to a peculiar convergence of domestic and international factors in both countries, including change in the rigid ideological perspectives of China, and the United States under the Nixon administration seeking allies to contain a USSR that was perceived to be getting stronger. The takeaway from these chapters is that accommodation is a very rare event in world politics and that the particular set of circumstances that led to it in these cases in the past need not repeat in future cases.

The remaining chapters of Part II deal with two cases of failure: the Allied powers versus Germany and the United States versus Japan in creating peaceful accommodation in the first half of the twentieth century. What caused the failure in these cases to prevent a power transition war and encouraged the status quo powers and rising powers not to seek peaceful avenues? What would have produced a positive power transition of these states? Or was war inevitable given the constellation of forces shaping international order during this era? In Chapter 8, Martin Claar and Norrin Ripsman argue that the British response to rapidly rising Germany shows declining states are more likely to contain rising challengers if they perceive the challengers as posing imminent major threats to their core interests and if the domestic political coalitions of the declining state expect their interests to be furthered through containment of or war with the challenger. It is clear that the British containment strategy was not successful in the end, while a deterrent strategy lacked credibility. In Chapter 9, Jeffrey Taliaferro offers a somewhat critical view of the US policy of neither containing nor accommodating Japan's power expansion to the rest of Asia. The Roosevelt administration seems to have used the 1940–41 crisis with Japan as a way of entering WWII.

In Part III, the aspirations, strategies, and potential for accommodation of four leading states – China, India, Brazil, and Russia – are presented in order to explore what would make their accommodation a feasible option in the years to come. These states are used here as samples, as each offers a test case for power transitions and accommodation without war. There is no assumption that they are the only likely candidates, but they certainly hold many parameters of potential rise from our vantage point in 2014. In Chapter 10, Kai He argues China's rise is a bargaining process between Beijing and other powers. Neither an overly optimistic nor an overly pessimistic view is accurate, as the outcome will depend heavily on how the different players and China bargain with one another. One challenge is that this bargaining may also depend on domestic politics, as we noticed in the past European context. In Chapter 11, Aseema Sinha contends that India is partially integrated in the world order largely due to a change in the policy attitudes of the United States. She ascribes non-state actors such as diaspora and business groups a major role in the accommodation process but sees lingering constraints on a full accommodation. In Chapter 12, David Mares offers a succinct analysis of Brazil's efforts at greater international influence using soft power and the threat of seeking more hard power. Finally, in Chapter 13, Nicola Contessi contends that Vladimir Putin has resorted to both carrots and sticks to restore Russia's great power status and that these have generated instability. He cautions that the West's containment strategy has not been effective and is likely to lead to more assertive behavior by Russia. All these states are currently engaging in bargaining strategies, some more assertively than others, to remake the system in their favor or to induce the leading powers to offer them a greater voice in the system.

One additional issue here is the possibility for other states such as Turkey and Indonesia to become candidates for accommodation, as the BRICS countries are seeking today. How will the United States, as the dominant power, engage these states? In Part IV and Chapter 14, Theodore McLauchlin analyzes the various strategies used by rising and status quo powers and makes some recommendations for theory and policy on what constitutes a power transition and what generates peaceful or conflictual transitions in international politics.

2 Realism, balance of power, and power transitions

Steven E. Lobell

In Chapter 1, T.V. Paul raises several important questions about the emerging BRICS states (Brazil, Russia, India, China, and South Africa) and what the major IR theories say about whether they will be accommodated by the established great powers.[1] For Paul, accommodation means "the emerging power is given the status and perks" of being a great power by the established powers in the international system.[2] He asks what strategies the leading states and the rising powers can use to avoid war and to promote peaceful systemic transformation, and what strategies will lead to the rise of a revisionist state bent on system change.

Balance of power theory argues that changes in the distribution of power are often dangerous and that aggregate power is fungible, and some offensive realists contend that the more power a state possesses, the more it can get whatever it wants.[3] Balance of power has been carried forward into the post-Cold War period to anticipate and forecast the power trends for the rising BRICS states. For instance, the 2013 Department of Defense annual report to Congress states that China increased its defense spending by as much as 20 percent from the previous year.[4]

---

[1] On the rise of the BRICS and Next 11 (N-11) states, see Fareed Zakaria, *Post-American World and the Rise of the Rest* (New York; Penguin Books, 2009); Alan S. Alexandroff and Andrew F. Cooper, eds., *Rising States, Rising Institutions: Challenges for Global Governance* (Washington, DC: Brookings Institution Press 2010); Charles A. Kupchan, *No One's World: The West, the Rising Rest, and the Coming Global Turn* (New York: Oxford University Press, 2012); Henry R. Nau and Deepa Ollapally, eds., *Worldviews of Aspiring Powers: Domestic Foreign Policy Debates in China, India, Iran, Japan, and Russia* (New York: Oxford University Press, 2012); Kristen P. Williams, Steven E. Lobell, and Neal G. Jesse, eds., *Beyond Great Powers and Hegemons: Why Secondary States Support, Follow, or Challenge* (Stanford: Stanford University Press, 2012).

[2] See Chapter 1.

[3] Joseph M. Grieco, *Cooperation among Nations: Europe, America, and Non-Tariff Barriers to Trade* (Ithaca: Cornell University Press, 1990).

[4] Office of the Secretary of Defense, Department of Defense, *Annual Report to Congress: Military and Security Developments Involving the People's Republic of China 2013* (DOD Report on China, 2013). Available at: www.defense.gov/pubs/2013_china_report_final.pdf. See also Richard A. Bitzinger, "China's Double-Digit Defense Growth: What it Means for a Peaceful Rise," *Foreign Affairs*, March 19, 2015. Available at:

According to IHS Jane's, China's defense spending is expected to double by 2015.[5] Based on current trends, the Stockholm International Peace Research Institute (SIPRI) forecasts that by 2035, China's defense spending will surpass the United States'.[6] More broadly, IHS Jane's expects that by 2021, Asia Pacific military spending, including China, India, and Indonesia, could surpass the United States'.

A similar power trend is reported for relative economic power. Both the United Nations and Goldman Sachs report that the BRICS, including China, Brazil, and India, are primed to make substantial gains on the United States.[7] The 2013 UN Human Development Report finds that by 2020, the BRICS will surpass the aggregate GDP of the United States and Europe.[8] According to Goldman Sachs, China's GDP will match America's by 2027, will match the leading Western nations' by 2032, and will then continue to pull ahead into 2065.[9] In less than forty years, Goldman Sachs predicts the BRICS economies together could be larger than the G6 economies. The National Intelligence Council (NIC)'s Global Trends 2030 report corroborates these military and economic diffusion trends.[10]

This chapter addresses what the shifts in material capabilities of the BRICS mean for the established great powers. Specifically, is conflict between the established great powers and the emerging BRICS inevitable? Is Sino-American great power competition, counterbalancing, and contestation likely, due to an unfortunate tragedy of great power

www.foreignaffairs.com/articles/143275/richard-a-bitzinger/chinas-double-digit-defense-growth.

[5] "China to Exceed Combined Defence Budget of All Other Key Defence Markets in APAC by 2015," *IHS Jane's Pressroom*, February 2012. Available at: press.ihs.com/press-release/defense-risk-security/china-exceed-combined-defence-budget-all-other-key-defence-marke.

[6] "China's Military Rise: The Dragon's New Teeth," The Economist (April 7, 2012). Available at: www.economist.com/node/21552193.

[7] On Brazil, see Andrew Hurrell, "Brazil: What Kind of Rising State in What Kind of Institutional Order?" in *Rising States, Rising Institutions: Challenges for Global Governance*, eds. Alan S. Alexandroff and Andrew F. Cooper (Washington, DC: Brookings, 2010), 105–27. On India, see Sumit Ganguly, ed., *India as an Emerging Power* (London: Frank Cass, 2003).

[8] UNDP, "Human Development Report 2013: The Rise of the South: Human Progress in a Diverse World," *United Nations Development Programme* (2013). Available at hdr.undp.org/en/2013-report.

[9] "Dreaming with BRICs: The Path to 2050," Goldman Sachs Report, no. 99, October 1, 2003; "The Long-Term Outlook for the BRICs and N-11 Post Crisis," *Goldman Sachs Report*, no. 192, December 2009; "The Rise of the BRICS and N-11 Consumer," *Goldman Sachs Report*, December 2010. All available at: www.goldmansachs.com/our-thinking/archive/brics-dream.html.

[10] National Intelligence Council, *Global Trends 2030: Alternative Worlds*. Available at: www.dni.gov/index.php/about/organization/national-intelligence-council-global-trends.

politics, as John Mearsheimer warns?[11] Is the "Thucydides Trap," or hegemonic war, between a rising China and a declining United States certain?[12] Do the BRICS need to become peer or near-peer rivals to pose a major danger? Finally, do different types of capabilities, such as military, economic, and technological, matter in determining an emerging BRICS' status in international politics?

US-Chinese territorial, military, and economic competition is on the rise. Territorial and maritime disputes include China's nine-dashed map, which comprises the U-shaped line (the so-called "nine-dash line") that claims the bulk of the South China Sea and Beijing's unilaterally declared East China Sea Air Defense Identification Zone (ADIZ). Sino-American military contestation is also on the rise. Since the 1990s, rather than directly challenging the United States, China has advanced its anti-ship missiles, short- and medium-range ballistic missiles, cruise missiles, stealth submarines, and cyber and space arms to challenge US naval and air superiority, especially in China's littoral waters. Finally, economically, Sino-American contestation has resulted in competing regional trade organizations.

Although Sino-American relations have witnessed an uptick in competition, it is possible for the United States and China to avoid the Thucydides Trap:[13] the historical pattern of a rising state challenging the ruling power's order – Athens' challenge to Sparta's or Germany's challenge to Britain's, which in both instances resulted in hegemonic and major war.[14] In February 2012, then Vice President Xi Jinping introduced the concept of a "new model of major power relations."[15] US Secretary of State

---

[11] John J. Mearsheimer, *The Tragedy of Great Power Politics* (New York: W.W. Norton, 2001). See also Aaron L. Friedberg, *A Contest for Supremacy: China, America, and the Struggle for Mastery in Asia* (New York: W.W. Norton, 2011).

[12] On the effect of unipolarity on a rising China, see Zhu Feng, "China's Rise will be Peaceful: How Unipolarity Matters," in *China's Ascent: Power, Security, and the Future of International Politics*, eds. Robert S. Ross and Zhu Feng (Ithaca: Cornell University Press, 2008), 34–54; Avery Goldstein, "Parsing China's Rise: International Circumstances and National Attributes," in Ross and Feng, *China's Ascent*, 55–86.

[13] For recent applications of power transition theory to China's rise, see Douglas Lemke and Ronald Tammen, "Power Transition Theory and the Rise of China," *International Interactions* 29, No. 4 (2003), 269–71; Steve Chan, "Is There a Power Transition between the US and China? The Different Faces of National Power," *Asian Survey* 45, No. 5 (September/October 2005), 687–701; Ronald L. Tammen and Jacek Kugler, "Power Transition and China-US Conflicts," *Chinese Journal of International Politics* 1, No. 1 (2006), 31–55.

[14] Graham Allison, "Avoiding the Thucydides Trap," *Financial Times* (August 22, 2012). Available at: belfercenter.ksg.harvard.edu/publication/22265/avoiding_thucydidess_trap.html.

[15] Rudy deLeon and Yang Jioeman, eds., *US-China Relations: Toward a New Model of Major Power Relationship* (Washington, DC: Center for American Progress, 2014). Available at: cdn.americanprogress.org/wp-content/uploads/2014/02/ChinaReport-Full.pdf.

Hillary Clinton later stated that "together the United States and China are trying to do something that is historically unprecedented, to write a new answer to the age-old question of what happens when an established power and a rising power meet?"[16] In recent testimony before Congress, US Assistant Secretary of State for East Asian and Pacific Affairs Daniel Russel stated that "there are those who argue that Cold War-like rivalry is inevitable and that the United States and China are condemned to a zero-sum struggle for supremacy, if not conflict. I reject such mechanistic thinking."[17]

Offensive realism and defensive realism offer different answers to whether accommodation of the BRICS is possible, whether a BRICS can become a legitimate stakeholder, whether the process will be peaceful or war-prone, what responses the established great powers will give, and what strategies the rising and declining states will pursue.[18] Offensive realism challenges the optimism of a new model of major power relations. The core assumptions of offensive realism are that all major states seek to maximize power (including the BRICS and even Brazil), status quo powers are rare, and conquest often pays. The import is that peaceful accommodation of a rising BRICS state is rare, though possible. To become a stakeholder, though not necessarily a legitimate one, an emerging state must expand through war and territorial conquest to dominate other states as a major power, or even a regional hegemon.

In contrast, the core assumptions of defensive realism are that states seek to maximize security, conquest rarely pays, status quo states can identify one another, and security-seeking states are common. The import is that gradual accommodation is possible for a moderate and restrained BRICS, which can become accepted as a legitimate stakeholder in the international system, and not through war or conquest, provided it is a security-seeking state and does not upset the positions of the established major powers. For instance, defensive realists maintain that deep American global engagement in the face of emerging BRICS will unnecessarily provoke soft balancing in the form of foot-dragging and

---

[16] deLeon and Jiemian, *US-China Relations*, 23.

[17] Daniel R. Russell, "The Future of US-China Relations." Testimony before the Senate Foreign Relations Committee, Washington, DC, June 25, 2014. Available at: www.state.gov/p/eap/rls/rm/2014/06/228415.htm.

[18] For a review of offensive and defensive realism, see Steven E. Lobell, "Structural Realism/Offensive and Defensive Realism," in *The International Studies Compendium Project*, ed. Robert A. Denemark (Oxford: Wiley-Blackwell, 2010), 6651–69. For a review of the balance of power literature, see Jack S. Levy, "What Do Great Powers Balance Against and When?" in *Balance of Power: Theory and Practice in the 21st Century*, eds. T.V. Paul, James J. Wirtz, and Michael Fortmann (Stanford: Stanford University Press, 2004), 29–51.

opposition, and hard balancing in the form of counterbalancing alliances and military buildup.[19] Specifically, America's pivot to Asia, the Air–Sea Battle (ASB), and the Trans-Pacific Partnership (TPP) will result in balancing by China.[20] Moreover, the Congressional Research Service warns that with the pivot to Asia, the "PLA [People's Liberation Army] will become more determined to strengthen China's anti-access capabilities and more assertive about defending China's territorial claims, rather than less."[21]

The general logic of balance of power theory is correct. Shifts and transitions in power are dangerous and can provoke counterbalancing, preventive war, and hegemonic war. However, in presenting components of power theory, I maintain that balance of power theory is wrong about how states measure power and capabilities, forecast trends, and assess threats. More importantly, a new model of major power relations is possible.

In recasting balance of power theory, components of power theory provides an important fix, rather than an alternative explanation.[22] One fix is that states assess power trends based on specific components of power and whether they threaten vital geostrategic interests, rather than relative power distributions. A second fix is that what matters is whether the state has the appropriate elements of power to pose a major threat. The import of components of power theory is that shifts in the aggregate power of a BRICS state may not provoke counterbalancing, a BRICS state does not need to strive to be a peer competitor or near-peer competitor to pose a major threat, and more aggregate capability might not translate into greater security.

This chapter consists of four sections, which examine balance of power theory and the likelihood of peaceful accommodation of the BRICS. The

---

[19] T.V. Paul, "Soft Balancing in the Age of US Primacy," *International Security* 30, no. 1 (Summer 2005), 46–71.

[20] Robert S. Ross, "International Bargaining and Domestic Politics: US-China Relations since 1972," *International Security*, 38, no. 2 (January 1986), 255–87.

[21] *Pivot to the Pacific? The Obama Administration's "Rebalancing" Toward Asia*, Congressional Research Service Report, March 29, 2012, p. 8.

[22] On components of power theory, see Steven E. Lobell, "Threat Assessment, the State, and Foreign Policy: A Neoclassical Realist Model," in *Neoclassical Realism, the State, and Foreign Policy*, eds. Steven E. Lobell, Norrin M. Ripsman, and Jeffrey W. Taliaferro (Cambridge: Cambridge University Press, 2009), 42–74; Steven E. Lobell, "Britain's Grand Strategy During the 1930s: From Balance of Power to Components of Power," in *The Challenge of Grand Strategy: The Great Powers and the Broken Balance between the World Wars*, eds. Jeffrey W. Taliaferro, Norrin M. Ripsman, and Steven E. Lobell (Cambridge: Cambridge University Press, 2012), 147–70; Steven E. Lobell, "Bringing Balancing Back In: Britain's Targeted Balancing, 1936–1939," *Journal of Strategic Studies* 35, no. 6 (2012), 747–75.

first section discusses balance of power theory, the next two discuss offensive and defensive realism, and the final section discusses components of power theory and presents a new model of major power relations.

Balance of power theory

Derived from Kenneth Waltz's realism, balance of power structural realist theorists can be divided into offensive realists and defensive realists.[23] There are three core distinctions between these variations: whether the anarchic system encourages states to maximize security or to maximize power, whether conquest and territorial expansion pays, and whether states are primarily revisionist in their intentions, or at least assumed to be, or are motivated by security-seeking behavior. These three distinctions influence whether accommodation of the BRICS, and especially China, is possible, whether a BRICS can become a legitimate stakeholder in the international system, whether the process will be peaceful or war-prone, the responses of the established great powers, and the strategies the rising and declining states will pursue.

For offensive realists, security in the international system is scarce. The anarchic nature of the international system compels all major states, including the BRICS, to maximize their share of world power and to seek regional or global hegemony to increase the odds of survival.[24] John Mearsheimer is clear that "states quickly understand that the best way to ensure their survival is to be the most powerful state in the system."[25] Moreover, since a state's intentions are never clear or certain, and it might become more aggressive in the future, all of the major powers are motivated by a worst-case-scenario perspective, which creates a high

---

[23] For a review of this literature, see Benjamin Frankel, "Restating the Realist Case: An Introduction," in *Realism: Restatements and Renewal*, ed. Benjamin Frankel (Portland: Frank Cass, 1996), ix–xx; Benjamin Miller, *When Opponents Cooperate: Great Power Conflict and Collaboration in World Politics* (Ann Arbor: University of Michigan Press, 1995); Jeffrey W. Taliaferro, "Security Seeking Under Anarchy: Defensive Realism Revisited," *International Security* 25, no. 3 (Winter 2000/01), 128–61; Stephen M. Walt, "The Enduring Relevance of the Realist Tradition," in *Political Science: State of the Discipline*, eds. Ira Katznelson and Helen V. Milner (New York: W. W. Norton, 2002), 197–234; Daniel H. Nexon, "The Balance of Power in the Balance," *World Politics* 61, no. 2 (April 2009), 330–59.

[24] Peter Liberman, "The Spoils of Conquest," *International Security* 18, no. 2 (Fall 1993), 125–53; Randall L. Schweller, "Bandwagoning for Profit: Bringing the Revisionist State Back In," *International Security* 19, no. 1 (Summer 1994), 72–107; Eric J. Labs, "Beyond Victory: Offensive Realism and the Expansion of War Aims," *Security Studies* 6, no. 4 (Summer 1997), 1–49; Fareed Zakaria, *From Wealth to Power: The Unusual Origins of America's World Role* (Princeton: Princeton University Press, 1998); Mearsheimer, The Tragedy of Great Power Politics.

[25] Mearsheimer, *The Tragedy of Great Power Politics*, 33.

level of competition and rivalry. Accommodation of a rising state is rare, though it can occur when there is a common enemy. Finally, territorial expansion and geographic conquest often succeed and pay.

For defensive or positional realists, security in the international system is plentiful. The major powers are positionalists and maximize their security by preserving the existing balance of power.[26] Defensive realists maintain that the international system encourages the major states, including the rising BRICS, to pursue moderate and restrained behavior, and provides few incentives for territorial expansion. A security-seeking BRICS state could be accepted as a legitimate stakeholder in the international system. However, aggression, competition, and expansion by the rising BRICS is self-defeating and will provoke the security dilemma and counterbalancing behavior by an offshore regional great power, the other BRICS states, or even a Next 11 (N-11) state in the locale.

Offensive realism

For offensive structural realists, the anarchic nature of the international system is the invisible hand that encourages all major states to maximize their power. States are compelled to maximize power in order to become more secure in a world of anarchy; the best way for a state to increase its likelihood of survival is to become the most powerful state in the region or the system.[27]

Maximizing power entails aggressive foreign economic, political, and military policies. The goal is to alter the balance of power, to take

---

[26] Robert Jervis, "Cooperation under the Security Dilemma," *World Politics* 30, no. 2 (January, 1978), 167–214; Kenneth N. Waltz, *Theory of International Politics* (New York: Random House, 1979); Barry R. Posen, *The Sources of Military Doctrine: France, Britain, and Germany Between the World Wars* (Ithaca: Cornell University Press, 1984); Stephen M. Walt, *The Origins of Alliances* (Ithaca: Cornell University Press, 1987); Jack Snyder, *Myths of Empire: Domestic Politics and International Ambition* (Ithaca: Cornell University Press, 1991); Charles L. Glaser, "Realists as Optimists: Cooperation as Self-Help," *International Security* 19, no. 3 (Winter 1994/95), 50–90; Christopher Layne, "From Preponderance to Offshore Balancing: America's Future Grand Strategy," *International Security* 22, no. 1 (Summer 1997), 86–124; Stephen Van Evera, *Causes of War: Power and the Roots of Conflict* (Ithaca: Cornell University Press, 1999).

[27] For a critique of Mearsheimer's version of offensive realism, see Glenn H. Snyder, "Mearsheimer's World – Offensive Realism and the Struggle for Security," *International Security* 27, no. 1 (Summer 2002), 149–73; Douglas Lemke, "Great Powers in the Post-Cold War World: A Power Transition Perspective," in *Balance of Power: Theory and Practice in the 21st Century*, eds. T.V. Paul, James J. Wirtz, and Michael Fortmann (Stanford: Stanford University Press, 2004), 52–75. See also Patrick James, "Elaborating on Offensive Realism," in *Rethinking Realism in International Relations: Between Tradition and Innovation*, eds. Annette Freyberg-Inan, Ewan Harrison, and Patrick James (Baltimore: Johns Hopkins University Press, 2009), 45–62.

advantage of windows of opportunity to gain more power, to gain power at the expense of other major states, including the established ones, and to weaken potential competitors through preventive wars or other delaying tactics, in order to arrest their ascent.[28] As Mearsheimer tells us, great powers are rarely satisfied with an "appropriate amount" of power, will rarely engage in only incremental change, and will rarely pass up opportunities to become the regional hegemon. Specifically, if a state selects to forgo an opportunity to expand, another rising power in the locale will act on it.[29] Thus, to become a stakeholder, and not necessarily a legitimate one, a state must expand through war and conquest to become either a major power among the powerful states or the most powerful state in the region.

For offensive realists, status quo states in the international system are rare. The underlying assumption is that states are never certain of one another's intentions, whether they can correctly assess the balance of power, and whether other states will use their offensive capabilities in the future to increase their relative power. Specifically, it is difficult for a state to assess how much relative power it must have over its rivals before it is secure, and it is difficult to determine how much power is enough into the future. Even in the absence of a specific or imminent threat, offensive realists argue that states will maximize power and influence because they are uncertain when or where the next challenger will emerge.[30]

Uncertainty about intentions and the fear of miscalculation mean that states adopt and prepare for the worst-case scenario when assessing other powers. The import is that states always regard each other with fear, mistrust, and suspicion, and all states view one another in the same way. The result is a constant security competition, even among states that have no reason to compete, and hence the title of Mearsheimer's book, *The Tragedy of Great Power Politics*. Thus, while an offshore regional hegemon might accommodate a buck-catching BRICS state in another locale, the relationship is driven by strategic calculations and a common enemy, and is not necessarily friendly or long-term; the offshore regional state will not view the accommodated state as a legitimate stakeholder and might be willing to unseat it in the future.

For offensive realists, conquest often pays. Expansion and conquest make states more secure, can pay huge dividends, and block other states from acquiring additional power. In terms of the profitability of

[28] A.F.K. Organski, *World Politics*, 2 edn. (New York: Knopf, 1968); Norrin M. Ripsman and Jack S. Levy, "Wishful Thinking or Buying Time? The Logic of British Appeasement in the 1930s," *International Security* 33, no. 2 (Fall 2008), 148–81.
[29] Zakaria, *From Wealth to Power*.   [30] Labs, "Beyond Victory."

expansion, Mearsheimer claims that states that initiate aggression win their wars 60 percent of the time.[31] According to Eric Labs, successful expanders are socialized and learn from the past or previous mistakes of other great powers.[32] Moreover, Peter Liberman finds that industrial resources can be "cumulative," and added easily and efficiently to existing material capability.[33] In addition, he finds that, in wealthy states, domestic resistance to occupation would have to be very costly to make conquest unprofitable.

Liberman also finds that wealthy, industrialized, and modern states make for good targets, which is good news for the BRICS. First, modernization increases the economic wealth produced. Second, modernization increases the efficiency of foreign coercion, because it centralizes control, facilitates the quick deployment of this power over wide regions, and gives hostage societies more to lose from opposition. Third, relatively low-cost investment in repression prevents most people in modern societies from participating in the collective acts required for resistance.[34]

For offensive realists, though states are relentless expanders, they are not mindless in their expansion.[35] States are prudent territorial expanders, especially given the real risk of undermining economic and industrial power through overexpansion, which is the basis for military power. States may forgo opportunities to increase their power because the costs are too high, because of diminishing returns from additional military resources, because it might undermine the national economy, or because building additional military forces will provoke a rival who can match the increase. Even great powers with abundant wealth have selected not to build militaries to conquer.

The distribution of power will affect the stability of the international system. Structural realists differentiate between bipolar and multipolar distributions of capabilities. Mearsheimer further distinguishes between balanced multipolar and unbalanced multipolar distributions. Most offensive and defensive realists agree that bipolar systems are more

---

[31] Mearsheimer, *Tragedy of Great Power Politics*, 149.   [32] Labs, "Beyond Victory," 13.

[33] Liberman, "The Spoils of Conquest." In contrast, see Jeffrey W. Taliaferro, "Neoclassical Realism and Resource Extraction: State Building for Future War," in *Neoclassical Realism, the State, and Foreign Policy*, eds. Steven E. Lobell, Norrin M. Ripsman, and Jeffrey W. Taliaferro (Cambridge: Cambridge University Press, 2009), 194–226.

[34] Liberman, "The Spoils of Conquest," 125–53.

[35] For Gilpin, who also argues that major powers are not mindless expanders, a major state will seek to change the international system as long as the expected benefits exceed the expected costs. Furthermore, the state will engage in territorial, political, and economic expansion until the marginal costs of greater expansion equal the marginal benefits. Finally, no state will seek to change the system when it is not profitable. Robert Gilpin, *War and Change in World Politics* (Cambridge: Cambridge University Press, 1981).

stable and less war-prone than multipolar systems, and that both are more stable than a unipolar system.[36]

For Mearsheimer, an unbalanced multipolar system generates the greatest instability and security competition among states. An unbalanced multipolar order contains a potential regional hegemon. Pressure to expand is great for the potential regional hegemon, because it strives to become a regional hegemon in order to increase its odds of survival. Moreover, because of its relative power standing, a potential regional hegemon has a good chance of dominating and controlling the other great powers in the locale. Pressure to expand is further heightened in regions with continental powers that have large land armies.

In an unbalanced multipolar order, an offshore regional hegemon will accommodate an emerging buck-catcher (great power, BRICS, or N-11) in order to check the potential regional hegemon from becoming a peer rival. The rationale is that a peer regional hegemon might support a rival or cause problems in the backyard of the regional hegemon. Thus, the offshore regional hegemon prefers at least two great powers in other locales. However, this does not imply the offshore regional power will accept the accommodated buck-catcher as a legitimate stakeholder or that it cannot be deposed in the future.

In balanced multipolar systems, security competition is also high, but less so than in unbalanced multipolar systems. For Mearsheimer, intra-regional buck-passing is common among the BRICS and N-11 states in a balanced multipolar system, and even more so if there are natural geographic barriers such as mountains, deserts, rivers, or jungles. Moreover, power maximizers will face less opposition and greater opportunities to expand while the other major powers are engaged in passing the buck and debating who will bear the burden of balancing the aggressor.

A bipolar system is the most stable system.[37] The simplicity of bipolarity reduces the dangers from miscalculations and uncertainty. Moreover, bipolarity is more efficient, since balancing occurs through internal mobilization and buck-passing is not an option as there is no buck-catcher available.

Geography, as a structural modifier, can also contribute to the level of systemic stability and a state's security. Mearsheimer contends that insular states like the United Kingdom, the United States, and perhaps Brazil and South Africa are more secure and less vulnerable to invasion

---

[36] Although Karl Deutsch and David Singer counter that multipolar systems are more stable: see Karl W. Deutsch and J. David Singer, "Multipolar Power Systems and International Stability," *World Politics* 16, no. 3 (April 1964), 390–406.

[37] Copeland asserts the opposite: see Dale C. Copeland, *The Origins of Major War: Hegemonic Rivalry and the Fear of Decline* (Ithaca: Cornell University Press, 2000).

than continental states such as Russia, India, Germany, and China, due to the stopping power of water, which makes it difficult for states to project their power over long distances. Continental great powers are more likely to make bids for regional hegemony and are more likely to face counterbalancing coalitions.

For offensive and defensive realists, the choice of balancing and buck-passing is a function of the structure of the international system. In a bipolar system, a great power must balance against a rival because there is no other great power to catch the buck.

In multipolar systems, and especially balanced distributions, states often buck-pass. Buck-passing is most common when there is no potential regional hegemon and the rival states do not share a common border. The more relative power the potential hegemon controls, the more likely it is that the other great powers in the region will form a counterbalancing coalition. For instance, an attempt by a BRICS state to achieve local dominance will provoke the other regional BRICS or N-11 states to counterbalance; China's rise will be countered by India and Russia, as well as Japan, South Korea, and Vietnam. If the regional BRICS or N-11 states in strategic locales are unable to restore the balance, then an offshore regional hegemon will enable the other BRICS states as a counterbalancing buck-catcher to prevent a peer-rival from emerging.

Defensive realism

For defensive realists, anarchy encourages states to adopt defensive, moderate, and restrained behavior in most instances.[38] The reasons are several-fold: expansion is self-defeating because it provokes coun-terbalancing behavior; conquest rarely pays; the offense–defense military balance often favors the defender and the defense over the offensive; and socialization and lessons from history teach states that maximizing power is pathological and results in self-encirclement, imperial overex-tension, and overstretch. For defensive realists, aggression is rare and is only necessary to counter instances of aggression or when differences are irreconcilable.[39] Thus, for a rising BRICS, peaceful accommodation is possible, and becoming a legitimate stakeholder is likely for a state

---

[38] Jervis, "Cooperation under the Security Dilemma"; Glaser, "Realists as Optimists."

[39] For a critique of defensive realism, see John A. Vasquez, "The Realist Paradigm and Degenerative versus Progressive Research Programs: An Appraisal of Neotraditional Research on Waltz's Balancing Proposition" *American Political Science Review* 91, no. 4 (December 1997), 899–912; Zakaria, *From Wealth to Power*; Jeffrey W. Legro and Andrew Moravcsik, "Is Anybody Still a Realist?" *International Security* 24, no. 2 (Fall 1999), 5–55.

that maximizes security and preserves the existing distribution of power among the established states.

For defensive realists, conquest rarely pays, and contributes instead to pathological outcomes such as self-encirclement and imperial over-stretch. Aggression and conquest are self-defeating because they provoke counterbalancing behavior and encourage opposition. Defensive realists largely accept Waltz's assumption that balances of power recurrently form in the international system and that imbalances of power are not durable or stable. As Stephen Walt notes, "If balancing is more common . . . then states are more secure because aggressors will face combined opposition. Status quo states should therefore avoid provoking countervailing coalitions by eschewing threatening foreign and defense policies."[40] Thus, as Snyder reminds us, "the balance of power that arises out of international anarchy punishes aggression; it does not reward it."[41]

Defensive realists identify several additional problems with aggression and conquest: modern nationalism makes conquest costly, because it "spurs the defenders to fight harder" and makes it hard to subdue and manipulate people in defeated states; repression will provoke massive popular resistance and uprisings; and modern information economies are hard to subjugate.[42] Moreover, the nuclear revolution and second-strike capability make it risky to attack a nuclear great power.[43] Finally, control over politically hostile societies is expensive; the price of maintaining empire, and especially the high levels of defense spending, will erode a great power's economic wealth; and the gains from conquest are rarely additive.[44]

For defensive realism, the security dilemma is one tragedy of anarchy. According to John Herz and Robert Jervis, one state's attempt to increase its own security due to the anarchic nature of the international system can inadvertently threaten other states and make them less secure, and thereby provoke them to augment their power.[45] As Jervis tells us, "many of the means by which a state tries to increase its security decrease the security of others"; further, "an increase in one state's security decreases

[40] Stephen M. Walt, "Alliance Formation and the Balance of World Power," *International Security* 9, no. 4 (Spring 1985), 4.

[41] Snyder, *Myths of Empire*, 11.

[42] Christopher Layne, "The Unipolar Illusion Revisited: The Coming End of the United States' Unipolar Moment," *International Security* 31, no. 2 (Fall 2006), 7–41.

[43] Robert Jervis, *The Meaning of the Nuclear Revolution: Statecraft and the Prospect of Armageddon* (Ithaca: Cornell University Press, 1990).

[44] Carl Kaysen, "Is War Obsolete?: A Review Essay," *International Security* 14, no. 4 (Spring 1990), 42–64.

[45] John H. Herz, *Political Realism and Political Idealism: A Study of Theories and Realities* (Chicago: University of Chicago Press, 1951); Jervis, "Cooperation under the Security Dilemma."

the security of others."[46] For defensive realists, motivated by security-seeking behavior, the outcome is an unintended hostility spiral among states that harbor no aggressive or revisionist intent.[47]

There are several peaceful rise strategies that the BRICS and the established states can use to reduce the security dilemma. These include: increasing the joint gains from cooperation; increasing the costs of non-cooperation; reducing the unilateral gains from the sucker's payoff; and increasing the costs of mutual defection.[48] Charles Glaser's contingent realism adds to the discussion by arguing that under many conditions, rival states can achieve a higher level of security through cooperation than through arms competition, aggression, and territorial expansion. For instance, he maintains that "when the risks of competition exceed the risks of cooperation, states should direct their self-help efforts toward achieving cooperation."[49]

For defensive realists, security-seeking states are common. Moreover, it is possible for security-seeking states that are satisfied with the status quo to signal their benign intent to one another and to identify one another. For Glaser, states that limit offensive capabilities through arms control, unilateral defense, and unilateral restraint, especially when the offense has the advantage, can communicate their benign intentions and motives to other states. Concomitantly, this behavior can increase their security by preventing the security dilemma, unnecessary hostility spirals, and dangerous arms races.[50]

For defensive realists, the international system rarely encourages security-seeking BRICS or the established great powers to maximize their power.[51] Defensive realists use the "fine-grained structure of power" or "structural modifiers" such as geography, technology, and other factors to explain most instances of expansion, aggression, and war.[52] According to Stephen Van Evera's findings, when technology makes conquest easier, states are less secure and less likely to cooperate or engage in diplomacy; states cannot increase security without threatening others; there are greater incentives for preemption, striking first, and "opportunistic expansion"; and strategies of security through expansion should be widespread even for status quo powers, who must behave like aggressors

---

[46] Jervis, "Cooperation under the Security Dilemma," 169, 186.

[47] Robert Jervis, "Realism, Liberalism, and Cooperation: Understanding the Debate," *International Security* 24, no. 1 (Summer 1999), 42–63.

[48] Robert Jervis, "From Balance to Concert: A Study of International Security Cooperation," *World Politics* 38, no. 1 (October 1985), 58–79.

[49] Glaser, "Realists as Optimists," 60.   [50] Ibid., 68–69.

[51] Jervis, "Realism, Liberalism, and Cooperation."

[52] Glenn D. Snyder, "Process Variables in Neorealist Theory," *Security Studies* 5, no. 3 (Spring 1996), 168–71; Van Evera, *Causes of War*, 7–8.

in order to defend themselves against aggressors. For defensive realists, instances of offensive advantage are a rare occurrence. Moreover, the defender usually has a net advantage.

When technology makes conquest more difficult, states are more secure, have a more relaxed view, can wait for unambiguous signs of aggression, can make themselves more secure without threatening other states, and, in the case of status quo states, can cooperate fairly easily and engage in diplomacy.[53] For Robert Jervis, defense dominance will "render international anarchy relatively unimportant."[54] Thus, for defensive realists, when the defense is dominant, states have little incentive to engage in territorial expansion.[55]

A second structural modifier for defensive realists is geography, which can make aggression easier or more difficult. In land warfare, natural buffers and barriers, the size of territory, and difficult terrain aid the defender against superior numbers. For Mearsheimer, the stopping power of water makes it more difficult for states to project their power over long distances. Furthermore, the loss-of-strength gradient or the logistical burden of projecting power over a long distance tends to reduce the relative fighting power of the attacker.

For Waltz and for defensive realists, socialization to the norms of peaceful conflict resolution and the learning of lessons from history are important deterrents to expansion and aggression, especially for the BRICS states that are newly emerging on the regional or global stage. As Walt notes, "If balancing is the norm and if states understand this tendency, aggression is discouraged because those who contemplate it will anticipate resistance."[56] Similarly, Christopher Layne states that "one of history's few incontestable lessons is that the pursuit of hegemony invariably is self-defeating."[57]

Finally, defensive realists account for ambitious attempts of expansion and conquest as the product of domestic- and individual-level pathologies. Leaders might inflate threats to mobilize domestic resources, perceptions of the balance of power can affect state behavior, and aversion to loss can lead to risky diplomatic and foreign military intervention.[58]

---

[53] Jack S. Levy, "The Offense/Defense Balance of Military Technology: A Theoretical and Historical Analysis," *International Studies Quarterly* 28, no. 2 (Spring 1990), 222–30.

[54] Jervis, "Cooperation under the Security Dilemma," 187.

[55] Ibid., 187.   [56] Walt, "Alliance Formation."

[57] Christopher Layne, *The Peace of Illusions: American Grand Strategy from 1940 to the Present* (Ithaca: Cornell University Press, 2006).

[58] Thomas J. Christensen, *Useful Adversaries: Grand Strategy, Domestic Mobilization, and Sino-American Conflict, 1947–1958* (Princeton: Princeton University Press, 1996); Melvyn P. Leffler, *A Preponderance of Power: National Security, the Truman Administration, and the Cold War* (Stanford: Stanford University Press, 1992); William Curti

According to Aaron Friedberg, states find it difficult to assess relative power, which often lags behind shifts in the real distribution of power.[59] Instead of steady, robust, and efficient balancing behavior (through either internal military buildup or counterbalancing alliances), a state's adjustment is likely to be irregular and jerky, and to occur in bursts. For Randall Schweller, underbalancing runs contrary to the core prediction of structural realism.[60] Schweller maintains that underreactions to dangerous shifts in relative power occur because actors' preferences are more influenced by domestic rather than international concerns, and therefore do not create incentives to adopt a balancing policy, or else the potential domestic political risks and costs of balancing are deemed too high. Thus, domestic constraints can prevent states from balancing in a timely and systematic manner in response to dangerous changes in relative power.

Components of power theory

The international system sets the broad parameters for interstate behavior. Moreover, the general logic of balance of power theory that shifts in power can provoke counterbalancing and great power war is well supported. However, balance of power theory is wrong about how states measure power and capabilities, forecast power trends, and assess threats. The danger is that Washington risks overreacting or underreacting to possible surpassing by the BRICS in 2021, 2027, or 2035. Moreover, neither the Thucydides Trap nor Mearsheimer's tragedy of great power politics is inevitable between the United States and China. Rather, a new model of major power relations is possible, as emphasized by Evan Medeiros, the Senior Director for Asian Affairs in the National Security Council:

We see the concept as a way to encourage – to ensure that China's rise is a force of stability in the region . . . When we say a "new model," the question is, what's new? And my point is it's new only insofar as we are able to develop patterns of interaction and habits of cooperation that allow us to avoid the historic trap of an established power and a rising power inevitably coming into conflict.[61]

Wohlforth, *The Elusive Balance: Power and Perceptions During the Cold War* (Ithaca: Cornell University Press, 1993); Thomas J. Christensen, "Perceptions and Alliances in Europe, 1865–1940," *International Organization* 51 no. 1 (Winter 1997), 65–97; Jeffrey W. Taliaferro, *Balancing Risks: Great Power Intervention in the Periphery* (Ithaca: Cornell University Press, 2004).

[59] Aaron L. Friedberg, *The Weary Titan: Britain and the Experience of Relative Decline, 1895–1905* (Princeton: Princeton University Press, 1988).

[60] Randall L. Schweller, *Unanswered Threats: Political Constraints on the Balance of Power* (Princeton: Princeton University Press, 2006).

[61] Yoichi Kato, "Interview/Evan Medeiros: China's Attempt to Isolate Japan worsens Bilateral Relations," *The Asahi Shimbun* (April 6, 2014). Available at: ajw.asahi.com/article/views/opinion/AJ201404060018.

China is a rising power. However, Beijing's aggregate material capability, overall military spending, and composite index of power – measurements that are often cited and used to highlight that China will challenge America's rule – are not good indicators for assessing China's power trends, future Sino-American enmities, and the likelihood for counterbalancing. More important is which specific components of China's national power are increasing, whether they challenge vital American interests, and whether these specific components are appropriate and useful against the United States.

Components of power theory advances two fixes that recast balance of power theory. One is that states assess power trends based on specific components of power and whether they threaten vital geostrategic interests.[62] When state leaders assess another state to forecast future power trends, they ask themselves which components or elements of its national power are increasing and whether they will peak above or below their own components of national power. Moreover, state leaders ask themselves whether specific components of power will peak above critical thresholds and redlines of power. Finally, state leaders ask whether these components of power threaten vital national interests.

For instance, for the United States, the foundation of its military security is its Command of the Commons. Command of the Commons allows Washington to extend its reach far beyond its waters' edge. Command of the Commons represents the United States' command over the globe's sea, space, and air. According to Barry Posen, this includes nuclear attack submarines, surface fleets (including aircraft carriers), satellite communications and anti-satellite technology, fighter and bomber aircraft, air- and sealift capacity, and missile and anti-missile technology.[63] This ability is supported by a network of bases, landing and air rights, and combat centers. The United States should balance against any state – great power, BRICS, or N-11 – that attempts to challenge its Command of the Commons by building a capability beyond what is required for its defense.

In contrast to the expectations of balance of power theory, a new model of major power relations can explain why there is no significant counterbalancing in Asia against the United States despite America's unprecedented strength. Historically, land powers, including France, Germany, and Russia, have not identified the naval components of power of a state

---

[62] On measuring vital interests, see Daryl G. Press, *Calculating Credibility: How Leaders Assess Military Threats* (Ithaca: Cornell University Press, 2005), 25–28, in which he divides interests into three categories: vital interests, important interests, and concerns.

[63] Barry R. Posen, "Command of the Commons: The Military Foundation of US Hegemony," *International Security* 28, no. 1 (Summer 2003), 5–46.

as a major challenge to their vital interests. In disaggregating China's power trends, Beijing is a continental land power. First, it shares borders with fourteen neighboring states, some of whom have nuclear weapons and large land armies, and Beijing has engaged in border disputes and wars. Second, China faces both interior border disputes on its northern and western frontiers and internal security challenges, including terrorism, separatism, and extremism. Third, as a land power, the PLA's demand for interior and internal security will constrain the development of the real assets necessary to become a blue-water maritime power. According to Robert Ross, China allocates the bulk of its defense spending to the PLA, with about one-tenth going to the People's Liberation Army Navy (PLAN).[64] For this reason, the United States should respond differently if Beijing moves to develop an ambitious blue-water naval program and supporting naval bases in the Pacific, or chooses to expand the land-based element of the PLA. Only the former component should matter for the United States, though the latter would provoke Russia and India. Thus, for China and other continental powers, counterbalancing against America's Command of the Commons is an inefficient use of resources that can better be directed toward interior border security and internal threats.

For Washington, one element of concern with China's power is that Beijing is acquiring anti-access and area denial (A2AD) capability.[65] Starting in the 1990s, China directed resources toward A2AD, including anti-ship missiles, short- and intermediate-range ballistic missiles, cruise missiles, stealth submarines, and cyber and space weapons, in order to challenge US superiority, especially in its littoral seas. The danger is that Beijing does not need to become a peer or even a near-peer naval competitor with the United States and its allies to pose a major danger to America's vital interests. States are driven by windows of opportunity and vulnerability in terms of specific components of power. If American statesmen expect that a major Sino-American hegemonic war will not occur until the intersection of the aggregate power curves of a rising China and a declining United States, then they will be too late in preparing for war. For this reason, Avery Goldstein is wrong to say that while China is "one of a small handful of states that may have the necessary ingredients to emerge one day as a peer competitor... The distance China must travel before it has the economic and military foundation of power comparable to those of the United States is great... While China's

---

[64] Robert S. Ross, "China's Naval Nationalism: Sources, Prospects, and the US Response," *International Security* 34, no. 2 (Fall 1990), 46–81.
[65] Ross, "China's Naval Nationalism."

capabilities have grown impressively compared with its own past, the strides it is making in 'closing the gap' with the United States are so far rather small."[66] Similarly, Barry Posen is mistaken to state that "the US military advantage in the sea, in the air, and in space will be very difficult to challenge – let alone overcome."[67] China does not need to overcome the United States. Instead, as discussed further on, in disaggregating China's material capability, what matters is whether China has the appropriate elements of power to challenge the United States. Thus, China might challenge the United States when it believes it has sufficient strength in a particular element of power, and well before any transition in overall power with the United States occurs.

The second fix of components of power theory is that, on this view, more important than an aggregate capability score or a composite index of power in assessing power trends is whether the state has the appropriate or necessary components of national power to pose a major danger. In the 1950s, the United States had a near monopoly on atomic weaponry. However, President Eisenhower's containment strategy of Massive Retaliation lacked fungibility, usefulness, and credibility in fighting the wars of liberation that it confronted with the collapse of the European empires. Similarly, despite the growth in China's aggregate defense spending, Beijing does not have a blue-water navy, but just commissioned its first aircraft carrier and carried out its first at-sea landings, and has no integrated carrier task group. Washington should monitor China's naval power trends, and specifically the supporting production, plant, skilled labor, and capacity to construct a green- or a blue-water navy, to determine whether Beijing is able to challenge America's Command of the Commons. Moreover, Washington should ask whether these specific components of power are increasing and whether they will peak above or below America's components of national power and above critical thresholds and redlines.

The import of these two fixes to balance of power theory is severalfold. First, for Washington, if no components or elements of China's or another BRICS state's power pose a threat to the United States, then they should not provoke American counterbalancing or a preventive war, despite their growing aggregate material capabilities. For now, much of China's defense spending remains focused on interior border security, internal security, and the PLA, rather than on PLAN or the PLA Air Force – all elements and power trends that do not challenge US vital interests.

---

[66] Goldstein, "Parsing China's Rise," 61.
[67] Posen, "Command of the Commons," 21.

Second, on assessment, a weaker state with a lower military capability score might be more threatening to the United States than is China, depending on the mix of its components of power.

Third, in contrast to arguments that emphasize aggregate shifts in material capabilities alone, China does not need to become a peer or even a near-peer competitor to pose a major danger to the United States. In contrast to David Shambaugh's findings, China does not need to possess a comprehensive toolbox of capabilities.[68] Rather, as a partial power, what matters is whether China has the correct elements. The same holds for other BRICS, such as Russia.

Fourth, American leaders should assess power trends based on components or elements of national power, rather than balancing against aggregate shifts and transitions in material capability alone. Specifically, relative American military or economic decline, even if the United States is surpassed by China in 2027 or 2035, does not mean that it is necessarily less secure. Nor does pouring more money into defense spending or boosting overall military capability necessarily make the United States more secure, especially if such spending is directed against the wrong elements of China's power or if the United States engages in broad and inefficient counterbalancing.

Conclusion

This chapter addresses what the major IR theories say about whether the emerging BRICS states will be accommodated by the established great powers. Specifically, is counterbalancing and contestation an unfortunate tragedy of great power politics? Is the Thucydides Trap certain? Do the BRICS need to become peer or near-peer rivals to pose a major danger?

Offensive realism and defensive realism offer different answers to whether peaceful accommodation of the BRICS is likely, whether a BRICS can become a legitimate stakeholder in the international system, whether the transition will be peaceful or war-prone, how the established great powers will respond, and what alternative strategies rising and declining states will pursue. The core assumptions of offensive realism are that all major states seek to maximize power, status quo powers are rare, and conquest often pays. The implication is that peaceful accommodation is rare. To become a stakeholder, an emerging state must expand through war and territorial conquest to dominate other states. In contrast, the core assumptions of defensive realism are that

---

[68] David Shambaugh, "China Engages Asia: Reshaping the Regional Order," *International Security* 29, no. 3 (Winter 2004/05), 94.

states seek to maximize security, conquest rarely pays, and status quo states are common. The import is that gradual accommodation is possible for a restrained BRICS, which can be accepted as a legitimate stakeholder in the international system provided it is a security-seeking state and does not upset the positions of the established major powers.

In recasting balance of power theory and presenting a new model of major power relations, I argue that components of power theory is more useful in assessing systemic and subsystemic power trends. I accept the general logic of balance of power theory, and especially that shifts in aggregate power and changes in the distribution of capabilities are dangerous. However, offensive and defensive realism miss how states assess power trends. In assessing power trends, what matters is (1) the specific components or elements of a state's power and whether they threaten vital interests, and (2) whether the state has the appropriate elements of power to pose a major threat.

3 Globalization, interdependence, and major power accommodation

Philip B.K. Potter

Those who are optimistic about the potential for accommodation between major powers often resort to arguments about the pacifying influence of economic interdependence. If one accepts this view and gives credence to the deepening ties of globalization, it is natural to anticipate that the accommodation of those states assessed as current cases in Part III (China, Russia, India, and Brazil) might proceed more peacefully than the historical cases outlined in Part II. For example, it has been widely argued in American policy and academic circles that the United States and China are less likely to get into serious conflict as China rises because of the extensive trade interdependence between them. As Madeline Albright observed in her announcement of the Clinton administration's decision to renew China's Most Favored Nation trade status, "we have in our era an unprecedented opportunity to integrate the world around basic principles of democracy, open markets, law *and a common commitment to peace.*"[1]

Proponents of this position tend to argue that that there is meaningful quantitative empirical evidence linking interdependence to peace (or at least to the lessened probability of conflict). Bruce Russett, a primary producer of this quantitative work in support of the liberal position, clearly articulates this stance, drawing the conclusion in a policy-oriented review of his work that conflict is unlikely in interdependent relationships because "if we bomb the cities or factories of a close trading partner – where we also are likely to have heavy private investments – we are bombing our own markets, suppliers, and even the property of our own nationals."[2]

The trouble with this conclusion is that there is actually very little that most of the quantitative work in this domain can say about the

---

[1] Madeleine Albright, "Secretary of State Madeleine Albright Luncheon Remarks," Wilmington, DE, May 19, 1997. Emphasis added.

[2] Bruce Russett, "What Else Causes War?" *Boston Review* (October/November 1997). Available at: new.bostonreview.net/BR22.5/russett.html.

accommodation of rising powers such as China.[3] In the vast majority of cases, the findings that underpin the linkage between interdependence and peace tie measures of trade to the incidence of relatively low-level conflict events.[4] Moreover, to get the statistical power needed to make inferences from these data, the regressions are typically time-series, cross-sectional aggregations of all countries over many years. While appropriate for establishing the general relationship between trade and conflict, almost every aspect of this arrangement undermines the applicability of the findings to the more significant question of major power accommodation in the present age. Inevitably, major power relationships will be outliers in a population of all states when it comes to both trade and conflict. Furthermore, small-scale militarized events are not what analysts should care most about when it comes to the success or failure of accommodation. Finally, these regressions generally have little to say about whether interdependence is the cause or consequence of peaceful behavior.

Aside from the challenges of extending extant arguments about the link between trade and conflict to great power accommodation, there are additional serious questions about the very nature of interdependence. As I have noted, financial interactions are the most common subject of inquiry, but what types of financial interaction matter and how should they be quantified? Is it simply trade that pacifies, or should investment be prioritized? How should we account for the differences between trade in manufactured goods, services, and primary resources? What about interdependencies aside from trade, such as communication and mobility? Globe-shrinking technologies are, after all, much of what separates this age of globalization from those that have preceded it.

These challenges in the existing literature mean that this chapter is somewhat pessimistic when it comes to the current state of what can be said with confidence about the relationship between interdependence and the accommodation of the rising powers that animate this volume. As I will outline, the interplay between independence and accommodation appears to be very context dependent – to the point that it seems to cut in opposite directions in some of the most highly salient cases (e.g., in the cases of China and Russia). There are, however, lessons that can be learned and applied from the extant literature, as well as avenues for new

---

[3] This is putting aside entirely the minority of quantitative work that finds no relationship (or even a positive relationship) between trade and conflict.

[4] This most commonly takes the form of the relationship between trade dependence (measured as some variant of (imports + exports)/GDP) and militarized interstate disputes from the Correlates of War Project.

research that could begin to clarify the causal processes linking various types of interdependence to major power accommodation.

What do we know about trade interdependence?

The idea that there might be a meaningful, causal linkage between trade and peace has a distinguished intellectual pedigree, which is commonly traced back to the work of Kant and Montesquieu.[5] Adam Smith built on these ideas in his arguments for free trade, maintaining that international commerce reduces friction and violent conflict by allowing each side to benefit from transactions.[6] Schumpeter took a similar perspective, suggesting that capitalist motives would give rise to a class of rationalist individuals "likely to be essentially of an unwarlike disposition."[7]

Broadly speaking, this "pacification through trade" argument is closely associated with the liberal school of thought, and Norman Angell's prediction that war among major powers has become so costly as to be futile – famously followed by the outbreak of World War I (WWI).[8] The setback was short-lived both for Angell (he went on to win a Nobel Prize) and for the argument itself, as modern versions of the liberal thesis remain dominant in the discourse on interdependence and conflict.

The world wars, however, remain the primary challenge to any simplistic or automatic linkage between trade interdependence and accommodation. As discussed in more detail in Chapters 8 and 9 of this volume, Germany and Japan were both substantial traders in the international system. Arguably, the failure of trade to facilitate accommodation with

---

[5] Immanuel Kant, *Perpetual Peace and Other Essays on Politics, History and Morals* (Indianapolis: Hackett Publishing Company 1983); Montesquieu, *Spirit of the Laws* (Cambridge: Cambridge University Press, 1989).

[6] Adam Smith, *The Wealth of Nations*, ed. Edwin Cannan (New York: Random House, 1994).

[7] Joseph A. Schumpeter, "Economic Theory and Entrepreneurial History," in *Essays on Economic Topics of Joseph A. Schumpeter*, ed. R.V. Clemence (Port Washington: Kennikat Press, 1951). A full review of the interdependence literature is beyond the scope of this chapter. For a more complete treatment, see Katherine Barbieri and Gerald Schneider, "Globalization and Peace: Assessing New Directions in the Study of Trade and Conflict," *Journal of Peace Research* 36, no. 4 (July 1999), 387–404; Arthur A. Stein, "Governments, Economic Interdependence, and International Cooperation," in *Behavior, Society, and Nuclear War*, vol. 3, eds. Philip E. Tetlock, Jo L. Husbands, Robert Jervis, Paul C. Stern, and Charles Tilly (New York: Oxford University Press, 1992), 243–324; Edward D. Mansfield and Brian M. Pollins, "The Study of Interdependence and Conflict: Recent Advances, Open Questions, and Directions for Future Research," *Journal of Conflict Resolution* 45, no. 6 (December 2001), 834–59; Susan M. McMillan, "Interdependence and Conflict," *International Studies Review* 41, no. 1 (May 1997), 33–58.

[8] Norman Angell, *The Great Illusion: A Study of the Relation of Military Power in Nations to their Economic and Social Advantage* (New York: Knickerbocker Press, 1991).

Germany is the more damning of the two, since German trade was both more extensive and more balanced than Japan's.

Liberal arguments linking trade and peace have taken a variety of related forms. Early on, Staley suggested that economic exchange represented an alternative to military exploits as a means of obtaining resources and prosperity.[9] Richard Rosecrance built on this logic, asserting that as international trade and the markets that support it mature, military action becomes an inefficient means of obtaining the requirements for growth, thus rendering territorial expansion obsolete.[10] In all of these formulations, emerging peace is contingent on the growth of liberal trading regimes. Where tariffs or other barriers to interdependence increase, these theorists seem to suggest that conflict could arise.[11]

With time, discussion of interdependence and conflict was integrated into the broader context of the "liberal peace." The liberal peace is a set of ideas about the ingredients for international cooperation loosely derived from the "three definitive articles" in Immanuel Kant's *Perpetual Peace*. This literature began with democracy and the democratic peace, but eventually spread to a broader analysis of the other two legs of what Russett and John Oneal term the "Kantian tripod" – economic interdependence and international organizations.[12] As the name implies, the idea is that each leg of the tripod (democracy, extensive trade, and international organization membership) is independent and essential.

At the opposite end of the spectrum from the liberal expectation that trade promotes peace are realists such as Kenneth Waltz who anticipate either no meaningful relationship between trade and conflict, or that trade might actually generate more domains for competition and unequal gain, and through that avenue actually increase the probability of conflict.[13]

---

[9] Eugene Staley, *The World Economy in Transition* (New York: Council on Foreign Relations, 1939).

[10] Richard Rosecrance, *The Rise of the Trading State: Commerce and Conquest in the Modern World* (New York: Free Press, 1986).

[11] Jacob Viner, *International Economics* (Glencoe: Free Press, 1951).

[12] John R. Oneal and Bruce Russett, "The Kantian Peace: The Pacific Benefits of Democracy, Interdependence, and International Organizations, 1885–1992," *World Politics* 52, no. 1 (October 1999), 1; John R. Oneal and Bruce Russett, "Clear and Clean: The Fixed Effects of the Liberal Peace," *International Organization* 55, no. 2, (Spring 2001), 469; John R. Oneal, Bruce Russett, and Michael L. Berbaum, "Causes of Peace: Democracy, Interdependence, and International Organizations, 1885–1992," *International Studies Quarterly* 47, no. 3 (September 2003), 371–93; John R. Oneal and Bruce M. Russett, "The Classical Liberals Were Right: Democracy, Interdependence, and Conflict, 1950–1985," *International Studies Quarterly* 41, no. 2, 267–93; Bruce Russett, John R. Oneal, and David R. Davis, "The Third Leg of the Kantian Tripod for Peace: International Organizations and Militarized Disputes, 1950–85," *International Organization* 52, no. 3 (Summer 1998), 441.

[13] Kenneth N. Waltz, "The Myth of National Interdependence," in *International Corporation: A Symposium*, ed. Charles P. Kindleberger (Cambridge, MA: MIT Press, 1971), 205–23.

The intellectual roots of this position are just as distinguished as those of the liberal argument. To take one example, Alexander Hamilton's Federalist Paper No. 6 is largely dedicated to debunking the notion that the "spirit of commerce has a tendency to soften the manners of men and to extinguish those inflammable humors which have so often led to wars."[14] Barry Buzan makes a similar case that interdependence does not matter one way or the other in a world dominated by security concerns.[15] To the point that states occupy themselves with trade and commerce in the short term, it represents an illusory calm before the storm and should not capture the primary attention of those attempting to understand the international system. Norrin Ripsman and Jean-Marc Blanchard echo this argument about the fundamental irrelevance of trade to the high politics of international affairs.[16] Robert Gilpin goes further, claiming that reluctant restraint is not the only way that states might react to the costs imposed by their interdependence with potential adversaries.[17] If the highest imperative for a state is survival in an anarchic world, then interdependence can also be viewed as a "vulnerability" that must be addressed by any means necessary – including violence.

Ripsman and T.V. Paul argue against the entire notion that global-ization, and the interdependencies that contribute to it, are eroding the primacy of the nation state.[18] This argument in many ways bears the closest relationship with the questions at hand in this chapter, since its underlying story is that interdependence and globalization have done little to change the fundamental relationship between great powers and their competitors. The implication is that if interdependence had limited success at facilitating accommodation in the past (as is seemingly the case in the instances of Germany and Japan), then there is relatively little reason to think that things should go better this time around.

Beginning in the late 1980s, many hoped that the emergence of large-N statistical analyses in political science would conclusively resolve the debate over the nature of the relationship between interdependence and conflict. Unfortunately, the empirical results have been notably mixed, and therefore on their own do not provide clear guidance with regard to

[14] Quoted in Stephen G. Brooks, *Producing Security: Multinational Corporations, Global-ization, and the Changing Calculus of Conflict* (Princeton: Princeton University Press, 2005).
[15] Barry Buzan, "Economic Structure and International Security: The Limits of the Lib-eral Case," *International Organization* 38, no. 4 (Autumn 1984), 597–624.
[16] Norrin M. Ripsman and Jean-Marc F. Blanchard, "Commercial Liberalism under Fire: Evidence from 1914 and 1936," *Security Studies* 6, no. 2 (Winter 1996), 4–50.
[17] Robert Gilpin, *War and Change in World Politics* (Cambridge: Cambridge University Press, 1981).
[18] Norrin M. Ripsman and T.V. Paul, *Globalization and the National Security State* (New York: Oxford University Press, 2010).

the question of accommodation. The preponderance of empirical findings indicates a negative relationship between economic exchange and
conflict.[19]

The aforementioned work by Russett and Oneal (sometimes together,
sometimes separately, and sometimes with other collaborators) forms the
backbone of the quantitative evidence supporting the liberal position.
They find a consistently negative relationship between interdependence
and conflict, both at the bivariate level and in the broader context of
the liberal peace.[20] Russett and Oneal reach this conclusion by modeling
the relationship between the dependence on trade within a pair of states,
measured in terms of total trade divided by GDP, and the probability
that they will come into conflict, measured with "militarized interstate
disputes" from the Correlates of War Project, over a very long period of
analysis of more than 100 years. As I noted at the outset, however, this
evidence is difficult to extend to the question of accommodation for at
least three reasons. First, the possibility of reverse causality looms large.
Second, aggregate findings generated from a sample of all states obscure
the peculiarities of major and rising powers. Third, and finally, militarized
interstate dispute is arguably a largely irrelevant outcome variable when
it comes to accommodation.

Others have contested this body of quantitative evidence in support
of the liberal peace. Edward Mansfield and Jon Pevehouse, for example,
argue that trade is related to the presence of regional trading institutions,
and that once these institutions are accounted for, there is little evidence
of a relationship between economic interdependence and conflict.[21] Also
claiming that previous models are underspecified, Erik Gartzke finds that
state preferences, as indicated by UN voting patterns, better predict the

[19] Key works include David A. Baldwin, "Interdependence and Power: A Conceptual
      Analysis," *International Organization* 34, no. 4 (Autmn 1980), 471–506; Barry Jones and
      Peter Willetts, *Interdependence on Trial: Studies in the Theory and Reality of Contemporary
      Interdependence* (New York: St. Martin's Press, 1984); Edmund Dell, *The Politics of
      Economic Interdependence* (New York: Palgrave Macmillan, 1987); William K. Domke,
      War and the Changing Global System (New Haven: Yale University Press, 1988); James N.
      Rosenau and Hylke Tromp, *Interdependence and Conflict in World Politics* (Brookefield:
      Avebury, 1989); Edward D. Mansfield, *Power, Trade and War* (Princeton: Princeton
      University Press, 1994).
[20] Oneal and Russett, "Clear and Clean"; Oneal and Russett, "The Kantian Peace";
      Oneal *et al.*, "Causes of Peace"; Oneal and Russett, "The Classical Liberals Were
      Right"; Russett *et al.*, "The Third Leg"; John R. Oneal, Brad Lian, and James H.
      Joyner, Jr., "Are the American People 'Pretty Prudent'? Public Responses to US Uses
      of Force, 1950–1988," *International Studies Quarterly* 40, no. 2 (June 1996), 261–79;
      Bruce Russett and John Oneal, *Triangulating Peace: Democracy, Interdependence, and
      International Organizations* (New York: W.W. Norton, 2001).
[21] Edward D. Mansfield and Jon C. Pevehouse, "Trade Blocs, Trade Flows, and Interna-
      tional Conflict," *International Organization* 54, no. 4 (Autumn 2000), 775–808.

outbreak of conflict than trade interdependence.[22] Katherine Barbieri argues (using models broadly similar to those employed by Russett and Oneal) that trade, at least under some circumstances, promotes conflict, and that liberal work in this area suffers from measurement errors.[23] Others have questioned the veracity of liberal findings on trade and peace by criticizing the applicability of the cross-sectional and time-series models typically used by researchers.[24]

Predictably, these divisions over the most basic attributes of the relationship between trade and conflict introduced a malaise into the entire research program. As Barbieri and Schneider note, "if the relationships we identify in disparate research efforts are truly robust, they should hold up under seemingly related concepts of interdependence and under different conditions captured by our choice of domain and control variables."[25] Yet they do not.

There are several plausible explanations for the discrepancies in the empirical findings, including the trade measures used, differences in the use of contiguous or "politically relevant" dyads, different countries in the data sets, and differences in the period of analysis. According to replications of the empirical evidence by other scholars, the immediate distinction between the models primarily arises from the variations in the countries and years used in the analyses.[26] It is unclear, however, what researchers and those interested in the question of major power accommodation should make of this result. Reasonable people can, and do, vehemently disagree about which formulation is correct. But if the relationship between interdependence and conflict is truly important and warrants such attention, it seems reasonable to expect a more durable finding that is relatively constant across relatively broad swaths of time and space. The lack of such consensus makes it essentially impossible for academics, and especially policymakers, to reach useful conclusions.

---

[22] Erik Gartzke, "Preferences and the Democratic Peace," *International Studies Quarterly* 44, no. 2 (June 2000), 191–212. In later work, Gartzke finds evidence for a relationship between economic openness and peace: Erik Gartzke, "The Capitalist Peace," *American Journal of Political Science* 51, no. 1 (January 2007), 166–91.

[23] Katherine Barbieri, *The Liberal Illusion: Does Trade Promote Peace?* (Ann Arbor: University of Michigan Press, 2002).

[24] Nathaniel Beck, Jonathan N. Katz, and Richard Tucker, "Taking Time Seriously: Time-Series-Cross-Section Analysis with a Binary Dependent Variable," *American Journal of Political Science* 42, no. 4 (October 1998), 1260–88. However, more methodologically sophisticated rebuttals appear to have reestablished the liberal thesis in the face of this argument: D. Scott Bennett and Allan C. Stam, "A Universal Test of an Expected Utility Theory of War," *International Studies Quarterly* 44, no. 3 (September 2000), 451–80.

[25] Barbieri and Schneider, "Globalization and Peace."

[26] William J. Dixon, "Commercial Liberalism on Trial," *International Studies Review* 5, no. 3 (September 2003), 364–66.

Obviously, this lack of confidence in the empirical evidence linking trade and conflict does not bode well for any extension of liberal arguments about interdependence to the question of major power accommodation. However, as I have noted, the challenges run far deeper. The unfortunate implication is that, despite decades of work on interdependence and conflict, the specifics as they relate to accommodation are relatively underdeveloped in the literature.

Trade interdependence and major power accommodation

How, then, should we think about the role of trade interdependence when it comes to the accommodation challenges that presently confront the international system? The anecdotal evidence suggests that the relationships are complex, interactive, and highly contingent on both the nature of trade and the position of the state in question. The implication is that there is unlikely to be a single, simple relationship that applies equally in all the cases that we scrutinize here. The contrast between the Russian and Chinese cases clearly illustrates this reality.

As described in greater detail in Chapter 13, Russia trades extensively if one simply considers the measure typically employed in the quantitative interdependence and conflict literature – the volume of exports and imports divided by GDP. However, the specifics of that trade are important when it comes to peace, conflict, and, ultimately, accommodation. Energy exports to Europe (rather than manufactured goods or services) constitute the preponderance of Russian trade. As a result, investment and broader economic integration are relatively low when compared to states with similar volumes of trade. This arrangement appears to lend Russia a coercive advantage over Europe (at least in the short term), a dynamic that has clearly played out in the series of crises and threats that occurred in the aftermath of the ouster of Ukrainian president Viktor Yanukovych in 2014. It is certainly true that in the medium to long term, Russia is highly dependent on the foreign exchange that its gas exports generate, but in compellent situations the short-term asymmetries trump those long-term benefits. Due to these asymmetric goals, the nature of Russian trade arguably makes peaceful accommodation more challenging, and serves to fuel conflict rather than mitigate it.

This situation stands in apparent contrast to the Chinese case spelled out by Kai He in Chapter 10. In this instance, at least under some circumstances, trade appears to have had a stabilizing influence on the relationship with the United States and has arguably contributed to the successful (thus far) accommodation of China's meteoric rise. Again, the distinction may owe to the nature of this trade, which is enormous – over US\$560 billion in 2013.[27] Rather than being driven by a unidirectional exchange of resources for cash, integrated supply chains and substantial capital investment characterize the Sino-US trade relationship.

Drawing on this insight, Chinese scholars charged with thinking about the nature of China's rise to great power status have taken to describing the country's relationship with the United States as that of competitors. The idea here is that the typical dichotomy between nations being either friends or enemies is a false one. The combination of substantial interdependence with divergent interests means that it is possible for the United States and China to compete in a "healthy" way that does not escalate to violence. This is, in a sense, the essence of peaceful accommodation. In many regards, the emergence of this school of thought underlines the stability of the relationship, which derives at least in part from the depth of the trade interdependencies between the states.

The curious thing is the extent to which dependency appears to have very different consequences in these two cases. In the Russian case, academics, pundits, and politicians tend to speak about the mutual hostage situation generated by European reliance on Russian gas, and about the Russian government's reliance on these revenues increasing both the probability and consequences of conflict. In the Chinese case, the mutual hostage situation associated with bilateral trade dependence and fiscal interdependencies generated by China's massive holdings of US debt (due to substantial trade imbalances) is more often credited with promoting peace and stability. Again, this underlines the extent to which the nature of interdependence matters and the serious distinctions that are obscured by the "one-size-fits-all" approach necessitated by the application of aggregate data to the question.

Non-trade interdependencies

Despite the starkly divergent conclusions of the realist and liberal camps when it comes to the link between trade and conflict, most scholars share common ground with regard to the core mechanism by which they theoretically tie interdependence to either conflict or its absence. Although this mechanism is rarely spelled out in great detail, it is widely assumed that states' reactions to interdependence are driven by an implicit calculation of the relative costs and benefits of trade and conflict. If such rationalist cost–benefit analysis is an appropriate modeling assumption, then it makes sense to assess interdependence in terms of trade as a

---

[27] Trade in goods on a nominal basis. Figure from the US Census Bureau.

measure of cost. However, in our increasingly globalized world, trade is far from the only interaction between states.

Cost is not the only mechanism that might underpin a relationship between interdependence and conflict. One particularly well-developed alternative explanation is based on familiarity between states and the depth of their societal interaction. Simply put, the ties between societies generated by the frequent interaction of individuals might alter the very nature of the relationship between states, rather than the value of that relationship. Karl Deutsch is often associated with the notion that the close contact that inevitably accompanies any sort of cooperative international interaction promotes peace. As Deutsch describes it, "closeness" harkens to an increased "sense of community," produced by a density of interactions.[28] Deutsch emphasizes that regional integration benefits security by improving the overall tenor of relations through improvements in communication links between policymakers.

As it turns out, Kant's *Perpetual Peace* (the foundation of liberal, cost-based discussions of the relationship between interdependence and conflict) actually supports this closeness mechanism. The discussion of trade and conflict in *Perpetual Peace* is limited to just two short passages. Recent authors draw almost exclusively from the second of these, portions of which have been widely quoted:

[t]he spirit of commerce, which is incompatible with war, sooner or later gains the upper hand in every state. As the power of money is perhaps the most dependable of all the powers (means) included under the state power, states see themselves forced, without any moral urge, to promote honorable peace and by mediation to prevent war wherever it threatens to break out.[29]

Kant does not clearly articulate the mechanism by which trade compels states to "promote an honorable peace," but reading it as an issue of cost and economic interest is reasonable. However, the widely ignored first reference to the pacifying effect of international commerce is considerably more explicit about the underlying mechanism, and here the issue is one of closeness. Speaking on the historic terms of trade among societies, Kant tells us:

Salt and iron ... were perhaps the first articles of commerce for the various peoples and were sought far and wide; in this way a *peaceful traffic among nations was established, and thus understanding, conventions, and peaceable relations were established* among the most distant peoples.[30]

---

[28] Karl W. Deutsch, *Political Community at the International Level.* (Salt Lake City: ECKO House Publishing, [1954] 2006), 41–44.

[29] Immanuel Kant. *Perpetual Peace* (Minneapolis: Filiquarian Publishing, 2007), 39.

[30] Ibid., 35. Emphasis added.

Here Kant is not writing about how the benefits of trade come to outweigh the benefits of conflict; rather, he is quite clear about the transformative effect of closeness stemming from interaction. That is, peace arises from familiarity and habitually cooperative co-existence. Yet, despite its place in the originating literature, the idea that contact can, in and of itself, engender more peaceable relations reemerges only sporadically, typically as a non-systematic aside without any sort of empirical test.

This question of mechanism matters a great deal because, in the present age of globalization, states are interacting on multiple dimensions simultaneously. There are interactions such as trade that aggregate naturally to a cost-based conception of what might lead to peaceful accommodation, and there are intersocietal interactions in terms of communication and mobility, which are much more logically associated with ideas about the central role of closeness.

This stands in meaningful contrast to Kant's time, in which trade was one of the only peaceful international interactions that permeated societies beyond the highest elites. Moreover, most trade was accomplished in person, and it inevitably carried with it a good deal of interpersonal interaction. In short, "soft" interdependencies and trade interdependence were, in effect, nearly perfectly collinear. In this context, it was quite reasonable to think of interdependence exclusively in terms of commerce and trade, regardless of whether the underlying mechanism was one of cost or closeness. However, since that time, the world economy has steadily changed, while the way we think about interdependence has failed to keep apace.

The lesson is that when we consider independence in our rapidly globalizing international system (and particularly its potential relationship with major power accommodation), we are inevitably talking about much more than simple trade. In other words, commerce is far from the only interaction between states, and, in the context of globalization, it is not necessarily the most transformative. Beginning with the Industrial Revolution and continuing through our current era, forces have emerged that have both limited the interactions required for even larger volumes of trade and allowed for much closer interactions between societies outside the economic arena. A typical modern trade interaction might involve a multinational corporation placing an electronic order with a Chinese manufacturer, loading a container in China, shipping it to the United States via a third-party cargo vessel, offloading in Long Beach, and, finally, making a payment by electronic bank transfer. While it is possible that such interdependencies would raise the costs of conflict for potential adversaries, it is equally possible that such impersonal and transient trade linkages do not have the binding effects that are sometimes ascribed to them. Moreover, it could be that the deeper interactions between states at the interpersonal and policy levels matter a great deal more when it comes to matters of war and peace.

In many regards, the idea that interdependence means more than trade already permeates discussions on the subject. For example, the very observation that we live in an era of globalization – an expansive concept that includes simple trade, but also incorporates such diverse elements as the "monetization" of the world economy, increased foreign direct investment, growth in the number and influence of multinational corporations, and social and political interactions at the level of the individual – has fueled recent scholarship on interdependence.[31]

Early neoliberal work had some of this flavor as well, and pushed the discussion of interdependence away from myopic attention to trade alone, though in many ways this legacy has been forgotten. In their seminal 1977 book, *Power and Interdependence*, Robert Keohane and Joseph Nye developed the concepts of "asymmetrical interdependence" and "complex interdependence."[32] At the center of their understanding of international politics is the belief that states are connected on a variety of dimensions, ranging from institutions to corporations. They see no hierarchy among issues or dimensions of interaction, thereby challenging the realist expectation that security concerns dominate international politics. Keohane and Nye did not operationalize these concepts, nor did they directly test the relationship between interdependence and conflict; however, they did predict that military conflict will not occur when complex interdependence is achieved between states. In many regards, this more nuanced notion of interdependence is a precursor of what I propose is required in order to account for the deeper interdependencies associated with globalization and the extension of the question to accommodation.

Despite this increasing mismatch between trade as an exclusive measure of interdependence and the reality of an increasingly globalized world, the empirical literature on interdependence and conflict often cites globalization as a motivating concern, but then limits itself to bilateral trade in the theory and analysis. For example, Barbieri and Gerald Schneider observe that "'globalization' has largely superseded the term 'economic interdependence' to describe the rapidly growing links between nations, economies and societies," but then limit their discussion and analysis to the relationship between trade and conflict.[33] They are correct that globalization has subsumed international trade but neglect

---

[31] See, e.g., Brooks, *Producing Security*.

[32] Robert O. Keohane and Joseph S. Nye, *Power and Interdependence* (Boston: Little Brown, 1977).

[33] Barbieri and Schneider, "Globalization and Peace."

the reality that it includes much more, and does so for reasons that correspond to important (and potentially measurable) changes in the international system. The point is that, while, in earlier periods, trade and contact may have been relatively congruent, in an era of increasing globalization, this is no longer the case. Developmental and technological advances have created more direct vectors for societal interaction through direct communication and interpersonal contact, which might directly impact interstate relations – vectors that can be effectively isolated, operationalized, and tested.

It has been noted that deep trade networks in Europe did very little to prevent the outbreak of the world wars. Thus, when we are looking for reasons to think that the current attempts at accommodation might go somewhat better, it makes sense to assess the part of our globalized system that is genuinely novel. What then might be included among the most significant non-trade interdependencies? I argue that, to the extent that the current era of globalization differs meaningfully from those that precede it, it is because of advances in communication and travel, which have effectively shrunk the globe and made it possible for far more extensive interaction to take place between individuals from distant societies. Examples of the operationalizable aspects of this individual-level interaction include communication (measured in terms of things like telecommunication network traffic) and mobility (measured in terms of air traffic, student exchange, and so on).

"Soft" interdependencies and accommodation

To illustrate this point graphically, consider Figure 3.1, which maps all the states in the system with high mobility (in terms of total air traffic) between them (I arbitrarily define mobility as high when it exceeds 1 percent of total joint population within a pair of states). Notably, from 1976 to 2010 there are no instances of militarized disputes within this group.

Figure 3.1 has a number of noteworthy attributes. There are clear indications of regional clustering in Northern and Western Europe, North America, Asia, and even the Middle East, which evoke Deutsch's concept of "security communities." However, there are also important linkages across regions, such as the link between Japan and the United States.[34] The links are also not just between developed democracies, but also include a number of autocracies, such as Bahrain, the United Arab

---

[34] Substantial traffic between the United States and Japan involves the popular island destinations of Saipan, Guam, and Hawaii. However, the volume exceeds 2 percent of joint population even when these destinations are excluded.

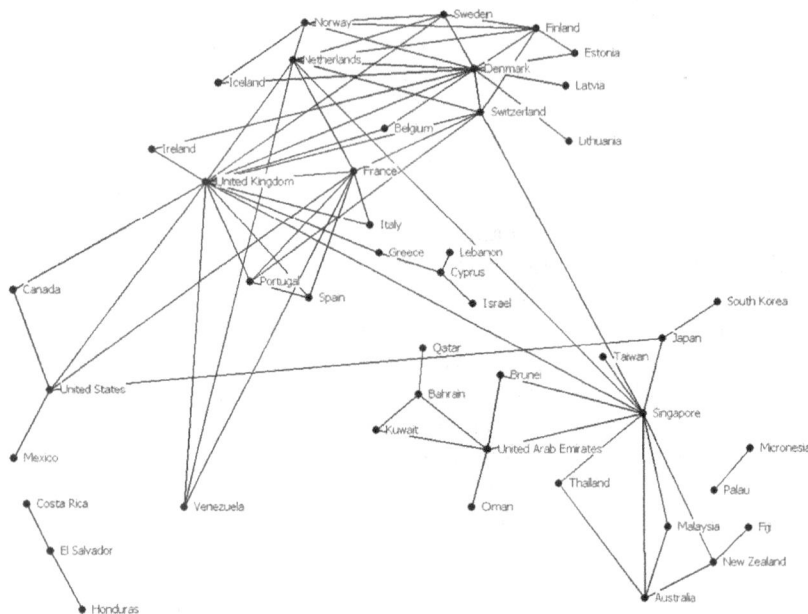

Figure 3.1 High-mobility (1 percent joint population) dyads, 2005

Emirates (UAE), and Singapore, as well as developing but stable countries such as Honduras and El Salvador. In general, this figure offers
reassuring face validity when it comes to our expectations regarding relatively peaceful international relationships, something that is not always
apparent in similar pictures of trade networks. That said, Figure 3.1
also raises troubling issues of reverse causality, which plague nearly all
inquiries into the interplay between interdependence and conflict. Is it
that nations don't come into conflict with those nations that they deal
with a lot, or that they don't deal with nations with which they will come
into conflict?

What is entirely absent from Figure 3.1, however, is any hint of the
current crop of emerging powers. In some sense, this is unsurprising given
their relatively large populations and comparatively low developmental
status, but if we think that deep cultural and interpersonal exchanges
might help the cause of peaceful accommodation, then this is an ominous
sign.

Arguably, this situation is improving, particularly with regards to
China. It has been widely noticed that, with growing wealth, the emerging Chinese middle class is developing an impressive appetite for international travel – particularly to the United States and Europe. Even more

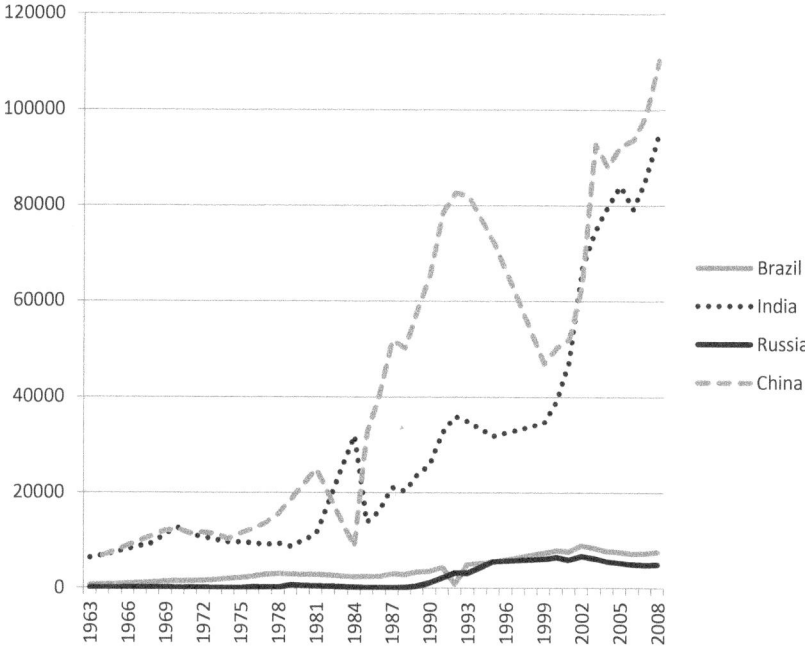

Figure 3.2 Foreign students in the United States, 1963–2008

importantly, China has a longstanding tradition of sending very large volumes of students abroad, particularly to the United States. Figure 3.2 shows the volume of foreign students sent to the United States from China, India, Brazil, and Russia.

The most notable thing about Figure 3.2 is the distinction between India and China, on the one hand, and Brazil and Russia, on the other. While this is just one measure of interpersonal interaction, there is a striking divergence between these trends, with the former sending huge and very rapidly increasing volumes of students (even when normalized for population) when compared to the latter. Interestingly, figures such as this one suggest a meaningful distinction in the likelihood of accommodation for Russia and China – one that is less apparent in the trade data.

Conclusion

There is an important distinction between saying that trade or globalization is (or is not) associated with peace and saying that it can be actively used as a policy instrument to accommodate rising powers. Yet, the notion that economic interdependence can pacify interstate relations has informed some of the most significant policy decisions of the twentieth century, and continues to influence policymaking today. The European Union finds its origins in the explicit assumption that the economic interdependence generated by the integration of French and German coal and steel capacities would stifle conflict and promote cooperation. This expectation was also a very real motivation behind the United States' loosening of trade restrictions with China in 1969, Nixon's advances toward that nation in the 1970s, and current US policy in that area. Similarly, Henry Kissinger's strategy of détente with the Soviet Union was, in part, driven by the sense that interdependence would soothe Soviet unpredictability. This is not to say, however, that there is a policy consensus on this issue, any more than there is an academic consensus. For example, the US Cold War strategy of containment was based on an entirely opposite expectation about the effects of interdependence.

The question of major power accommodation, however, is less well traveled in these debates, and it is somewhat less clear how effective the active use of interdependence as policy might be in this domain. That said, the ongoing relationship between the United States and China suggests (so far) that it is at least benign, and possibly quite helpful. As a result, the worst fears of realist theories about the implications of globalization have seemingly not materialized, at least thus far in this particular case at this particular time.

That being said, myopic attention to trade might obscure the importance of a broader swath of interdependences that invoke both cost and closeness mechanisms. While far from definitive, it seems relevant that the two states that are arguably most rapidly integrating into the existing international order (China and India) are relatively high when it comes to both symmetrical trade and investment relationships and interpersonal exchanges and contact. In contrast, the one that is lagging the furthest behind when it comes to accommodation (Russia) has trade relationships dominated by resource exchange and much more limited engagement with the outside world at an interpersonal level.

Does any of this have implications for policy planners, particularly those in the United States contemplating a more multipolar world, where accommodation might be necessary? I believe that it does, but at this point there is little consensus within this community. That is, while it is increasingly widely accepted that policy planners in the United States must accept the emergence of both new global powers such as China and regionally dominant powers such as Brazil, there is much less agreement about some of the most basic dimensions of the American response. This is particularly the case when it comes to the sorts of policies that either bolster or undermine interdependence.

The conflicting views that Albright alludes to in the quote with which I opened this chapter arise from dramatically different ideas about the efficacy of engagement and interdependence as tools of international diplomacy, with some linking interdependence to peaceful accommodation and others tying it to the exacerbation of inevitable conflict. However, in addition to the implications for overt policies of engagement and accommodation, these statements also imply divergent views on the significance of the growing interdependence and interaction that naturally accompanies the emergence of new powers in an era of globalization. Do these ties of globalization foster cooperation, or provide new domains for conflict? Do they wed newcomers to the existing global order and thereby satisfy them as stakeholders, or do they simply fuel the ascent of these countries and thereby hasten the day when they will be in a position to upset this order? If ties pacify and accommodate, then they should be encouraged, but if they breed conflict and competition, then those who advocate for walls might have the right idea.

The arguments I have made here, however, also suggest that a previously overlooked type of engagement – cultural engagement – could further these accommodative goals as well. In many regards, this is already occurring. The massive flow of Chinese students to the United States documented in Figure 3.2 has produced an elite cohort in China with much closer ties to the United States than would otherwise be the case (this despite the fact that many of them never returned to China). While it remains to be seen whether China will be successfully accommodated into the international system, it is difficult to imagine that elites with deep and positive experiences with the United States would do anything but help that cause. The other side of the coin is that, though it would probably only be a small step toward the larger goal, incremental progress on drawing out Russian societal engagement abroad might be just as important as rebalancing Russia's trade asymmetries.

4   What would E.H. Carr say?
How international institutions address peaceful political change

Krzysztof J. Pelc

> While therefore resort to war for the purpose of altering the status quo now usually involves the breach of a treaty obligation and is accordingly illegal in international law, no effective international machinery has been constituted for bringing about changes by pacific means.
>
> E.H. Carr

E.H. Carr is invariably described as the father of twentieth-century realism. As often happens to seminal writers, he is also misremembered, his writings reduced to a handful of aphorisms. Carr is forever the enemy of the utopians, the critic of Woodrow Wilson's fourteen points and the League of Nations' folly. This trend is not helped by the fact that his main opus, *The Twenty Years' Crisis*, has grown scarce on graduate syllabi. The fashion these days leans toward the work of Carr's fellow early realist, Hans Morgenthau, who put forward a more systematic treatment of some of the ideas he shared with Carr.

Carr's topic was peaceful change. As he claimed, "to establish methods of peaceful change is therefore the fundamental problem of international morality and of international politics."[1] The main complaint that emerges from *The Twenty Years' Crisis* is over the lack of some "international machinery," as per the epigraph to this chapter, that might enable change by peaceful means. Carr's writings are thus highly germane to the set of questions being asked in this volume.

Writing in the interwar period, Carr was preoccupied by how the rise of an emerging power might be dealt with without resorting to war. The first notable point, then, is that he did not see conflict as an inevitable outcome of even large-scale political change. His view was also thoroughly modern in this respect: he saw conflict as an inefficient means of reallocating

I am grateful to the editor, the participants of the *Rising Powers* workshop, and three anonymous readers for useful comments. I also thank Marc L. Busch, who gave me my now dog-eared copy of *The Twenty Years' Crisis* on news of my admission to graduate school.

[1] E.H. Carr, *The Twenty Years' Crisis, 1919–1939: An Introduction to the Study of International Relations* (London: Macmillan, 1946), 222.

resources and settling disagreements among states. Yet the futile attempts to legislate war through the League of Nations represented for him a *utopia*, that is, "an ideal to be aimed at, though not wholly attainable."[2]

It may thus surprise some to reread the note on which *The Twenty Years' Crisis* ends. The hard-nosed realist revealed himself to have had hope for a solution. One that, by his own admission, also has a distinct utopian quality. Yet, he explained:

> it stands more directly in the line of recent advance than visions of a world federation or blue-prints of a more perfect League of Nations. Those elegant superstructures must wait until some progress has been made in digging the foundations.[3]

In this chapter, I want to propose a rereading of Carr's view of rules binding state behavior, and identify exactly what is meant by these necessary "foundations." I claim that the conclusion to *The Twenty Years' Crisis*, especially, stands in opposition to common readings of his work. In this conclusion, Carr actively engages with the prospect of binding international institutions and establishes conditions for their ability to ease peaceful political change. The crux of Carr's claims about international law, in particular, rests on the possibility of law taking into account the protean nature of politics. Much as he argued that economics could not be conceived of as separate from political power, so too was it necessary for law to recognize that which was antecedent to it. Carr had in mind a reflexive aspect of international law, whereby the law could somehow adjust itself, or suspend itself entirely, when faced with political necessity. Yet he fell short of fully articulating a mechanism by which this might be achieved.

Today's international institutions, I argue, feature provisions that attempt just such an adaptation to uncertainty. In this chapter, I focus on two institutional features. First, international law has long recognized, and codified formally in 1969, the principle according to which fundamental, unexpected change can lead to a suspension of a country's legal obligations. I examine documents surrounding the negotiation of the corresponding clause in the Vienna Convention on the Law of Treaties (VCLT), the text that to this day provides the framework for most international agreements. My goal is to show that negotiators saw Article 62 as a solution to the very type of problem that Carr outlined. Far from an isolated provision, Article 62 is symptomatic of the open-contract nature of today's global governance. International law is a collection of second-best solutions. Much as Carr indicated, today's institutions

---

[2] Ibid., 222.   [3] Ibid., 239.

recognize how the inclusion of some measure of wiggle-room for politics to operate in is the necessary precondition for the rules to constrain state behavior in the first place. Second, I examine the role courts can play in ensuring a balance between political needs and legal requirements. Both these elements – flexibility provisions that mimic Article 62 and the court as an independent international actor – go some way in answering Carr's challenge and give us a sense of how institutions might play a role in facilitating political change by peaceful means. Despite going down in history as the foremost critic of the attempt to legislate affairs between states, Carr gave us a useful measure by which to reflect on today's system of global governance, and its ability to deal with change.

Carr's objections to law and morality in international relations were not absolute. Not only did he foresee a role for law in dealings between states, but he saw it as the one potential means of ensuring peaceful change. He outlined the essential features of a viable international legal system, and he saw none of these satisfied in the international rules of the day. Most presciently, he maintained that no legal system could exist without recognizing its inherently political function. In its essence, Carr's critique was not of rules per se, but of their *design*.

The exercise of reading Carr into today's system of global governance has an interesting corollary. The way in which current provisions of international law can be shown to heed political factors, as I claim Carr was calling for, has the unexpected effect of throwing in doubt the idealized view of law as fully binding political impulses. In other words, the optimal imperfections of law that Carr would find salutary should also lead champions of today's liberal institutionalism to reexamine their premises. This amounts to a return to the old debate about the epiphenomenality of international law, but with a twist: in order for rules to affect country behavior, they must also cede to state necessity in some agreed-on circumstances.

This chapter proceeds as follows. I begin with an overview of Carr's well-known, skeptical take on binding law among states, and how it relates to his views on peaceful change. I then focus on the conclusion to *The Twenty Years' Crisis*, where I argue Carr not only left open a role for law, but saw in it the only possible solution to peaceful political change. Finally, I consider today's international rules in light of Carr's argument, and ask whether these have responded to the challenges he raised. I give special consideration to the role of the "Fundamental Change of Circumstances" clause of the VCLT, and that of the court-as-actor in international law. This discussion has implications about reading Carr's work, as well as about contemporary views of international law as a mechanism for binding states.

Carr and international law

When Carr lays out the realist position of law, labeling it as such, he is careful not to come out as wholly subscribing to it himself. He depicts it as one possible conception of law, according to which law is an expression of the will of the state, an instrument of coercion by which stronger nations impose their will on weaker ones. Law cannot aspire to morality in this sense, since it is a temporary reflection of relations among states. As Otto von Bismarck had it, it is merely "a constatation of a definite position in European affairs."[4] Yet, Carr goes on to say, breaking with the strict realist view, no set of laws can be enforced by power alone. What is needed is akin to what we call "self-enforcement" today, which comes from some shared recognition of the law serving the common good. Much of Carr's reasoning from here onwards is concerned with securing this shared recognition in the international realm.

The realist insight that Carr does insist on is the absence of an inherent morality to law. Rendering commands legal does not make them morally sound, Carr reasons. He is at his vaguest when discussing the prerequisites of such a morality, speaking of the need for an international "political community of nations." What Carr seems to have in mind is acquiescence, something we might today call "legitimacy." The weakness of law reflects the weakness of the international community. Yet, nowhere is this seen as immutable. It is precisely such moral validity that must be sought as a means of achieving self-enforcement.

Moral validity cannot be attained without recognizing the source of international law. There can be no such thing as the rule of law in IR that is distinct from the rule of powerful countries within the small international community. Carr's main point in this respect is that international rules, more so than municipal (i.e., domestic) law, are the product of state interaction, and that politics are thus antecedent to the law. "The ultimate authority of law derives from politics."[5] As Carr points out, treaties among states, which are essentially contracts among actors within the international community, are considered part and parcel of international law, whereas no one would conceive of a private contract between two individuals as constituting municipal law. Carr's point stands to this day: international law is the product of bargaining among states.

Carr sees a crucial transformation in states' attitude toward treaties under international law, one he believes is taking place before his very

---

[4] Otto von Bismarck, *Gedanken und Erinnerungen*, vol. ii (Germany: Herbig Verlag, 2004), 258.
[5] Carr, *The Twenty Years' Crisis*, 180.

eyes: writing in the late 1930s, he points to the end of World War I (WWI) as a threshold beyond which treaties became binding on states.[6] If anything, it is surprising that Carr, a historian, trained in taking the long view, does not hesitate to date a fundamental shift in states' attitude as taking place less than two decades prior. As Carr puts it:

in spite of the universal recognition by all countries that treaties are in principle legally binding, international law before 1914 was reluctant to treat as absolute the binding character of treaty obligations.[7]

Previously, sovereign nations had been thought to have an unconditional right to suspend their treaty obligations. In the words of Teddy Roosevelt, "the nation has as a matter of course a right to abrogate a treaty in a solemn and official manner for what she regards as a sufficient cause."[8] This is also the spirit of Bismarck's view, previously referenced. The state, simply by virtue of its supreme position in international affairs, could never be fully bound. To be sure, those countries favored by the content of a treaty vehemently insisted on its binding nature, but those who were on the losing end of the same treaty had few qualms about breaking their obligations, as soon as power politics afforded them the opportunity to do so. Starting with the end of WWI, however, Carr describes the emergence of a consensus that treaty obligations are legally binding on states.

Yet Carr does not see this legalization of international affairs as a necessarily positive transformation. The distinction he observes between the period prior to 1919 and the post-1919 world is that as international law grows to encompass the law of treaties, leaders actually grow *more* likely to flout their obligations. In such instances, leaders often admit that their actions constitute breaches of law. Yet they invoke higher grounds to justify them: they make their arguments on the basis of morality, stability among nations, even *peace*. In today's terms, they seek to unilaterally delegitimize the rules they are breaking. Carr's point is that the legal provisions of his day did not sufficiently take into account political factors that made compliance impractical. The result was that leaders went ahead and broke their obligations by referring to principles outside of the laws that bound them. The inability of law to rise to the level of a shared morality meant that countries could admit to breaking their legal

---

[6] It is worth noting that most of the treaties Carr had in mind, e.g., the Straits Convention, which bound Russia's maritime activities and was signed at the conclusion of the Crimean War, tended to be bilateral in nature, and locked in the preferred state of the world of a war's victors.

[7] Carr, *The Twenty Years' Crisis*, 182.   [8] Ibid.

obligations in the name of some loftier reason of state. The rigidity of the rules compromised their moral soundness.

In pushing this line of reasoning, Carr makes what amounts to an unambiguous empirical claim: the increase he observes in the repudiation of treaties since 1919, he argues, is "due in part to the well-intentioned efforts of the victorious Powers [of WWI] to strengthen those rules and to interpret them with greater rigidity and precision."[9] As evidence of a link between the greater rigidity of international rules and the resulting increased likelihood of their being broken, Carr cites the British suspension of the Anglo-American War debt agreement in 1933. Britain faced increasing balance-of-payments issues that made it difficult to come up with the necessary dollars to finance its obligations, and it abrogated the treaty. Britain justified this abrogation on what Carr insists are moral, rather than legal grounds: the government argued that the burden imposed by the agreement was "unreasonable."[10] The then Chancellor of the Exchequer, Neville Chamberlain, reminded the House of Commons that Britain had other "other obligations and responsibilities," suggesting that "millions of human beings across the world" would be worse off if Britain was made to continue with its payments.[11] The truth was that Germany's reparation payments were decreasing, and the world was in the grips of the Great Depression. Britain still saw a global role for itself, and believed that servicing its considerable debt obligations would get in the way of performing that role. Absent formal allowances for such exogenous difficulties, leaders in Britain – as well as in France, whose government had repudiated its own debt agreement with the United States a few months earlier – began to prod at the legitimacy of the original agreements. As Chamberlain put it to the House of Commons, on the occasion of Britain's last debt payment to the United States before suspending the agreement, "When . . . the War was over we were left with this huge debt to the United States, incurred for a purpose in the pursuit of which she as well as we had been engaged."[12] How just had the agreement been in the first place, Chamberlain was asking, and what was the political and *human* cost of continued compliance?

As Carr sees it, such unilateral suspensions of treaty were typical of the effects of the West's attempt to legalize international affairs, which lost sight of the politics underlying the rules. Insisting on rigid agreements

---

[9] Ibid., 185.   [10] Ibid., 186.
[11] *Reparations and War Debts*, HC Deb December 14, 1932, vol. 273, cc. 353–486. Available at: hansard.millbanksystems.com/commons/1932/dec/14/reparations-and-war-debts-1#column_354.
[12] Ibid.

had the unforeseen effect of making it easier to exit. Paradoxically, the inability of rules to recognize the political forces from which they emerged made it easier to call into question their legitimacy.

Contemporary students of international institutions will find much to agree with in Carr's claim about the empirical consequences of legalization. In their aptly titled article, "Is the Good News About Compliance Good News About Cooperation?",[13] George Downs, David Rocke, and Peter Barsoom remind us that as countries make deeper commitments, they necessarily grow more likely to cheat, all things equal, and this is why we need an increase in enforcement to maintain a stable level of cooperation. Depth, in their telling, is the difference between behavior under an agreement and what behavior would have been absent that agreement. Largely building on this work, the depth/rigidity literature outlines a similar tradeoff to what Carr envisions.[14] One cannot increase the ambition of countries' commitments without also allowing for additional policy space to face changing circumstances. Without that additional flexibility, an increase in commitments will lead to an increase in the odds of abrogation.[15] Similar findings have found an equally interesting inverse relationship, looking to the economic sphere: when countries have access to some measure of wiggle-room, or flexibility, they end up making more ambitious commitments.[16] In light of this recent theory, Carr's claims sound plausible: following WWI, the utopian desire to expand the reaches of law, while insisting on its inflexibility, made it more acceptable to flout international law, as its claim on moral validity was weakened. To pretend that international law can be distinct from politics is to expose it to the vagaries of politics.

Whether Carr's empirical point was ultimately correct is difficult to assess. Did the frequency with which governments suspended treaties increase post-WWI, and was it due the increased legalism of international

---

[13] George W. Downs, David M. Rocke and Peter N. Barsoom, "Is the Good News About Compliance Good News About Cooperation?" *International Organization* 50, no. 3 (Summer 1996), 379–406.

[14] Leslie Johns, "Depth versus Rigidity in the Design of International Trade Agreements," *Journal of Theoretical Politics* 26, no. 3 (July 2014), 468–95.

[15] B. Peter Rosendorff, "Stability and Rigidity: Politics and Design of the WTO's Dispute Settlement Procedure," *American Political Science Review* 99, no. 3 (August 2005), 389–400; B. Peter Rosendorff and Helen V. Milner, "The Optimal Design of International Trade Institutions: Uncertainty and Escape," *International Organization* 55, no. 4 (Autumn 2001), 829–57; Leslie Johns, "Depth versus Rigidity"; Krzysztof J. Pelc, "Seeking Escape: The Use of Escape Clauses in International Trade Agreements," *International Studies Quarterly* 53, no. 2 (June 2009), 349–68.

[16] Jeffrey Kucik and Eric Reinhardt, "Does Flexibility Promote Cooperation? An Application to the Global Trade Regime," *International Organization* 62, no. 3 (July 2008) 477–505.

rules? Considering the events leading up to World War II (WWII), this seems at least plausible, though it bears remembering that nineteenth-century European affairs had largely consisted of treaties signed and almost immediately rescinded. Even in the examples Carr mentions, such as the Anglo-American and French-American debt agreements, actors on the American side seemed well aware of the political underpinnings of the agreement, and the consequences of insisting on payment. Hoover was the first to recognize the stakes in insisting on continued debt payments, and early on he proposed a moratorium on debt payments from Britain. Continuous bargaining over the terms of the treaty, which is what Carr argues was missing, is actually not far off as a description of the facts in these two cases.

Offering a definitive answer to this question is thankfully not the task of this chapter. Rather, I am interested in Carr's premise: As the scope and rigidity of law increases, does it become more difficult to defend its moral validity? Is the legitimacy of law derived from its flexibility? As Carr puts it in another work, *Nationalism and After*, in which he is even more critical of efforts to legislate world affairs:

Any so-called international order built on contingent obligations assumed by national governments is an affair of lath and plaster and will crumble into dust as soon as pressure is placed upon it.[17]

In other words, the fact that countries exchange commitments that are beneficial at the time of signing does not mean that these commitments will become self-enforcing. As soon as pressure is increased – Carr seems to have in mind mostly domestic pressure – the government will give in and break its commitment.

Thus, we arrive at the crux of the matter. Considering Carr's critique of the West's behavior during the interwar period, his objections to law among states are over issues of *institutional design*. Carr does not reject the possibility of binding international law out of hand. Indeed, he readily recognizes the need for "effective international machinery" that might address political change in a peaceful manner. Rather, he puts forth two separate objections. The first is that there must be some recognition of the political nature of international law. The second is more concrete, and an outgrowth of the first. When circumstances change, and the burden of compliance with law grows unbearable, the law must recognize that countries cannot remain strictly bound. Today, we might refer to such a prospect as "involuntary defection," borrowing Putnam's phrase.[18]

[17] E.H. Carr, *Nationalism and After* (London: Macmillan, 1945), 31.
[18] Robert D. Putnam, "Diplomacy and Domestic Politics: The Logic of Two-Level Games," *International Organization* 42, no. 3 (Summer 1988), 427–60.

Traditionally, addressing this possibility has fallen under the rubric of *necessity* in law. How might law allow for responses to exigency, without forsaking its own force? The challenge Carr sees is: How can the rigidity of the law deal with uncertainty and with unforeseeable changes to come?

Financial and economic commitments . . . may be accepted by governments in all good faith, but without full understanding of their consequences; and should these eventually turn out to be detrimental to the standard of living or level of employment in one of the contracting countries, they will be dishonoured, as Great Britain dishonoured her financial obligations to the United States in 1933.[19]

The full "understanding of their consequences" refers to the inability of negotiators to predict the future circumstances under which they will be required to perform their obligations. In Carr's view, domestic obligations, when they arise, will invariably trump international obligations. When we speak of revisionist nations, we often have in mind countries whose domestic expectations and international position are out of sync. In these cases, Carr predicts, leaders will not hesitate to break international commitments to meet domestic expectations. How can international law reconcile itself with this fact?

The politics of necessity in international law

The question before us is the same as the one Carr was facing. How does the set of covenants, treaties, and agreements that make up international law adapt to global shifts of power, or other unexpected developments? If the law is the reflection of one state of the world, favorable to the dominant powers of one era, does it not *stand in the way* of peaceful political change, by making adjustments more difficult? Law's rigidity makes the global regime akin to a steel bridge: How can such a bridge adapt to changing temperatures without giving way?

One place to start looking for answers is in the text that serves as the legal framework to most international treaties and multilateral agreements today: the VCLT, signed in 1969. What has been called the most controversial provision of the Convention is Article 62, titled "Fundamental Changes of Circumstances."[20] Article 62 states that "A fundamental change of circumstances . . . not foreseen by the parties" can be grounds for suspending a treaty obligation, if those circumstances

---

[19] Carr, *Nationalism*, 30–31.
[20] David Kennedy, "The Sources of International Law," *American University International Law Review* 2, no. 1 (1987), 1–96.

were central to the treaty, and if the change "radically" transforms the obligations under the treaty. If there is any doubt as to the aims of the provision, the International Law Commission, which was charged with drafting the text, repeatedly refers to the Article as "an instrument of peaceful change."[21]

The existence of Article 62 constitutes a tremendous concession of law to politics. The question is whether the provision adds to stability or diminishes it.[22] The allowance in the VCLT for fundamental change is a recognition that commitments take place in a particular context, and that the legitimacy of those commitments – what Carr would call their "moral validity" – is contingent upon that context. In an extreme case, an agreement between the victors and the losers of a war may lose its validity in short order. The broader implication of Article 62 is that, given the inherent uncertainty of the social world, no contract between parties can predict and provide for every possible state of affairs. Some policy space must thus be granted to allow for fundamental, unforeseeable change. If the designers of treaties could predict every state of the world, then they could also include a provision dictating behavior for every case. They cannot, and that is why there is a need for clauses that seek to define the range of situations that would warrant revision, or abrogation altogether, of the treaty.

Carr was witnessing a major political shift during the writing of *The Twenty Years' Crisis*, with the rise of revisionist Germany, and Britain's growingly apparent inability to maintain its nineteenth-century hegemonic function. The drafters of the Article 62 provision were also highly aware of the meaning of political change, albeit of a very different order. The year 1968, during which most of the negotiations took place, was a time of widespread domestic turmoil, from Paris to Prague, as well as the tail end of a significant wave of decolonization – new states were born, and with them the map of global power politics was being redrawn. Today, as we witness the emergence of great economic powers that are progressively demanding the renegotiation of the global compact, we can ask whether the design of international rules has risen to Carr's challenge.

---

[21] United Nations Conference on the Law of Treaties. Second Session, Twenty-Second Plenary Meeting, April 9 el Games, Ca. Document A/CONF.39/SR.22.

[22] As the Dutch representative stated, the "fundamental change" provision "was the only article in the draft which contained a number of ambiguous terms. It was impossible, for example, to know with certainty what was meant by such terms as 'fundamental,' 'with regard to,' 'foreseen,' 'essential basis,' 'radically,' or 'the scope of obligations,' and it would be dangerous to employ such expressions in a legislative text." In United Nations Conference on the Law of Treaties. First Session. Vienna, March 26–May 24, 1968. Official Records. Sixty-Third Meeting. May 10, 1968. 367, paragraph 20.

The International Law Commission's commentary on its discussions about Article 62 is instructive, as it explicitly outlines the objective behind the inclusion of the clause. The Commission reasoned that international treaties might come to represent an "undue burden" on states, and "the dissatisfied state might ultimately be driven to take action outside the law."[23] These are words Carr could have written himself, and it is the issue that concerns us in this volume. The existence of Article 62 is a testament to the notion that there are cases in which non-compliance is inevitable, and that in those cases the law may find it preferable to accommodate the breach, rather than to oppose it. As a legal observer of the time put it, "The community interest may be best served, regardless of the parties' earlier shared expectations, by putting an end to obligations which come to be felt so burdensome that attempts to exact their performance threaten general stability and peace."[24]

Article 62 is not only a legal provision under which the law predicts circumstances that might call for the suspension of a treaty; it is designed to affect bargaining outcomes between states. As the Commission commented, the Article "could serve a purpose as a lever to induce a spirit of cooperation in the other [obdurate] party."[25] The Commission thus reveals the full intent of the clause. Article 62 is designed not only to address unexpected changes that temporarily make continued compliance impractical, such as droughts, famines, or domestic upheavals, but it also aims at resolving the consequences of a fundamental shift of power between states. The Commission reasoned that if the status quo power "were obdurate in opposing any change, the fact that international law recognized no legal means of terminating or modifying the treaty . . . might impose a serious strain on the relations between the States concerned."[26] Article 62 was a solution to this concern: in recognizing that states' legal commitments are the result of bargaining, the VCLT thus takes into account, to paraphrase Carr, the political antecedents of law.

Article 62 takes sides. A state having made a set of commitments in a period of relative weakness may later find itself with sufficient power to challenge those commitments if they come to be seen as imposing an "undue burden." Article 62 unambiguously has in mind such shifts of

---

[23] United Nations, "Draft Articles on the Law of Treaties with Commentaries," in *Yearbook of the International Law Commission*, vol. II (New York: United Nations, 1966), 258.

[24] Oliver J. Lissitzyn, "Treaties and Changed Circumstances (Rebus Sic Stantibus)," *The American Journal of International Law* 61, no. 4 (October 1967), 897.

[25] International Law Commission, *Yearbook of the International Law Commission*, vol. II. (New York: United Nations, 1966), 258.

[26] Ibid.

power. The clause thus comes down on the side of the revisionist, rather than the status quo, power.[27] Insofar as its objective is the maintenance of peace, it recognizes that the maintenance of the status quo – "stability," in the common sense of the word – can come at the expense of stability in the greater sense of peace. As such, Article 62 is an astonishingly pragmatic bit of international law. It also constitutes a formal legal response to the concerns raised by Carr. As political motives are incorporated into law, the incentive for state leaders to raise higher objectives outside the law to justify their breaches decreases. The trick, of course, is to strike the right balance: all of behavior can easily be covered by the rules, if these are made sufficiently lax, but law then becomes meaningless. The challenge is to bind state behavior sufficiently, while allowing breaches when political pressure grows unmanageable. Article 62 of the VCLT, together with the jurisprudence that has emerged around its interpretation, is an attempt at striking this balance.[28]

Article 62 is not unique. I have considered it here because the availability of the drafting texts allows us a rare glimpse at the reasoning of its creators, and because it pertains to what may be the foundational text of international law. Yet the same reasoning is likely to be at the basis of similar provisions across a range of issue-areas. Article 62 is thus merely an archetype of a widely prevalent type of legal provision. Whether derogation clauses in human rights agreements[29] or safeguards and escape

---

27 This raises issues that had already been foreseen by one of Carr's contemporaries, the jurist Charles C. Hyde. Speaking of the changed conditions clause in 1945, he writes, "Reliance therefore, on a change of conditions which refers merely to the development of the power of such a State to a point where it may safely ignore the terms of its agreement, is an appeal to force rather than to law." Charles C. Hyde, *International Law Chiefly as Interpreted and Applied by the United States* (Boston: Little, Brown and Company, 1945), 1524.

28 The significance of Article 62 should not be overstated. References to the provision in interstate affairs have been few. That, per se, is not enough to dismiss its impact. The existence of the clause itself may well be enough to affect outcomes of states bargaining in the shadow of the "Fundamental Change" clause, since countries may try to avoid resorting to it. States may prefer yielding to a demand for suspension of an obligation from a partner, rather than risk setting a lasting precedent that might increase invocations of Article 62. Such is the risk of clauses allowing a suspension of the rules. As the Commission itself recognized, "The circumstances of life are always changing and it is easy to allege that the changes render the treaty inapplicable." In an effort not to erode the contours of the exception, countries may accede more willingly to demands by revisionist powers than they would otherwise. It is thus difficult to assess with any certainty the true impact of the provision on state behavior. There is little doubt, however, that the aim of Article 62 is to address the very aspects of international law that led Carr to question its effectiveness. International Law Commission, *Yearbook*, 760.

29 Emilie M. Hafner-Burton, Laurence R. Helfer, and Christopher J. Fariss, "Emergency and Escape: Explaining Derogations from Human Rights Treaties," *International Organization* 65, no. 4 (October 2011), 673–707.

clauses in trade agreements, global governance is a collection of second-best solutions. It is a recognition of the fact that entirely rigid rules will be abrogated at the first bump in the road, precisely because law cannot afford to be wholly separate from politics. Wherever hard constraints on country behavior are found in law, there are also provisions that offer states wiggle-room to deal with political exigency.

International law, courts, and change

Article 62 of the VCLT recognizes how fundamental changes of "critical" circumstances may call for a suspension of the treaty, but it remains a blunt tool. It is not designed for the micro-adjustments to international agreements that the changing social realm requires on an ongoing basis. Moreover, Article 62's willful vagueness – how else to accommodate change of an unknown nature? – calls for an institutional mechanism capable of addressing it, applying it to concrete settings, and resolving disagreements over its meaning.

International courts are tasked with just such interpretations. And though it is never their formal mandate to perform the types of micro-adjustment that international institutions may require, they often end up doing just that. In this section, I consider how courts walk the line between accommodation and constraint that Carr had in mind when outlining a role for law in international affairs.

Some adjustments by courts are uncontroversial. International law necessarily leaves some issues unaddressed, often because those issues could not have been foreseen at the time the rules were designed. In these cases, the task of filling the gap may fall on judges. Applying existing rules to changing scientific knowledge, for instance, provides many opportunities for judges to engage in gap-filling. If such "interstitial" legislating[30] by judges is accomplished in such a way that the designers of the agreement would agree with the outcome, then there is little controversy. Courts in these cases act as loyal agents to the institution's principals.

More interesting, however, are cases where judges internalize the likely objections of governments in rendering rulings over sensitive issues. In the EU setting, where interactions between the national and the supranational levels are especially intense, scholars have found that courts in some cases tailor their decisions to the political sensitivities of countries.[31]

---

[30] In a famous opinion, Judge Holmes offered that judges do legislate, but that they do so interstitially.

[31] Geoffrey Garrett, R. Daniel Kelemen, and Heiner Schulz, "The European Court of Justice, National Governments, and Legal Integration in the European Union," *International Organization* 52, no. 1 (Winter 1998), 149–76.

Despite the fact that the very authority of judges comes from their being perceived as wholly removed from political considerations, the continued relevance of courts in large measure depends on their ability to take these considerations into account.[32]

What this means is that courts have a function in legitimizing change, and in shaping its distributional consequences. Most often, we expect concessions to politics to take the form of deference to the status quo power. In the case of the North American Free Trade Agreement (NAFTA), for instance, a 2002 decision in an early investment case in favor of the United States drew wide criticism from jurists. The consensus among observers was that NAFTA judges had yielded to pressure from an unfavorable Congress. As one legal observer put it at the time, "if Loewen had won, we might not have a Chapter 11 [the dispute settlement provision for investment] today, and maybe that's why the tribunal decided the way it did."[33] In other words, judges saw the stability of the legal regime at stake, and chose not to challenge the superpower's interests.

In such cases, courts uphold the status quo, by yielding to the status quo power. Yet courts' political sensitivity means that they may just as well recognize shifting political power, and act accordingly. This is seen most clearly in domestic contexts, when high courts precede legislatures in recognizing societal shifts. Social issues like gay marriage are prime recent examples: when it comes to such politically sensitive issues, legislatures may have an incentive to wait for courts to rule before amending legislation. In these instances, it is courts that write the first page of history.

An important area where a role for international courts in ushering change is slowly emerging is self-determination. The advisory opinion of the International Court of Justice (ICJ) thus played a role in shaping global attitudes over Kosovo's self-determination, despite the opinion's great restraint, in a way that converged expectations on what would make for legitimate secession in the future. The Court did not pronounce itself on Kosovo's statehood per se, and strategically abstained from setting too strong a precedent, yet in so doing it claimed, for instance, that lawful secession cannot result from outside intervention. This effectively delegitimized subsequent secession movements in South Ossetia and Abkhazia – and, at time of writing, Crimea – and conversely bolstered

---

[32] Anne-Marie Burley and Walter Mattli, "Europe Before the Court: A Political Theory of Legal Integration," *International Organization* 47, no. 1 (Winter 1993), 41–76.

[33] Michael D. Goldhaber, "Balancing Act," *The American Lawyer*, August 1, 2009. Available at: www.americanlawyer-digital.com/americanlawyer-ipauth/tal200908ip?folio=5#pg5.

the claims of other territories, like Chechnya.[34] The Court also refused to extend the prohibition on the use of force against territorial integrity to domestic secessionist movements, confirming the view that the proscription concerns only dealings *between* states.[35] Although it remained circumspect, the Court left itself space for more expansive pronouncements in self-determination cases to come.

The fact that countries care enough about the rulings of courts to expend resources on shaping their outcomes suggests that rulings matter for converging expectations, in a way that can slow down or accelerate large-scale political change. Spain was notably among the few EU countries that voted against Kosovo, fearing repercussions on the independence movements within its own borders. Such concerns are an acknowledgment of the Court's strength – even in a case where the ruling itself was narrow and limited, and where there was great emphasis on the uniqueness of Kosovo's situation, in an effort to keep it from serving as a precedent. Courts can thus not only serve as (de)legitimators of ongoing change, but also affect calls for subsequent change. It is likely, in fact, that their greatest influence operates through a gradual change of countries' expectations over a series of opinions, rather than through single rulings that change the course of history.

The fact that, in highly politicized disputes, the power of international courts is curtailed by the tolerance of member states is traditionally seen as a reality to bemoan – evidence of the weakness of international law. Rarely is it recognized as a means of striking the much-needed balance between the rigidity of law and political necessity. The oft-derided weakness of law thus also makes it more adaptable to change, as international courts are made to react to shifts in the geopolitical landscape. This adaptability may be the required feature for the international legal system's continuity.

The greater point is that the interpretive judicial process provides wiggle-room. Courts are meant to be credible third parties put in place to provide objective assessments of the matter before them, but they are inevitably also political actors, and are thus prone to political biases. This need not be a bad thing. The sensitivity of courts to countries' interests means that they acknowledge the "political antecedents" of the law. It means that they can provide some of the flexibility that is necessary for the meaning of the law to evolve in accordance with its political context.

---

[34] Chatham House, "Kosovo: The ICJ Opinion – What Next? Summary of the International Law Discussion Group meeting held at Chatham House on Tuesday, September 21, 2010." Available at: users.ox.ac.uk/~sann2029/ChathamH_kosovo_ICJ_Paper.pdf.
[35] Ibid.

Conclusion

E.H. Carr – this intellectual father of realism, this anti-utopianist who reminded us that "there are men that govern . . . but there are no laws that govern" – ended his magnum opus on a hopeful twist that saw a role for law in international relations.[36] Carr foresaw the possibility of a mechanism that would facilitate political change through peaceful means. And despite his skepticism over the possibility of binding commitments on states, he saw formal constraints on states as the solution. Yet, an obstacle stood in the way, which he faulted for the increase in the widespread repudiation of international commitments he witnessed in the late 1930s. International institutions had to recognize their political antecedents, rather than aspiring to an absolute morality they could not credibly attain, it being the outcome of bargaining among states. International law had to be designed in such a way as to allow room for political necessity. The hardest thing for law to do is to imagine its inapplicability. Yet, that is precisely what Carr was asking of global governance, if it was to be an effective constraint on state behavior.

In this chapter, I have described two features of international law that go some way toward addressing Carr's concerns. The first is the formalization of the *rebus sic stantibus* doctrine in the form of Article 62 of the VCLT, among a range of formal provisions seeking to offer countries some policy space in unexpected circumstances. The thought behind this central provision of international law should give one pause. Not only is it a concession of law to politics, but it ultimately comes down on the side of revisionist states. It stands in recognition of the fact that investing too much in the preservation of the status quo risks global instability. The law needs some "give", and Article 62, and other provisions like it, from human rights agreements to trade and investment agreements, are meant to provide it. Carr was writing fluently about a concept that has attained acceptance among scholars only recently: if a "first-best" solution is unattainable, it is not truly first-best. In view of the source of change in global politics, this recognition inevitably comes at the expense of established powers, in the interest of stability.

Second, I have outlined how courts in international law have a role to play in facilitating the micro-adjustments that institutions go through as the social context in which they evolve changes. This function is far from uncontroversial. The claim I have made is that what is often seen as the weakness of international judges – their vulnerability to political pressure – may also be a means of walking the line between legal rigidity

---

[36] Carr, *The Twenty Years' Crisis*, 178.

and political need. Courts have an underappreciated function to play in easing large-scale political change.

What still keeps international courts today from playing a decisive role in this respect, much as it did in Carr's time, is some form of compulsory jurisdiction over interstate disagreements. Even the ICJ, the "World Court," relies on countries willfully accepting jurisdiction under Article 36 of its statute. Without compulsory jurisdiction, the very instances that stand to benefit the most from third-party adjudication are likely never to receive it, and to be left to political bargaining.

The troublesome conclusion of this chapter's argument is that international institutions are a second-best solution. States make binding commitments to one another, and create mechanisms to monitor and enforce those commitments. Yet these mechanisms cannot be rigid and flawless, lest they fail at the first bump in the road, when states find themselves unable to perform their obligations. International rules, paradoxically, gain from pricking themselves with well-designed exceptions.

Carr claimed the interstate rules of his day ignored their political origins at a risk. Looking at international governance today, there is no lack of recognition of the political forces underlying it. One sober takeaway is that this imperfect enforcement function may be as good as international law gets. By increasing its scope and formalization, as current champions of liberal institutionalism call for, we risk the same outcome Carr observed in the interwar period: with insufficient policy space left to sovereign countries, international law risks losing some of its compliance pull. Faced with increased rigidity, it became easier, rather than harder, for governments during the interwar period to question the rules' foundations. In the face of political change, more law may come at the expense of stability.

5 The responsibility to accommodate
Ideas and change

Mlada Bukovansky

T.V. Paul notes in Chapter 1 that constructivist IR scholarship has not developed a theory of power transitions. Despite the fact that once such a statement gets put into print, someone is bound to come forward and contest it, the claim is plausible enough if one views constructivism not so much as a theory of international politics, but rather as a set of onto-logical and epistemological commitments respecting the role of ideas in constituting social and political life, including (but not limited to) inter-national politics. Beyond the assertion that ideas are central to making a society what it is, there are many different forms of constructivism. At the most general level, a constructivist perspective brings at least three things to the table in analyzing the problem of peaceful accommodation: (1) a delineation of the ideational contours of the society or order into which emerging powers should be accommodated; (2) a more refined understanding of the *identities* of those involved, especially considering the question of who is doing the accommodating, and who is to be accommodated; and (3) some specification of the role of ideas in the *process* of accommodation. This chapter deploys a constructivist ori-entation in reviewing and assessing approaches grounded primarily in the liberal and realist traditions, but including also the international society school, security communities literature, and the "practice turn" in IR, with the aim of fleshing out these three dimensions of the problem of accommodation. My analysis leads me to conclude that ultimately, accommodation is a moral responsibility falling both on the dominant and the aspiring powers. With so much at stake, both hegemon and aspirant must draw on some common stock of ideas in order to intentionally develop meaningful practices of accommodation; institutions alone will not "solve" the problem of accommodation.

Although, because of their focus on the role of ideas, construc-tivists tend to emphasize that international order is malleable *in principle* because it is a social construct, they are unified neither in how they conceptualize the current international order, nor in regard-ing the *actual* malleability of international society at any given time, nor about the *process* by which international orders are transformed.[1] Does a constructivist view of accommodation mean that the rising powers will change through interaction with the dominant powers and be thus accommodated (and necessarily transformed) in the process? Or does constructivist accommodation mean that the social order will itself change to suit the aspirations and identities of the rising powers? Or will the existing order disintegrate into competing civilizational blocs precisely because the gaps between ideas and identities are simply too vast to bridge through repeated interaction? Any of these hypotheses could be generated by a constructivist approach. Further, the question of "who accommodates whom" may be productively explored by a theoretical orientation that is known for prioritizing identity.[2]

Different forms of constructivism are likely to generate different solutions to – and indeed, different conceptualizations of – the problem of peaceful accommodation, and the underlying questions of order and the process of change. Many constructivists either explicitly or implicitly adopt a liberal approach to international order and its transformation; the work of a smaller subset dovetails more readily with the realist approach (and some realists in turn have become comfortable evoking the role of ideas[3]); and yet a third division embraces a more postmodern, critical orientation. Constructivism has also generated intellectual developments, including the security communities literature[4] and the practice turn in IR theory,[5] which may shed further light on the problem of accommodation.

Finally, though I will not dwell on this, constructivists are a methodologically diverse group, as some constructivists accept and deploy a

---

[1] Patrick T. Jackson and Daniel H. Nexon, "Paradigmatic Faults in International-Relations Theory," *International Studies Quarterly* 53, no. 4 (December 2009), 907–30. Alastair I. Johnston, *Social States: China in International Institutions, 1980–2000* (Princeton: Princeton University Press, 2008) offers a constructivist theory of socialization on which one could build a theory of peaceful accommodation, if not power transition.

[2] Some of these questions are productively explored by Maximilian Terhalle, "Reciprocal Socialization: Rising Powers and the West," *International Studies Perspectives* 12, no. 4 (November 2011), 341–61. On identity, there is a vast literature, but a good place to begin is Ted Hopf, *Social Construction of International Politics: Identities and Foreign Policies, Moscow, 1955 and 1999* (Ithaca: Cornell University Press, 2002). See also Mlada Bukovansky, "American Identity and Neutral Rights from Independence to the War of 1812," *International Organization* 51, no. 2 (Spring 1997), 209–43.

[3] For example, see Randall L. Schweller and Xiaoyu Pu, "After Unipolarity: China's Visions of International Order in an Era of US Decline," *International Security* 36, no. 1 (Summer 2011), 41–72.

[4] Emanuel Adler and Michael Barnett, eds., *Security Communities* (Cambridge: Cambridge University Press, 1998).

[5] Emanuel Adler and Vincent Pouliot, "International Practices," *International Theory* 3, no. 1 (February 2011), 1–36; Vincent Pouliot, "The Logic of Practicality: A Theory of Practice of Security Communities," *International Organization* 62, no. 2 (April 2008), 257–88.

scientific method aiming at causal explanations, while others remain res-
olutely interpretive. The methodological differences should be kept in
mind because, for the more scientifically minded constructivists, addressing the problem of accommodation might require rigorous hypothesis
generation and testing, whereas for the more critical and interpretive
branch, the value added by a constructivist approach is to be found in
probing intellectual histories and drawing inferences and normative priorities from an assessment of how certain ideas helped to shape certain
social realities. This chapter falls more into the latter camp, for practical
rather than for dogmatic reasons (i.e., this chapter does not develop a
case study).

Because of the lack of a readily distinguishable constructivist theory of
power transition, it is worth exploring what a constructivist orientation
might offer in terms of reinterpreting or elaborating on liberal and realist
approaches to power transition, as these two traditions so strongly shape
our understanding of what international order actually is.[6] A focus on
the more liberal dimensions of constructivism can review how the now
voluminous work on norms and the social construction of international
politics has enhanced our understanding of international order, and in
particular the means by which such order becomes internalized in the
identities of its members. An exploration of constructivist dimensions of
realism, in turn, denaturalizes without rejecting the reality of the practices
of *realpolitik*. Power struggles are not just material, nor does assessment
of material distributions of capability yield reliable insights on peaceful
change. A constructivist orientation is particularly suited to recapturing
some of the rich strands of classical realism, and also to elaborating
on the close affinity between some strands of realism and the English
school or international society tradition. Such reinterpretation should
yield insights on how to accommodate the status claims of rising powers
without creating insecurity.

In exploring the ideological dimensions of the realist and liberal traditions of thought, as well as work which transcends or bridges these
traditions, I will focus on how each tradition conceptualizes international order, the character and process of accommodation, and how each
addresses the identity question of "who accommodates whom." The next
section revisits some definitional issues as a way to set the stage for the
different interpretations of the accommodation problem explored in the
rest of the chapter.

---

[6] I use the term "traditions" rather than "paradigms" or "theories" advisedly, for reasons
I hope will become clear in the course of this discussion. See also the use of the term
"tradition" in Daniel H. Deudney, *Bounding Power: Republican Security Theory from the
Polis to the Global Village* (Princeton: Princeton University Press, 2008).

The vocabulary of accommodation

Chapter 1 articulates working definitions of the relevant terms used in this project, but a constructivist perspective may offer some additional and hopefully useful commentary on the vocabulary being used. All the terms involved in the question of whether rising powers may be peacefully accommodated are potentially contestable; the meanings attributed to "rising," "accommodation," and even "peacefully" can vary according to the theory and perspective being deployed. As already stated, to get at the question of accommodation, we need to specify the character of the order into which rising powers should be accommodated, or, alternatively, within which rising powers must accommodate a declining hegemon to prevent it from using violence to stem its own decline: Is the order an anarchic balance of power, a hierarchy or hegemony, an international society, an institutionalized liberal order, or a capitalist world system? And would the order fundamentally change with the process of accommodation?

Even the definitions of "rise," and the corresponding "decline," are not obvious, because changes in material capability alone cannot yield accurate predictions about the power and status relationships in the system. In an essay in *International Security*, for example, Alastair Iain Johnston interrogates and contests the widespread "meme" whereby China is deemed to be demonstrating a "new assertiveness" in its foreign policy.[7] His discussion raises the question of how we should interpret "rise." Is the growth of material capability adequate to constitute a rise which must be accommodated, or must the rise be accompanied by assertiveness and status-seeking? Or, to give this question an identity spin: Is it possible for a rising power to be a status quo power, or should we expect all rising powers to be revisionist?[8] In his book *Social States*, Alastair Johnston himself makes the case that, despite its rising capabilities, from the 1990s until today, China developed into a status quo state on most foreign-policy issues.[9] Clearly, something other than material capability must be assessed in order to evaluate the character of a country's "rise" in the international system, and the related likelihood of peaceful accommodation between that country and the dominant power or powers. If, to follow through on the China example, the preservation of the core international norm of sovereign territorial integrity remains central to

---

[7] Alastair Iain Johnston, "How New and Assertive is China's New Assertiveness?" *International Security* 37, no. 4 (Spring 2013), 7–48.

[8] An interesting take on this question can be found in Schweller and Pu, "After Unipolarity."

[9] Johnston, *Social States*, 207. Compare with Schweller and Pu, "After Unipolarity."

international order, then presumably China can both rise in material power and remain a status quo power with respect to this core aspect of international order.

Moreover, the debate over whether or not the United States is in decline, whether or not the current world order is unipolar, and, if so, how long it is likely to stay that way, indicates that, if "rising" is to be relative to something else, we cannot really specify what "rise" means unless we have a sense of the corresponding "fall."[10] The question of whether and how much the United States is in decline is especially relevant to the question of accommodation, because presumably, to have peaceful change, it is not only the rising powers which need to be accommodated. The declining hegemon must also be accommodated, lest its relative decline generate so much insecurity that the threat of war comes not from the challenger or challengers, but from the dominant but declining power. As Randall Schweller and Xiaoyu Pu point out, balancing is a drastic course in an established unipolar system, and in such a system revisionism is an extremely dangerous and costly path to take, as it challenges not only the hegemon but all those states invested in the international order. This would reinforce the idea that, at least for a time, it is the rising powers who must do the accommodating, with respect not only to the hegemonic state, but to all those invested in the existing world order.[11] Accommodation, then, is something to be practiced on both sides of the equation: by the hegemon and by the challengers. One cannot assume that all rising powers are revisionist, nor that all hegemonic powers are status quo – especially if they feel threatened.

Even the "peace" that is part of peaceful accommodation can be interpreted in a number of ways. The obvious meaning is, of course, absence of major or "systemic" war. But what about the possibility of doing violence to a rival by crippling their information technology systems in ways which render their other capacities unusable? If cyber warfare becomes common, is the international system still peaceful? Moreover, is change peaceful if the process entails the drastic uprooting of societies so that large percentages of a country's population are unable to sustain their livelihoods? Many changes wrought by wild fluctuations in business cycles have been "peaceful" in the sense that they did not yield great power war, but they may nevertheless have resulted in revolutions, mass migrations, and other forms of drastic adjustment that have been violent

---

[10] Stephen G. Brooks and William C. Wohlforth, *World Out of Balance: International Relations and the Challenge of American Primacy* (Princeton: Princeton University Press, 2008).

[11] Schweller and Pu, "After Unipolarity."

at the core. So, to generate a more sustainable peace, the forms of accommodation needed may go beyond traditional security issues and reflect concern about the economic and general well-being of ecologies and societies. From this perspective, a broad array of institutions engaged in economic and environmental governance could be relevant to the problem of accommodation.

It is also quite clear in my mind, though I can give only a moral and not an empirical justification for this view, that certain forms of peace are simply not worth having, and thus not every pathway to "peaceful accommodation" is acceptable. In particular, I would not want peace if it meant totalitarian rule over the planet. There may still be some impending transitions that would be worth fighting against, and thus peaceful accommodation may not actually be an end in itself. However, because peace, and especially the prevention of hegemonic war, is normally a valuable goal, we can certainly evoke a moral responsibility to accommodate so that such war does not happen.

Constructivist reading of the liberal tradition

There are several strands of liberalism, offering different takes on the problem of accommodation. Here I explore their ideological underpinnings for clues as to how ideas play a role in accommodation during power transition. The core issues explored here include liberalism as a belief in progress, socialization into liberal order, neoliberal institutionalism's emphasis on institutions as sources of cooperation, the character and spread of the "liberal peace," and the extent to which liberal order depends on US hegemony. I conclude the section by observing that the intellectual underpinnings of liberalism are rich and resonant enough to offer good ideas about accommodation but need to be supplemented by realist attentiveness to power dynamics.

John Mueller's work on the obsolescence of great power war invokes, albeit vaguely, the role of ideas in delegitimizing war as a tool of statecraft.[12] The notion that war among "developed countries" is fading away (as slavery and dueling faded away in prior eras) because people no longer believe it to be reasonable does seem, on the face of it at least, to be an idea-based theory. Mueller belongs in the liberal tradition of thought, because his thesis is strongly grounded in a liberal conception of human progress. However, his work never identifies specific mechanisms

---

[12] John E. Mueller, *Quiet Cataclysm: Reflections on the Recent Transformation of World Politics* (New York: HarperCollins College Publishers, 1995); John Mueller, "The Obsolescence of Major War," *Bulletin of Peace Proposals* 21, no. 3 (July 1990), 321–28.

by which war has ceased to seem "reasonable" (something which Neta Crawford's book on decolonization does attempt to do[13]). The changes are part of some grand historical process that just seems to happen, especially, it must be noted, in "developed" states. Although Mueller does not specify what it means to be "developed," it seems reasonable to posit that he means liberal states. The very fact that Mueller focuses on practices like dueling, slavery, and war and finds that human beings no longer see them as "reasonable" suggests an implicit but fairly strong assumption of progress along liberal lines. But we must look to other theories to get at a more precise understanding of mechanisms that might facilitate peaceful accommodation.

One significant orientation of liberal IR theories toward emerging powers looks to socialize those powers into a liberal international order composed of regimes and institutions, which many, but not all, liberal theorists would argue have been created under the auspices of US leadership or hegemony.[14] Although the dominant states in the system "accommodate" rising powers by allowing them membership in liberal institutions such as the World Trade Organization (WTO), sometimes on special terms, the emerging powers must accommodate themselves (that is, comply with and conform) to an already existing order, which for the most part they did not have the opportunity to shape on its inception. In the socialization-to-liberal-order view of accommodation, then, it is primarily the rising powers which must accommodate themselves to an existing order, but the reasons for them to do this are presented as good ones, in accord with their own self-interest: economic growth, wealth creation, and, of course, peace. Within these institutions, however, there may exist accommodations for the rising powers in the form of exceptions and arrangements, such as the classification of countries in the WTO, and also in the International Monetary Fund (IMF) and the World Bank (WB), as less developed and thus deserving of "special and differential treatment" or laxer loan terms. This means that some countries are not expected to fully comply with the rules until they achieve a state of development that enables them to do so. Once they

---

[13] Neta C. Crawford, *Argument and Change in World Politics: Ethics, Decolonization, and Humanitarian Intervention* (Cambridge: Cambridge University Press, 2002).

[14] This is most fully presented in G. John Ikenberry, *Liberal Leviathan: The Origins, Crisis, and Transformation of the American World Order* (Princeton: Princeton University Press, 2011). On socialization, see G. John Ikenberry and Charles A. Kupchan, "Socialization and Hegemonic Power," *International Organization* 44, no. 3 (Summer 1990), 283–315; Jeffrey T. Checkel, "Why Comply? Social Learning and European Identity Change," *International Organization* 55, no. 3 (Summer 2001), 553–88; Ann Kent, "China's International Socialization: The Role of International Organizations," *Global Governance* 8, no. 3 (July–September 2002), 343–64.

do, they are expected to take on full obligations and bear the full costs of membership.

In my view, some significant weaknesses of the "socialization through institutions" approach include its complacency about the character, depth, and sources of the existing order, and its failure to adequately emphasize the possibility that emerging powers might prefer to see themselves as constructing a new order rather than acquiescing to an existing one.[15] A rising power's potential preference for being a norm-maker rather than simply a norm-taker raises a host of issues. The difficulties that have emerged in adjusting voting rights in the IMF, for example, or in altering the composition of the UN Security Council to reflect new power realities, show that the existing institutional order may not be accommodating enough. A very real drama is playing out at this writing as a cascade of US allies commits, against the will of the United States, to joining the Asian Infrastructure Investment Bank (AIIB), which is being started with Chinese leadership and capital.[16] Since the AIIB is being explicitly touted as an alternative to the WB, it provides at least a sliver of evidence that China has aspirations to reworking certain institutional aspects of the international economic order, even as it embraces a form of capitalism. And it appears as though US allies are scrambling to accommodate China, irritating the United States in the process.

To the extent that rising powers see themselves merely as norm-takers rather than norm-makers, their investment in any existing order could easily be more instrumental and strategic, rather than a matter of deep identification with the principles of that order. Schweller and Pu deploy James C. Scott's ideas about everyday forms of resistance to suggest that China may be paying lip service to the liberal order while finding ways short of direct confrontation to challenge its legitimacy.[17] However, even the issue of passive resistance fails to capture the dynamic that appears to be happening with the AIIB: on one level, the emerging bank itself promises to be part of a global capitalist system, and so presumably is not a revisionist project vis-à-vis that system; on another, perhaps more superficial level, it is a challenge to the global capitalist system's basis in US hegemony. This again raises the question of the character of the order into which rising powers are being accommodated. Are the institutional manifestations of that order (the Bretton Woods institutions) identical with and constitutive of it, or are there deeper dimensions to

---

[15] See Terhalle, "Reciprocal Socialization."
[16] Jamil Anderlini, "UK Move to Join China-Led Bank a Surprise Even to Beijing," *Financial Times* (March 26, 2015). Available at: www.ft.com/cms/s/0/d33fed8a-d3a1-11e4-a9d3-00144feab7de.html#axzz3WYpfgYOQ.
[17] Schweller and Pu, "After Unipolarity."

the order (global capitalism) that can endure under a different set of institutional arrangements? The implicit answer in contemporary liberal IR discourse seems to favor existing institutional manifestations, though Marxist-inspired accounts may have very different answers,[18] and Chapter 4 of this volume further suggests that we need to view international law and institutions in a far more flexible fashion than most liberals recognize.

This question of the depth of the existing order becomes particularly problematic if we acknowledge the strong presumption that liberal order is composed of liberal states. Integrating rising powers into a liberal order is a proposition that contains within it the assumption that such integration will cause changes within those rising powers: they will become more liberal, that is, more democratic and more open to transnational flows, not only of goods, services, and capital, but also of people and information.

From a liberal perspective, then, the question of accommodating rising powers is usually about integrating those powers into a preexisting order composed primarily of cooperative international institutions. In strong forms of liberalism, such cooperative institutions are liberal in character, though this is not always made explicit, nor always assumed. In some forms of neoliberal institutionalism, for example, any institution seems to be preferable to no institution, insofar as institutions lengthen the shadow of the future, reduce transaction costs, and so on, making cooperation more likely.[19] And the security communities literature explores a variety of institutional arrangements, not all of them necessarily liberal in character.[20] To take the most obvious example: the United Nations, though it pays lip service to many liberal principles, such as human rights and democracy, nevertheless does not itself fully embody these principles, nor was it created by liberal states exclusively to reflect their views of a desirable order; its structure and principles are very much compromises between liberal and non-liberal views of politics and order. And, as already suggested, it is entirely possible that some deep structure of global capitalism is sustainable over time without being contingent on the survival of the Bretton Woods institutions.

Many accounts of liberal international order put significant emphasis on the role of US hegemony in generating that order after WWII, thus

---

[18] Philip S. Golub, "From the New International Economic Order to the G20: How the 'Global South' is Restructuring World Capitalism from Within," *Third World Quarterly* 34, no. 6 (2013), 1000–15.

[19] Robert O. Keohane and Lisa L. Martin, "The Promise of Institutionalist Theory," *International Security* 20, no.1 (Summer 1995), 39–51.

[20] Adler and Barnett, *Security Communities*.

imbuing it with a liberal character due to the liberal credentials of its primary sponsor. But a longer historical view surely shows that the United States did not invent liberalism; nor has it been the only exemplar of liberal principles in the world.[21] Many ideological aspects of the liberal international order – respect for human rights, encouragement of open markets, rule of law, peaceful settlement of disputes, and so on – have a much longer lineage, and are more broadly diffused in ways that are not contingent on US leadership. This does not mean that the principles implement themselves, especially internationally, nor that they were sufficient to prevent the rise of totalitarianism and world war during past times of power transition.[22] This is why analysts put so much emphasis on the need for a leader to render those liberal principles meaningful and operative in the world. But, as Robert Keohane noted some time ago, it may be possible for those principles to endure "after hegemony."[23]

Further, hegemony as a social fact rests somewhat uneasily alongside the strains of liberalism most concerned with restraining arbitrary power (or Judith Shklar's "liberalism of fear"[24]). Those writers who embrace unipolarity buttress their case by pointing out the liberal character of the order sustained by the United States.[25] But liberal theory counsels caution toward situations in which leaders operate without checks and balances.[26] By sidelining the intellectual content of liberal political philosophy, neoliberal institutionalism and much of the security communities literature made peace with structural realism, but at the price of further reflection about the character and content of international institutions. Privileging institutions and emphasizing institutionalization of world politics may be a useful way to counter structural realism's pessimistic assertions about the consequences of anarchy, but once we acknowledge that "anarchy is what states make of it,"[27] it follows that

---

[21] For a short introduction, see John Gray, *Liberalism* (Minneapolis: University of Minnesota Press, 1986). See also James L. Richardson, *Contending Liberalisms in World Politics: Ideology and Power* (Boulder: Lynne Rienner, 2001).

[22] For a strong argument about the failure of liberalism in interwar Europe, see Mark Mazower, *Dark Continent: Europe's Twentieth Century* (New York: Vintage, 2000).

[23] Robert O. Keohane, *After Hegemony: Cooperation and Discord in the World Political Economy* (Princeton: Princeton University Press, 1984).

[24] Judith N. Shklar, "Liberalism of Fear," in *Liberalism and Moral Life*, ed. Nancy L. Rosenblum (Cambridge: Harvard University Press, 1989), 21–37; see also N.J. Rengger, *International Relations, Political Theory, and the Problem of Order: Beyond International Relations Theory?* (London and New York: Routledge, 1999).

[25] Ikenberry, *Liberal Leviathan*; Stephen G. Brooks, G. John Ikenberry, and William C. Wohlforth, "Don't Come Home, America: The Case against Retrenchment," *International Security* 37, no. 3 (Winter 2012/13), 7–51.

[26] A useful essay is Quentin Skinner, *Liberty Before Liberalism* (Cambridge: Cambridge University Press, 1998).

[27] Alexander Wendt, "Anarchy is What States Make of It: The Social Construction of Power Politics," *International Organization* 46, no. 2 (Spring 1992), 391–425.

even war is a social institution. From a constructivist perspective, which advocates a sociological approach to world politics, it is difficult to imagine a state system that does not have some sort of institutional contours, and some of these may be violent. So institutions in and of themselves are not the solution to the problem of peaceful accommodation.

To remain true to its liberal core, liberal institutionalism needs to be – and, indeed, usually is – discerning about the content and structure of specific institutions. Clearly, some international institutions are more liberal than others. Core elements of liberalism as a political philosophy include the need for restraints on arbitrary power, commitment to the rule of law, and prioritization of individual rights and liberties over those of the collective.[28] On that last point at the very least, the United Nations falls far short, whatever supposed progress has been made in doctrines qualifying sovereignty, such as the Responsibility to Protect (R2P). Moreover, the institutionalization of international monetary and trade relationships may not be adequate to restrain arbitrary power, neither within those institutions, such as the IMF, governed by weighted voting, nor within the world of global finance, where market players arguably heft the most weight of all. Nor is institutionalization of trade negotiations any sort of hedge against manipulation, domination, and hypocrisy.[29] And, from a Marxist-influenced critical perspective on the world political economy, the liberalism of an economic system whose institutions, in the wake of the global financial crisis of 2008, seem primarily concerned with bailing out large financial institutions rather than protecting individuals can surely be called into question.

The point here is that liberal institutionalism may be too sanguine about the positive role international institutions play in constructing international order. Rising powers may have strong interests in engaging at least some multilateral institutions and becoming responsible stakeholders in those institutions. But healthy skepticism is warranted when it comes to the character of the socializing effects of membership in these institutions. For example, research on authoritarian leaders' strategies shows that they actively resist certain types of norm diffusion if they see them as threatening to their hold on power.[30] There appears to be plenty of evidence that non-liberal states are engaging international institutions in a highly selective manner, resisting those aspects which would liberalize

---

[28] Here I follow Rengger's useful review in Rengger, *International Relations*, chapter 3.

[29] Mlada Bukovansky, "Institutionalized Hypocrisy and the Politics of Agricultural Trade," in *Constructing the International Economy*, eds. Rawi Abdelal, Mark Blyth, and Craig Parsons (Ithaca: Cornell University Press, 2010), 68–90.

[30] Karrie J. Koesel and Valerie J. Bunce, "Diffusion-Proofing: Russian and Chinese Responses to Waves of Popular Mobilizations against Authoritarian Rulers," *Perspectives on Politics* 11, no. 3 (September 2013), 753–68.

their domestic politics. Moreover, states can be socialized into bad behavior as easily as into good behavior. Surely constructivism's core insight about the social construction of world politics should alert us to this. But this insight often seems to be missing from IR scholarship about institutions – even constructivist literature. I think this is because, too often, constructivists assume that the order created after 1945 under the auspices of US hegemony is actually a liberal order. I am suggesting here that such an assumption can be contested, and that there are much older, pre-liberal elements to our international order worth emphasizing, especially sovereignty and territorial integrity norms. Institutional complexes such as the United Nations, and many security organizations besides, embody pre-liberal or non-liberal elements that may attract non-liberal powers without thereby socializing them into anything that can reasonably be called a liberal international order.

Still, many constructivist works do focus on liberal institutions, and privilege these as the most worthy of spreading and securing over time. Works dealing with the spread of human rights norms are the most prominent example, but so too is work on European integration. In the democratic peace literature, a liberal international order is grounded in liberal states which form a pacific union with some level of international institutionalization, and there are "thin" liberal accounts and "thicker" constructivist accounts of how such an order works.[31]

Constructivist liberals tend to have a richer understanding of the substance of liberal institutions and liberal order than do liberals proceeding from rationalist individualism; for constructivists, liberal order is not simply the product of iterated self-interested bargaining, but rather a manifestation of shared identity and purpose. Moreover, whether through processes of communicative action or socialization, liberal order penetrates the identities of liberal states in such a way that they see its fundamental principles not as something externally imposed, but rather as a deeply internalized part of who they are.

It is not clear, however, whether liberal order can do this for non-liberal states, though Johnston's work suggests that perhaps it can.[32] From a constructivist liberal perspective, one key problem is to determine whether international interactions between liberal states and rising non-liberal

---

[31] Michael W. Doyle, "Liberalism and World Politics," *American Political Science Review* 80, no. 4 (December 1986), 1151–69; Bruce Russett, *Grasping the Democratic Peace: Principles for a Post-Cold War World* (Princeton: Princeton University Press, 1993); John M. Owen, "How Liberalism Produces Democratic Peace," *International Security* 19, no. 2 (Fall 1994), 87–125; Michael E. Brown, Sean M. Lynn-Jones, and Steven E. Miller, *Debating the Democratic Peace* (Cambridge, MA: MIT Press, 1996).

[32] Johnston, *Social States*.

states can yield domestic transformation within the latter, so that their structures and institutions develop checks and balances, mechanisms of representation, and rule of law that respects individual rights and freedoms. This question is amenable to empirical investigation, obviously, and at this point there seems to be just as much cause for pessimism as for optimism.

Another problem for a liberal perspective is how to assess the character of US hegemony. The question of what restrains the hegemon, and whether it is willing to be bound by the rule of law, is an important one from a liberal perspective. If one side of liberal accommodation is the socialization of emerging powers into liberal order, surely the other side is the continued demonstration by the leading power (or powers) that it is (or they are) willing to be bound by the rules of that order – something not always evident in the behavior of the United States, nor indeed of the European powers in institutions such as the UN Security Council and the IMF. Resistance by the major powers of institutional changes which would dilute their bargaining leverage in key global arenas shows a reluctance to engage in meaningful accommodation: the AIIB case is worth watching carefully on this score, as it may be construed as a response to the failure of existing international financial institutions to accommodate Chinese aspirations to leadership. Conversely, the willingness to make such changes in existing institutions, or even to join alternative institutions generated under the auspices of a rising power, could be a very strong accommodating signal by the hegemon. To consider more closely the power dynamics evoked by this discussion, we need help from the realist tradition.

Building on the realist tradition

Realist theory, especially classical realism, offers a rich trove of ideas for considering problems of accommodation, the primary ones being respect for the predominance of security concerns and the centrality of competition for status, wealth, and especially material power as driving forces in international politics.[33] Taking these concerns seriously makes accommodation far more challenging than simple socialization or institutionalization, especially when one considers the complexities of the concept of power, power cycles, and power transition. As is the case in the liberal tradition just discussed, the question of unipolarity – or international hierarchy – and how to interpret it haunts the realist discourse. While there may still be some proponents of a materialist realism who

---

[33] For an insightful review of varieties of realism, see Chapter 2.

predict that balancing behavior is inevitable even under conditions of US preponderance, there are plenty of realists who have now either overtly or covertly rejected such determinism.

This opens up new ways to think about power competition, recognizing that such competition is socially constructed in at least some senses, which in turn invites consideration of such issues as soft balancing, for example, or other forms of status-seeking short of overt balancing of the hegemon.[34] Even when realist scholars do not overtly theorize the role of ideas, one can find in realist work plenty of references to soft power, legitimacy, (mis)perception, emotions, irrationality, and other idea-laden concepts. Perhaps most importantly for conceptualizing accommodation, debates about the proper contours of grand strategy are, among other things, debates about how to interpret the international system in order to act in such a way as to sustain one's country's power and interests, which too must be interpreted, while recognizing that others will be doing the same for their own country's power and interests.[35] Realism today is almost never a purely materialist theory. When contrasted with the hardline rationalism of certain strands of neoliberal institutionalism, moreover, realism appears to have a good deal more in common with at least some strands of constructivism.

Realists themselves have differed substantially in how they perceive the possibilities of peaceful change.[36] One significant strand, recently presented by William Scheuerman,[37] stresses how realist thinkers have envisioned a world state as a resolution to the security dilemmas posed by anarchy. Constructivists such as Alexander Wendt,[38] and also writers such as Daniel Deudney,[39] have granted substantial weight to the idea of the international system resolving itself into a hierarchy. There is a realist logic underlying such speculations, insofar as most realists share a skepticism about the possibility of peace without some sort of hierarchy,

---

[34] Daniel H. Nexon, "The Balance of Power in the Balance," *World Politics* 61, no. 2 (April 2009), 330–59.

[35] For example, consider the wide-ranging debate in *International Security* and the more popular foreign affairs journals, not to mention the blogosphere, about the desirability of US retrenchment in the post-Cold War, and then post-9/11 world. The "bookends" of this debate are Eugene Gholz, Daryl G. Press, and Harvey M. Sapolsky, "Come Home, America: The Strategy of Restraint in the Face of Temptation," *International Security* 21, no. 4 (Spring 1997), 5–48 and Brooks, Ikenberry, and Wohlforth, "Don't Come Home, America."

[36] See Chapter 2.

[37] William E. Scheuerman, "The (Classical) Realist Vision of Global Reform," *International Theory* 2, no. 2 (July 2010), 246–82.

[38] Alexander Wendt, "Why a World State is Inevitable," *European Journal of International Relations* 9, no. 4 (December 2003), 491–542.

[39] Deudney, *Bounding Power.*

and about the ability of any hierarchical order to endure in the absence of centralized military power.

If hierarchy is the only solution to world order, then the problem of accommodation becomes one of sustaining that hierarchy through some combination of co-optation and coercion. This view is perhaps best outlined in John Ikenberry's *Liberal Leviathan*, and also in Stephen Brooks and William Wohlforth's *World Out of Balance*. The fact that these three writers have collaborated in an article arguing for sustained US engagement in world order, evoking a combination of liberal and realist ideas to make a case for sustaining US primacy through global engagement, which they see as the best option for a peaceful world order, shows how in the United States realism and liberalism can be, and often are, fused into a single approach.[40] But Charles Doran's work on power cycles, as well as other analyses, such as that of Robert Gilpin, positing the inevitability of power transition in world history, suggest that other forms of accommodation might be needed should liberal hierarchy be unsustainable.[41] It is worth considering the role of ideas in those lines of realist thought which are less sanguine about the fusion of power and purpose embraced by supporters of the "Liberal Leviathan."

Despite the arguments of Brooks and Wohlforth,[42] the very fact that the question of US relative decline and accommodation of rising powers is preoccupying scholars and policymakers suggests that a world state or world empire under US auspices is not imminent, and that despite its preponderance of power, the United States still faces strategic challenges which necessitate some sort of accommodation and adjustment. In the volume *Special Responsibilities*, for example, our team of writers found much to be skeptical about in terms of the US exercise of responsibility and legitimate authority in areas as diverse as nuclear proliferation, climate change, and management of global finance. Material capability turned out to be a poor predictor of the exercise of authority and responsibility in these issue-areas.[43] Nor can the United States afford to act to sustain peace in every theater where armed conflict might arise, as has been made glaringly evident in the wake of its withdrawals from Iraq

---

[40] Brooks, Ikenberry, and Wohlforth, "Don't Come Home, America."

[41] Charles F. Doran, "Economics, Philosophy of History, and the 'Single Dynamic' of Power Cycle Theory: Expectations, Competition, and Statecraft," *International Political Science Review* 24, no. 1 (January 2003), 13–49; Robert Gilpin, *War and Change in World Politics* (Cambridge: Cambridge University Press, 1981).

[42] Brooks and Wohlforth, *World Out of Balance.*

[43] Mlada Bukovansky, Ian Clark, Robyn Eckersley, Richard Price, Christian Reus-Smit, and Nicholas J. Wheeler, *Special Responsibilities: Global Problems and American Power* (Cambridge: Cambridge University Press, 2012).

and Afghanistan, and in light of its failure to act with respect to civil war in Syria and forceful Russian territorial expansion in Georgia, and now Ukraine.

Setting aside the question of hierarchy, then, accommodation still needs to happen with respect to certain issue-areas and certain regions. Here we might draw on old *realpolitik* notions of spheres of influence, perhaps combined with insights from the literature on security communities,[44] and openly acknowledge that, in some theaters, accommodation means allowing those with strong interests and capabilities in the issue or region to take the lead, perhaps within some specified parameters of the loose sort evoked by the international society school.[45] The international society approach is after all experienced in blending insights of realism into a more socially conditioned view of international order. Scholars such as Martin Wight, Hedley Bull, and, more recently, Andrew Hurrell and Barry Buzan, among others, are well versed in the history and practice of realist statecraft and power politics, but they recognize and often explicitly analyze the societal constraints on such power politics.[46]

The core norms of international society vary at any given time, but as Ian Clark has effectively demonstrated, they always include some articulation of principles delineating rightful membership, and rightful conduct.[47] Bull and Wight focused on systems of great powers, but in the post-Cold War world a more pressing issue has been whether international society can be sustained under conditions of hegemony, and what that would look like.[48] In my view, the absence of great power rivals who through their interaction develop habits of respect for one another's interests and status may make the international system appear more peaceful, but at a cost. That cost may best be described by the Greek word *hubris* – the danger is that the preponderant power loses the habit of interacting with equals. If we consider the findings of the practice turn in IR theory, discussed later, such a habit may be a bad thing to lose.

---

[44] Adler and Barnett, *Security Communities*.

[45] Hedley Bull, *The Anarchical Society: A Study of Order in World Politics* (London: Macmillan, 1977).

[46] Martin Wight, *Systems of States*, ed. Hedley Bull (London: Leicester University Press, 1977); Bull, *The Anarchical Society*; Barry Buzan, *From International to World Society? English School Theory and the Social Structure of Globalisation* (Cambridge: Cambridge University Press, 2004); Andrew Hurrell, *On Global Order: Power, Values, and the Constitution of International Society* (New York: Oxford University Press, 2007).

[47] Ian Clark, *Legitimacy in International Society* (Oxford: Oxford University Press, 2005), 5.

[48] Ibid.

A particularly interesting take on accommodation under conditions of hegemony can be found in E.H. Carr's *The Twenty Years' Crisis*.[49] In the chapter on peaceful change, Carr suggests that a model of bargaining between capital and labor might serve as an analogy for the problem of peaceful change in IR.[50] He is skeptical about the emergence of any sort of legislative process whereby disputes could be reliably settled at the international level – which one could take to mean that merely reweighting the votes in the IMF, or even perhaps recalibrating the membership and voting arrangements in the Security Council, may not cut it.[51] Carr has a deep skepticism about the ability of international institutions to create the conditions for peaceful change, a skepticism consistent with his view of the League of Nations. For him, bargaining is a more appropriate model for generating the changes needed to accommodate the power aspirations of potential challengers – though, as Pelc notes, that bargaining might optimally take place within an appropriately flexible legal framework. Importantly, Carr focuses on bargaining between dominant status quo, and potentially revisionist, states. Any hegemon must anticipate the rise of revisionist powers, and thus must accommodate those powers if war is to be avoided. That is why Carr points out, in a different chapter, the need for self-sacrifice by the hegemon if a hegemonic order is to endure.[52] Further, peaceful change as Carr sees it has a moral dimension, which he sketches as a "spirit of give and take," again using the term "self-sacrifice."[53] Can such moralizing by a purported realist offer some useful insights into the problem of accommodation today?

Although Carr appears to dismiss international institutions,[54] it may be that the international institutions of our day embody a degree of adaptability that makes them more effective bargaining arenas than was the League in Carr's.[55] If we acknowledge the importance of bargaining among unequals as an important key to peaceful change under conditions of hegemony, we might also find reasons to support institutional configurations which make that bargaining both possible and meaningful in its accommodation of the aspirations of weaker but rising powers.

[49] E.H. Carr, *The Twenty Years' Crisis, 1919–1939*, 2 edn. (New York: Harper Torchbooks, 1964); see also Charles Jones, *E.H. Carr and International Relations: A Duty to Lie* (Cambridge: Cambridge University Press, 1998); Scheuerman, "The (Classical) Realist Vision."

[50] Carr, *The Twenty Years' Crisis*, 212.   [51] See Chapter 4.

[52] Carr, *The Twenty Years' Crisis*, 68.   [53] Ibid., 220.

[54] Although the fact that he devotes so many pages to the League, and a chapter to international law, suggests some ambiguity.

[55] See Chapter 4.

From that perspective, more bargaining weight in the IMF, WB, and UN Security Council, as well as membership in the more informal regulatory clubs and regimes governing world politics, is not a trivial thing to pursue, and the United States should be working hard on policies to facilitate such accommodation.[56] From this perspective, the burden of responsibility to accommodate lies disproportionately on the shoulders of the hegemon.

Conclusion

The line of thought which focuses on the processes involved in the construction of security communities and other practices of global governance has taken a turn that is relevant to the problem of accommodation as I have presented it to this point. This approach evolved out of the work of constructivist thinkers such as Emmanuel Adler, but has further developed in the "practice turn" in IR theory, where practices are conceptualized in a thick and idea-laden manner, as "socially-meaningful patterns of action which, in being performed more or less competently, simultaneously embody, act out, and possibly reify background knowledge and discourse in and on the material world."[57] In many respects, the practice turn is a logical outgrowth of constructivism, and yet, as Vincent Pouliot has demonstrated, it departs from constructivist theory in its rejection of what he calls the "representational bias" present in constructivist (as well as liberal and realist) thought.[58] While practices are imbued with practical and intersubjective knowledge, such knowledge cannot and should not be abstracted from its instantiation in action; it does not reside in some milieu separate from the realm of action, guiding such action, as representational theories (whether rationalist or constructivist) imply. Rather, action proceeds from largely unarticulated background knowledge. I believe that accommodation must be practiced, that habits of accommodation should be developed in arenas where they have not been already, and that the action takes place in the realm of politics and diplomacy; we cannot expect institutions to automatically solve the problem of accommodation. But Pouliot's emphasis on the tacit and unreflective nature of practice, valuable as it is, may not be entirely appropriate to the concept of accommodation, because accommodation presumably should

---

[56] On the importance of informal clubs, see Daniel W. Drezner, *All Politics is Global: Explaining International Regulatory Regimes* (Princeton: Princeton University Press, 2008).

[57] Adler and Pouliot, "International Practices," 4.

[58] Pouliot, "The Logic of Practicality."

be practiced with intention and purpose, with a conscious sense of responsibility.

Insofar as the practice of accommodation is conducted through diplomacy, it may proceed from largely inarticulate background knowledge, rather than communicative or instrumental rationality.[59] Moreover, the language of status can go quite a long way toward describing the central stakes in the practice of international competition, and there may be something about status that is pre-rational, or at least not entirely amenable to rational bargaining.[60] But the arenas in which diplomacy and status competition takes place, be they international institutions or clubs, or even domestic political arenas, are structured to give differential power and status to different players, and we need to be aware that accommodation might require conscious efforts to ameliorate these power differentials. Further, to speak of peaceful accommodation is to speak of a set of practices in terms of a higher goal and an undesirable alternative should that goal not be achieved: bluntly put, peaceful accommodation should fend off hegemonic war. Analysts, and especially policymakers, must thereby imbue this practice with moral resonance. What is at stake is not peace at any price (for it is possible to imagine a peace without accommodation), but rather a peaceful process whereby changes in global power distributions are lubricated and cushioned by accommodating practices. Successful accommodation must somehow satisfy the status claims of aspiring powers without thereby aggravating the status anxieties and legitimate interests of the power or powers doing the accommodating.

In situations where the practice of accommodation is playing out between hegemonic powers and those who aspire to a greater role in regional or other kinds of governance and security arenas, with all the tension and insecurity that arises in eras of power transition, some sort of mindfulness that is neither purely instrumental, nor yet completely habitual and inarticulate, must necessarily come into play. This is what I think Carr is getting at when he calls for a spirit of give and take. Rationalists might emphasize the "give and take" part of the phrase, and rightly turn their focus onto bargaining, but perhaps the "spirit" is just as important. In order to peacefully accommodate rising powers, the hegemonic power (or powers) must practice *purposive and skillful* accommodation, and the rising powers must be similarly purposive and skillful in presenting their

---

[59] Vincent Pouliot, "Setting Status in Stone: The Negotiation of International Institutional Privileges," in *Status in World Politics*, eds. T.V. Paul, Deborah Larson, and William Wohlforth (Cambridge: Cambridge University Press, 2014), 192–215; Pouliot, "The Logic of Practicality."

[60] Paul, Larson, and Wohlforth, *Status in World Politics*.

status claims in a manner that is capable of being accommodated. It is the responsibility of the relevant actors involved in power transition to develop and sustain practices of claiming and accommodating one another in this transition, and, for this, the actors need to draw on ideological and perhaps even moral resources which render them capable of doing so.

Some of these ideological and moral resources can be found in international norms and institutions, even in the idealistic goals of those institutions – human rights, self-determination, free flow of goods, services, and capital – which cynics are so fond of deriding because they have never been fully realized. Dominant and rising powers must draw on some common store of ideas in articulating status and leadership claims, and negotiating changes in the structure of authority. To go back to the example of the AIIB, the fact that the United States and China are in conflict over the institutional configurations of global finance does not mean that they lack a common commitment to continued financial globalization and its regulation. Or, in the case of the United Nations, there may be differences in emphasis on and interpretation of sovereignty, but the fundamental value of sovereignty remains a common commitment. But the moral resonance of sovereignty ultimately rests on the flourishing of people and place.

If accommodation is to be a sustainable practice when the most fundamental power rankings in world politics are at stake, it must also entail a morally resonant dimension of meaning, beyond rational strategic objectives. Accommodation perceived by any side as merely strategic (or, worse, hypocritical) is not likely to create the sorts of condition in which the status aspirations of the respective parties will be satisfied. At stake is the creation and sustenance of a security community, but if an existing security community can sustain itself through largely habitual practice, an emergent one requires a degree of intentionality, and that intentionality must be construed in moral terms in order to motivate difficult and costly action. The most resonant language through which to articulate the moral dimension of accommodation may, I think, be found not in liberalism alone, but in a liberalism supplemented by a form of republican realism, where the core imperative is *a desire not to be dominated.*[61] The proper complement to the desire not to be dominated is the willingness to exercise self-restraint. Both dominant and rising powers have responsibilities pertaining to accommodation: the hegemon must be prepared to signal self-restraint, and the aspirants a willingness to be satisfied with

---

[61] Skinner, *Liberty Before Liberalism*; Philip Pettit, *Republicanism: A Theory of Freedom and Government* (Oxford: Oxford University Press, 1997).

a position that falls short of wiping out one's rival. The responsibility to accommodate is thus a moral responsibility, and it falls on all actors involved in power and status competition, because what is at stake is not just relative position, but the well-being of whole societies, and indeed ecosystems.

Part II

Historical cases

6   Seizing the day or passing the baton?
Power, illusion, and the British Empire

Ali Zeren and John A. Hall

Some of the fierceness of the reaction of the United States to the foul attacks of 9/11 has often been ascribed to the inviolate condition of this great continental hegemon. Nothing could be further from the truth. In 1812, British forces occupied Washington and gleefully burnt down the White House. Further, Great Britain supported the South during the Civil War – or, more precisely, the British state supported the South, even though many of the Lancashire cotton workers most affected supported the North. Gladstone later apologized for this, but his predecessors had been positively keen to see the breakup of the Union. Very much in this spirit, the British state did all it could to stand in the way of American expansion to the west – not surprisingly, as a continental power would have had the capacity to gobble up Canada. In a nutshell, we have here a history of war, friction, and deeply opposed interests. But it is just as clear that peace has since broken out between these two powers. Great Britain and the United States fought together in many wars in the twentieth century, from the world wars to more varied conflicts – most obviously and recently in Iraq and Afghanistan, but just as importantly, if covertly, in Iran, when toppling Mohammad Mosaddeq. If the burning of the White House stands at one extreme, at the other is American reverence for Winston Churchill and the much-trumpeted mutual regard of Margaret Thatcher and Ronald Reagan.

So this is a case – perhaps, indeed, the case – of peaceful accommodation between a declining and a rising power. It has been thoroughly studied, with most scholars agreeing on a basic explanatory frame.[1] We begin with the most recent account, that of Charles Kupchan, given that

---

[1] Lionel M. Gelber, *The Rise of Anglo-American Friendship: A Study in World Politics, 1898–1906* (Oxford: Oxford University Press, 1938); Kenneth Bourne, *Britain and the Balance of Power in North America, 1815–1908* (Berkeley: University of California Press, 1967); Charles S. Campbell, *From Revolution to Rapprochement: The United States and Great Britain, 1783–1900* (New York: John Wiley & Sons, 1974); Steven E. Lobell, "Britain's Paradox: Cooperation or Punishment Prior to World War 1," *Review of International Studies* 27, no. 2 (April 2001), 169–86.

it offers the most powerful general model for understanding the relations, both violent and peaceful, between rising and established powers.[2] Kupchan moves from considerations of the balance of power to assertions that stable peace has come to depend upon societal integration and cultural commonality. We offer mild critique. The dream of "Anglo-America" was and is far more British than American. This point can usefully be highlighted immediately.

For one thing, it is important to remember divisions within the United States. Franklin Roosevelt never visited the British Isles during the war, despite Churchill's pleading, because he feared a backlash among Irish-American and German-American voters. Domestic concerns mattered more than Anglo-America. For another, there was Suez. Dwight Eisenhower was not prepared for a moment to be drawn into that morass and used all the considerable powers available to him to bring Britain and France to heel within a matter of days. We offer detailed description of one key moment when American self-interest overrode commonality to drive this consideration home. In a sense, this is close to Kupchan's starting point, in that it stresses power. It differs from his position merely in suggesting that a truly common culture was never established – with attempts at such creation coming much later than he suggests. Our core argument is, then, that the transition was one in which power was "seized" by the United States.

That position gains support when we consider the flip side to the picture. There were British figures who genuinely hoped to create a single Anglo-American society. One thinks in this regard of Churchill's proposal for shared passports. But British policy is best seen in strategic rather than normative terms. Its classic statement remains that of Harold Macmillan when serving as the British liaison to American forces in North Africa in 1942:

[We] are the Greeks in this American empire. You will find the Americans much as the Greeks found the Romans – great big, bustling people, more vigorous than we are and also more idle, with more unspoiled virtues but also more corrupt. We must run [this HQ] as the Greek slaves ran the operations of the Emperor Claudius.[3]

Britain has sought, to use the phrase of the former Conservative Foreign Secretary Douglas Hurd, "to punch above its weight" – to remain at the

---

[2] Charles A. Kupchan, *How Enemies Become Friends: The Sources of Stable Peace* (Princeton: Princeton University Press, 2010), especially chapter 3.

[3] Alastair Horne, *Harold Macmillan, Volume One: 1894–1956* (New York: Viking, 1988), 160. This sounds impressively scholarly, but in fact it demonstrates ignorance: the Greeks did not do very well in the Roman Empire. Perhaps Macmillan learned this himself, given his disappointments when dealing with Kennedy in connection with nuclear weapons: first Skybolt, and then Polaris.

table of the great powers – through serving as the junior partner to the liberal hegemon. Given what has been said about American power, a judgment can be rendered about this position: it was prone to illusion, failing to realize that the relationship between the United States and Great Britain was only really special to one side. This ought to have been clear for many years. Perhaps Barack Obama's clear preference for Britain within the European Union will at last make it so. Of course, there were always hardheaded members of the British elite who did not fall for the illusion in question, and it may be that their voice is gaining in strength. The refusal of the British Parliament to offer support to Obama's proposed military strike against Syria in 2013 points in that direction. So, too, does the comment made to the BBC on that occasion by Crispin Blunt, a Conservative Member of Parliament and former army officer, that he was "delighted that we relieved ourselves of this imperial pretension."[4] All of this suggests that there is little sense in talking about "passing the baton" of liberal hegemony. It is very important not to accept such language. For one thing, Great Britain never exercised hegemonic power, being but one of a small number of great powers; the situation of the United States, both at the end of World War II (WWII) and still more from 1989, has been entirely different.[5] For another, the manner in which the United States took powers from Great Britain was altogether more brutal.

This chapter goes beyond these mild but necessary correctives. Most importantly, we seek to open discussion by raising a question that we do not then answer in any definitive manner. The issue is that of the nature of "accommodation," or, perhaps better here, "transition." It behooves us to remember that ancient historians no longer speak of the Fall of Rome, stressing institutional continuities and continuing legacies in a sustained transition. In this regard, it is worth asking whether the British embrace affected the worldview of the United States. Even if decisions were and are made in Washington, might it be the case that something of an imperial agenda was created by Great Britain? This, after all, was the claim of the Nye Commission after World War I (WWI), accusing Britain of having pulled America into the war against the Bolsheviks. It has often and accurately been noted that there are different strands to American foreign policy. Most obviously, there has been a decided tension between the avoidance of entanglements abroad and the desire to play a major part on the world stage. The world policy has triumphed, even if it is all too easy to detect even today voices privileging isolationism.

[4] Gideon Rachman, "Politics: A Leader Humbled, a Nation Cut Down to Size," *Financial Times* (August 30, 2013). Available at: www.ft.com/cms/s/0/3e92a36a-11a3-11e3-8321-00144feabdc0.html#axzz3X1hqJqbS.

[5] John A. Hall, *International Orders* (Cambridge: Polity Press, 1996).

The question that then arises is simple: Was Britain in part responsible for the complete entry of the United States onto the world scene? To raise this question is to bring back into consideration constructivist concerns – despite the fact that the general argument insists that considerations of power mattered most of all – so as to see if there might be something to them at some sort of subliminal level.

The conclusion begins by summarizing the argument. It then asks whether general lessons can be learned from the British-American accommodation. The variables involved most certainly have wide use, but the specificities of the case suggest that most can be learned by contrast rather than copying.

Kupchan's account

Kupchan argues that Anglo-American rapprochement took place in four stages, roughly between 1895 and 1906. The first stage was that of "unilateral accommodation" by Britain.[6] In 1895, President Cleveland insisted that the United States would play the predominant role in dealing with Venezuelan borders. Two motives lay behind his actions: party advantage and the simple desire to follow his immediate predecessors in staking a claim to status in the world polity – something that had become possible by the end of the century, as economic growth had allowed Civil War debts to be paid off.[7] Britain backed down, seeking in the ensuing years to avoid conflict at all costs. This is not surprising. Extensive British power in the nineteenth century was always potentially fragile. The country was, after all, but a small island, its possession of so much territory something of a freak. The defeat of the French in the great imperial contest of the late eighteenth and early nineteenth centuries had allowed Britain to expand, and the maintenance of its empire resulted thereafter from, in turn, exhaustion and then balance among its European rivals.[8] Most of its rule was but skin deep. "The weary titan," to use Joseph Chamberlain's expression, was all too aware of the gap between its resources and commitments.[9] A combination of German rivalry (seen, above all, in the initiation in 1898 of the program to build a high-seas fleet), the Russian military threat in the east to India,

---

[6] Kupchan, *How Enemies Become Friends*, 74.

[7] Fareed Zakaria, *From Wealth to Power: The Unusual Origins of America's World Role* (Princeton: Princeton University Press, 1998).

[8] John Darwin, *After Tamerlane: The Rise and Fall of Global Empires* (London: Penguin, 2007); Paul Kennedy, "Why Did the British Empire Last So Long?" in *Strategy and Diplomacy, 1870–1945*, ed. Paul Kennedy (London: George Allen and Unwin, 1983).

[9] Joseph Chamberlain, Address in the Imperial Conference of 1902, in Julian Amery, *The Life of Joseph Chamberlain*, vol. IV (London: Macmillan, 1956), 421.

Japan's naval strength, and the Boer Wars forced Britain to make strategic choices. What mattered most of all was the European threat, and this
accordingly led to a treaty with Japan and to understandings with the
United States, which allowed the Royal Navy to concentrate its forces
and attention on home waters. Kupchan's argument has an additional
nuance. British actions during the dispute and in the years that followed
sought more than mere dispute resolution. Every attempt was made to
exhibit warm cooperation: this was meant to demonstrate a deliberate
effort to reduce rivalry, perhaps thereby to hide the underlying weakness
of the British position. In general, "the British were hopeful that doing
so would constitute an important first step in turning an implacable
adversary into a potential friend."[10]

The positive reception of the new, softer British line within the United
States led to the regular arbitration of subsequent disagreements between
the two powers. Both British claims regarding damages to sealing vessels
and the dispute over the border between Alaska and Yukon were settled
in this way, by the setting up of arbitration tribunals. Kupchan considers
genuinely "reciprocal restraint" a second stage in the changing relationship between Britain and the United States. American support of the
British during the Boer Wars is taken as a sign of reciprocation by the
United States. One very crucial example of peaceful accommodation and
concessions is that of the abrogation of the Clayton–Bulwer Act and its
replacement in 1901 by the Hay–Pauncefote Treaty, allowing the United
States to build and fortify a canal in Central America.[11] This meant
that Britain had effectively surrendered all naval control and superiority
in the Gulf and eastern Atlantic, and allowed the United States naval
influence in the Pacific – a development of such significance that it is
indicative of the extent to which "accommodation" was highly skewed in
favor of the United States. Further, Britain alone among the European
powers backed the United States in its war with Spain, in ousting the
Spanish from Cuba, and in supporting American colonial expansion in
the Caribbean and Pacific, notably in the Philippines and Hawaii. But
Kupchan's argument is once again subtle. British support in the Spanish-
American war and in the Pacific was not just "friendship"; to the contrary, it also furthered British interests. The "open-door" policy in China
and power balancing in East Asia were also welcomed, Kupchan argues,
because British officials held that the United States and Britain shared
common interests: American acquisition of power, and its more general
rise to great power status, was preferable to any alternative. Whatever the
precise motivations involved, the consequence was considerable. Benign

---

[10] Kupchan, *How Enemies Become Friends*, 78.   [11] Ibid., 78–80.

perceptions of American actions by British officials were reciprocated in the United States, resulting in a change of attitude and the emergence of a view, among high-level politicians, diplomats, and officials, of congruence between US and British interests.[12]

Kupchan argues that generalized trust "spread outward from the exclusive realm of politicians, diplomats, and military officials to engage a wider range of actors on both sides."[13] "Societal integration," in which bureaucrats, the media, economic interests, and private citizens also played a role, is taken to be a third stage in the process of accommodation. Rapprochement between the naval establishments in Washington and in London clearly played an enormous part. But Kupchan also makes much of increased linkages in the private economic sector: Britain became the largest export market for the United States, above all because of cotton, while the United States was the leading venue for British direct foreign investment. The general picture is of an increase in British-American friendship via the shaping of public discourse by private economic agents on both sides. This was followed by personal travel and by linkages of all sorts in the press and the media.

All of this is seen as bringing about a big transformation in public sentiment on both sides by the turn of the century. From this comes the fourth and final stage in the process, termed "the generation of a new narrative," comprising three distinct elements. First, both British and American elites began to adopt a narrative of friendship between the two countries, starting from 1896 in the case of the British and from 1898 on the American side, replacing the previous discourse of hostility. Second, this new narrative was strongly based on a discourse of racial and cultural affinity. Intellectual and literary networks benefitting from the publishing revolution of the 1890s were able to spread "Anglo-Saxonism" through transatlantic publishing houses with joint centers in New York and London.[14] Alongside this discourse of kinship and common heritage, finally, emerged the notion that war between the two countries was unthinkable, fratricidal in character, and so all but impossible. And this was not just an ideological change. War plans between the two powers ceased to be made, although the United States did continue to plan for conflict with Canada until a much later date. The rapprochement

---

[12] "This mutual shift in assessments of each other's broader motivation constituted a critical turning point; geopolitical competition was not just abating, but it was giving way to a shared sense of confidence that the two countries had congruent interests and common goals." Ibid., 82.

[13] Ibid., 85.

[14] Ibid., 98–99. Of particular importance were such magazines as *Scribner's*, *Atlantic Monthly*, *North American Review*, *Fortnightly Review*, *Century Magazine*, and *Nineteenth Century*.

between 1895 and 1906 as a whole is seen as laying the groundwork for the emergence of an eventual security community between Britain and the United States.

Although this constitutes the explanation for *how* peace came about, Kupchan considers questions concerning *why* it occurred. Three main conditions are held to have been crucial, namely institutionalized restraint, the compatibility of social orders, and cultural commonality.

The first factor is a type of democratic peace argument, resting on the proposition that it was enabled by the fact that the United States and Britain were both liberal polities, with institutions structured to "check power, ensure rule of law, and discourage exploitation of political advantage."[15] The argument is that this commonality manifested itself in the conduct of foreign policy and created mutual credibility since "such commitments . . . had to pass muster among legislators and the public."[16] It also follows that this credibility was achieved not only by transparency but also because it was balanced with pluralism and political flexibility within both British and American domestic political arenas.

Second, democratization and liberalization on the British side, particularly after the 1884 franchise reform, as well as the resolution of the North–South conflict in the United States (in which Britain had supported the South), created compatible social orders. Political liberalization on the British side is held to have diluted anti-American attitudes of the traditional class, while also leading Americans to see "Britain as a country that shared its social and political proclivities – a change in perception that helped replace a sense of social estrangement with one of affinity."[17]

Finally, Kupchan claims that the emphasis on cultural commonality was not somehow a pragmatic gesture intended to sway public opinion. Rather, officials and opinion-makers held such beliefs sincerely and deeply. The important role cultural fusion played derives from the following:

Cultural affinity appears to have mattered most during the early and late stages of rapprochement. At the outset of the process, as Britain searched for adversaries that it could potentially convert into friends, it singled out the United States at least in part due to cultural commonality and the familiarity and comfort that it bred. It was strategic necessity that prompted London to attempt reconciliation with Washington. But Britain's latent sense of kinship with America helps explain why London worked hardest to befriend the United States rather than other challengers.[18]

[15] Ibid., 105. [16] Ibid. [17] Ibid., 109. [18] Ibid., 110.

The mild critique

There is no doubt but that a vision of Anglo-America was created at the end of the nineteenth century.[19] Elites on both sides of the Atlantic became closely linked. Henry Adams, Brooks Adams, Teddy Roosevelt, Mahan, and Hay stood on one side of the relationship, Macmillan, Bryce, Churchill, and Spring Rice on the other. Then there was Kipling. Although born in India, he had spent several years in Vermont before moving permanently to Sussex, and he was sufficiently well connected to send a poem that he completed on November 22, 1898 directly to Roosevelt. A word of context is in order before quoting from three of the seven stanzas. "Recessional," written the year before on the occasion of the Jubilee, had warned of British decline, thereby giving special meaning to this new poem.

The White Man's Burden
The United States and the Philippine Islands

Take up the White Man's Burden—
Send forth the best ye breed—
Go bind your sons to exile
To serve your captives' need;
To wait in heavy harness
On fluttered folk and wild—
Your new-caught, sullen peoples,
Half devil and half child . . .

Take up the White Man's Burden—
And reap his old reward:
The blame of those ye better,
The hate of those ye guard— . . .

Take up the While Man's Burden—
Have done with childish ways—
The lightly proffered laurel,
The easy ungrudged praise.
Comes now to search your manhood
Through all the thankless years,
Cold-edged with dear-brought wisdom,
The judgement of your peers.

On January 12, 1899, Roosevelt sent the poem to Henry Cabot Lodge, endorsing its view of "expansionism," and it was first published in the *Sun* on February 5, 1899, the day before the Senate moved toward taking the

---

[19] Christopher Hitchens, *Blood, Class and Empire: The Enduring Anglo-American Relationship* (New York: Farrar, Strauss and Giroux, 1990) is a brilliant and amusing account of the "special relationship."

Philippines under American control.[20] If this stresses the linkages of race and the dreams of empire, it is as important to stress those of class. An immediate linkage here was the marriage of American heiresses to members of the British elite, not least in the cases of Churchill and Macmillan. This is the world of Henry James, deeply attracted to Europe, finding a depth in social class that he felt to be lacking in the United States.

It would be extremely easy to fill page after page with details of such linkages – of Walter Annenberg as Ambassador to London commissioning books on the Roman Empire, of John Travolta dancing with Princess Diana, and of Caspar Weinberger being knighted by the Queen. But a flood of detail of this sort would mislead. The American elite was rarely interested in the notion of some sort of shared condominium, in "Anglo-America" *tout court*. The story that needs to be told is that of American power, objectively present and subjectively welcomed. Mahan and Brooks Adams made it perfectly clear that they wished to replace Britain, seen as a declining power. Similar sentiments were present in the determination to make the Panama Canal an American preserve, by cutting out British rights in the Hay–Pauncefote Treaty.[21] Adam Tooze's brilliant account of the remaking of the global order between 1916 and 1931 carries the story forward, demonstrating how ruthless was the behavior of the United States once its financial ascendancy was both secure and obvious.[22] The spirit of what is involved can be caught in the image of Dean Acheson jumping on a table filled with delight in front of his officials in 1947 after receiving a telegram from London saying that Britain could not handle the situation in Greece. Here we have a member of a new elite (many of its members educated in Groton School), keen to run the world, not least as it blamed the horrors of WWII on its own failure to do so in the interwar period.[23]

The importance of power can best be illustrated by considering a single issue at some length, namely, that of the debates surrounding the creation of the architecture for the postwar political economy of the capitalism.[24] The story was first told by Richard Gardner in a

[20] Ibid., chapter 3.
[21] Steven E. Lobell, *The Challenge of Hegemony: Grand Strategy, Trade, and Domestic Politics* (Ann Arbor: University of Michigan Press, 2003), chapter 3.
[22] Adam Tooze, *The Deluge: The Great War, America and the Remaking of the Global Order 1916–1931* (New York: Viking, 2014).
[23] Dean Acheson, *Present at the Creation: My Years in the State Department* (New York: W.W. Norton, 1969). Walter Isaacson, *The Wise Men: Six Friends and the World They Made* (New York: Simon and Schuster, 1986) is a classical portrait of Acheson and his immediate colleagues; that is, of a group which came close to creating a ruling class for the United States.
[24] An alternative would have been to follow the ups and downs in the relationship of Roosevelt and Churchill revealed in their wartime correspondence, some details of which are in Hitchens, *Blood, Class and Empire*, chapters 7 and 8.

path-breaking volume dealing not just with financial matters but also with the creation of multilateral trade arrangements; further details about the struggle over the international financial system are now available in Benn Steil's account of the central relationship involved – that between John Maynard Keynes and Harry Dexter White.[25]

The situations of Great Britain and of the United States in the years after 1918 could not have been more different. The United States did not join the League of Nations, retreating thereby to isolationism, wholly obsessed with its own concerns. One element involved at the time was the activities of the Nye Commission: this eventually blamed Churchill for involving the United States in the attempt to dislodge the Bolsheviks. Suspicion toward Britain was perhaps not surprising, as it was at this time that the British Empire expanded to its maximal point, principally through gaining territories of the erstwhile Ottoman Empire. But size hid exceptional fragility. Keynes realized this during the war, only too aware of the precariousness of state finances. It may well be, as French critics pointed out, that there was nothing inherently wrong with the provisions of the Treaty of Versailles, as Keynes had so famously claimed. A harsh treaty would have brought order had France and Britain been prepared to enforce it. But they were not, thereby allowing a steam of concessions that failed to satisfy Germany, while seemingly admitting that the provisions of the Treaty were unjust. Hence, the interwar period was marked by continuing geopolitical instability, despite the presence of a treaty – exactly the opposite situation, of course, to that at the end of WWII, bereft of a treaty but with the balance of power made crystal clear. In these circumstances, trade could not possibly regain the position that it had held before 1914. The collapse of the Gold Standard and the rise of protectionism followed.

Cordell Hull saw things in a different light, claiming that it was the breakdown of trade that led to vicious geopolitics – that is, replacing geopolitical facts with an economistic alternative. The importance of the difference can be seen in the terms of the Lend–Lease arrangements agreed in 1941. Hull's position had everything to do with Article VII seeking to end imperial preferences. There was much debate around this article, but considerable clarity as to British feelings: Keynes referred to the "lunatic" position of Hull, while Churchill was of course wholly devoted to the Empire. But Churchill was always prone to believing in

---

[25] Richard N. Gardner, *Sterling-Dollar Diplomacy: Anglo-American Collaboration in the Reconstruction of Multilateral Trade* (New York: Columbia University Press, 1956); Benn Steil, *The Battle of Bretton Woods: John Maynard Keynes, Harry Dexter White, and the Making of a New World Order* (Princeton: Princeton University Press, 2013). Their arguments receive strong support from Raymond F. Mikesell, "The Bretton Woods Debates: A Memoir," *Essays in International Finance* 192 (March 1994), 1–68.

the good nature of the United States, and so fudged the matter in the House of Commons, suggesting that there was no likelihood of the clause being enforced.

This is the celebrated background to the clash between Keynes and White, the key proponents of the British and American plans for a post-war world economic order. It is as well to remember the personalities involved. The utter brilliance, often acerbic, always ingenious, of Keynes is legendary. It is important to remember his famous quip to a critic, admitting that he changed his position when the facts changed. He had envisioned protectionism in the 1930s – becoming thereafter a suspicious quantity in the eyes of many American policymakers – but moved in the opposite direction during the war. Less appreciated is the extent to which he always had English interests at heart. White's background has been hinted at for many years but is only now fully known: leftist in politics, the purveyor of American secrets for Soviet ears, always keen to find a place within the international arena for Russia. Nonetheless, the initial plans that each produced had elements in common, notably the seeds for both the International Monetary Fund (IMF) and the World Bank (WB). But beyond the desire to produce a set of rules that would allow the international political economy to work smoothly lay clear differences.

The Clearing Union envisaged by Keynes was characteristically inge-nious, not least in the proposal for a world currency, the Bancor, which would be used to facilitate the transactions of states. The most impor-tant element in the proposal for consideration here is the fact that the plan was designed to create stability by dealing not just with debtors, but with creditors as well. Chronic debtors would be forced to depre-ciate their currency and to raise interest rates, to sell gold, and to limit exports of capital. Chronic creditors, on the other hand, would be forced to appreciate their currency, and then to pay fines to the central bank's reserve fund.[26] White had no interest whatsoever in such a scheme. The United States would emerge from the war as the great creditor nation, and it had no interest in creating a system that would diminish its power. White's plan was wholly different: to make the American dollar the inter-national medium of exchange, albeit backed by gold reserves. Such a sys-tem would, of course, give the United States advantages far greater than Britain had enjoyed under the Gold Standard. A single power could print money within capitalist society, and very significant seigniorage would be reaped from the pricing of world commodities in its own currency.

But the clash of these two personalities mattered less than the prevail-ing structure of power. Keynes was defeated in the 18 months before the meetings at Bretton Woods. This was symbolically seen in New

---

[26] Steil, *The Battle of Bretton Woods*, 144.

Hampshire: White carefully sidelined Keynes to the WB discussions, placing himself in charge of those dealing with the IMF. And White orchestrated everything else: he leaned on country after country in order to gain the necessary votes for passage, and he had his way on a whole series of issues – from the voting rights on both the WB and the IMF, to the location of both organizations in Washington, DC.

This is the world within which we have lived, and whose contours still structure our existence. The system has most certainly served to help the United States. In the 1960s, the United States did not raise taxes to pay for Great Society programs and the war in Vietnam; instead, it printed money, and thereby unleashed the great postwar inflation.[27] These years made it obvious that White's plan was deeply flawed, so the inability to back the dollar with gold led in 1971 to "the closing of the Gold Window." But the world has continued to bank in dollars, with the United States retaining advantage by sending the dollar up or down to suit its domestic situation.[28] Logically, one might say that the United States should have regretted the inability to punish creditors – first Japan, and then China. But this is not so: the United States has the guns still, and thereby gains butter provided by other states. This was certainly true in the cases of Germany, Saudi Arabia, and Japan. And a slightly different embrace has been at the center of the world's political economy more recently: in return for access to its markets, China has sustained the profligate habits of the hegemonic power, and it is chary about restraining these, as the monies it is owed would thereby depreciate rapidly in tandem with the collapse of the dollar. The great currency imbalances of the world economy are closely related to the bubble in the American housing market, and thereby to the great crash of 2008. The ability to print money that others again absorbed saved the American economy. But that very success is now causing terrible problems in emerging economies: as capital returns to invest in a reviving United States, it becomes ever harder for those economies to service debts taken at the height of the world liquidity crisis. Seigniorage remains, and it does little, as Keynes had realized, to provide stability for capitalist society as a whole.

Concentration on this particular case has been designed to show that the lack of conflict involved as Britain declined and America triumphed is best explained by the brute facts of power. That is the key consideration, and it accords with Kupchan's account of events in and around 1895. The fact that the struggles described here take place in the 1940s does, however, cast doubt on the extent to which shared cultural

---

[27] Michael R. Smith, *Power, Norms and Inflation* (New York: Aldine de Gruyter, 1992).
[28] Susan Strange, *Casino Capitalism* (Oxford: Basil Blackwell, 1986).

understandings, as compared to power, really mattered. And much could be added here. The extent to which economic ties lead to cultural understanding can always be questioned. More strikingly, in military affairs, the attempt to create "Anglo-America" was very much an ongoing British dream in the early years of the Cold War, hampered, one can add, by popular dislike of Great Britain within the United States.[29]

Second thoughts

There can be no doubt but that the United States inherited a mass of problems left in the wake of British decline, from civil war in Greece to the secession of Bangladesh from Pakistan, and from Cyprus to Vietnam. Perhaps the two greatest problems, haunting American and world affairs to this day, concern Israel and Iran. At the center of attention here is the suspicion that Britain might have actively sucked the United States into these rather varied conflicts, in a way that privileged its own interests at the expense of a rather supine United States. That had been the claim at the end of WWI about the role of Churchill in involving the United States in an anti-Bolshevik crusade. And Churchill appears again in entirely believable claims that the sinking of the *Lusitania* was less than an accident, a consequence of his insistence that the ship be used to carry arms in an area known to be patrolled by German submarines. Then there is Attlee's presumption at the time of the Korean War that Britain could expect American support if it launched a nuclear weapon – leading, on this occasion at least, to severe dressing down by Acheson.[30] So, is there any truth to this position? Did Anglo-American social solidarity lead to distortions of the foreign policy of the United States, thereby, of course, suggesting a measure of truth to the perspective of social constructivism? In order to get real purchase on the matter, it is necessary to consider a single but very important case in some detail: that of the toppling of Mossadeq.

The initial reluctance of the British to renegotiate the Anglo-Iranian concession of 1933 quickly escalated to a crisis situation by the beginning of 1951. Between March 15 and May 2, 1951, Mosaddeq's nationalization bill went through the *Majlis*, with unanimous support becoming law on the latter date. The American view of the escalation of conflict stressed British incompetence. Dean Acheson summarized this position in his memoirs: "Never had so few lost so much so stupidly and so fast."[31]

[29] Henry Butterfield Ryan, *The Vision of Anglo-America: The US-UK Alliance and the Emerging Cold War 1943–1945* (Cambridge, Cambridge University Press, 1987).
[30] The episode is recounted in Hitchens, *Blood, Class and Empire*, chapter 13.
[31] Acheson, *Present at the Creation*, 503.

The British hardline position rested on the argument that allowing nationalization to take place, regardless of the terms of compensation, would jeopardize all Britain's foreign investments. The American perspective on this was that such intransigence on the side of the British was quite pointless after the government of Saudi Arabia had successfully received a fifty–fifty concession on the contract of the Arabian-American Oil Company (ARAMCO) in 1950. Following this, no Middle Eastern government would settle for any less.[32] But the guiding principle behind American opposition to the recalcitrant British was the communist threat; that is, the potential replacement of Britain by the Soviets – a manifestation of the obsessive anti-communism that at this time was starting to dominate the United States' entire foreign policy. "Britain might drive Iran to a Communist *coup d'etat*, or Iran might drive Britain out of the country," Acheson wrote later, stressing that "either would be a major disaster. We were deeply concerned."[33] Following nationalization, Britain reacted by sending more troops to its bases in the Middle East and dispatching additional warships to the Gulf, which immediately prompted Acheson to warn the British that the United States would support the use of military force "only on invitation of the Iranian government, or Soviet military intervention, or a Communist *coup d'etat*, or to evacuate British nationals in danger of attack."[34] What the United States feared was that an extended suspension of the activities of the Anglo-Iranian Oil Company (AIOC, later to become British Petroleum) and the loss of the foreign exchange it had previously provided could bring about a collapse of the Iranian economy and a potential communist takeover.

What complicated the issue, however, was that protection of British national interests and the preservation of cooperation between Britain and the United States were then seen as a cornerstone of American foreign policy in the Middle East. President Truman made this clear in a letter to former Ambassador Henry R. Grady:

We had Israel, Egypt, Near East defense, Sudan, South Africa, Tunisia, the NATO treaties all on the fire. Britain and the Commonwealth nations were and are absolutely essential if these things are successful. Then on top of it all we have Korea and Indochina. Iran was only one incident.[35]

---

[32] William Roger Louis, *The British Empire in the Middle East, 1945–51* (Oxford: Clarendon Press, 1984). This view was also held by George C. McGhee, Assistant Secretary of State for the Near East, South Asia, and Africa. But both Acheson, *Present at the Creation* and Louis, *The British Empire* make it clear that the British position was resistant to change.

[33] Acheson, *Present at the Creation*, 506.

[34] Ibid. It is also the case that the United States did not want to sanction the Soviets to similarly apply military intervention in Azerbaijan over its own claims to oil rights there.

[35] Truman to Henry Grady, November 27, 1952, Grady Papers, Harry S. Truman Library, Independence, MO.

National Security Council 136/1 outlining US policy regarding Iran underlined the fact that the American stance and goals with regard to Iran were wholly shaped by the desire to preserve the stability of Iran in order to prevent a Soviet takeover and a consequent increase of the USSR's influence over the Middle East in general.[36] More crucially, it also clearly and unequivocally stated that, in carrying out these goals, the United States would:

(1) Maintain full consultation with the United Kingdom.
(2) Avoid unnecessarily sacrificing legitimate United Kingdom interests or unnecessarily impairing United States-United Kingdom relations.
(3) Not permit the United Kingdom to veto any United States actions which the United States considers essential to the achievement of the policy objectives set forth above.[37]

This dual consideration – the fear of communism and the need to support Britain – shaped American actions in the months following the breakout of the crisis. On the one hand were multiple loans and credits issued to both Britain, for the loss of potential revenue, and Iran, for relief of emergency foreign exchange. On the other were continual efforts to keep both sides negotiating. The first attempt to help sustain negotiations was the mission headed by Averell Harriman, which began in mid-July 1951, but ended when the British walked out at the beginning of September. Subsequent brokerage attempts by Acheson at the United Nations and, later, during North Atlantic Treaty Organization (NATO) meetings in Europe were all broken off by the British – on the ground that "Mosaddeq was never definite enough on price to give the British a proposal capable of development."[38] Acheson would later acknowledge in his memoirs that the adamant British position ruled out further discussions and the possibility of any face-saving retreat for Mosaddeq, who "knew that the British wanted a fight to the finish and [who] took the declaration of a fight to the finish with dignity."[39]

The "Personal & Private" letter of October 3, 1951, from the Permanent Under-Secretary at the Ministry of Fuel and Power, Sir Donald

---

[36] David S. Painter, *Oil and the American Century: The Political Economy of US Foreign Oil Policy, 1941–1954* (Baltimore: Johns Hopkins University Press, 1986); "United States Policy Regarding the Present Situation in Iran," NSC 136/1, November 20, 1952 (sanitized copy), FR 1952–1954, 10: 529–32.

[37] "United States Policy Regarding the Present Situation in Iran," NSC 136/1, November 20, 1952 (sanitized copy), FR 1952–1954, 10: 529–32.

[38] Acheson, *Present at the Creation*, 511. It is worth recalling that the British resolution at the United Nations ended up with a great victory for Mosaddeq, who came to make the case of Iran himself.

[39] Ibid.

Ferguson, to the Lord Privy Seal, Richard Stokes, succinctly summed up the majority perspective of the British cabinet. First, it suggested their belief in the impossibility of reaching a settlement with Mosaddeq under any circumstance, as they firmly held that Mosaddeq's real concern was not financial but rooted in a complete hatred of the British and a desire to remove them entirely from Iran. Second, they thought that allowing the prevailing situation to continue would put all British enterprises and trading activities at risk, by encouraging any other foreign government to unilaterally repudiate contracts with the British. The letter also clearly stated that it was unlikely that Iran would go communist, given that there was no significant internal communist threat. In turn, the proposed course of action was to wait it out "and let Persia and other countries see the disastrous economic consequences to her of her action."[40] The same perspective – that a deal could not be made with Mosaddeq, meaning that he must be replaced – was presented to Acheson via Eden. Acheson considered the British view to be directly opposed to his own.[41] Following a year of "trench warfare" from the end of 1951 to fall 1952, the Americans showed signs of losing patience with the "obstructive" British position, as Acheson later made clear:

Within our government my own colleagues in the State Department and in Treasury and Defense had come to the conclusion that the British were so obstructive and determined on a rule-or-ruin policy in Iran that we must strike out an independent policy or run the gravest risk of having Iran disappear behind the Iron Curtain and the whole military and political situation in the Middle East change adversely.[42]

In order to force the British hand (and to shoot two birds with one stone), the State Department, in the middle of an ongoing Justice Department investigation against major oil companies for allegations of anti-trust violations, decided that individual purchases of Iranian oil should be left to individual judgment, thereby allowing American companies to buy Iranian oil.[43] Further, the State Department drew up plans for a potential US$100 million advance to Iran for future purchases of oil, to be moved and marketed by American oil companies alone or in conjunction with AIOC.[44] "We would make every effort to act with the British," Acheson later explained, "but time was short and soon we might have no alternative to acting in the best manner to save Iran. This stirred up turgid waters in London."[45]

---

[40] Louis, *The British Empire*, 682–85.
[41] Acheson, *Present at the Creation*, 680.   [42] Ibid., 682.
[43] US Department of State Bulletin, vol. XXVII, December 15, 1952, 496.
[44] Acheson, *Present at the Creation*, 683.   [45] Ibid.

Just as it seemed that an alternative and independent American policy was forming, much to the dislike of the British, two factors pulled the United States back to the old course. The first was the stance of the major American oil companies. In a meeting with Acheson and McGhee in October 1951, the top executives of Standard Oil of New Jersey, Standard Oil of New York, Gulf, Standard Oil of California, and Texaco all raised arguments similar to those of Britain, emphasizing the violation of contractual relations and the threat that successful nationalization would pose to all American investments abroad. Accordingly, they recommended backing the British.[46] A year later (and this time in the midst of the Justice Department investigation), Acheson met again with the oil companies, on December 4 and 9, 1952. Their willingness to consider an alternative plan had not increased. The companies did not want to absorb Iranian production. For one thing, it would require cutbacks and readjustments elsewhere, with reactions from these other concessions all too likely.[47] For another, an agreement on price and compensation did not seem to be nearing a resolution.[48] It would take a big concession on the side of the American government – in the form of easing up on the anti-trust lawsuit initiated by Truman and then backed by Eisenhower – to secure the major oil companies' cooperation even after the coup, in order to move and absorb the production of Iranian oil.

The second factor, a change in British tactics, mattered much more. The British consciously played up the communist threat, and were successful in thereby bringing in the United States. The important figure is C.M. Woodhouse, the chief MI6 officer in Iran at the time, who traveled to Washington after the British were expelled on November 1, 1952.[49] Highlighting the communist threat, Woodhouse suggested a joint operation to remove Mosaddeq (to be engineered with coordinated uprisings of Rashidian and Bakhtiari tribes) to both the CIA and the State Department. The proposal found some support among high-level CIA officials, specifically Walter Bedell Smith (head of CIA), Frank Wisner (head of covert operations), Allen W. Dulles (Deputy Director, CIA), and Kermit Roosevelt (head of CIA operations in the Middle East). However, mid-level operatives and Iran specialists, including the CIA station chief

---

[46] Painter, *Oil and the American Century*, 188; Acheson, *Present at the Creation*, 684.

[47] Mark J. Gasiorowski, "The 1953 Coup d'Etat in Iran," *International Journal of Middle Eastern Studies* 19, no. 3 (1987), 261–86. Saudi Arabia and Kuwait would have had to cut back production.

[48] And according to Acheson, *Present at the Creation*, 684, they "disliked even the appearance of hovering like vultures over the carcass of Anglo-Iranian."

[49] Christopher M. Woodhouse, *Something Ventured* (London: Granada, 1982), esp. 117–18. See also Stephen Kinzer, *All the Shah's Men* (New Jersey: John Wiley & Sons, 2003), 150–55.

in Tehran, were all opposed to the idea.[50] The prevailing assessment by CIA analysts at the time was that a communist takeover of Iran by TUDEH was not likely before the end of 1953, especially as the economy, having recovered throughout 1952, was not in danger of imminent collapse.[51] Further, the State Department noted that while Truman (and Acheson) would not accept the plan, the recently elected Eisenhower might.[52] Dulles (who was slated to become the CIA director, and whose brother, John Foster Dulles, would be named the Secretary of State) recommended sitting on the plan until Eisenhower assumed power.[53] The British playing of the communist card did indeed work once Eisenhower was inaugurated. The Soviet threat had been a key issue in the 1952 elections, and Eisenhower had accused the Democrats of being soft on communism, above all in losing China. Hence, the new administration quickly sought to act: planning started immediately once Eisenhower took office, with the top US and British officials meeting on February 3, 1953, two weeks after the inauguration. From this meeting emerged the decision to develop and implement a plan to overthrow Mosaddeq and install Zahedi. The plan was codenamed AJAX/TPAjax; it was to be led by Kermit Roosevelt, who had been key in bringing Woodhouse's plans to the CIA and in swaying opinions therein.

Even though the United States had the capabilities of its own BEDAMN network, at work in Iran for more than a decade, the execution of the operation also relied on the assets that MI6 turned over to the CIA, particularly the Rashidian network. Furthermore, though the CIA carried out the whole operation, including the housing of Zahedi in a CIA safe house, the original plan was provided by Britain. More critically, the decisive British contribution was that of undermining Mosaddeq throughout his whole premiership, helping in the division of the National Front and in eroding his popular base. The British desire to remove Mosaddeq was of long standing, as can be seen in the previous three attempts to oust him. The American position, on the other hand, had remained directly opposed until the beginning of 1953, and even then the shift of opinion took place only at the highest levels within the CIA. Emphasis is needed on one vital matter: both British internal exchanges and the Iran specialists in the CIA did not assess the communist threat as

[50] Gasiorowski, "The 1953 *Coup d'Etat*."
[51] Gasiorowski's information in "The 1953 *Coup d'Etat*" is derived from "Probable Developments in Iran Through 1953," NIE-75, November 13, 1952; Department of State, Office of Intelligence and Research, "Iran's Political and Economic Prospects Through 1953," OIR No. 6126, January 9, 1953; National Security Council, "United States Policy Regarding the Present Situation in Iran," NSC 136/1, November 20, 1952.
[52] Gasiorowki, "The 1953 *Coup d'Etat*," 270.
[53] Painter, *Oil and the American Century*, 189–90.

a significant issue.[54] This was quickly vindicated by the ease with which Iranian forces dispensed with TUDEH following the *coup d'etat*.

The toppling of Mossadeq shows the autonomous impact of Britain upon the policy of the United States.[55] First, Britain's actions went against American ideas, but Britain got away with this as the United States wished to prop up British power. Second, Britain played the card that drew in the United States, even though it knew that the communist threat was not serious. America was sucked into a conflict that it initially had sought to manage, and had done so with skill and intelligence. Judgment is needed. The toppling of Mossadeq proved to be a disaster. For one thing, it unleashed an obsessive anti-communism that characterized much of American foreign policy thereafter. For another, the behavior of the Pahlavis in power led to the Islamic revolution with which the West struggles to this day. Furthermore, it also shows us that the process of transition that started in the 1890s was still ongoing by the 1950s and 1960s.

Conclusion

The main argument has been straightforward. The ordering of the liberal part of the world polity in the twentieth century owes little to British skill, and certainly did not result from Britain's "passing of the baton" of world leadership in such a way as to allow it to maintain a good deal of influence over world affairs. To believe all that was to be subject to an illusion. Many in Britain have been so subject, not least Tony Blair, not just in his actions but in his very voice – deeper, gravelly, Churchillian – when seeking to support Bush the Younger. Here we have the remains of an imperial agenda. The British would have been best advised to remember the useful quip of Oscar Wilde to the effect that while it is desirable to have illusions, it is more important never to seek to realize them. What has mattered in this whole history has been brute power. The United States seized the day when it was able to do so, and has held a hegemonic position thereafter, acting habitually in its own interest.

[54] For instance, Sir Donald Ferguson's letter to Richard Stokes; see too Louis, *The British Empire*, and, for many details, William Roger Louis and James Bill, eds., *Musaddiq, Iranian Nationalism and Oil* (Austin: University of Texas Press, 1988). Interestingly, Churchill stressed the communist threat very early on when out of power, both in correspondence with Herbert Morrison and when speaking in the Commons. See Martin Gilbert, *Churchill: A Life* (London: Pimlico, 2000), 895.

[55] Ryan, *The Vision of Anglo-America* makes very similar points for an earlier period, demonstrating the way in which British ideas about Poland and Greece influenced the United States as WWII ended, setting agendas that were not really those that America wanted.

Nonetheless, we have tried to keep an open mind. Most obviously, we have suggested that there may be some truth to constructivist notions. It may be that some actions went beyond national interest, at least when seen in stark and limited terms. The United States was sucked into Iran under an aegis not of its own choosing. Equally, it may be the case that Reagan helped Thatcher in the conflict over the Falklands because he felt the relationship between the two countries to be "special." We cannot yet investigate that episode, as documents are not available. But against any positive finding, one would have to set Reagan's bombing of Libya: Thatcher was informed about this only when American planes, launched from British bases, were already in the air. Whatever role "affinity," whether political, institutional, or cultural, may have played, it was in no way a symmetrical perception. The references to commonality were most of the time constructs of British hopes, rather than of American realities, let alone acceptances. Maybe it would be better to consider them primarily as Britain's justification for choices that had to be made in a world that was slipping away from it.

In conclusion, it is worth asking if this transition holds lessons for the future. Two considerations come to mind, both suggesting a negative answer. First, rapprochement between the United States and Britain was made easy by the sheer fact of geographical distance. Here were spheres of influence that had no need to collide. But the world has changed. Now all countries are closer, given the character of modern weapons, thereby removing this particular easement. Second, thought needs to be given to nationalism within rising powers. This certainly caused difficulties within German society, and it may well be affecting Chinese behavior. In retrospect, we can see how very easy it was to manage this element within the United States, given the speed of its rise to world power. Situations of relative equality are harder to manage, as was the case with the Anglo-German rivalry, and as may yet become true in relations between China and the United States.

7   The US accommodation of Communist China

Lorenz M. Lüthi

The admission of the People's Republic of China (PRC) to the United Nations in October 1971 and the concurrent Sino-American rapprochement in the period from 1969 to 1979 suggest that the existing international order was easily capable of accommodating Communist China after more than two decades of international isolation. Under which conditions did this accommodation actually occur? Neither the international organization in New York nor its host country accommodated Communist China because it had become a rising power. In terms of steadily increasing economic or military power, the PRC was neither ascending nor declining in 1971, when it joined the United Nations, nor even in 1979, when it obtained full American diplomatic recognition. Much of the country's meteoric rise happened *after* these events. How do we explain this case of accommodation, then?

For more than two decades after 1949, the United Nations was the central location both in the American attempt to keep Communist China outside of the global system and in the worldwide movement toward integrating it into the family of nations. The entry of the PRC into the United Nations in October 1971 marked its *full* accommodation by that international institution; in its wake, Communist China obtained a permanent seat in the Security Council, instantly transforming it into a major stakeholder in global governance. At roughly the same time, however, the PRC obtained only *limited* accommodation by the United States; bilateral relations did not develop further for another seven years. In fact, the American limited accommodation of Communist China in 1971–72 was largely an attempt to achieve – unsuccessfully – strategic advantages in the Vietnam War (1964–1975), and to accommodate – successfully, at least for a while – the rise of the Soviet Union to strategic parity. *Full* US accommodation of the PRC at the turn of 1978–79 occurred against the background of domestic developments in China and the bilateral need for cooperative containment of Soviet-supported Vietnamese expansionism in South East Asia.

The motivations for the United States to accommodate Communist China after 1969 rested in the American desire to avoid war in the long term. However, this required the PRC to accept the existing normative world order, that is, the United Nations. In fact, Communist China's entry into the world over the course of the 1970s marked the country's transition from revolutionary challenger to status quo power. Still, the world in 1971, and the United States in 1978–79, accommodated a country with the largely *untapped potential of a future rising power*.

Two pairs of reasons – one on the Chinese and one on the American side – explain why accommodation occurred in the period 1969–79. First, starting in the late 1960s, Mao Zedong reduced China's ideological commitment to world revolution by abandoning the goal of overthrowing the international system, led by what he considered the hegemonic United States. The change signaled China's readiness to be accommodated by the outside world. Second, parallel developments in the international system assisted in making the Chinese accommodation possible. Since 1960, the PRC has moved away from close association with the socialist world to opening up toward the international system. By the early 1970s, the majority of the members of the United Nations considered the continued exclusion of the PRC from their midst an anachronism of the Cold War. Third, the United States, the major obstacle to PRC accommodation, changed its policy toward Communist China in 1969. The new US president, Richard M. Nixon, understood that excluding the demographically largest country in the world from international affairs was inherently counterproductive. He also realized that American economic and military power was declining in relation to the rising Soviet Union – a development for which the US commitment to the Vietnam War was partially responsible. By 1971–72, the Nixon administration hoped to exploit rapprochement with the PRC to help both manage the rise of the Soviet Union to strategic parity and find an exit from the Vietnamese quagmire. Yet, the nascent Sino-American rapprochement in 1971, triggered by Henry Kissinger's famous secret visit to China in July, broke the dam for the vast majority of UN members to extend *full* accommodation to the PRC. In October, the General Assembly voted for Communist Chinese membership and simultaneously expelled the Republic of China (ROC) on Taiwan from its midst. And finally, while Richard Nixon's visit to Communist China in February 1972 was highly symbolic on a global scale, it only produced a *limited* accommodation of the PRC by the United States. *Full* accommodation occurred only with the establishment of full diplomatic relations on January 1, 1979, and with Deng Xiaoping's visit to Washington four weeks later.

Scholars in general overestimate the significance of Nixon's visit to the PRC in February of 1972. It neither "changed the world" nor constituted a "turning point."[1] Chinese admission to the United Nations had happened four months before, and full Sino-American diplomatic recognition was another seven years into the future. Yet, 1972 is so firmly lodged as a major crossroads in our collective memory that the scholarly literature on Sino-American relations almost completely falls into publications dealing with the period up to the early 1970s and works covering the following years.[2] Only a few books, usually with a periodical focus larger than the Cold War, span either side of the Nixon visit.[3] While several publications deal with the Nixon visit itself, only one focused study on the crucial period of Sino-American diplomatic recognition at the turn of 1978/79 and Deng Xiaoping's subsequent visit to the White House in February 1979 has appeared.[4]

Apart from general treatments of Sino-American relations, a significant number of specialized studies has appeared covering the pre-1972 period. Western scholars have written on American strategic concerns,[5] the US economic blockade,[6] and Washington's policy of keeping Beijing out of the United Nations.[7] In comparison, Chinese-language publications on Sino-American relations, suffering from incomplete

---

[1] See, for example, Margaret MacMillan, *Nixon in China: The Week that Changed the World* (New York: Penguin, 2006); Chris Tudda, *A Cold War Turning Point: Nixon and China, 1969–1972* (New Orleans: Louisiana State University Press, 2012).

[2] For the first group, see Roderick MacFarquhar, ed. *Sino-American Relations, 1949–1971* (New York: Prager, 1972); Chen Jian, *Mao's China and the Cold War* (Chapel Hill: University of North Carolina Press, 2000); Xia Yafeng, *Negotiating with the Enemy: US-China talks During the Cold War, 1949–1972* (Bloomington: Indiana University Press, 2006); Robert S. Ross and Jiang Changbin, eds., *Re-examining the Cold War: US-China Diplomacy, 1954–1973* (Cambridge: Harvard University Press, 2001). For the second, see James Mann, *About Face: A History of America's Curious Relationship with China, from Nixon to Clinton* (New York: Vintage, 2000); William C. Kirby, Robert S. Ross, and Gong Li, eds., *Normalization of US-China Relations: An International History* (Cambridge: Harvard University Press, 2005).

[3] John King Fairbank, *The United States and China*, 4 edn., revised and enlarged (Cambridge: Harvard University Press, 1983); Warren I. Cohen, *America's Response to China: A History of Sino-American Relations*, 5 edn. (New York: Columbia University Press, 2010).

[4] The lack of literature on this episode is largely due to the long-time inaccessibility of American documentation and the continued Chinese black-out of virtually all information. See Enrico Fardella, "The Sino-American Normalization: A Reassessment," *Diplomatic History* 33, no. 4 (September 2009), 545–78.

[5] Gordon H. Chang, *Friends and Enemies: The United States, China, and the Soviet Union, 1948–1972* (Stanford: Stanford University Press, 1990); John Lewis Gaddis, *Strategies of Containment: A Critical Appraisal of American National Security Policy during the Cold War*, revised and enlarged edition (Oxford: Oxford University Press, 2005), 67–68, 114–15, 120–22, 154–56, 192–94, 229–30.

[6] Zhang Shu Guang, *Economic Cold War: America's Embargo against China and the Sino-Soviet Alliance, 1949–1963* (Stanford: Stanford University Press, 2002).

[7] Sydney D. Bailey, "China and the United Nations," *The World Today* 27, no. 9 (September 1971), 365–72; Evan Luard, "China and the United Nations," *International Affairs* 47, no. 4 (October 1971), 729–44.

access to primary sources, mostly focus on narrating events.[8] However, both Western and Chinese scholars have written specialized studies on various aspects of the 1972–79 period, such as cooperation against the Soviet Union,[9] trade issues,[10] Deng Xiaoping's role in opening China,[11] and Vietnam's rise as a regional and strategic threat.[12]

Chinese ideology, late 1940s to early 1970s

Since the PRC considered itself a challenger to the existing international order for two decades after its foundation in 1949, its accommodation by the outside world – either *limited* or *full* – was difficult. Initially, Communist China had hoped to become a member of the United Nations – the ultimate symbol of the international order.[13] Failing to displace its rival, the ROC on Taiwan, the PRC not only reemphasized its negative attitude, but even went to war against the United Nations during the Korean War.[14]

Communist Chinese behavior derived from the ideological articulation of the country's role in international affairs. Refining the Stalinist ideological view that the world was divided into two hostile camps,[15] the supreme

8   Tao Wenzhao, *ZhongMei guanxishi, 1949–1972 [History of Sino-American Relations, 1949–1972]* (Shanghai: Renmin chubanshe, 1997); Gong Li, *Kuayue honggou: 1969–1979 nian ZhongMei guanxi de yanbian [Bridging the Chasm: the Evolution of Sino-American relations, 1969–1979]* (Zhengzhou: Henan renmin chubanshe, 1992); Chen Dunde, *Shengli zai 1971: Xin Zhongguo chongfan Lianheguo jishi [Victory in 1971: Record on How New China Returned to the United Nations]* (Beijing: Shijie zhishi chubanshe, 2004); Chen Dunde, *Mao Zedong, Nikesong zai 1972 [Mao Zedong and Nixon in 1972]* (Beijing: Jianfangjun wenyi chubanshe, 2009); Chen Dunde, *Qihang zai 1979: ZhongMei jianjiao shilu (xuji) [Start of the Journey in 1979: The Records of Establishing Sino-American Relations (Continuation)]* (Beijing: Shijie zhishi chubanshe, 2002); Qian Jiang, *Deng Xiaoping yu ZhongMei jianjiao fengyun [Deng Xiaoping and the Fast-changing Situation of the Establishment of Sino-American Diplomatic Relations]* (Beijing: Zhonggong dangshi chubanshe, 2005).
9   Wang Zhongchun, "ZhongMei guanxi zhengchanghua jincheng zhong de Sulian yinsu (1969–1979)" ["The Soviet Factor in the Process of Sino-American Normalization (1969–1979)"], *Dangde wenxian* 2002/4, 50–60.
10   William Burr, "'Casting a Shadow' Over Trade: The Problem of Private Claims and Blocked Assets in US-China Relations, 1972–1975," *Diplomatic History* 33, no. 2 (April 2009), 315–49. Gong Li, "1972 nian yilai ZhongMei jingji maoyi guanxi de fazhan" ["Developments in Sino-American Economic and Trade Relations since 1972"], *Waijiao Xueyuan Xuebao* 2000/1, 25–31.
11   Gong Li, "Deng Xiaoping yu 1977 nian zhihou de ZhongMei guanxi" ["Deng Xiaoping and Sino-American Relations after 1977"], *Meiguo yanjiu* 2001/2, 7–20.
12   Li Junjie, "ZhongMei cong duikang dao huanhe guocheng zhong de Yuenan yinsu" ["The Vietnam Factor during the Process from Antagonism to Conciliation of Sino-US Relation"], *Linyi shifan xueyuan xuebao* 2 (2004), 115–20.
13   Bailey, "China and the United Nations," 365.
14   Chen Jian, *China's Road to the Korean War: The Making of the Sino-American Confrontation* (New York: Columbia University, 1994).
15   Iosip D. Stalin, "Two Camps," February 22, 1919, in *Works, vol. 4: November 1917–1920* (Moscow: Foreign Languages Publishing House, 1953), 240–44.

Chinese Communist leader, Mao Zedong, developed the Theory of the Intermediate Zone in 1946. According to his view, the world was divided into the peace-loving, progressive socialist camp headed by the Soviet Union and the aggressive, reactionary capitalist-imperialist camp led by the United States. Moreover, the two camps struggled for control over the intermediate zone – the colonized and decolonizing world – with China as the ultimate prize.[16] In this struggle, the nascent PRC decided to "lean to one side."[17] As this phrase suggests, the emerging Sino-Soviet alliance was not to be a permanent arrangement, but was supposed to be a temporary means to help China modernize and retake its rightful place in the world.[18]

By the late 1960s, the deadlock of the domestic turmoil created by the Cultural Revolution (1966–76) and the resulting complete international isolation of the PRC caused Chairman Mao to rethink the revolutionary character of China's foreign relations. For example, at the turn of 1965/66, many of the sub-Saharan African states had suspended or even terminated recently established relations due to Chinese ideological radicalism in international affairs.[19] And by 1967, Beijing had recalled most of its ambassadors, sent large numbers of its foreign ministry cadres to the Chinese countryside for reeducation, and left its embassies abroad with a skeleton staff tasked with spreading Cultural Revolution propaganda.[20]

Mao's call for a reduction of propaganda in foreign relations in 1968 preceded the redispatch of ambassadors to selected, mostly non-socialist, countries in 1969, the return of cadres to the foreign ministry in Beijing or embassies and consulates abroad, and the reform of the foreign policy in 1970–71.[21] Despite the de-emphasis of ideology in the conduct of foreign relations, Chinese Communist dogma remained an important source of external behavior. Chinese leaders continued to consider the state, which they had founded in 1949, a force for progressive change

[16] Niu Jun, *From Yan'an to the World: The Origin and Development of Chinese Communist Foreign Policy* (Norwalk: EastBridge, 2005), 286–89; Mao Zedong, "Talk with the American Correspondent Anna Louise Strong," August 1946, in *Selected Works*, vol. 4 (Beijing: Foreign Languages Press), 97–101.

[17] Bo Yibo, "The Making of the 'Lean-to-One Side' Decision," *Chinese Historians* 5, no. 1 (Spring 1992), 57–62.

[18] Lorenz M. Lüthi, *The Sino-Soviet Split: Cold War in the Communist World* (Princeton: Princeton University Press, 2008), 38.

[19] Alaba Ogunsanwo, *China's Policy in Africa, 1958–1971* (Cambridge: Cambridge University Press, 1974), 194; Alan Hutchison, *China's African Revolution* (London: Hutchinson, 1975), 103–32.

[20] Ma Jisen, *The Cultural Revolution in the Foreign Ministry of China* (Hong Kong: The Chinese University Press, 2004), 73–77.

[21] "New Ambassadors of the PR China," August 8, 1969, *Politisches Archiv des Auswärtigen Amtes-Ministerium für Auswärtige Angelegenheiten* [*Political Archive of the Foreign Office-Ministry für Foreign Affairs*], Abteilung Ferner Osten – Sektor China, C 186/74, 68–69.

in international affairs.[22] Furthermore, the Cultural Revolution had created a dysfunctional and ideologically charged domestic political system, whose recurrently erupting factional struggles had unpredictable influences on the conduct of Chinese foreign relations until Mao's death in 1976 and the end of the Cultural Revolution soon thereafter.[23]

China's turn away from the socialist camp toward the world at large, 1960s

As a result of its decision to "lean to one side," the newly established PRC concluded the Friendship and Alliance Treaty with the Soviet Union on February 14, 1950. The accord provided the PRC both with immediate military protection against the feared American military reintervention in China and with a certain degree of economic aid.[24] Although, or maybe because, Soviet economic aid was smaller than expected, New China embarked on an industrial modernization campaign largely based on self-efforts.[25]

De-Stalinization, which officially started in the Soviet Union in February 1956, and the resulting thaw in relations with the United States provided the basis for the emerging Sino-Soviet split. Mao quickly understood that Nikita S. Khrushchev's criticism of Stalin's mistakes could also be used against him. As early as March 1956, he tried to shape the discourse on de-Stalinization in China in a manner that focused on the mistakes which Stalin supposedly had made in relation to the Chinese revolution.[26] Consequently, Mao started to consider himself, and not the "immature" Khrushchev, as the rightful heir to Stalin's primary position at the head of the socialist camp.[27] No wonder that the Great Leap Forward (1958–60), a program designed to propel China into the communist future ahead of the Soviet Union, was an ideological challenge to Khrushchevian leadership.[28] In its self-perception as a revolutionary power, New China also could not accept the limited Soviet cooperation, mostly on nuclear arms limitation, with the supposedly imperialist and reactionary United States.[29] Once Soviet economic aid programs started to wind down and Chinese repayment obligations picked up by the late

---

[22] King C. Chen, ed., *China and the Three Worlds: A Foreign Policy Reader* (White Plains: M.E. Sharpe, 1979), 39.

[23] See, for example, the Lin Biao Affair: Chen, *Mao's China*, 269–71.

[24] For the text of the agreements, see Harold Hinton, *People's Republic of China, 1949–1979*, vol. 1 (Wilmington: Scholarly Resources, 1980), 123–26.

[25] Lüthi, *The Sino-Soviet Split*, 37–38.   [26] Ibid., chapter 2.

[27] Yan Mingfu in Ding Ming, "Huigu ge sikao: Yu ZhongSu guanxi qinlizhi de duihua" ["Review and Reflections: Interviews with Those Who Witnessed Personally Sino-Soviet Relations"], *Dangdai Zhongguo shi yanjiu* 2 (1998), 24.

[28] Lüthi, *The Sino-Soviet Split*, chapter 3.   [29] Ibid., 135–38.

1950s, Mao concluded that the partnership with the Soviet comrades had run its course.[30]

By the beginning of the Cultural Revolution in 1966, Sino-Soviet relations had diminished to the bare minimum of diplomatic relations needed to resolve problems occurring as the result of routine intercourse.[31] In the first two years of the Cultural Revolution, Mao and his radical acolytes used physical attacks on the so-called Soviet revisionists – diplomats and citizens living in the PRC – to whip up ideological radicalism at home.[32] While Soviet leaders were afraid that this climate would lead to an armed attack on the Soviet Union by radicalized youth heeding Mao's revolutionary calls,[33] military conflict eventually emerged over disputed border territories. The clashes on the frozen Ussuri River in March 1969 occurred as a result of the mutual militarization of the joint border after 1966.[34] Early in 1969, the Chinese side had decided on a punitive action to teach the Soviet revisionists a "bitter lesson" for their border transgressions in previous years.[35] The ambush of March 2, 1969, which cost thirty-one Soviet lives, stunned Moscow.[36] Although the PRC had no intention to follow up with more military actions,[37] the Soviet Union embarked on a punitive attack against China on March 15, which cost over one hundred lives on both sides combined.[38]

Subsequent Soviet military threats, even with a nuclear strike, powerfully drove home the fact that the PRC was not only *completely isolated* in

---

[30] "An Outline for a Speech on the International Situation, December 1959," in David Wolff, "'One Finger's Worth of Historical Events': New Russian and Chinese Evidence on the Sino-Soviet Alliance and Split, 1948–1959," *Cold War International History Project*, Working Paper 30 (2000) 73–74; Lüthi, *The Sino-Soviet Split*, 152–53.

[31] Ibid., 299.

[32] Sergey Radchenko, *Two Suns in the Heavens: The Sino-Soviet Struggle for Supremacy, 1962–1967* (Washington, DC: Woodrow Wilson Center Press, 2009), 177–80; Vladimir Semichastnyi, *Bespokoinoe serdtse [Restless Heart]* (Moskva: Vagryus, 2002), 327–28.

[33] Semichastnyi, *Bespokoinoe*, 328.

[34] Thomas W. Robinson, "The Sino-Soviet Border Conflict," in *Diplomacy of Power: Soviet Armed Force as a Political Instrument*, ed. Stephen S. Kaplan (Washington, DC: Brookings, 1981), 272.

[35] Barbara Barnouin and Yu Changgen, *Chinese Foreign Policy during the Cultural Revolution* (London: Kegan Paul International, 1998), 88; Li Ke, and Hao Shengzhang, *Wenhua dagemingzhong de renmin jiefangjun [The People's Liberation Army during the Cultural Revolution]* (Beijing: Zhonggong dangshi ziliao chubanshe, 1989), 319–21; Yang Kuisong, "Sino-Soviet Border Clash of 1969: From Zhenbao Island to Sino-American Rapprochement," *Cold War History*, 1, no. 1 (August 2000), 24–30.

[36] Arkady N. Shevchenko, *Breaking with Moscow* (New York: Alfred A. Knopf, 1985), 164–65.

[37] Gao Wenqian, *Wannian Zhou Enlai [Zhou Enlai's Last Years]* (Niu Yue: Mingjing chubanshe, 2003), 402.

[38] M. Taylor Fravel, *Strong Borders, Secure Nation: Cooperation and Conflict in China's Territorial Disputes* (Princeton: Princeton University Press, 2008), 201–02.

the world but also encountering an *existential threat* to its political, and even physical, survival.[39] Not only did Beijing face the possibility of large-scale war with the Soviet Union, but critical words about the PRC by the new American President, Richard M. Nixon, seemed to indicate that the United States would not change its hostile attitude toward Communist China.[40] Fearing "large-scale conflict,"[41] Mao Zedong decided to use the impending 9th National Congress in April to reconstitute the party institutions broken by the Cultural Revolution. However, the mostly charismatic nature of his leadership was insufficient to unite the fractured rump-party, and thus, after the congress, he continued to face an unstable domestic setting, which did not facilitate the reform of China's foreign policy.[42]

In parallel to the deterioration of relations with the Soviet Union since the late 1950s, the PRC had been opening up toward the outside world. As already mentioned, the PRC had tried to obtain membership in the United Nations from the very beginning. In the early 1950s, only the socialist states and a handful of Western and newly independent states had recognized the PRC.[43] Initially, Beijing tried to enforce its entitlement to representation in the international organization through moral appeals to the international community, but in the context of the Cold War division of the world, its efforts went nowhere.[44] The numerical superiority of pro-Western members and the quirks of agenda-setting in the General Assembly allowed the United States to block the admission of Communist China to the United Nations for over two decades.[45]

---

[39] Gong Li, "Chinese Decision Making and the Thawing of US–China Relations," in *Re-examining the Cold War: US–China Diplomacy, 1954–1973*, eds. Robert S. Ross and Jiang Changbin (Cambridge: Harvard University Press, 2001), 323.

[40] Xiong Xianghui, "Dakai ZhongMei guanxi de qianzhou: 1969 nian siwei laoshi dui guoji xingshi yanjiu he jianyi de qianqianhouhou" ["Prelude to the Opening of Sino-American Relations: The Whole Story of the Study and Recommendations on the World Situation of the Four Teachers in 1969"], *Zhonggong dangshi ziliao* 42 (1992), 56.

[41] Zhonggong zhongyang wenxian yanjiushi bian [CCP Central Documents Research Office, ed.], *Zhou Enlai nianpu, 1949–1976 [A Chronicle of Zhou Enlai's Life: 1949–1976]*, vol. 3 (Beijing: Zhongyang wenxian chubanshe, 1997), 284–85.

[42] Lorenz Lüthi, "Restoring Chaos to History: Sino-Soviet-American Relations in 1969," *The China Quarterly* 210 (June 2012), 384–86.

[43] For recognition dates, see Ben She and Yi Ming, *China's Foreign Relations: A Chronology of Events, 1949–1988* (Beijing: Foreign Languages Press, 1989).

[44] Bailey, "China and the United Nations," 365.

[45] For example, the United States used the two-thirds rule to put important issues on the agenda to block choke any discussion on PRC membership. Also, admission itself required the two-thirds majority of all those voting (abstentions were not counted). Consequently, the United States was able to prevent even votes on admission for the 1950s and for most of the 1960s. See Bailey, "China and the United Nations," 366–67; Luard, "China and the United Nations," 729–35.

Rapprochement with the non-socialist world eventually occurred as the result of the collapse of Sino-Soviet economic relations in 1960. In the wake of this collapse, the PRC focused on trade with the economically advanced capitalist states, mainly Japan, Canada, Australia, and the West European countries. China's goals were twofold: the purchase of grain to feed its starving population after the collapse of the Great Leap Forward, and the acquisition of modern production technologies.[46] The PRC was willing, for this double purpose, to ignore the diplomatic relations many of these states maintained with the ROC on Taiwan. The fact that economic relations flourished in the first half of the 1960s helped the PRC to establish very *limited* accommodation, with the prospect of *full* accommodation later on.[47] In this context, Mao Zedong refined his Theory of the Intermediate Zone, arguing that China's arch enemies – the United States and the Soviet Union – were struggling over two intermediate zones – one in the Afro-Asian-Latin American world and the other in developed Europe (comprising both halves of the divided continent). While Mao decided to focus on the first zone for the purpose of promoting world revolution, he also called on the establishment of economic links to the western half of the second zone for the purpose of China's modernization.[48]

The ideological radicalism which Mao had imposed at home since 1962 in his struggle for domestic supremacy undermined the strategy of mobilizing international support for the PRC. China's anti-American policies, anti-Soviet propaganda, and anti-Indian positions (after the Sino-Indian war in 1962) had alienated the Afro-Asian world to such a degree that it turned away from the PRC.[49] Furthermore, the Cultural Revolution slowed down trade with the developed capitalist world, though the negative impact was far smaller than in the country's relations with the third world.[50]

China's retreat from ideological radicalism in international affairs during the 1968–69 period, as mentioned earlier, increased its chances to obtain admission to the United Nations. While the support of leftist and secular regimes in the Arab world for China's admission was secure,

---

[46] Xiao Donglian, *Qiusuo Zhongguo: Wenge qian shi nian shi [In Search for China: The History of the Decade before the Cultural Revolution]*, vol. 2 (Beijing: Hongqi chubanshe, 1999), 759–61, 919; Dangdai Zhongguo congshu bian [Contemporary China Series, ed.], *Dangdai Zhongguo duiwai maoyi [Contemporary China: Foreign Trade]*, vol. 1 (Beijing: Zhongguo shehui kexue chubanshe, 1992), 31.

[47] For the development of trade relations, see *Dangdai Zhongguo duiwai maoyi*, 371–88.

[48] Mao Zedong, "Two Intermediate Zones (1963/9, 1964/1, 7)," in *Mao Zedong wenji [A Collection of Mao Zedong's Papers]*, vol. 8 (Beijing: Renmin chubanshe, 1999), 343–44.

[49] Lüthi, *The Sino-Soviet Split*, 328–29.

[50] *Dangdai Zhongguo duiwai maoyi*, vol. 2, 371–88.

the PRC needed the votes of the conservative governments in the Middle East. The end of the Chinese backing of insurgencies and independence movements in this region allowed the PRC to improve relations with countries that had not yet recognized Communist China.[51] Henry Kissinger's secret visit to Beijing in July 1971, which will be covered later, broke the dam against admission of the PRC to the United Nations. Even if a positive outcome of the vote in the UN General Assembly was not assured for the crucial ballot in late October 1971, the support of the socialist, Asian, Middle Eastern, and West European states turned out to be essential for the narrow victory. Sub-Saharan Africa mostly voted against PRC membership, and the Americas split their votes. In the end, by 1971, the world – or at least a large majority of the UN members – was ready to extend *full* accommodation of Communist China, including permanent membership in the Security Council.[52]

Developments in US containment policy toward limited accommodation, 1949–1972

Ultimately, changes in US Cold War policy opened the path to the accommodation of the PRC – albeit only on a *limited* basis by 1971–72. American reasons to seek rapprochement were complex. The roots of US Cold War policy toward the PRC lay in the last period of the decades-long Chinese civil war. On the basis of the World War II (WWII) alliance with the *Guomindang*-led ROC, the United States supported the internationally recognized government against an internal Communist rebellion in the immediate postwar years. Despite some initial worries, Washington continued to support the ROC after its loss on the mainland and reestablishment on Taiwan in 1949.[53]

Much of the confrontational US policy toward China in the 1950s derived from the idea of straining the Sino-Soviet alliance to the breaking point. During the thaw of American-Soviet relations in the mid-1950s and the emerging Sino-Soviet disagreements only some years later, Washington hoped to wean Moscow away from Beijing.[54] Internal

---

[51] John Calabrese, "Peaceful or Dangerous Collaborators? China's Relations with the Gulf Countries," *Pacific Affairs* 65, no. 4 (Winter 1992–93), 471–72; "Peking Reported in Drive to Play Key Role in Mideast and Africa," *The New York Times* (October 17, 1971), 3.

[52] Lorenz M. Lüthi, and Chen Jian, "China's Turn to the World," in *The Regional Cold Wars in Europe, East Asia, and the Middle East: Crucial Periods and Turning Points*, ed. Lorenz M. Lüthi (Washington, DC/Stanford: Woodrow Wilson Press/Stanford University Press, 2015), 160.

[53] Chang, *Friends and Enemies* 12–17.

[54] John Lewis Gaddis, *Long Peace: Inquiries into the History of the Cold War* (New York: Oxford, 1987), 164–87; Chang, *Friends and Enemies*, 46–48, 192–94.

American assessments of the developing Sino-Soviet split in the early 1960s spoke about the potential of exploiting the situation but were cautious about quick results.[55]

Although Beijing and Washington signaled to each other in 1965 that they would like to keep the unfolding Vietnam War localized,[56] they had both supported their respective allies in Indochina since the 1950s, and continued to do so into the mid 1970s. Yet, the war had a major economic impact on both countries. Starting in 1965, the PRC spent much of its construction budget to relocate strategic industries from the southern and coastal provinces to the interior.[57] In the United States, the seemingly unending Vietnam War not only created popular disaffection but also caused high budget deficits and a long-lasting recession.[58] By 1968, the Vietnam War had developed into a stalemate.

In the US presidential election of 1968, a demoralized Democratic Party nominated the leftist Vice-President Hubert Humphrey against the centrist Republican and former Vice-President Richard M. Nixon. Campaigning on the vague platform of ending the Vietnam War, but without providing any details, Nixon won the election in November of 1968.[59] The new president had spent his time out of office between early 1961 and early 1969 traveling the world and discussing international affairs with many political leaders in Europe, the Middle East, and Asia.[60] In 1967, he had published his famous article "Asia after Viet Nam" in *Foreign Affairs*, in which he sketched his vision for future US policies in East Asia. Nixon called on Americans to look beyond the "small country" of Vietnam, where the United States was stuck in a costly quagmire, toward "the rest of Asia [which] has been undergoing a profound, an exciting and on balance an extraordinarily promising transformation." While he was concerned about China's nascent nuclear weapons project, he did *not* fear the PRC because the country had become a military or economic powerhouse – on the contrary, he was primarily apprehensive about the ideological basis of China's aggressive foreign policy and the impact of the country's continued involuntary isolation from the rest of the world. Thus, he proposed that it was time to "come urgently to

[55] "Record of the PPS Meeting," February 8, 1961, *Foreign Relations of the United States, 1961–1963*, vol. V (Washington: United States Government Printing Office, 1998), 62.
[56] Lorenz M. Lüthi, "Reading and Warning the Likely Enemy: A Commentary: Signalling Across Four Continents," *The International History Review* 35, no. 4 (2013), 807–16.
[57] Lorenz M. Lüthi, "The Vietnam War and China's Third-Line Defense Planning before the Cultural Revolution, 1964–1966," *Journal of Cold War Studies* 10, no. 1 (Winter 2008), 26–51.
[58] Arthur M. Okun, "The Great Stagflation Swamp," *Challenge* 20, no. 5 (Fall 1977), 8.
[59] Gaddis, *Strategies of Containment*, 272.
[60] See the collection "Wilderness Years" in the Nixon Presidential Library, Yorba Linda.

grips with the reality of China . . . we cannot afford to leave China forever outside the family of nations, there to nurture its fantasies, cherish its hates and threaten its neighbors." For the future president, it was crucial "to persuade China that it must change . . . [from] its imperial ambitions . . . toward the solution of its domestic problems."[61] Accommodation, in his eyes, was nothing else than helping the PRC evolve from a revolutionary power with an ideologically defined set of global goals into a post-revolutionary power focusing on its own economic development.[62] Of course, this transition would also help the United States reduce the level and financial burden of its commitments to East Asia, particularly to Vietnam.

As newly elected president, Nixon faced three major international crises in early 1969: the war of attrition in the Middle East, the ongoing Vietnam War, and the eruption of the Sino-Soviet border clashes. Despite his 1967 vision of seeking rapprochement with the PRC, he decided to focus on West and South East Asia first. Over the course of 1969, his policy toward China eventually came into focus. Henry Kissinger, Nixon's national security adviser, believed that the Sino-Soviet military clashes did not force the United States to choose one or the other side but enabled it to play them against each other, with the ultimate aim of having good relations with both. Thus, by late 1969, Washington sent signals to Beijing that it was interested in the resumption of informal ambassadorial talks in Warsaw.[63]

Yet, events in Indochina intervened in the smooth development of rapprochement. The coup in Cambodia, which brought a pro-Western government to power in March 1970, led the PRC to step back from seeking rapprochement, at least temporarily. By the spring of 1971, however, both sides used two chance events – the friendly encounters of their table tennis teams at the world championship in Japan and Pakistani mediation – to organize the famous secret visit by Henry Kissinger to Beijing in July 1971. In its wake, the United States and the PRC announced the Chinese invitation of President Nixon to visit Beijing in February 1972.[64]

At the same time, it was clear that the United States was using the *China card* to extract concessions from the Soviet Union over détente. While Washington tried to seek rapprochement with an isolated Beijing in the 1969–71 period, it simultaneously had to accommodate the rise of Moscow to strategic parity. From the late 1940s to the early 1960s, the United States had enjoyed nuclear superiority in the superpower conflict, despite intermittent periods of self-doubt. Yet, following the

---

[61] Richard M. Nixon, "Asia after Viet Nam," *Foreign Affairs* 46/1 (1967), 111, 120–21.
[62] Ibid., 111–25.   [63] Lüthi, "Restoring Chaos."   [64] Chen, *Mao's China*, 257–68.

Cuban Missile Crisis in October 1962, Moscow had massively invested into nuclear armament, with the result that it reached parity with Washington by the early 1970s and threatened to reach superiority in subsequent years.[65] By mid 1971, the Nixon administration had tried for some time to bring nuclear arms limitation talks (SALT) to a satisfactory end, and possibly to crown that achievement with a visit to Moscow by President Nixon.[66]

The publication of Kissinger's recent secret visit to Beijing in mid-July 1971, including the simultaneous announcement of Nixon's visit to China for early 1972, triggered two developments – one unintended by Washington, the other highly anticipated. First, as already mentioned, it broke the dam of the United States-led international opposition to PRC membership in the United Nations. Yet Washington was not willing to allow Beijing to replace Taipei without a fight. In the fall of 1971, it tried to rally what it believed were its supporters to prevent the replacement of the ROC by the PRC, including in the Security Council. American attempts included the idea of a double representation, which both halves of the divided China rejected.[67] The second development was the spurring of Moscow to make the necessary concessions in Soviet-American talks. In fear of being left out in the fast-changing developments in international affairs, the Soviet Union hastened in early August to invite Nixon to come to Moscow, possibly even before his recently announced trip to Beijing.[68] The White House and the Kremlin eventually agreed the summit should take place in May 1972, which put pressure on the Soviet Union to make concessions in the SALT negotiations beforehand.[69] Thus, through rapprochement with Beijing, Washington achieved accommodation of Moscow's strategic rise.

Although the Nixon visit to the PRC in February 21–28, 1972, seemed to flow from his 1967 *Foreign Affairs* article, the president's political focus had become markedly myopic by early 1972. In many respects, his publicly celebrated visit to Communist China was a *failure*, because it did not really open a new era of Sino-American relations. Concentrating

---

[65] Keith L. Nelson, *The Making of Détente: Soviet-American Relations in the Shadow of Vietnam* (Baltimore: Johns Hopkins, 1995), 51–54.

[66] "Oval Office Conversation No. 508–13, 2 June 1971," in *The Vietnam War Files: Uncovering the Secret History of Nixon-era Strategy*, ed. Jeffrey P. Kimball (Lawrence: University Press of Kansas, 2004), 163.

[67] Tudda, *A Cold War Turning Point*, 104–19.

[68] Lorenz M. Lüthi, "Beyond Betrayal: Beijing, Moscow, and the Paris Negotiations, 1971–1973," *Journal of Cold War Studies* 11, no. 1 (Winter 2009), 70.

[69] See the Soviet invitation letter: "189. Note from the Soviet Leadership to President Nixon," August 10, 1971, in *Soviet-American Relations: The Détente Years, 1969–1972*, eds. David C. Geyer and Douglas E. Selvage (Washington, DC: US Government Printing Office, 2007), 430–31.

on the ongoing Vietnam War at the expense of almost everything else, Nixon left Washington for Beijing with little hope of achieving anything. The longest and most acrimonious sections of his talks with Zhou circled around the ongoing war in Indochina.[70]

In the aftermath of the visit, relations did not develop. Not only were the strategic differences too large (despite the shared hostility toward the Soviet Union), but the hoped-for increase in trade also did not materialize, largely due to private US claims on properties nationalized in Communist China in the early 1950s.[71] The PRC itself did not consider Nixon's visit a major shift in international relations.[72] In fact, the Chinese leaders were unhappy about Soviet-American rapprochement, which started with Nixon's trip to Moscow three months after his visit to Beijing.[73] Ironically, the American accommodation of the Soviet Union for strategic reasons impeded the development of closer Sino-US relations beyond the fragile rapprochement of 1971–72. While the vast majority of UN members extended *full* accommodation to the PRC in October 1971, *full* American accommodation of Communist China had to wait for another seven years.

Full US accommodation achieved, 1972–1979

In the period immediately following Nixon's visit, the Chinese leaders revisited Mao's Theory of the Two Intermediate Zones from the early 1960s. In August 1973, the constitution of the Chinese Communist Party stressed that the overarching goal of PRC foreign policy was to "firmly unite" with "the proletariat, the oppressed people and nations of the whole world" for the ultimate goal of opposing "the hegemonism of the two superpowers."[74] Only a little later, Mao issued his new theoretical understanding of international relations. According to the new Theory of the Three Worlds, the two imperialist powers (the United States and the Soviet Union) formed the first world, the developed countries (the former European intermediate zones) made up the second, and the large rest (i.e., the former Asian-African-Latin American intermediate zone) composed the third.[75] Although the PRC continued to claim a

---

[70] Lüthi, "Beyond Betrayal," 76–80.   [71] Burr, "Casting a Shadow," 315–49.

[72] The rest of this paragraph paraphrases from Lorenz M. Lüthi, "Chinese Foreign Policy, 1960–79," in *The Cold War in East Asia, 1945–1991*, ed. Toshi Hasegawa (Stanford: Stanford University, 2011), 166–67.

[73] As Mao told President Ford in 1975. See "Secret, Memorandum of Conversation," December 2, 1975, *Digital National Security Archive*, KT01839, 5.

[74] Quoted in Chen, *China and the Three Worlds*, 39.

[75] Mao Zedong, "On the Question of the Differentiation of the Three Worlds," February 22, 1974. Available at: digitalarchive.wilsoncenter.org/document/119307; Mao Zedong, *On Diplomacy* (Beijing: Foreign Languages, 1998), 454.

leadership position in its zone, it now emphasized economic development and cooperation within the third world *over* communist revolution and confrontation, as Deng Xiaoping told the UN General Assembly in early 1974.[76]

In the absence of significant developments in Sino-American relations after 1972, Chinese foreign policy focused on Japan and West Europe. China's trade with Japan occupied a share of 16.5–25.7 percent of the country's overall trade in the early 1970s, with the United Kingdom and West Germany adding another 10 percent combined. Trade with the two "imperialist" powers remained irrelevant throughout most of that decade.[77] While Japan was an important provider of technology, Western Europe seemed to offer more than just economic benefits.[78] In the early 1970s, the PRC was interested in the European Community (EC) – today's European Union – because it believed that West European integration "improved [the] economic and political strength of smaller countries and therefore their ability to resist [the] imperialist pressure of [the] super powers."[79] The PRC welcomed the EC enlargement with Great Britain in 1972–73 largely because it seemed to strengthen West Europe even further, at the expense of the United States and the Soviet Union.[80]

Eventually, the year 1978 became central to the *full* accommodation of the PRC by the United States. Developments in three realms converged to produce an outcome that Beijing had awaited for seven years. First, Beijing went through a major policy transformation following Mao's death in 1976 and the quick end of the Cultural Revolution thereafter. This two-year period experienced the further reduction of ideological commitments by the PRC at home and abroad. In domestic politics, the rising Deng Xiaoping made the Four Modernizations (in agriculture, industry, science and technology, and the military) to his chief domestic policy goal by May 1978, after Mao's radical development ideology had stymied rational economic policies for almost a quarter of a century since 1954. Deng considered rapprochement with Washington a crucial

[76] Mentioned in "Soviet tells UN Détente Aids All," *The New York Times* (April 12, 1974), 12.

[77] *Dangdai Zhongguo duiwai maoyi*, vol. 2, 371–88.

[78] "Chinese Foreign Policy during the 1970's," December 16, 1974, National Archives of the United Kingdom, FCO 21/1230, "Foreign Policy of China," 11.

[79] "FM Moscow 302 FEB14/72," February 14, 1972, National Archives of the United Kingdom, FCO 21/974, "Foreign Policy of China," 3.

[80] "FM PEKING 140940Z," April 14, 1972, National Archives of the United Kingdom, FCO 21/974, "Foreign Policy of China," 1–2. See also "Chinese Foreign Policy," September 18, 1972, National Archives of the United Kingdom, FCO 21/975, "Foreign Policy of China, 1972," 11.

factor in making the new domestic policy a success, because the United States, as the technologically most advanced country, could offer China important know-how and investment.[81]

Second, the successful North Vietnamese military effort to reunify the country in early 1975 not only removed a continued source of Sino-American disagreements but also triggered far-reaching changes in East Asian politics. With reunification accomplished, Communist Vietnam's long-standing relations with the Chinese comrades to the north faltered. Each side suspected the other of hegemonic interests in Laos and Cambodia. The Vietnamese mistreatment of the Chinese ethnic minority in former South Vietnam as supposedly reactionary capitalists added fuel to the conflict. As Vietnamese-Cambodian border conflicts increased while Sino-Vietnamese relations folded in 1978, Beijing started to support Phnom Penh against Hanoi, while Vietnam sought a defensive alliance with the Soviet Union against the PRC in the run-up to its military intervention in Cambodia in late 1978.[82]

Third, the new US President Jimmy Carter faced major political shifts at home and abroad following his inauguration in early 1977. US-Soviet superpower détente faded once American public opinion came to consider Nixon's foreign policy of accommodating the Soviet Union unethical.[83] Although the Carter administration continued the SALT negotiations in the hope of curbing the Soviet trend of achieving nuclear superiority, the bilateral relationship deteriorated nevertheless.[84] Still, in his first two years in office, the president hesitated to seek normalization with either the former Cold War adversary PRC or the former war enemy Vietnam.[85] The Soviet support for the revolution in Ethiopia in 1977 and the coup in Afghanistan in 1978 triggered American interest in rapprochement with the PRC for strategic purposes. The United States hoped to establish a global counterweight against the Soviet Union, at the expense of the nascent American-Vietnamese normalization.[86]

[81] Lüthi, "Chinese Foreign Policy," 158.
[82] Lorenz M. Lüthi, "Strategic Shifts in East Asia," in *The Regional Cold Wars in Europe, East Asia, and the Middle East: Crucial Periods and Turning Points*, ed. Lorenz M. Lüthi (Washington, DC/Stanford: Woodrow Wilson Press/Stanford University Press, 2015), 230–32.
[83] Phil Williams, "Détente and US Politics," *International Affairs* 61, no. 3 (Summer 1985), 431–47.
[84] Zbigniew Brzezinski, *Power and Principle: Memoirs of the National Security Adviser 1977–1981* (New York: Farrar, Straus, Giroux, 1983), 50.
[85] Cécile Menétrey-Monchau, *American-Vietnamese Relations in the Wake of the War* (Jefferson: McFarland, 2006), 177–202.
[86] Lüthi, "Strategic Shifts in East Asia," 232–34.

On December 15, 1978, Washington and Beijing announced the establishment of diplomatic relations for January 1, 1979.[87] In between, on December 25, Vietnam invaded Cambodia.[88] The *full* accommodation by the United States of the PRC at the turn of 1978/79 flowed naturally from the three shifts in international politics just described. Over the course of 1978, Beijing had signaled to Washington its interest in resuming normalization talks, largely since Deng Xiaoping needed full accommodation to buttress the launch of his modernization programs at home and to contain Vietnamese expansionism in South East Asia.[89] Thereby, however, the People's Republic had shifted from a *revolutionary* supporter of Vietnam to an anti-Vietnamese *status quo power*. In turn, the United States was receptive to rapprochement for a range of global and regional reasons.

Unlike Nixon's trip to Beijing in late February 1972, Deng Xiaoping's visit to Washington almost exactly seven years later (January 29–February 5, 1979) was not symbolic but a *rite of passage*. Any invitation to the White House signifies American acknowledgment of the international standing of the guest. During the visit, Deng informed Carter of his commitment to contain Vietnam, including the launch of a short war to punish the southern neighbor for its invasion of Cambodia.[90] While Deng did not anticipate that this military action would dislodge Vietnam from Cambodia, it was designed as a Chinese signal to the members of Association of Southeast Asian Nations (ASEAN) that Beijing was serious about curbing Hanoi's expansionism in the future.[91] Carter neither approved nor rejected Deng's war plans, but warned his guest of the potential dangers to China's worldwide reputation.[92]

The three-week-long war (February 16–March 5) was a military, but not a political, disaster for the PRC.[93] In its wake, Hanoi and Moscow closed ranks even further, which cemented Vietnam's international isolation additionally. Thus, 1979 not only increased Moscow's financial overcommitment to Hanoi, but, with the Soviet intervention in Afghanistan

---

[87] "US and China Opening Full Relations; Teng will Visit Washington on Jan. 29," *The New York Times* (December 16, 1978), 1.

[88] Menétrey-Monchau, *American-Vietnamese Relations*, 218.

[89] Lüthi, "Strategic Shifts in East Asia," 230–32.

[90] Brzezinski, *Power and Principle*, 409–10.

[91] As Huo Guofeng told Helmut Schmidt in late 1979. See Helmut Schmidt, *Menschen und Mächte [Humans and World Powers]* (Berlin: Siedler, 1987), 378.

[92] "To Vice Premier Deng Xiaoping," January 30[31], 1979, *Jimmy Carter Library*, Atlanta Georgia [hereafter: JCL], Zbigniew Brzezinski Collection [hereafter: ZBC], Geographic File, Box 9, "China, [People's Republic of] – President's Meeting with [Vice Premier] Deng [Xiaoping 12-19-78 – 10-3-79]," 1–2.

[93] Robert S. Ross, *The Indochina Tangle* (New York: Columbia, 1988), 236; Lee Kuan Yew, *From the Third World to First* (New York: Anchor Press, 2000), 596.

at the end of the year, also triggered the superpower's eventual demise.[94] More importantly, Soviet policies in Asia in 1979 terminated superpower détente.[95]

While the Soviet Union entered into a period of decline in the 1980s, the PRC experienced the beginnings of its rise to global power. Institutionally, Beijing had achieved a leadership role in the world as early as October 1971 with permanent membership in the UN Security Council, but it initially used its newly found global power with great reluctance.[96] *Full* accommodation by the United States in early 1979 not only had an important psychological impact but also led to closer Sino-American economic cooperation.[97] Yet, much of China's economic rise in the 1980s was fueled by sensible reforms at home, particularly in the countryside, which started in 1978–79 after Mao's radicalism had delayed them in the preceding three decades.[98]

Most of China's rise to global power in reality occurred *after* the full American accommodation of the PRC in 1978–79. Given the sequence of events, China's economic ascent was *the result of, not the cause for US accommodation*. The economy of the PRC had remained sluggish on a low level throughout the 1970s; its performance in that decade was far inferior to the expansion unleashed by the Four Modernizations in the 1980s.[99] The country's military capabilities were equally underdeveloped. Apart from a very small defensive nuclear force, its conventional means suffered from two decades of neglect and proved wholly inadequate in the short punitive war against Vietnam in early 1979.[100]

Conclusion

The US accommodation of Communist China over the 1969–79 period provides several insights into the conditions necessary for such a process to succeed. The focus must be on both the goals and perceptions of those directly engaged in the process, as well as on the ever-shifting context in which accommodation eventually occurs. Primarily,

---

[94] Lüthi, "Strategic Shifts in East Asia," 236–37.
[95] Gaddis, *Strategies of Containment*, 348–49.
[96] Samuel S. Kim, "The People's Republic of China in the United Nations: A Preliminary Analysis," *World Politics* 26, no. 3 (April 1974), 306–323.
[97] *Dangdai Zhongguo duiwai maoyi*, 378.
[98] Kate Xiao Zhou, *How the Farmers Changed China: Power to the People* (Boulder: Westview, 1996).
[99] Lorenz M. Lüthi, "China's Wirtschaftswunder [China's Economic Miracle]," in *Erbe des Kalten Krieges: Studien zum Kalten Krieg*, Band 6 *[Legacy of the Cold War: Studies on the Cold War*, vol. 6], eds. Bernd Greiner, Tim B. Müller, and Klaas Voss (Hamburg: Hamburger Editionen, 2013), 447–62.
[100] Ross, *The Indochina Tangle*, 236.

accommodation is possible only if both sides are willing to engage with each other. In the Sino-American case, 1969 was crucial – Mao had just called for the reduction of ideology in foreign relations, and Nixon, who had envisioned helping the PRC transition from its radicalism and global isolation to economic development and international integration, had become President of the United States.

Yet the willingness on both sides to come to accommodation alone does not explain the eventual outcome; context matters, too. The existential threat to China's physical security and political survival following the Sino-Soviet border clashes in March 1969 convinced its leadership in Beijing to rethink basic assumptions on foreign policy. Equally, the United States faced a deteriorating international environment – albeit, not in such a stark dimension. Faced with the rise of the Soviet Union to nuclear parity and with a seemingly never-ending and economically costly commitment to the Vietnam War, Washington eventually decided on rapprochement with Beijing for strategic reasons.

But such unrelated strategic considerations also demarcated the limits of US accommodation toward Communist China in 1971–72. In the end, by early 1972, Washington had become more interested in better relations with Moscow than with Beijing. Even the full accommodation of the PRC by the world community in October 1971 did not convince the United States to follow suit completely. Full American accommodation of Communist China occurred only in the context of massive parallel changes in PRC domestic, East Asian, and global politics in the late 1970s. The further reduction of Chinese ideological radicalism after Mao's death, Deng's modernization policies, the collapse of Sino-Vietnamese and Vietnamese-Cambodian relations, and assertive Soviet policies from Ethiopia to Afghanistan to Vietnam provided the environment in which the full US accommodation of Communist China became possible in early 1979.

8 Accommodation and containment
Great Britain and Germany prior to the two world wars

Martin Claar and Norrin M. Ripsman

As Stephen Van Evera observes, impending power transitions can be conceptualized as windows of opportunity for existing great powers, but they do not always necessarily climb through these windows in order to wage preventive wars against rising states and forestall their rise. Thus, as T.V. Paul suggests in Chapter 1, though most IR theorists focus on the prospects of rising powers leading to confrontation, conflict and containment are not inevitable; great powers might accommodate rising powers peacefully.[1] The purpose of this volume is to explore the conditions under which great powers accommodate rising states and invite them into the great power club, and how such accommodations are made. In order to evaluate the phenomenon of accommodation comprehensively, however, it is useful to examine negative cases as well as positive ones, in order to determine the limits of accommodation and the factors that prevent it.[2] To this end, this chapter examines British responses to rising Germany prior to each of the world wars. These are particularly interesting cases, as British leaders began by accommodating rising Germany, but then switched to a policy of containment. By focusing on the events that inspired the British to change their policies, we hope to shed light on the factors that changed to inspire containment.

Departing slightly from Chapter 1, however, we conceptualize accommodation as an alternative to containment, rather than a full acceptance of the rising challenger and a reduction of tensions between the two states. If states attempt to contain a rising challenger and

---

[1] Stephen Van Evera, *Causes of War: Power and the Roots of Conflict* (Ithaca: Cornell University Press, 1999), 74–86. See also Henk Houweling and Jan Siccama, "A Two-Level Explanation of World War," in *Parity and War: Evaluations and Extensions of the War Ledger*, eds. Jacek Kugler and Douglas Lemke (Ann Arbor: University of Michigan, 1996).

[2] Our use of the terms "negative" and "positive" is not intended to denote connotation. We do not make the case that accommodation is *a priori* a normatively preferable strategy to containment. We simply mean to refer to positive and negative examples of the concept of "accommodation."

prevent its inclusion in the great power club, either through diplomatic means, economic sanctions, or even preventive war, that can hardly be understood as accommodation. We would argue, however, that accommodation is not inconsistent with balancing, as existing great powers might accept the rising challenger as part of the club while still aiming to limit its growth and its potential to pursue outright hegemony.[3]

Our purpose here is to examine what explains the shift from accommodation to containment in these cases. To this end, we begin with a very brief overview of the leading hypotheses on why states might decline to accommodate rising states. We then investigate British responses to rising Germany from 1900 to 1914 and from 1933 to 1939 to see which, if any, of these hypotheses best explains British behavior. If none of the hypotheses fully captures the logic of British policy, we will then consider the implications of these cases for theory development. We do not engage in careful theory testing, however. Our purpose is rather, as part of a collective project with the other contributors, who are studying other prominent cases of accommodative and conflictual responses to rising states, to generate cumulative knowledge about when and how states accommodate new great powers and when they do not.

In general, key variables that have been used to explain the reaction of great powers to rising challengers can be divided into two categories: environmental and volitional.[4] William Domke argues that geographical proximity and the degree of political influence that a state has over a particular region are the key environmental variables that condition the response to rising challengers. If the rising state is nearby and threatens to extend its influence to regions of importance to an existing great power, war is more likely and accommodation less so.[5] Furthermore, building on recent neoclassical realist research, the permissiveness of the state's geostrategic environment should also matter. If the existing great power operates within a permissive international environment – defined in terms of either a low-threat environment, or an environment in which the threat posed by the rising state would materialize only in the longer term – it may be more willing to accommodate the rising power. In contrast, if it faces a more restrictive environment, in which the threat posed by the

---

[3] This is similar to the argument that appeasement and balancing are not incompatible strategies. See Norrin M. Ripsman and Jack S. Levy, "Wishful Thinking or Buying Time? The Logic of British Appeasement in the 1930s," *International Security* 33, no. 2 (Fall 2008), 152–58.

[4] William K. Domke, *War and the Changing Global System* (New Haven: Yale University Press, 1988), 4.

[5] Ibid.; Robert Gilpin, *War and Change in World Politics* (New York: Cambridge University Press, 1981), 33.

rising state is serious and more immediate, containment or war should be more likely.[6]

Environmental factors frame the objective parameters of the transition, but how states respond to these circumstances depends on volitional factors, which pertain to internal characteristics of the states. These factors include domestic political environments, the attitudes of key decision-makers, and other perceptual factors. In general, if the states in question share similar domestic political structures and ideological outlooks, it may make accommodation more likely, whereas large differences between the states might make confrontation more likely.[7] Coalition politics in the existing great power should also matter. If the dominant domestic political coalition has economic interests that would be undermined by conflict with the rising power, it will be more likely to avoid confrontation. In contrast, coalitions whose interests would be promoted by conflict will prefer containment.[8]

The literature on power transitions suggests three broad, non-mutually-exclusive reasons why states might accommodate rising challengers: (1) if the challenger is not perceived as threatening to the declining great power's core interests, at least over the short term; (2) if, though threatening, it represents less of a threat than other potential challengers; or (3) if the balance of domestic coalitional interests prefer to cooperate with the challenger. The first two hypotheses are broadly consistent with realist balance of power and balance of threat theories, which suggests that states should be willing to shift alignments

---

[6] Jeffrey W. Taliaferro, Steven E. Lobell, and Norrin M. Ripsman, "Introduction: Neoclassical Realism, the State, and Foreign Policy," in *Neoclassical Realism, the State, and Foreign Policy*, eds. Steven E. Lobell, Norrin M. Ripsman, and Jeffrey W. Taliaferro (Cambridge: Cambridge University Press, 2009); Steven E. Lobell, Jeffrey W. Taliaferro, and Norrin M. Ripsman, "Introduction: Grand Strategy between the World Wars," in *The Challenge of Grand Strategy: The Great Powers and the Broken Balance between the World Wars*, eds. Jeffrey W. Taliaferro, Norrin M. Ripsman, and Steven E. Lobell (Cambridge: Cambridge University Press, 2012), 1–36.

[7] Mark L. Haas, *The Ideological Origins of Great Power Politics, 1789–1989* (Ithaca: Cornell University Press, 2005). In accordance with democratic peace theory, therefore, democratic states should be less concerned about power transitions involving other democracies and should be willing to accommodate rising democratic great powers. On democratic peace theory, see Bruce M. Russett, *Grasping the Democratic Peace* (Princeton: Princeton University Press, 1993); John M. Owen, "How Liberalism Produces the Democratic Peace," *International Security* 19, no. 2 (Fall 1994), 87–125; Fred Chernoff, "The Study of Democratic Peace and Progress in International Relations," *International Studies Review* 6, no. 1 (March 2004), 49–77.

[8] Steven E. Lobell, *The Challenge of Hegemony: Grand Strategy, Trade, and Domestic Politics* (Ann Arbor: University of Michigan Press, 2006). In this regard, the literature on nationalist versus internationalist coalitions is relevant. See, for example, Etel Solingen, *Regional Orders at Century's Dawn: Global and Domestic Influences on Grand Strategy* (Princeton: Princeton University Press, 1998).

in order to concentrate their resources on the greatest power or threat to their interests.[9] The third is consistent with a variety of theories that focus on domestic similarities, such as Mark Haas' theory of ideological distance or democratic peace theory.[10] At the same time, it is consistent with liberal and pluralist theories that seek to explain foreign policy in terms of the interests of the ascendant domestic political coalition. This accords well with Stephen R. Rock, who argues that accommodation is possible when the geostrategic and economic interests of two states conflict minimally, and when they share certain domestic political attributes, such as regime type or ideology, that encourage cooperation.[11]

By implication, declining states are more likely to contain rising challengers: (1) if they perceive the challengers as major threats who pose greater threats to core interests than others; (2) if these threats are imminent; and (3) if the domestic political coalition of the declining state expects its own interests to be furthered through containment of, or war with, the challenger. We now turn our attention to the British responses to rising Germany prior to the two world wars, to see whether this logic underlay their decisions to abandon accommodation and embrace containment and confrontation, or whether other factors mattered in addition to or instead of these.

Great Britain and Imperial Germany, 1900–1914

The British response to Germany's rapid rise in the decades after German unification can be divided into two distinct periods: an initial period of accommodation (until 1905) and a subsequent period characterized mainly by containment, eventually resulting in war. We argue that this variation resulted from different perceptions of the external environment during the two periods, and, in particular, changing perceptions of the

---

[9] On balance of power theory, see Edward Vose Gulick, *Europe's Classical Balance of Power* (New York: Norton, 1967); Hans J. Morgenthau, *Politics Among Nations*, 6 edn. (New York: McGraw-Hill, 1985); Kenneth N. Waltz, *Theory of International Politics* (Long Grove: Waveland Press, 1979); T.V. Paul, James Wirtz, and Michel Fortmann, eds., *Balance of Power: Theory and Practice in the 21st Century* (Stanford: Stanford University Press, 2004). Balance of threat theory is elaborated by Stephen M. Walt, *The Origins of Alliances* (Ithaca: Cornell University Press, 1987).

[10] See Haas, *The Ideological Origins*. On democratic peace theory, see Michael Doyle, "Kant, Liberal Legacies, and Foreign Affairs, part 1," *Philosophy and Public Affairs* 12, no. 3 (Summer 1983), 205–35; "Kant, Liberal Legacies, and Foreign Affairs, part 2," *Philosophy and Public Affairs* 12, no. 4 (Fall 1983), 323–53; Russett, *Grasping the Democratic Peace*; Owen, "How Liberalism Produces the Democratic Peace."

[11] Stephen R. Rock, *Why Peace Breaks Out: Great Power Rapprochement in Historical Perspective* (Chapel Hill: The University of North Carolina Press, 1989).

nature of the German challenge – which led to a change from a permissive environment for Great Britain to a more restrictive one – as well as changes in the composition of the British leadership.

Changes in the system and Britain in decline, 1900–1905

The British foreign policy mentality at the turn of the twentieth century was based largely upon the idea of British hegemony. Rival nations could do little more than accept the way that British policy established and dictated the world system dynamics. From 1900 to 1905, however, several events occurred both domestically and abroad which would shake the British hegemonic mentality, resulting in new perceptions of the system and rising Germany. These changes can be divided into three categories: economic challenges, military limitations, and domestic political shifts. Because of these changes, Britain's risk and rival assessments changed, resulting in direct confrontation with rising Germany – a state previously deemed non-threatening by Britain.

Economic capabilities are the basis of all power capabilities. Without a strong economy and good growth potential, a dominant state stagnates and declines.[12] Britain in 1900 remained at the pinnacle of economic power because of two factors: imperialism and the rapidity of industrialization in the British homeland.[13] British industrial exports accounted for approximately 30 percent of worldwide exports.[14] The resulting ability to control other states in the system via trade helped the British to forge the largest empire in history, encompassing parts of the Caribbean, Atlantic, Mediterranean, African, and Far East regions, plus much of India, and reinforced a feeling of superiority among British policymakers and citizens.

During the late 1890s, however, a struggle took place over the direction of the British economic posture, which affected policymakers' economic assessments.[15] The British economy began its shift from heavy industry to world banking, thereby limiting the number of skilled jobs and economic exports. Other nations were beginning to catch up to and overtake British industrial output and steel production. Most prominent among the rising challengers were longtime rival Russia, the United States, and

---

[12] A.F.K. Organksi, *World Politics* (New York: Alfred A. Knopf, Inc., 1958), 299–306.
[13] Paul Kennedy, *The Rise and Fall of the Great Powers* (New York: Random House, 1987), 226–28.
[14] Paul Kennedy, *The Realities behind Diplomacy: Background Influences on British External Policy, 1865–1980* (London: George Allen & Unwin Ltd, 1981), 22.
[15] Aaron L. Friedberg, *The Weary Titan: Britain and the Experience of Relative Decline, 1895–1905* (Princeton: Princeton University Press, 1988), 30–35.

upstart Germany.[16] Without the necessary industrial trade, the Empire's spread was also becoming a heavy burden on the British economy and accumulated national wealth. Managing the expenses for military dispatches and diplomats abroad was becoming exceedingly costly. These themes were picked up by Conservative policymakers, most prominently Joseph Chamberlain, who served as Secretary of State for the Colonies from 1895 to 1903. As he famously put it, Britain was a "weary titan staggering under the weight" of its own empire.[17] Thus, Conservative party members began to challenge the liberal expansionist ideas that pervaded British culture.

Policymakers were not ignorant of the issues facing their economy; quite the opposite, in fact. Lord Salisbury's government (1895–1902) commissioned a report on British productivity compared to that of other nations, which reported that "In neutral markets, such as our own colonies and dependencies, and especially in the East, we are beginning to feel the effects of foreign competition in quarters where our trade formerly enjoyed a practical monopoly. The increasing severity of this competition in our home and in neutral markets is especially noticeable in the case of Germany."[18] Despite this, Salisbury's commission, and one appointed later by the chief of the Board of Trade's statistical department, Robert Giffen, determined that British economic superiority was intact and could be maintained without fear.[19] The challenges faced were unlikely to result in a loss of control. But three years of guerrilla warfare during the Second Boer War (1899–1902) changed that assessment, as they left Britain in a severe financial crisis. The costs in terms of troops and finances were immense, forcing Britain to look for new revenue streams.[20]

Chamberlain in 1902 and Prime Minister Arthur Balfour in 1903 came to similar conclusions about a possible solution. Given Britain's stalling domestic economy, a new international trade arrangement was necessary. The solution was what Chamberlain called "reciprocal preference," or, in Balfour's words, "imperial cohesion."[21] Chamberlain and Balfour proposed a trade arrangement through which Britain and its colonies would pay decreased tariffs and non-Empire states would pay greater tariffs, thereby creating non-competitive market structures. Balfour's advisors,

[16] League of Nations, *Industrialization and Free Trade Report*, 13, in Friedberg, *The Weary Titan*, 26.
[17] Kennedy, *The Rise and Fall of the Great Powers*, 229.
[18] "Royal Commission on the Depression of Trade and Industry: Final Report," Parliamentary Papers 23 C4893 (1886), xi, in Friedberg, *The Weary Titan*, 39.
[19] Friedberg, *The Weary Titan*, 41, 44–45.
[20] Kennedy, *The Realities behind Diplomacy*, 35.   [21] Friedberg, *The Weary Titan*, 48–56.

Percy Ashley and Alfred Marshall, advised against such an arrangement, cautioning that trade was needed with non-Empire states, such as the United States and Germany, which were becoming more industrialized and innovative.[22] Chamberlain and Balfour's plans met with similar luke-warm responses from policymakers and voters. Consequently, decisions on an economic solution were postponed, economic stagnation contin-ued, and many cabinet ministers resigned between 1903 and 1905, when the ruling Conservatives were replaced by Liberals. By this time, how-ever, other changes had occurred and Germany had been left unchecked for too long, facilitating the German rise and resulting in a seemingly peaceful transition in economic power preponderance from Britain to Germany after 1905.[23]

While British economic capabilities were faltering, Britain found itself pulled into several land and sea conflicts. Between wars in foreign lands and helping allies to maintain dominance over traditional rivals, the British government began to realize how hard pressed it would be to maintain systemic hegemony via its military. To begin with, the country had spread its land forces too thinly across the globe. The army was pushed to its limit when Britain became involved simultaneously in the Boxer Rebellion and the Second Boer War. The government dispatched a sizable contingent to an international military force in China, success-fully securing peace and a trade foothold.[24] At the same time, another large troop dispatch was deployed to South Africa to maintain control over the colony there. This was the more costly military and economic investment, as the war was fought to a three-year standstill. The guerrilla tactics employed by Boer commandos caused massive troop losses and economic expenditures, all because the resources and trade benefits in the Transvaal were deemed valuable to the Empire.[25] Several smaller wars and rebellions during the period, such as the Last Ashanti War, the Somali Rebellion, the Conquest of Kano and Sokoto, the Sokoto Uprising, and the Third British-Zulu War, continued to drain British forces.[26]

It was the Indian Question of 1904, however, that drove the point home that British land forces were insufficient to maintain system dominance.[27] Troops, trade, and footholds to the Far East were threatened unless

---

[22] Ibid., 64–65.   [23] Kennedy, *The Realities behind Diplomacy*, 47–48.

[24] John Darwin, *The Empire Project: The Rise and Fall of the British World System, 1830–1970* (New York: Cambridge University Press, 2009), 259.

[25] Kennedy, *The Realities behind Diplomacy*, 112–13.

[26] Meredith Reid Sarkess and Frank Wayman, *Resort to War: 1816–2007* (Thousand Oaks: CQ Press, 2010).

[27] Friedberg, *The Weary Titan*, 231–32.

Britain could maintain control. As Lieutenant Colonel Altham warned, "[t]he loss of India by conquest would be a death blow to our prosperity, prestige and power... Second only to the security of the United Kingdom itself, comes the question of the defense of India."[28] Subsequently, Balfour sought to avoid a fight with Russia because "a quarrel with Russia anywhere or about anything [meant] the invasion of India."[29] War never occurred, despite several years of troop mobilization and parliamentary debate about how best to defend India. What restrained Russia from acting, however, was not British power, but the Russo-Japanese naval war, which ended in 1905. Nonetheless, the vulnerability to a Russian attack prompted a revelation about British land forces: "In the existing state of our army, it would be extremely difficult to secure the safety of the United Kingdom, to meet the demands of India, and to be prepared for troubles that might arise in other parts of the Empire."[30]

This idea of declining military might was further driven home by the simultaneous naval challenges the Royal Navy faced. Land forces had never been Britain's pride and joy, nor its primary means of defense and economic expansion. That role was given to the navy, which had secured colonies, helped protect and expand trade, and put Britain in a position of dominance for the better half of the 1800s. Even foreign observers were forced to remark that "[t]he Fleet... is certainly the most formidable force in all its elements and qualities that has ever been brought together, and such as no combination of other powers can rival. It is at once the most powerful and far-reaching weapon which the world has ever seen."[31]

To gain such a level of naval dominance, Britain had maintained what it termed the "two-power standard." This meant it maintained rough equivalence between itself and its top two competitors – traditionally France and Russia – combined.[32] Until 1905, Britain maintained greater than the two-power standard, with other states lagging far behind British vessel numbers and technologies.

Naval forces were distributed based on region. Britain viewed its naval forces in terms of three fronts: the North Sea and Mediterranean "homefront," the Eastern front, and the Western or Atlantic front.[33] The first challenge to naval supremacy came from the United States on the Western front. During the late 1890s, American naval forces drastically

---

[28] PRO, Cab. 3/1/1A, 49.
[29] BM, Add. Mss. 49727, Balfour to Lansdowne in Friedberg, December 12, 1901.
[30] PRO, Cab. 6/1/41D, "What Number of Troops Could Be Spared for India?" Roberts, March 23, 1904.
[31] *The Times*, June 25, 1897 in Paul M. Kennedy, *The Rise and Fall of British Naval Mastery* (London: Allen Lane Books, 1976), 205.
[32] Kennedy, *The Rise and Fall of British Naval Mastery*, 210.
[33] Friedberg, *The Weary Titan*, 171.

increased and threatened British control over the Atlantic and British interests in Canada and the Caribbean. The threat to British dominance grew following the Clayton–Bulwer Treaty and the building of the Isthmian Canal.[34] The American challenge drove home to naval strategy policymakers that "Britain unaided can hardly expect to be able to maintain in the West Indies, the Pacific, and in the North Atlantic stations, squadrons sufficiently powerful to dominate those of the United States and at the same time to hold the command of the sea in home waters, the Mediterranean, and the Eastern seas, where it is essential that she should remain predominant."[35] Consequently, First Lord of the Admiralty Selborne made it clear that the two-power standard was no longer feasible. Selborne thought this would be especially true if one of the traditional rivals were to be replaced by a new rival, such as the United States or Germany.[36] Despite calls for a new standard, the Cabinet's reply was to redistribute the fleet to protect Britain's two biggest interests – the Far East and the homefront – while relinquishing dominance in the Atlantic.[37] The American challenge, though, was just the beginning of the tectonic shift in global naval power during this period. The Far East would also be threatened.

British interests in the Far East had been secured through imperialism or alliances. In 1902, Britain had allied itself with Japan in order to increase its leverage in the region and augment its naval forces against Russia.[38] When Russia showed interest in the Korean Peninsula in 1904, which was under Japanese control, British interests were threatened as well. As Japan's ally, Britain supplied naval reinforcements, but worked diligently to avoid being drawn openly into the conflict. The reasoning was simple: if Britain were drawn into the war, then Russia would invoke the Franco-Russian Alliance, thereby bringing the Russo-Japanese War to the homefront. Thus, Britain and France began to work through their differences via the Entente Cordiale of 1904 to avoid such a world war.[39] In 1905, the Japanese defeated the Russians. Russia's defeat, which was a surprise for British policymakers, had profound strategic implications. Russian naval forces had been greatly weakened by the war, dropping them out of the top three naval powers. A central question for British strategists and policymakers, therefore, was: Who succeeded Russia as the third-ranked sea power?

---

[34] Kennedy, *The Rise and Fall of British Naval Mastery*, 212.
[35] PRO, Cab. 37/56/2, Admiralty to Foreign Office, January 5, 1901.
[36] Friedberg, *The Weary Titan*, 172–74.
[37] Kennedy, *The Rise and Fall of British Naval Mastery*, 212; Friedberg, *The Weary Titan*, 186–87.
[38] Kennedy, *The Rise and Fall of the Great Powers*, 249.   [39] Ibid., 251.

The most likely answer was Germany, which had rapidly increased its naval forces during the period. The number of German battleships had increased from 21 in 1896 to 31 in 1906, while the numbers of German cruisers had also increased and the German Navy had begun building dreadnought class ships.[40] This rapid German naval program convinced Selborne that Britain needed to reevaluate how it thought about naval power. Under these circumstances, Naval Intelligence told the Balfour Cabinet that "[i]f we are involved in difficulties with any other Nation, and Germany adopts a menacing attitude, it will be necessary to maintain a force in the North Sea sufficient to mask the German fleet. As the German Navy will be at that date a much greater danger to this country than the Fleet of Russia it is thought that in future all our calculations should refer to France and Germany rather than to France and Russia."[41]

The Cabinet was reluctant to recognize these changes. In reply to the War Office's recognition that the two-power standard was at an end, the Cabinet stated that "[u]nless . . . The War Office has misinterpreted the plan for strategical distribution of our naval forces . . . the conclusion appears to be unavoidable that the present strength of His Majesty's Navy would not suffice to defend on the high seas the interests of the Empire; in other words, that the Two Power Standard, up to which the country has been given to understand the Navy is maintained no longer exists."[42]

Despite the reluctant recognition of British decline, policymakers were loath to view Germany as a threat. The main reason for this state of denial toward Germany's rising economic and naval power was that Conservative party decision-makers had a vastly different perception of Germany from that of their Liberal predecessors, in large part due to the relationship that the leadership of the two states shared and to the Bismarckian policies that had been pursued by Germany. Under Bismarckian rule, Germany remained perpetually prostrated before Britain. Bismarck's policies did not seek power or territory; he did not attempt aggressive expansion.[43] Like the policies of Salisbury, Giffen, and Balfour, Bismarckian policies were intent on preserving the balance of power. While Britain focused on avoiding French and Russian challenges to

---

[40] Friedberg, *The Weary Titan*, 153.
[41] Selborne to Salisbury, *Selborne Papers*, May 18, 1907, 158; "From: Custance to Selborne," in Friedberg, *The Weary Titan*, 178.
[42] PRO, Cab. 5/1/3C in Friedberg, *The Weary Titan*, 188.
[43] Sir F. Lascelles to the Marquess of Salisbury, February 12, 1900, in *British Documents on the Origins of the War, 1898–1914*, eds. G.P. Gooch and Harold Temperley (London: HMSO, 1926–1938), vol. I, no. 311.

British dominance, Germany focused on avoiding Britain's wrath and war in Europe.[44] To project this perception, Bismarck fixated on internal state growth and reaffirmed numerous times that Britain had nothing to fear from Germany on any front. After Bismarck's removal in 1890, his policy of capitulation was continued under Wilhelm II until 1905, despite some minor disruptions such as the Transvaal and Samoa Questions. Even during these disagreements, Wilhelm II still expressed that he would prefer to obtain new colonies while maintaining a peaceful arrangement with England.[45] Wilhelm also maintained that Britain should get the lion's share, with Germany obtaining whatever was left over – an obvious prostration before the hegemon.[46]

For these reasons, aside from those few military advisors previously mentioned, none of the major decision-makers in Britain feared a German rise. In fact, Balfour seemed to like Germany and his German counterpart. He was noted as being fond of Wilhelm, as well as of Germany's culture and industrial advancements. He perceived no direct threat between the two countries, but wished for closer relations. Therefore, Balfour refused to admit that war between the two would ever be possible.[47] British decision-makers remained hopeful that relations with Germany would not result in conflict but stay amicable even in disagreements. In the Transvaal, Samoa, and China, Britain was even reassured by Wilhelm and Count Bulow that Germany "had no intention of doing anything disagreeable to England."[48] As such, Britain felt it could spread its focus to its colonies while maintaining the systemic status quo, since, despite German naval and economic growth, the Conservative government did not judge Germany to be a threat or rival.[49] In that regard, they judged that, despite the rise of Germany and other powers in Asia and the Americas, Britain still faced a permissive international system, since no major threats existed in British home waters or the critical European theater. Events following the Russo-Japanese War would alter that judgment, however.

---

[44] Frank McDonough, *The Conservative Party and Anglo-German Relations, 1905–1914* (New York: Palgrave Macmillan, 2007), 37–38; Kennedy, *The Rise and Fall of the Great Powers*, 232.

[45] Sir F. Lascelles to Mr. Balfour, August 22, 1898, *British Documents on the Origins of the War, 1898–1914*, vol. I, no. 87.

[46] Sir F. Lascelles to the Marquess of Salisbury, September 5, 1898, *British Documents on the Origins of the War, 1898–1914*, vol. I, no. 96.

[47] Paul Kennedy, *The Rise of the Anglo-German Antagonism, 1860–1914* (London: George Allen & Unwin Ltd, 1980), 254–55.

[48] Appendix: Memorandum of Mr. J.A.C. Tilley, *British Documents on the Origins of the War, 1898–1914*, vol. I, 328–29.

[49] McDonough, *The Conservative Party*, 39–40.

The new world order: Britain and Germany, 1905–1914

Beginning in 1905, several factors changed in the Anglo-German relationship, resulting in a move from ambivalence to outright antagonism. The first for both states were domestic factors – specifically, whose policies guided the relationship. In Britain, the Conservatives who favored Germany were no longer in power, as a result of the mishandled economic issues facing Britain. While not all Liberals were anti-German, the ascendance of the Liberal Party from 1905 to 1914 brought with it a contingent of policymakers who viewed Germany with greater skepticism in light of the German challenge to naval commercialism. These radical Liberal policymakers included Foreign Secretary Edward Grey, Prime Minister Herbert Asquith, Secretary of State Lord Haldane, and David Lloyd George, among other members of the Foreign Office.[50] This core group was vocal about and integral to Anglo-German relations. They had come to the conclusion that Germany was a threat, given the new power distribution in the system, because of their internationalist views and the fact that they listened quite closely to military advisers like Captain Philip Wylie Dumas.[51] Their opinion of Germany was so strong that the German Problem became a regular and serious topic of both the British government and the British public.[52] These domestic actors are arguably the principal source of Anglo-German antagonism in the post-1905 era, and subsequently the primary source for evaluating the Official Mind toward Germany and about the new power distribution.

Meanwhile, in Germany, Wilhelm II sought to step out from behind Britain and Bismarck's shadows in order to fulfill Germany's newfound manifest destiny. German industry had grown substantially between 1900 and 1914.[53] The German population had become highly educated, resulting in a greater number of skilled industrial workers, who produced larger quantities of steel and almost as much coal as Britain. German foreign trade numbers were almost equal to Britain's by 1914, bringing about virtual economic power parity with Britain.[54] Thus, Germany

---

[50] Zara S. Steiner, *The Foreign Office and Foreign Policy, 1898–1914* (Cambridge: Cambridge University Press, 1969), 70, 76–78, 89–89; Zara S. Steiner and Keith Neilson, *Britain and the Origins of the First World War*, 2 edn. (New York: Palgrave Macmillan, 2003), 38–43; Christopher Clark, *The Sleepwalkers: How Europe Went to War in 1914* (New York: HarperCollins, 2012), 202.

[51] Appendix II: Captain Dumas, R.N. to Sir F. Lascelles, January 29, 1907, British Documents on the Origins of the War, 1898–1914, vol. VI.

[52] Sir F. Lascelles to Sir Edward Grey, February 4, 1907, British Documents on the Origins of the War, *1898–1914*, vol. VI, no. 3.

[53] Darwin, *The Empire Project*, 273.

[54] Kennedy, *The Rise and Fall of the Great Powers*, 200–01.

sought to advance in the world system by gaining colonies, eschewing Bismarck's statesmanship method.[55]

Economic power parity, while significant, was not what rubbed British leaders the wrong way; rather, it was the increases in German naval power. Increasing proportions of the booming German budget were being funneled into German naval power as per recommendations by Admiral Tirpitz. By 1914, the German fleet had come closer to the size of the British fleet than had either of the traditional British rivals.[56] British policymakers kept tabs on this explosive naval growth, and the resulting fear reinforced the Liberal leadership's feelings that Germany was a direct threat to the homefront: the only thing Britain valued more than India.[57] This new German *Weltpolitik* strategy quickly became a source of tension with Britain.

Having increased all facets of power exponentially, German leaders found themselves in a position to expand Germany's systemic influence, especially with Russia's precipitous decline after 1905.[58] Wilhelm II began to assert that Germany "had tasks to accomplish outside the narrow boundaries of old Europe," in a dramatic change from Bismarckian Germany, which acted as a "saturated" power whose intent was not to buck the status quo.[59] With new capabilities and now opportunities, Germany began to enforce its will on others. Efforts were made to pressure the French in Morocco, to build the Baghdad Railway, and to secure influence over the Portuguese Islands. Financial attempts were made to expand into the Balkan, Turkish, and Near East markets in order to gain greater influence in Europe.[60] Whereas Germany had not posed direct challenges to British interests previously, now it was willing to risk harming its relationships with other great powers in order to gain influence. Add to this the increases in German naval power in European waters, and British policymakers were left with only one prevailing perception: "the whole trend of Germany's policy [shows] conclusive evidence that she is consciously aiming at the establishment of a German hegemony, at first in Europe, and eventually the world."[61]

The result of these coinciding changes to Britain and Germany was that, after 1905, Anglo-German tensions had increased considerably, as the growing German threat to British interests in Europe and home

---

[55] Appendix A: Memorandum of Mr. Eyre Crowe, January 1, 1907, British Documents on the Origins of the War, 1898–1914, vol. III.

[56] Kennedy, *The Rise of the Anglo-German Antagonism*, 416.

[57] Appendix B: Memorandum by Lord Sanderson, February 27, 1907, British Documents on the Origins of the War, 1898–1914, vol. III, 422–24.

[58] Kennedy, *The Rise of the Anglo-German Antagonism*, 311–12.

[59] Kennedy, *The Rise and Fall of the Great Powers*, 213–14.

[60] Ibid., 251–52.   [61] Appendix B: Memorandum by Lord Sanderson, 421.

waters presented British leaders with a more restrictive international environment. Britain's traditional rival, France, had receded as a threat since the two countries had entered into the Entente Cordiale. Likewise, Russia had become a smaller concern after the Russo-Japanese War.[62] Thus, after 1905, Britain shifted its attention from its traditional rivals and focused intently on the German Question.

Three major developments would solidify Germany as Britain's new rival before their 1914 confrontation. The first was the 1907 Anglo-Russian Entente, which eased lingering tensions between Russia and Britain. Britain sought to expand the Entente Cordiale to bring now-fallen Russia into the fold. Foreign Secretary Sir Edward Grey explained this move as a reflection of the government's desire to "see Russia established in the councils of Europe, and . . . on better terms with us [Britain] than she has been yet."[63] While technically this was successful for Britain, the Entente Cordiale was not without its difficulties. Relations with France and Russia were still tense at best, though the primary goal of securing the homefront was largely successful. There was, however, an unforeseen consequence of this extension. The Entente put extreme pressure on Germany by surrounding it with enemies, thereby inspiring further German military expansion.[64] Effectively, by securing Britain's other interests (especially Indian security), Britain ensured that Germany would become a new rival. But German fears did not even enter the British calculations. As Grey put it, "the Anglo-French Entente had been in no way directed against Germany . . . neither the late Government nor the present Government had the least intention of using it to the disadvantage of Germany."[65] Essentially, Britain was simply attempting to maintain the established world system and its own hegemony, even though it fueled German insecurity.

The German perception of the Entente inspired the second development in the antagonism spiral: the 1907–09 Anglo-German naval race. The Entente Cordiale created a threatening atmosphere in Germany, resulting in a need for increased military forces. Admiral Tirpitz, Wilhelm II's primary military advisor, brought about even greater expansion to the already formidable German fleet in response.[66] Production of

---

[62] Kennedy, *The Realities behind Diplomacy*, 133–34.

[63] Grey to Spring Rice, London, December 22, 1905, in Clark, *The Sleepwalkers*, 140.

[64] Kennedy, *The Rise and Fall of the Great Powers*, 252–53.

[65] Sir Edward Grey to Sir E. Egerton, December 27, 1906, British Documents on the Origins of the War, 1898–1914, vol. III, no. 206; Appendix B: Memorandum by Lord Sanderson.

[66] Captain Dumas to Sir F. Lascelles, January 14, 1907, British Documents on the Origins of the War, *1898–1914*, vol. VI, no. 1.

dreadnought class ships began, and most were kept in Britain's home-front waters. This extreme military buildup made British policymakers doubly nervous about their control over the North Sea and about Germany's "attempt to rival Britain" through her "policy of feverish shipbuilding."[67] This dual perception led to British attempts to reduce tensions through negotiations. Germany, in return for a non-violence agreement, requested that Britain remain neutral in the event of a European continental war – a request to which the British could not agree.[68] The British leaders' reluctance stemmed from their growing concern over German *Weltpolitik*, which had begun to alarm both Britain and France. Of particular concern was Germany's extortion of a weakened Russia to allow Austria-Hungary to gain control over Bosnia-Herzegovina. Russia, left without an option, acquiesced to the German demands, thereby reminding British policymakers how different – and threatening – Germany had become.[69]

The third development was the 1911 Agadir Crisis, in which France tried to gain sole control over the Moroccan colonies. Germany, France's co-claimant, became enraged but opted not to start a war; instead, it sent a single vessel to the region as a show of claim.[70] French policymakers viewed this as an act of war and began plans to mobilize, fully expecting Britain to come to their aid in accordance with the Entente. Although Grey and Asquith were reluctant to become involved, after the inflammatory "Mansion House speech" by David Lloyd George they initiated a British intervention, which ended the conflict before it could escalate further.[71] Negotiations were held between France and Germany, with France gaining control of Morocco in exchange for Germany gaining colonial control over parts of the Congo. The increased and unwarranted military escalations resulted in a palpable surge of patriotic and nationalistic feelings in all three nations, further increasing tensions.[72]

---

[67] Mr. Cartwright to Sir Edward Grey, August 19, 1907, British Documents on the Origins of the War, *1898–1914*, vol. VI, no. 24.

[68] Sir E. Goschen to Sir Edward Grey, June 26, 1909, British Documents on the Origins of the War, *1898–1914*, vol. VI, no. 183.

[69] Kennedy, *The Rise and Fall of the Great Powers*, 253.   [70] Clark, *The Sleepwalkers*, 207.

[71] Lloyd George insisted that "Britain should maintain . . . [h]er place and her prestige among the Great Powers of the world . . . [If Britain were forced to choose between peace on the one hand and the surrender of her international preeminence on the other,] then I say empathically that peace at that price would be a humiliation intolerable for a great nation like ours to endure." "Mr. Lloyd George on British Prestige," *The Times*, July 22, 1911, 7.

[72] Memorandum by Sir C. Hardinge, February 11, 1909, *British Documents on the Origins of the War, 1898–1914*, vol. VI, no. 145–1.

By 1912, after failures to ease these tensions with Germany over the German increases in naval forces and expansionism, the British were left in a position where the only tenable option was to sign the Anglo-French naval agreement.[73] This precautionary tactic was meant to contain Germany and tighten relations with France, thereby securing the home-front. In fact, it only inflamed Anglo-German tensions further.

The growing British policy of containing the German threat did not preclude attempts to defuse conflict through negotiations. Indeed, the 1912 Haldane Mission was one of two final attempts to abate the grow-ing Anglo-German enmity and return the European system to a peaceful state. Asquith and Grey sent Richard Haldane to Berlin to discuss a three-point plan to improve bilateral relations: first, the Germans had to slow or stop their naval increases and recognize British naval superi-ority; second, Britain would accept German colonial expansion so that the two could normalize relations; and third, both nations would assure one another that they had no aggressive designs toward the European continent.[74] These talks, lasting the better part of a year, failed, as the German policymakers with whom Haldane met, especially Tirpitz, Met-ternich, and von Kiderlen-Waechter, adamantly refused to slow German naval power growth.[75] Asquith concluded: "Nothing, I believe, will meet her [Germany's] purpose which falls short of a promise on our part of neutrality: a promise we cannot give."[76] German goals and ambitions were too threatening to leave unchecked, lest Britain tumble from its pinnacle completely.

This led to the final attempt by Britain to pacify the German fer-vor for expansion: offering up the former Portuguese colonies in North Africa in exchange for peace in Europe. In 1913, the two states success-fully reached an agreement that should Portugal's economy collapse, as appeared likely, Germany would take over the North African colonies previously under Portugal's control. However, disagreements over when to publicize the agreement and its finer points created lingering issues that eventually precipitated its collapse.[77] Thus, an agreement that might have cooled the heated tensions fell through.

In light of the failed negotiations, Britain was left in a position where its top military advisor, Winston Churchill, suggested that its best option

---

[73] Kennedy, *The Realities behind Diplomacy*, 134.

[74] Sir E. Goschen to Sir Edward Grey, February 9, 1912, *British Documents on the Origins of the War, 1898–1914*, vol. VI, no. 500.

[75] Diary of Lord Haldane's Visit to Berlin, February 10, 1912, *British Documents on the Origins of the War, 1898–1914*, vol. VI, no. 506.

[76] Asquith to Sir Edward Grey, April 10, 1912, *British Documents on the Origins of the War, 1898–1914*, vol. VI, no. 571.

[77] Clark, *The Sleepwalkers*, 335.

was to abandon naval positions in the Mediterranean and deploy British naval forces to the North Sea homewaters, where the majority of the German fleet was stationed.[78] This defensive mentality remained dominant among British policymakers for the remainder of the period, since they now recognized Germany as a systemic rival and a direct threat to Britain. Vigilance and a reliance on external power balancing became the only means of restraining the German threat, thereby containing the German force for the time being.

Conclusions from the reordered world, 1900–1914

This case suggests a few possible explanations for both accommodation and containment of rising states, relating to the existing great power's perception of the rising power, the transition environment, and both states' domestic make-up. Initially, absent a history of rivalry between the two states, accommodation was the British default toward Germany, as it concentrated on its traditional rivals Russia and France. Only after Germany began to challenge high-level British interests, such as the status quo in the colonial world and, most importantly, British supremacy on the high seas, did the British government begin to pursue a policy of confrontation toward Germany. This suggests that containment and preventive war might not always be the natural response to a rising challenger outside the context of a strategic rivalry.[79] Furthermore, when faced with a multiplicity of challengers, great powers might focus their attentions on long-term rivals and accommodate those with whom they have not previously been in conflict. Nonetheless, as Steven Lobell argues, when a rising non-rival pursues a conflictual policy and accumulates the components of power which most threaten a great power, that great power is more likely to respond with containment, hostility, and possibly preventive war.[80]

In addition, the environment within which the transition occurred is also important. British policy toward Germany did not become hostile until the environment of the transition changed. Until 1905, though Britain faced a number of challengers, the time frame of the challenge was longer-term, since not even its closest rivals could come near to overtaking it, making the environment a more permissive one. After 1905, however, the environment that Britain found itself in was highly restrictive. There was no longer a true two-power standard for the navy; now

---

[78] Kennedy, *The Rise and Fall of British Naval Mastery*, 224–29.
[79] Paul F. Diehl and Gary Goertz, *War and Peace in Enduring Rivalries* (Ann Arbor: University of Michigan Press, 2000), 5.
[80] Lobell, *The Challenge of Hegemony*, 153–58; and Chapter 3 in this volume.

there was a rapidly rising Germany with a rapidly growing navy near homefront waters. In this more restrictive and immediately threatening environment, Britain had little choice but to treat Germany as a potential enemy and contain German power.

Finally, partisan politics and coalition interests appear to have played a role in the transition. Under the stewardship of the Conservative Party, the British government was more attuned to threats to the Empire posed by Russia and France than the commercial threat posed by the Germans. After 1905, however, the politicians that dominated the Liberal foreign policy team, representing an internationalist, export-oriented business coalition, were much more concerned about the challenge the Germans represented in terms of global commerce, the merchant marine, and the navy, which protected British commerce.[81] Consequently, domestic political considerations in the responding state also impact upon the strategy it pursues vis-à-vis the rising challenger.

Great Britain and Nazi Germany, 1933–1939

After Adolf Hitler's accession to power in Germany, the British defense establishment determined that Germany constituted "the ultimate potential enemy against whom our 'long range' defence policy must be directed."[82] The Cabinet, too, viewed Nazi Germany as the principal threat to peace and stability in Europe and to British interests on the Continent.[83] As Norrin Ripsman and Jack Levy demonstrate, however, the British initially sought to accommodate rising Germany for several reasons not principally related to the degree of threat that Germany posed, nor to the preferences of the dominant political coalition. From 1933 to late 1934, British strategy attempted to allow a measure of limited German rearmament and equality within the confines of the Washington Disarmament Conference, in order to allow Germany to achieve some of its aspirations to revise the Versailles Treaty and return to the great power club on a more equitable basis. Despite Britain's fear of rising

---

[81] See Mark Brawley, "The Political Economy of Balance of Power Theory," in *Balance of Power: Theory and Practice in the 21st Century*, eds. T.V. Paul, James J. Wirtz, and Michael Fortmann (Stanford: Stanford University Press, 2004), 93; Lobell, *The Challenge of Hegemony*, 75–84.

[82] "Committee of Imperial Defence: Defence Requirements Sub-committee Report," D.R.C. 14, February 28, 1934, reproduced for the Cabinet in C.P. 64 (34) – CAB 24/247, 383; Wesley K. Wark, *The Ultimate Enemy: British Intelligence and Nazi Germany, 1933–1939* (Ithaca: Cornell University Press, 1985).

[83] See, for example, Foreign Secretary John Simon's briefings on Germany in "The Crisis in Europe," C.P. 52 (33), February 28, 1933 – CAB 24/239, 10–11; "The Foreign Policy of the Present German Government," C.P. 129 (33), May 16, 1933 – CAB 24/247, 44–50.

German power, its reasons for this strategy of accommodation were principally the fear that a policy of confrontation and preventive war would be disastrous for an unstable Depression-era British economy and would interfere with a substantially disarmed Great Britain's ability to defend simultaneously its homeland and its imperial possessions abroad.[84] As the Cabinet would observe again and again throughout the decade, Great Britain faced too many enemies in Germany, Japan, and Italy, and confronting Germany would undermine British power projection capability in the Mediterranean and the Pacific.[85]

Although it is true that public opinion during this period opposed a policy of military confrontation, public attitudes were far less consequential than the economic and geopolitical considerations identified by the Cabinet and British military experts. As Simon explained to Sir Robert Vansittart in December 1933, the public was heavily committed to a disarmament agreement rather than a confrontational policy. He judged, therefore, that "The loss of credit which the British Government would suffer in the eyes of the public if there is no international agreement which can be called a disarmament convention will be something tremendous," and might result in electoral defeat.[86] Nonetheless, as Ripsman and Levy demonstrate, "the Government was willing to satisfy public opinion only as long as their demands did not place national or imperial security in jeopardy," and in the event of a pressing strategic need for a harder-line policy, they probably could have swayed public opinion.[87]

By 1935, after Germany withdrew from the Disarmament Conference, and once it became clear that Hitler was rearming at a far faster pace than the British had anticipated, rather than shifting to a policy of

---

[84] Norrin M. Ripsman and Jack S. Levy, "British Grand Strategy and the Rise of Germany, 1933–1936," in *Broken Balances: Grand Strategy in the Interwar Years*, eds. Jeffrey W. Taliaferro, Norrin M. Ripsman, and Steven E. Lobell (Cambridge: Cambridge University Press, 2012), 171–92. On the impact of British military weakness, see Gustav Schmidt, *The Politics and Economics of Appeasement: British Foreign Policy during the 1930s*, trans. Jackie Bennett-Ruete (New York: St. Martin's Press, 1986), 383; Malcolm S. Smith, "Rearmament and Deterrence in Britain in the 1930s," *Journal of Strategic Studies* 1, no. 3 (December 1978), 313–37.

[85] See, for example, Paul Kennedy, *Strategy and Diplomacy, 1870–1945* (London: George Allen and Unwin, 1983), 18; Paul W. Schroeder, "Munich and the British Tradition," *Historical Journal* 19, no. 1 (March 1976), 224.

[86] Simon to Vansittart, December 23, 1933, enclosure to Vansittart to Baldwin, December 29, 1933, Papers of Stanley Baldwin, Cambridge University Library, Cambridge, vol. 121, 133–34.

[87] Ripsman and Levy, "British Grand Strategy," 184. See also Catherine Krull and B. J. C. McKercher, "The Press, Public Opinion, Arms Limitation, and Government Policy in Britain, 1932–34: Some Preliminary Observations," *Diplomacy & Statecraft* 13, no. 3 (September 2002), 126; Paul W. Doerr, *British Foreign Policy 1919–1939* (Manchester: Manchester University Press, 1998), 164.

containment or preventive war, Britain continued to accommodate Nazi Germany through the strategy of appeasement, though for a different set of reasons. During this period, Britain sought to limit German challenges through strategic concessions, such as the Anglo-German Naval Agreement (1935) allowing Germany a limited navy, British acceptance of the Rhineland remilitarization, and the coercive inclusion of Austria in the German Reich – all proscribed by the Versailles Treaty – because of the perceived British incapacity to wage war (and, consequently, to contain Germany with threats of force) pending British rearmament, which would take time. The high-water mark of appeasement (or, perhaps, its low point) was Neville Chamberlain's acquiescence in German demands on Czechoslovakia at the September 1938 Munich conference, because he and the majority of the Cabinet accepted the Chiefs of Staff Intelligence subcommittee's estimation that British rearmament had not yet reached the point where they could contemplate war with Germany.[88] In Foreign Secretary Lord Halifax's words, "Quite frankly, the moment is unfavourable, and our plans, both for offence and defence, are not sufficiently advanced."[89] Thus, as Ripsman and Levy have demonstrated, appeasement during this period was about buying time for rearmament and containment, and was therefore complementary to an eventual balancing strategy in the long run.[90]

What then explains the British strategy shift from appeasement/ accommodation to containment and war after Munich? On one hand, intelligence information from a variety of sources beginning in late 1938 indicated that the British had run out of time, as the Germans were bent on an imminent challenge. Notably, the Committee on Imperial Defence convened in December 1938 to consider alarming evidence that Hitler was considering a bolt-out-of-the-blue air attack against Great Britain in retaliation for the military victory over Czechoslovakia that Hitler believed Chamberlain had cheated him out of at Munich.[91] In early January 1939, in addition to rumors of an attack on London, a stream of evidence suggested that a German invasion of Holland was

---

[88] Cabinet 15 (38), March 22, 1938 – CAB 23/93, 32–34.
[89] Halifax to Phipps, March 23, 1938, enclosure 2 in CP 76 (38), March 23, 1938 – CAB 24/276, 19.
[90] Ripsman and Levy, "Wishful Thinking or Buying Time?" 148–81.
[91] See Norrin M. Ripsman and Jack S. Levy, "From Appeasement to Confrontation: Explaining the Shift in British Strategy from 1938 to 1939," Paper Presented at the 2011 International Studies Association Conference, Montreal, Canada, March 16–19, 2011; G. Bruce Strang, "The Spirit of Ulysses? Ideology and British Appeasement in the 1930s," *Diplomacy & Statecraft* 19, no. 3 (September 2008), 506; Minutes of the 342nd meeting of the Committee of Imperial Defence, December 16, 1938, CAB 2/8, 98–103.

imminent.[92] In this context, Hitler's March 1939 invasion of the Czechoslovakian rump state further confirmed that Hitler had rapidly increased the pace of his challenges. If the British strategy to this point had been to buy time for rearmament, it was now clear that there was no further time to buy.

At the same time, the British began to be convinced both that their rearmament efforts had begun to bear fruit and that the Germans, economy was vulnerable to a wide blockade of the North Sea in the event of war. On the first issue, military planners reported to the Cabinet that the British military had finally closed gaps in coastal defenses and the British ability to repel a German air attack.[93] On the latter issue, British intelligence had concluded that the pace of German rearmament had outstripped available resources and that a protracted war effort would impose a great strain on the German economy.[94] Consequently, there was less of a need to postpone a confrontation with Germany. In this context, the British began in 1939 to shift from accommodation to confrontation, concluding that it was necessary to make a clear commitment to Holland and other vulnerable Western countries, to ramp up joint military cooperation with France and, eventually, to extend guarantees to vulnerable Eastern states, as well.[95]

In this case, therefore, the initial decision to accommodate stemmed more from British incapacity in the face of multiple threats, rather than from any expectation that Germany posed no significant threat to British interests or that it faced a particularly permissive security environment. Nonetheless, successive German challenges and growing evidence that the time frame of the German challenge had shortened made the environment all the more restrictive for Great Britain after September 1938. Accommodation was abandoned, therefore, once the Germans demonstrated that accommodation was unlikely to bear further fruit, while British incapacity was alleviated through rearmament.

---

[92] Doerr, *British Foreign Policy 1919–1939*, 241; Peter Neville, *Hitler and Appeasement: The British Attempt to Prevent the Second World War* (New York: Palgrave MacMillan, 2006), 156; Cabinet 35 (33), May 17, 1933 – CAB 23/76, 88.

[93] Willamson Murray, "Appeasement and Intelligence," *Intelligence and National Security* 2, no. 4 (October 1987), 60; Jeffrey L. Hughes, "The Origins of World War II in Europe: British Deterrence Failure and German Expansionism," *Journal of Interdisciplinary History* 18, no. 4 (Spring 1988), 876; Wark, *The Ultimate Enemy*, 213.

[94] "Germany," Directorate of Military Intelligence Memorandum, August 1938 – WO 190/644, 3; "Note on Germany's Present Position and Future Aims," 13. See also "Statement by the Secretary of State for Foreign Affairs to the Cabinet," CM 2 (39), January 25, 1939, CAB 23/97, 66; Norman H. Gibbs, *Grand Strategy, vol. 1: Rearmament Policy* (London: H.M.S.O., 1976), 533.

[95] Ripsman and Levy, "From Appeasement to Confrontation."

Conclusion

In both of these cases, the British government was initially inclined to accommodate rising Germany. In the late 1890s and early twentieth century, the British concluded that containing Germany would be difficult and that accommodation would be reasonable, given the multiplicity of challengers that Britain faced. Under these circumstances, the lack of a history of rivalry with Germany made it natural to focus on threats from Britain's traditional rivals, Russia and France. Only after Germany persisted in challenging British dominance over the high seas, as a leading commercial power, and in the colonial world did the British slide into a clearly defined rivalry with Germany. In the 1930s, though the British and the Germans had by then developed a history of rivalry, Britain initially settled on accommodation of German demands to revise the Versailles order in part because of the concern that the British Empire – substantially disarmed as it was after World War I (WWI) – faced too many enemies in Japan, Italy, and Germany. Thus, the British concluded that it would be unwise to provoke war with Germany through a strategy of containment, at least until they had rearmed sufficiently to face these threats. Accommodation and appeasement were therefore consequences of both weakness and a multiplicity of threats.

Furthermore, both cases also illustrate that the switch from appeasement to containment occurred as a result of actions by the rising state that demonstrated it intended to challenge the more powerful state's interests. Prior to WWI, it was the German decisions to challenge British naval supremacy and seek colonial gains that convinced British leaders that Germany constituted a serious threat to British interests. Similarly, Hitler's demonstration that he would not moderate his challenges in response to British appeasement, together with evidence of his growing hostility to Great Britain, contributed greatly to the British shift from appeasement to confrontation in 1938–39.

In this regard, both cases illustrate that accommodation as a strategy is more likely when the leaders of the existing great power perceive that they are faced with a more permissive environment, where the time frame of the rival challenge is off in the future. When adversary behavior – indications of hostility and a short-term desire to harm the existing great power's interests – indicates that a challenge is imminent, containment and confrontation are more likely to result.

The implications of these cases for the contemporary era, if they are generalizable, appear to be twofold. First, there is no reason to believe that the United States and other leading global powers, having no history of rivalry or conflictual relations with many of today's rising challengers, such as India and Brazil, will be alarmed by their rise or will attempt to contain or confront them. Nonetheless, other challengers, such as China and Russia, whom the United States is likely to view with greater suspicion on historical grounds, are less likely to be accommodated. Second, to a great extent, the choice of accommodation or containment may rest with the challengers themselves. If a rising power sends signals that its goals are non-threatening, it might coax the existing great powers to accommodate its rise. Conversely, if the rising states present themselves as challengers and potential rivals, confrontation may result.[96] In this regard, China's expansive definition of its maritime sphere of influence and Russia's adventurism in Ukraine are ominous developments.

[96] See Andrew Kydd, "Sheep in Sheep's Clothing: Why Security Seekers Do Not Fight Each Other," *Security Studies* 7, no. 1 (Autumn 1997), 114–55; Evan Montgomery, "Breaking out of the Security Dilemma: Realism, Reassurance, and the Problem of Uncertainty," *International Security* 31, no. 2 (Fall 2006), 151–85; Shiping Tang, *A Theory of Security Strategy for Our Time: Defensive Realism* (London: Palgrave Macmillan, 2010).

9 Did the United States and the Allies fail to accommodate Japan in the 1920s and the 1930s?

Jeffrey W. Taliaferro

At first glance, the steady deterioration of relations between the United States and Japan in the late 1930s, culminating in the Japanese Combined Fleet's attack on the US Pacific Fleet at Pearl Harbor, Hawaii, on December 7, 1941 and the US entry into World War II (WWII), would appear to be the textbook case of failure by an established great power (the United States) to either peacefully accommodate or successfully deter a rising challenger (Japan). The United States viewed Japan's search for autarkic economic development through territorial expansion in China and, later, South East Asia as predatory and dangerous.

Instead of acquiescing to Tokyo's territorial ambitions in East Asia or finding a way to peacefully integrate Japan into a Western-led international system, the administration of President Franklin D. Roosevelt resorted to coercive diplomacy after the outbreak of the second Sino-Japanese War in July 1937. The United States lacked the military forces and the domestic support necessary to stop the Japanese military advance in China, but nevertheless had ample coercive leverage. By 1939, Japan depended on the United States for 80 percent of its fuel products, more than 90 percent of its gasoline, more than 60 percent of its machine tools, and about 75 percent of its scrap iron.[1] As the United States, joined by the United Kingdom and the Netherlands, tightened the economic screws in 1940 and 1941, Japanese leaders pursued further conquests in South East Asia, eventually seizing the French and Dutch colonies in Indochina and the East Indies and threatening the British colonies in Singapore, Hong Kong, and Malaysia, as well as the Philippines (then a US commonwealth). After the Roosevelt administration deployed the US Pacific Fleet to Hawaii and imposed a de facto oil embargo in late July 1941, ostensibly as a deterrent, Japanese leaders adopted a two-track strategy: enter into high-level negotiations with Washington for

[1] Michael A. Barnhart, *Japan Prepares for Total War: The Search for Economic Security, 1919–1941* (Ithaca: Cornell University Press, 1987), 144–46.

a resumption of bilateral trade and recognition of Japanese territorial acquisitions since 1937, but also secretly prepare for war with the United States.

Roosevelt told a joint session of Congress the day after the Pearl Harbor attack: "The United States of America was suddenly and deliberately attacked by naval and air forces of the Empire of Japan. The United States was at peace with that nation, and, at the solicitation of Japan, was still in conversation with its government and its Emperor toward the maintenance of peace in the Pacific."[2] In asking Congress for a declaration of war, Roosevelt implied his administration desperately sought to avoid war in the Pacific and remained committed to negotiated settlement to the Sino-Japanese War and the resumption of Japanese-American trade. Instead, the government of Prime Minister General Tōjō Hideki and the chiefs of staff of the Japanese Imperial Army and Imperial Navy decided to initiate a preventive war against the United States, even while talks in Washington between Secretary of State Cordell Hull and Japanese Ambassador Nomura Kichiasburō were ongoing. Moreover, leaders in Tokyo decided to wage war knowing that, even with their recent conquests in South East Asia, the Japanese Empire lacked the economic and military capabilities to win a prolonged conflict and that any US-Japanese war would likely last several years.

In Chapter 1, T.V. Paul states how accommodation among great powers "involves mutual adaptation and acceptance by established and rising powers, and the elimination or substantial reduction of hostility between them." He writes further, "The accommodation of a rising power simply implies that the emerging power is given the status and perks associated with the rank of great power in the international system . . . It does not assume deep friendship or lack of competition."[3]

Accommodation is inextricably linked to status. Elsewhere, T.V. Paul, Deborah Welch Larson, and William C. Wohlforth define status in international politics as the "collective beliefs about a given state's ranking on valued attributes (wealth, coercive capabilities, culture, demographic position, sociopolitical organization, and diplomatic clout)."[4] Status, in

---

[2] Franklin D. Roosevelt, "Address to Congress Requesting a Declaration of War with Japan," December 8, 1941. Gerhard Peters and John T. Woolley, *The American Presidency Project.* Available at: www.presidency.ucsb.edu/ws/?pid=16053.

[3] See Chapter 1.

[4] Deborah Welch Larson, T.V. Paul, and William C. Wohlforth, "Status and World Order," in *Status in World Politics*, eds. T.V. Paul, Deborah Welch Larson, and William C. Wohlforth (New York: Cambridge University Press, 2014), 7. Other recent treatments of status in international politics include: Deborah Welch Larson and Alexei Shevchenko, "Status Seekers: Chinese and Russian Responses to US Primacy," *International Security* 34, no. 4 (Spring 2010), 63–95; William C. Wohlforth, "Unipolarity, Status Competition, and Great Power War," *World Politics* 61, no. 1 (January 2009), 28–57.

turn, is manifested in two distinct but closely related ways: first, as membership in a well-defined group of actors; and second, as relative standing within that group. Whether it involves membership in a club or relative standing within a social hierarchy, status is simultaneously collective, subjective, and relative. Furthermore, in both senses, the conferral of status can come only through the voluntary deference of other actors.[5] Accommodation involves mutual status adjustment, as well as the willingness to share leadership roles through the accordance of relevant institutional rules and privileges, something that established powers rarely afford to newcomers.[6]

Did the United States, and to a lesser extent Britain, France, and the Netherlands, lose a "window of opportunity" to peacefully accommodate a rising Japan in the 1930s? Alternatively, was Japan simply beyond the point of accommodation without major territorial adjustments in East Asia that the United States, Britain, and the other European colonial powers were not prepared to offer? I contend that in the 1930s, and especially after the outbreak of the second Sino-Japanese War in July 1937, Japan was beyond the point of accommodation with respect to its territorial demands in East Asia. The window of opportunity for the United States and Britain to accommodate Japan by redressing Tokyo's regional security concerns and aspirations had closed by the mid-1920s, as I discuss later in the chapter.

That said, war between Japan and the United States and Britain was not inevitable in the late 1930s and did not even become likely until the imposition of the American oil embargo in late July 1941. As I have argued elsewhere, the Roosevelt administration manipulated the 1940–41 crisis with Japan as an indirect route to bringing the United States into the European war against Germany. President Roosevelt and Secretary of State Hull even rebuffed efforts by the Japanese prime minister, Konoe Fumimaro, and his successor, Tōjō, to negotiate a settlement that might have avoided war between the United States and Japan in late summer and autumn 1941.[7] Indeed, upon closer examination, the record of Japanese expansion in the 1930s and the ensuing 1940–41

---

[5] Larson, Paul, and Wohlforth, "Status and World Order," 7–8.   [6] See Chapter 1.

[7] Jeffrey W. Taliaferro, "Strategy of Innocence or Calculated Provocation? The Roosevelt Administration's Road to World War II," in *The Challenge of Grand Strategy: The Great Powers and the Broken Balance between the Wars*, eds. Jeffrey W. Taliaferro, Norrin M. Ripsman, and Steven E. Lobell (Cambridge: Cambridge University Press, 2012), 193–223. Other recent variants of the "back door to war" thesis include John M. Schuessler, "The Deception Dividend: FDR's Undeclared War," *International Security* 34, no. 4 (Spring 2010), 133–65; Marc Trachtenberg, *The Craft of International History: A Guide to Methods* (Princeton: Princeton University Press, 2006), 79–139. The classic treatment of the thesis is Charles Callan Tansill, *Back Door to War: The Roosevelt Foreign Policy, 1933–1941* (Westport: Greenwood Press, 1975).

United States–Japan crisis does not fit neatly into the rising challenger versus status quo hegemon framework.

In the 1930s, Japanese leaders did not see their country as a "rising" challenger, but rather as a great power on the precipice of relative decline in an increasingly threatening strategic environment in East Asia. Drawing upon neoclassical realism, I contend that fear of perceived losses in Japan's relative power and international status drove much of the grand strategic thinking in Tokyo throughout the 1930s and especially in the 1940–41 period.[8] The international system – that is, the relative distribution of material power and anticipated power trends – set the parameters of Japanese grand strategic adjustment. Yet those systemic forces were mediated through the prism of Japanese leaders' subjective assessments of the international environment and the constraints imposed upon them by domestic institutions.

Japanese leaders perceived their country as facing strong and conditional systemic constraints in East Asia, especially after the start of the Great Depression. Chief among these systemic constraints were the resurgence of Soviet military presence in East Asia, the political turmoil in China, which might have prompted the Soviet Union or the Western great powers to try to exploit the power vacuum on the Asian mainland, and the growing fear that, since future wars would likely be attritional struggles like World War I (WWI), Japan was increasingly vulnerable to embargo by foreign suppliers of oil, tin, iron ore, and other raw materials – namely, the United States, Britain, France, and the Netherlands.

Before we continue, several caveats are in order. What follows is not an effort to test competing hypotheses that might explain the failure of the United States, Britain, and other established powers to either accommodate or deter (or contain) a "rising" Japan in the 20 years between the two world wars. Nor do I test competing hypotheses that might explain variation in Japanese grand strategy during the period. Rather, my purpose is merely to illustrate the difficulties of successful accommodation or deterrence from the perspective of the dissatisfied power.

Due to space constraints, I largely focus on Japanese grand strategic adjustment from the 1920s to the early 1940s. As Chapter 1 suggests, Japan has traditionally been seen as the "rising" challenger to the

---

[8] For overviews of neoclassical realism, see Gideon Rose, "Neoclassical Realism and Theories of Foreign Policy," *World Politics* 51, no. 1 (October 1998), 144–77; Jeffrey W. Taliaferro, Steven E. Lobell, and Norrin M. Ripsman, "Introduction: Neoclassical Realism, the State, and Foreign Policy," in *Neoclassical Realism, the State, and Foreign Policy*, eds. Steven E. Lobell, Norrin M. Ripsman, and Jeffrey W. Taliaferro (New York: Cambridge University Press, 2009), 1–41.

international status quo in East Asia in the first half of the twentieth century. Japanese leaders unquestionably had revisionist aims and pursued expansionist foreign and security policies, but my central claim is that fear of relative decline and loss of international prestige drove those leaders' calculations and strategic choices in the 1930s and early 1940s. The dependent variable, therefore, is Japanese grand strategic adjustment from the end of WWI until the outbreak of WWII in the Pacific.

Furthermore, since one of my points of contention is that the United States, Britain, France, and the Netherlands did not in fact miss a "window of opportunity" to accommodate Japan's territorial ambitions in East Asia (or at least accommodate Japan symbolically) in the late 1930s, but rather in the 1920s, it seems more sensible to focus on Japanese grand strategy than on the strategies of the "established" great powers. Although the United States had roughly eight times as much potential power as Japan in 1941 and would go on to defeat and dismantle the Japanese Empire in 1945, in the interwar period the United States "punched well under its weight" relative to every other great power in terms of military expenditures (both in absolute terms and as a percentage of gross domestic product), military personnel, army divisions, tanks, and combat aircraft.[9]

The remainder of this chapter is organized as follows. The next section briefly defines grand strategy and strategic adjustment. A brief discussion of neoclassical realism follows in the third section, where I explicate the hypothesized causal relationship between "objective" shifts in the relative distribution of power in the international system and changes in particular great powers' strategic environments, on the one hand, and the politics of grand strategic adjustment, on the other. The fourth section outlines Japanese grand strategy in the 1920s – the era of the so-called Taishō hybrid grand strategy or Shidehara diplomacy – when, arguably, the United States, Great Britain, France, and other powers had an opportunity to accommodate Japan's great power status at least symbolically, if not in terms of actual acknowledgment of Japanese security claims on the Asian mainland and in the Pacific. In the fifth section, I examine how systemic forces filtered through the medium of Japanese elites' calculations to produce the strategic expectation of creating a New Order in East Asia in the late 1930s and the various military and diplomatic initiatives toward that end, culminating in the decision for war with the United States in November 1941. Chief among these were decisions to: (1) expand the Japanese Empire into the Dutch East Indies to acquire the

---

[9] John A. Thompson, "Conceptions of National Security and American Entry into World War II," *Diplomacy & Statecraft* 16, no. 4 (November 2005), 671–97.

oil and raw materials needed to continue the war in China; (2) use diplomacy and, later, military force to stop the flow of arms to the Kuomintang (KMT or Chinese Nationalist) regime of Chiang Kai-shek; (3) conclude a military alliance with Germany and Italy as a means of deterring the United States and Britain; and (4) ultimately wage a preventive war – knowing that Japan could not win a prolonged conflict with the United States and that any US-Japanese conflict might last several years. The conclusion briefly discusses some implications for the accommodation or containment of emerging powers in the twenty-first century.

Grand strategy and grand strategic adjustment

Elsewhere, Norrin Ripsman, Steven Lobell, and I define grand strategy as a set of principles or a blueprint that organizes and animates all aspects of a state's relations with the world beyond its borders for the purposes of securing itself and maximizing its interests.[10] Grand strategy encompasses more than just military doctrine, force posture, and weapons acquisition decision. It is more than the particular foreign policies that one state may pursue toward another state or an entire geographic region at any given point in time. Instead, grand strategy shapes (or, at least, ought to shape) the parameters of the foreign, economic, and military strategies that states pursue toward all external actors. Grand strategy is a future-oriented enterprise – it requires the continual assessment of external threats and external opportunities, as well as the specific material, political, and ideological objectives of the state. The foreign policy executive – which Ripsman, Lobell, and I define as the top decision-makers within the state who are charged with the formulation of foreign and security policies – has the task not only of assessing current international threats and opportunities and identifying the resources (both material and human) needed to redress or exploit them, but also of assessing threats and opportunities that may (or may not) arise in the future, and the possible resources and strategies required to meet them. At the same time, grand strategy need not be limited to the mitigation of international threats, and often encompasses the pursuit of objectives far beyond the preservation of a state's physical security, territorial integrity, and political autonomy.

[10]   Steven E. Lobell, Jeffrey W. Taliaferro, and Norrin M. Ripsman, "Introduction: Grand Strategy between the World Wars," in *The Challenge of Grand Strategy: The Great Powers and the Broken Balance between the World Wars*, eds. Jeffrey W. Taliaferro, Norrin M. Ripsman, and Steven E. Lobell (Cambridge: Cambridge University Press, 2012), 14–15.

Any state's grand strategy includes three interrelated and dynamic political processes, typically involving the foreign policy executive, a set of support state institutions, and various domestic interest groups: the politics of threat assessment, the politics of grand strategic adjustment, and the politics of implementation. In the interest of space, I will not go into detail here.[11]

Neoclassical realism: systems, clarity, and strategic environments

Neoclassical realism, like neorealism (or structural realism), proceeds from the supposition that the international system, specifically anarchy or the absence of a universal sovereign and the relative distribution of material capabilities, defines the parameters of the external strategies those states will likely pursue. However, whereas neorealism largely focuses on the external constraints imposed by system polarity and anticipated power trends, neoclassical realism also emphasizes the clarity of a particular state's strategic environment. There are two important aspects of clarity: (1) the degree of clarity about the systemic constraints and opportunities a state faces; and (2) the degree of clarity about the appropriate or optimal responses to those constraints and opportunities.[12]

The proximate cause of the emergence of modern Japan was the demise of the Sino-centric interstate system that had existed in East and South East Asia for the previous 500 years.[13] Technological change and diffusion in the West, specifically the advent of the steamship and advances in firearms, increased those states' ability to project military power over longer distances. By the mid-nineteenth century, a single global interstate system largely subsumed the previously autonomous systems in other regions of the globe.[14] Thus, modern Japan was "born" into a highly

---

[11] For more information, see Taliaferro, Lobell, and Ripsman, "Introduction," 31–32.

[12] Norrin M. Ripsman, Jeffrey W. Taliaferro, and Steven E. Lobell, "Conclusion: The State of Neoclassical Realism," in *Neoclassical Realism, the State, and Foreign Policy*, eds. Steven E. Lobell, Norrin M. Ripsman, and Jeffrey W. Taliaferro (New York: Cambridge University Press, 2009), 282–87.

[13] See David C. Kang, *East Asia before the West: Five Centuries of Trade and Tribute, Contemporary Asia in the World* (New York: Columbia University Press, 2010).

[14] Barry Buzan and Ole Wæver, *Regions and Powers: The Structure of International Security* (Cambridge: Cambridge University Press, 2003); David B. Ralston, *Importing the European Army: The Introduction of European Military Techniques and Institutions into the Extra-European World, 1600–1914* (Chicago: University of Chicago Press, 1990), chapter 6.

competitive and geographically expanding multipolar international system. That system's center of gravity was in Europe, where most of the other great powers were located. Systemic constraints on great powers and non-great powers alike were often strong and conditional.[15]

During the period between 1850 and 1941, Japan confronted three impending power shifts in East Asia and across the globe, and corresponding rules established by the great powers to govern the international system: (1) the collapse of the Sino-centric international system and the imposition of imperial rule over large portions of East and South East Asia by the Western powers in the mid-nineteenth century; (2) the weakening of the European imperialist order in East Asia during WWI and the United States' emergence as a major military and economic player in the region; and, finally, (3) the onset of the Great Depression (and with it, the breakdown of global trade) and the resurgence of Soviet military power in East Asia in the early 1930s. Each of these power transitions precipitated major adjustments in Japan's grand strategy.

Pre-WWII Japan actually pursued three distinct and successive grand strategies: (1) a grand strategy of emulation and regional consolidation pursued for the entire Meiji period (also called the Meiji consensus of "rich nation, strong army"); (2) a "hybrid" grand strategy during much of the Taishō period, marked by attempts to exploit the power vacuums in East Asia created by WWI, the Bolshevik Revolution and Russian Civil War, and China's descent into near state failure, on the one hand, and attempts to bolster Japan's global stature by adherence to the new liberal international order championed by the United States and Britain, on the other; and (3) a grand strategy of concerted autarky and military expansion in Manchuria, the northern provinces of China, and, later, South East Asia during the early Shōwa era (the so-called Konoe consensus or the "New Order in East Asia").[16]

Only prewar Japan's latter two grand strategies – the Taishō hybrid strategy in the 1910s and 1920s and the Konoe consensus or quest for a New Order in East Asia in the 1930s – are relevant to the present volume, since the European great powers and the United States really began to recognize Japan as a rising power in East Asia (and a potential great power) only after the 1904–05 Russo-Japanese War. Nonetheless,

---

[15] See Stephen G. Brooks and William C. Wohlforth, *World out of Balance: International Relations and the Challenge of American Primacy* (Princeton: Princeton University Press, 2008), 13–15.

[16] See Richard J. Samuels, *Securing Japan: Tokyo's Grand Strategy and the Future of East Asia* (Ithaca: Cornell University Press, 2007), 13–28. This typology of Japanese grand strategies does not exactly coincide with the reigns of Japan's modern emperors.

from the Meiji Restoration onward, enhancement of Japan's international status, and its eventual recognition as an "equal" by the Western great powers, especially Britain, France, and the United States, was the overriding strategic objective of the Japanese foreign policy executive.

This begs the question of what might have communicated Britain, France, the United States, and the other powers' acceptance of Japan as a full-fledged member of the "great power club."[17] Paul defines full accommodation as the "recognition of a rising power's position in a leadership role in the conduct of international politics in both security and economic areas, through appropriate status recognition within global institutions and consultative mechanisms where its voice is given substantial weight among its peers."[18] This definition suggests two subsidiary questions: First, during WWI and the decade that followed, what exactly did Japan seek from the "established" great powers? Second, what were the United States, Britain, and others actually prepared to offer Japan?

There were several areas of contestation between Japan and the established great powers, including naval armaments, international trade, the League of Nations, Japanese immigration to the United States, and the role of perceived racial hierarchies in underpinning all of them.[19] However, I submit that the most significant area of dispute between Japan and the West, and the one that I address at length in this chapter, revolved around Japan's claim of an exclusive sphere of influence on the Asian mainland – principally in China. On this point, Japanese leaders believed their claims legitimate and quite reasonable, both given their country's relative capabilities and geographic proximity to the mainland and given the precedents set by the "established" great powers. After all, the British Empire had long claimed exclusive spheres of influence in various parts of the globe that were geographically distant from the British Isles, such as the Indian subcontinent. Since the declaration of the Monroe Doctrine in 1832, the United States had claimed the entire western hemisphere as its sphere of influence. Similarly, civilian and military leaders in Tokyo

---

[17] Arguably, this is a counterfactual question, since, as I discuss further on, the United States, Britain, and other powers were not, in fact, willing to fully accommodate a rising Japan in the 1910s and 1920s. On the use of counterfactuals in qualitative social science research, see Philip Tetlock and Aaron Belkin, eds., *Counterfactual Thought Experiments in World Politics: Logical, Methodological, and Psychological Perspectives* (Princeton: Princeton University Press, 1996).

[18] See Chapters 1 and 3.

[19] For two recent studies on the impact of Western racial hierarchies and perceived status immobility on pre-WWII Japanese foreign policy, see Zoltán I. Búzás, "The Color of Threat: Race, Threat Perception, and the Demise of the Anglo-Japanese Alliance (1902–1923)," *Security Studies* 22, no. 4 (November 2013), 573–606; Steven Ward, "Race, Status, and Japanese Revisionism in the Early 1930s," *Security Studies* 22, no. 4 (November 2013), 607–39.

sought Western great powers' recognition of a Japanese sphere of influence in East Asia, principally in China. This was a particular "status marker" that the United States, Britain, and other powers, who had their own economic interests in China, were simply never prepared to cede to Japan.[20]

Perhaps had the Western great powers been willing to recognize an informal Japanese sphere of influence in northern China (in addition to the existing Japanese colony in Korea and the leased territory in South Manchuria, acquired from Russia after the 1904–05 Russo-Japanese War) during WWI or the 1920s, they might have accommodated Japan. Again, such recognition was not something that the United States, Britain, and France (let alone Bolshevik Russia, which was Japan's principal antagonist in the region) were prepared to offer, as explained later in the chapter. Furthermore, the onset of the Great Depression marked a real turning point in Japanese leaders' conception of their country's security requirements. As discussed further on, mid-level army officers, nationalist politicians, and some civil servants made arguments in the 1920s about the strategic necessity of autarkic economic policies and territorial conquest in China. After the collapse of world markets in 1930–31, those arguments began to receive a more sympathetic hearing at the highest levels of Japan's military and civilian leaderships. And ultimately, it was Japan's pursuit of a New Order in East Asia in the 1930s – which entailed an effort to impose direct Japanese rule in central and coastal China (proper) after 1937 – and the resulting opposition of the United States and Britain that precipitated the outbreak of the Pacific War.

Taishō grand strategy: East Asian ambition or Western diplomacy, 1912–1926

During the Taishō era, Japanese grand strategy pursued two paths that became increasingly mutually exclusive. In East Asia, Japan attempted to fill power vacuums in northern China and the Russian Far Eastern Provinces resulting from the collapse of the Qing (Manchu) dynasty in 1912 and the Bolshevik Revolution in 1917. On the world stage, Japan sought to enhance its stature as a "modern" great power and an equal to the West by participating in the new liberal international order championed by President Woodrow Wilson. Yet, the Twenty-One Demands that Japanese Foreign Minister Katō Takaaki issued to China in

---

[20] On "status markers" see Larson, Paul, and Wohlforth, "Status and World Order," 10.

January 1915 and the 80 000 Japanese troops that the cabinet of Prime Minister Terauchi Masatake dispatched as part of the Siberian intervention in 1918 had the unintended effects of stoking Chinese nationalism, incurring the enmity of the new Bolshevik regime in Moscow, and exacerbating American and British suspicion of Japan simultaneously. These events reflected two enduring (and unresolved) questions: Should Japan seek acceptance by the Western great powers through participation in the League of Nations and by agreeing to naval arms limitations? Alternatively, should Japan unilaterally seek security through territorial expansion in East Asia?[21]

On the eve of WWI, Foreign Minister Katō favored keeping Russia out of Manchuria by maintaining the 1902 Anglo-Japanese alliance, even if doing so meant declaring war on Germany (which Japan did in August 1914). Field Marshal Yamagata Aritomo, the "father" of the Japanese Imperial Army, a former chief of the Army General Staff, and a two-time former prime minister, and his protégé, General Tanaka Giichi, another future army chief of staff and prime minister, actually welcomed the outbreak of war in Europe as an opportunity to develop an "autonomous" military program and to push Westerners out of East Asia, possibly through a Sino-Japanese alliance. As the war in Europe ended, the navy wanted to increase the size of the fleet to deal with the multiple threats posed by the combined United States, British, and German fleets, while the army planned for renewed hostilities with Russia, but considered the United States and China as secondary threats. The 1918 revision of the Imperial Defense Policy simply incorporated both services' military strategies, without any attempt to reconcile them with each other or with diplomatic initiatives undertaken by the cabinet of Prime Minister Hara Takashi (Kei).[22]

During the final year of WWI and in the immediate postwar period, Japanese leaders had to contend with new international threats and opportunities. The Russian Revolution and the 1918 Treaty of Brest-Litovsk between Russia and Germany threatened Japan's control of German territories seized in 1914 and jeopardized the concessions obtained from the tsarist government in 1916. Furthermore, the Terauchi cabinet and the military leadership, like their counterparts in London, Paris, and

---

[21] James W. Morley, *The Japanese Thrust into Siberia, 1918* (New York: Columbia University Press, 1957), 310; Kenneth B. Pyle, *Japan Rising: The Resurgence of Japanese Power and Purpose*, 1 edn. (New York: Public Affairs, 2007), 150; Samuels, *Securing Japan*, 17.

[22] Frederick R. Dickinson, *War and National Reinvention: Japan in the Great War, 1914–1919* (Cambridge: Harvard University Press, 1999), 36–48; Pyle, *Japan Rising*, 140–42.

Washington, genuinely feared the spread of Bolshevism. On the other hand, the collapse of the tsarist Russian army gave Japan an opportunity to expand it influence in Siberia and northern China, as hedge against a future resurgence of Russian power.[23]

Turmoil in China posed another threat to Japanese interests. The Chinese Republic's control over northern Manchuria and other parts of the country was non-existent. The Japanese army and government engaged in an intricate game of power politics with various Chinese warlords.[24] Meanwhile, Japan's relations with the Western great powers became more complex. The Anglo-Japanese alliance, a cornerstone of Japanese diplomacy and defense policy since 1902, came up for renewal or replacement in 1921. It was obvious that Britain was highly unlikely to join Japan in a possible war against the United States. Therefore, Japan would have to find some security mechanism to replace it.[25]

Lastly, growing American strategic and economic interests in East Asia and the Pacific posed a particular challenge for Japanese elites. The causes of friction in US-Japanese relations in the late 1910s and early 1920s revolved around continued US insistence on the "Open Door" in China, the size of the Japanese force deployed as part of the 1918 Siberian intervention, naval armaments, and later, the US Congress's passage of the 1924 Immigration Act, which slashed the quota of Japanese allowed to immigrate to the United States.

It is fair to say that so-called militarists within and outside the Japanese foreign policy executive were wary of the growth of US power in East Asia and were implacably hostile toward Wilson's liberal internationalist vision from the outset. Wilson's rejection of the Japanese proposal for inclusion of racial equality in the League of Nations' Covenant was a bitter blow and served to confirm the hypocrisy of the Anglo-American powers.[26] Yet, aspects of Wilson's "new diplomacy" resonated with some politicians and diplomats, such as Hara Kei (until his assassination in 1921) and, especially, Baron Shidehara Kijūrō, Japan's ambassador to Washington from 1919 to1924, foreign minister from 1924 to 1926, and

[23] See Hosoya Chihiro, "The Tripartite Pact," in *Deterrent Diplomacy: Japan, Germany, and the USSR, 1935–1940*, ed. James W. Morley (New York: Columbia University Press, 1976), 149–158; Morley, *The Japanese Thrust into Siberia*, 55 and 94; Ian H. Nish, *Japanese Foreign Policy, 1869–1942: Kasumigaseki to Miyakezaka* (London: Routledge, 1977), 106–11.

[24] John Whitney Hall and Marius B. Jansen, *Studies in the Institutional History of Early Modern Japan* (Princeton: Princeton University Press, 1968), 512–17.

[25] Charles A. Kupchan, *How Enemies Become Friends: The Sources of Stable Peace* (Princeton: Princeton University Press, 2010), Chapter 4. See also Ian H. Nish, *Alliance in Decline: A Study in Anglo-Japanese Relations, 1908–23* (London: Athlone Press, 1972).

[26] See Ward, "Race, Status, and Japanese Revisionism," 629–31.

prime minister from 1930 to 1931. "Shidehara diplomacy" represented Japan's first attempt at an economics-oriented foreign policy.[27]

Far from accepting Wilson's rhetoric at face value, however, Shidehara (among other Japanese leaders) reached a number of conclusions based upon sober assessments of the international balance of power. Japan could more easily achieve prosperity and security through free trade with the Western great powers, rather than through continued territorial expansion in East Asia. While Shidehara did not advocate surrendering Japanese colonies in Taiwan and Korea, he was prepared to return to China parts of Shandong seized from Germany in 1914 in exchange for US and British recognition of Japan's interests elsewhere in China. He even advocated active Japanese participation in the League of Nations as a means to secure those objectives.

Shidehara also recognized the futility of a naval arms race with Britain and the United States. During WWI, all of the great powers embarked upon massive naval armament programs. None of them could sustain the pace of naval expansion or maintain large battleship fleets in peacetime, but each needed assurances that limitations on future naval construction would not disadvantage them in future competition. Shidehara was willing to have Japan's naval strength frozen in a subordinate position, but in exchange Britain, the United States, France, and Japan would have to pledge mutual respect for one another's East Asian mandates and colonies and agree to resolve disputes peacefully.

The 1921–22 Washington Conference convened by Secretary of State Charles Evans Hughes produced a network of multilateral treaties that set parameters for defense and economic relations in the Pacific for the next decade. A Four-Power Pact replaced the Anglo-Japanese alliance and committed the signatories to respect the status quo in the Pacific and to consult with one another if the security interests of any one power were threatened. The 1922 Naval Arms Limitation Treaty imposed a moratorium on construction of battleships and heavy cruisers and adopted a tonnage ratio for existing capital ships of 10 for the United States and Britain, 6 for Japan, and 1.75 for France and Italy. Furthermore, it obligated the signatories not to build additional naval bases in the Pacific Ocean, except on Hawaii, Singapore, and the Japanese islands. The Nine-Power Treaty obligated the parties to respect Chinese sovereignty, maintain the Open Door in trade, and cooperate to help the Republic of China regain control over its territory.

Shidehara advocated a policy of non-intervention in China's domestic politics, recognizing that the KMT under Chiang would likely succeed

---

[27] Samuels, *Securing Japan*, 23–24.

in reunifying the country and that such a development would be compatible with Japanese economic interests, as long as the KMT kept the communists under control. Japan, he argued, could expand its influence in China through trade, investment, and ostensible compliance with the Open Door principle, rather than by supporting various Chinese warlords or resorting to excessive military force and "gunboat diplomacy."[28] Shidehara's China policies ran directly counter to the actions of the Kwantung Army, including its support for Chang Tso-lin's separatist regime in Manchuria.[29]

Soviet Russia's renewed military presence in Siberia by 1925 prompted the Army General Staff to push for the construction of five new railway lines in northern Manchuria to reinforce the Kwantung Army. When the local warlord, Chang Tso-lin (the "old marshal"), reneged on a deal with the Japanese government-owned South Manchurian Railway (SMR) by casting his lot with the KMT in May 1928, Prime Minister Tanaka ordered the Kwantung Army into Mukden (Shenyang) to disarm him. A month later, Col. Kōmoto Daisaku, a staff officer assigned to the Kwantung Army HQ, arranged to have the railway car in which Chang rode blown up as the train entered Manchuria. Chang's son and successor Chang Hsueh-ling (the "young marshal") pledged his allegiance to the Republic of China in 1929 (though he would later betray Chiang Kai-shek in 1936) and refused to allow the SMR to build any railways through his territory. The murder of the elder Chang and the army's subsequent refusal to conduct an investigation led to Tanaka's resignation and effectively ended any chance of an "independent" Manchuria friendly to Japan. The cover-up set the stage for the next crisis two years later.[30]

Finally, the onset of the Great Depression and Congress's passage of the Smoot–Hawley Tariff Act in 1930, which closed American markets to Japanese exports, marked a turning point in US-Japanese relations. The intent of Smoot–Hawley was to protect domestic manufacturers from

[28] Akira Iriye, *After Imperialism: The Search for a New Order in the Far East, 1921–1931* (Boston: Athenaeum, 1969), 56–88; Akira Iriye, "The Failure of Economic Expansionism: 1918–1931," in *Japan in Crisis: Critical Essays on Taishō Democracy*, eds. Bernard S. Silberman and Harry D. Harootunian (Princeton: Princeton University Press, 1974), 237–69; Robert Gordon Kaufman, *Arms Control During the Pre-Nuclear Era: The United States and Naval Limitation between the Two World Wars* (New York: Columbia University Press, 1990); Samuels, *Securing Japan*, 24–25.

[29] For the origins of the Kwantung Army, see Akira Iriye, *Japan and the Wider World: From the Mid-Nineteenth Century to the Present* (London: Longman, 1997), 1–16.

[30] Barnhart, *Japan Prepares for Total War*, 30–31; Iriye, *Japan and the Wider World*, 14–16; see also Katsumi Usui, "The Role of the Foreign Ministry," in *Pearl Harbor as History: Japanese-American Relations, 1931–1941*, eds. Dorothy Borg and Shumpei Okamoto (New York: Columbia University Press, 1973), 339–40.

foreign competition, rather than to punish Japanese encroachments into Manchuria. The unintended consequence, however, was that it encouraged Japanese expansionists who pressed for economic advantage by military conquest.[31]

It is important to remember that the international system did not preordain increased tensions among Japan, China, and the United States in the 1920s, any more than the 1919 Paris Peace Settlement made the outbreak of WWII twenty years later "inevitable." Leaders in Tokyo, like their counterparts in other capitals, made strategic calculations based upon subjective assessments of relative power and anticipated power trends, but always subject to domestic constraints. Systemic constraints on Japan were far weaker in the 1920s than they would be in the 1930s. As neoclassical realism would expect, these weaker systemic constraints had three implications for Japanese grand strategy. Since the international system provided little unambiguous information about the "optimal" strategies, there was considerable disagreement within the Japanese foreign policy executive over the appropriate way to secure national interests, the tradeoffs between short-term military security and longer-term economic prosperity, and the time horizons for redressing the latent threat posed by Bolshevik Russia and the US and British navies and the more immediate threat posed by China's turmoil.[32]

Japanese grand strategy in the 1930s: the New Order in East Asia

With the onset of the Great Depression, three "nightmare" scenarios in East Asia preoccupied civilian politicians, civil servants, and military planners in Tokyo. First, drawing upon the "lessons" of Germany's defeat in WWI, Japanese officials became increasingly fearful that the United States, Britain, and the Netherlands might cut off the raw materials upon which the Japanese economy depended. The onset of the Great Depression and the subsequent adoption of protectionist policies by the United States and Britain undermined arguments that economic growth through trade was a viable means for Japan to achieve security.[33] As the historian Akira Iriye writes, "The collapse of the American market,

---

[31] Edward S. Miller, *Bankrupting the Enemy: The US Financial Siege of Japan before Pearl Harbor* (Annapolis: Naval Institute Press, 2007), 51.

[32] For a discussion, see Mark R. Brawley, *Political Economy and Grand Strategy: A Neoclassical Realist View* (New York: Routledge, 2009), chapter 1.

[33] Dale C. Copeland, "Economic Interdependence and the Grand Strategies of Germany and Japan, 1925–1941," in *The Challenge of Grand Strategy: The Great Powers and the Broken Balance between the World Wars*, eds. Jeffrey W. Taliaferro, Norrin M. Ripsman, and Steven E. Lobell (Cambridge: Cambridge University Press, 2012), 137–38.

the decline of trade in China, and the failure to achieve any degree of constructive cooperation with the powers in China, all meant the removal of the basic rationale for Japan's economic diplomacy."[34] One could speculate that a partial reopening of its markets to Japanese exports would have been a tangible way for the United States to accommodate Japan. However, lowering tariff barriers never received serious discussion in Washington or any other major capital. Instead, the great powers responded to the economic downtown by creating narrow trade and finance blocs.

Second, Japanese army planners were extremely wary of the resurgence of Soviet military power in the Far East following the upheaval of the 1918 Bolshevik Revolution and the 1922–24 Russian Civil War. Indeed, in the decades following the 1904–05 Russo-Japanese War, the Army General Staff in Tokyo assumed it would be only a matter of time before Russia (formally the Soviet Union from 1922) recovered the military capability to threaten Japan's colony in Korea and its leased territories in southern Manchuria and South Sakhalin, and by extension the Japanese home islands.[35]

Third, officials in Tokyo became increasing concerned that continued political turmoil in China proper would spill over into southern Manchuria or invite other great powers – the USSR, Britain, France, or, more implausibly, the United States – to seek to fill the power vacuum and to protect their own interests in the region. Consequently, beginning in 1931, Japan embarked upon a campaign of measured expansion into Manchuria. Later, the Japanese army pushed into the northern provinces of China proper. The stated goal of expansion on the Asian mainland was autarky, and thereby greater economic security vis-à-vis the Western great powers, as well as greater strategic depth vis-à-vis the Soviet Union.[36]

The Shōwa grand strategy of the "New Order in East Asia" grew out of prolonged debates within the Japanese foreign policy executive about the nature of external threats and the appropriate strategies to counter them, followed very often by epic battles between the Imperial Army and the Imperial Navy over resource allocation and strategic priorities. As mentioned earlier, many of these strategic concepts originated with

---

[34] Iriye, *After Imperialism*, 283.

[35] Jonathan Haslam, *The Soviet Union and the Threat from the East, 1933–41: Moscow, Tokyo, and the Prelude to the Pacific War* (Pittsburgh, PA: University of Pittsburgh Press, 1992), 7–37; Ōhata Tokushirō, "The Anti-Comintern Pact," in *Deterrent Diplomacy: Japan, Germany, and the USSR, 1935–1940*, ed. James W. Morley (New York: Columbia University Press, 1976), 9–111.

[36] This section selectively draws upon Jeffrey W. Taliaferro, *Balancing Risks: Great Power Intervention in the Periphery* (Ithaca: Cornell University Press, 2004), 94–131.

mid-level army officers in the 1920s. By the early 1930s, more senior military officers, civil servants, and politicians had embraced them. The core elements of this grand strategy were largely in place by the mid-1930s. However, the "formal" proclamation of the creation of a "New Order in East Asia" (*Tōa Sin Chitsujo*) as the overriding grand strategic aim came relatively late, in a speech delivered by Prime Minister Konoe in November 1938,[37] in which he argued that henceforth Japanese grand strategy would strive to "secure international justice, perfect joint defense against communism, and create a new culture . . . The establishment of a new order in East Asia . . . is the exalted responsibility with which our generation is trusted."[38] Konoe further stated, "Our empire wholly trusts the [Western great] powers to add themselves to this new situation in East Asia by accurately recognizing the real intention of our empire."[39] This remained the core objective of Japanese grand strategy during the "caretaker" cabinets of Baron Hiranuma Kiichirō, General Abe Nobuyake, and Admiral Yonai Mitsumasa, in office between January 1939 and July 1940.

In August 1940, after the (second) Konoe cabinet and the military chiefs of staff approved the deployment of Japanese troops to French Indochina and the use of coercive diplomacy to secure larger oil shipments from the Dutch East Indies, Konoe and Foreign Minister Matsouka Yōsuke broadened the New Order into the grandiose vision of creating a "Greater East Asia Co-Prosperity Sphere," a Japanese empire stretching from Sakhalin and Manchukuo in the north to the Dutch East Indies, French Indochina, and other European colonies in South East Asia.[40]

Mid-level army officers such as Ugaki Kazunari, Kosio Kuniaki, Suzuki Teichi, Nagata Tetsuzan, and most notably Ishiwara Kanji first and most forcefully articulated arguments in favor of autarky and territorial expansion in the 1920s. The notion that Japan could best provide for its long-term security through empire and autarky had its origins in the lessons these officers (and others) drew from the German defeat in WWI. Since future wars would likely be attritional conflicts, victory would largely depend on a state's ability to mobilize economic resources. This would

[37] Usui Katsumi, "The Politics of War, 1937–1941," in *The China Quagmire: Japan's Expansion on the Asian Continent, 1933–1941*, ed. James W. Morley (New York: Columbia University Press, 1983).

[38] Quoted in Hosoya Chihiro, "Retrogression in Japan's Foreign Policy Decision-Making Process," in *Dilemmas of Growth in Prewar Japan*, ed. James W. Morley (Princeton: Princeton University Press, 1971), 91.

[39] Cited in Nobuya Bamba, *Japanese Diplomacy in a Dilemma: New Light on Japan's China Policy, 1924–1929* (Vancouver: University of British Columbia Press, 1972), 376.

[40] Samuels, *Securing Japan*, 28.

require the complete mobilization of national economies for warfare and dramatic increases in the extractive capacity of the state. States not self-reliant in raw materials, especially oil, iron ore, rubber, tin, and food-stuffs, were acutely vulnerable to economic blockade. In an age of "total warfare," economies of scale and the acquisition of large tracts of territory were not only desirable, but also critical for a great power's very survival. For Japan, expansion into regions such as Manchuria, followed by several years of intense industrial development in peacetime, seemed the most reasonable means of attaining economic self-sufficiency and thereby enhancing Japan's strategic position in East Asia. In the mid-1920s, a clique of "total war" army officers, many of whom had studied in Germany, began to lobby for territorial expansion abroad and coordinated industrial planning at home to attain economic self-sufficiency and thus security.[41]

A good number of politicians, civil servants, diplomats, and academicians reached similar conclusions about Japan's security requirements. Chief among them were Konoe and Matsuoka, both of whom had served in the Japanese delegation to the 1919 Paris Peace Conference led by Saioniji.[42] In November 1933, Konoe, then president of the House of Peers, created the Shōwa Research Association (*Shōwa Kenkyūkai*), his personal think tank and shadow cabinet. The Shōwa Research Association, which eventually included leading academics such as Tokyo University professor Rōyama Masamichi and the disillusioned former liberal journalist Ishibashi Tanzan, became the major source of advocacy research on wartime mobilization, corporatist economic policies, and the necessity of Japanese expansion.[43]

After resigning from the diplomatic service in 1922, Matsuoka went on to become the vice president of the SMR, in which capacity he negotiated the abortive deal with Chang Tso-lin for the construction of five new railway lines through Manchuria in 1928. He subsequently became Japan's chief delegate to the Assembly of the League of Nations in Geneva, where he staged a dramatic walkout in February 1932 in protest of the Lytton Commission Report condemning the Japanese annexation of Manchuria. David J. Lu observes that Matsuoka came to symbolize a mixture of "national trauma and schizophrenia" that gripped Japan in the aftermath

---

[41] On the origins "total war" planning, see Barnhart, *Japan Prepares for Total War*, 22–49; Mark R. Peattie, *Ishiwara Kanji and Japan's Confrontation with the West* (Princeton: Princeton University Press, 1975), 223–65.

[42] See Yoshitake Oka, *Konoe Fumimaro: A Political Biography* (Tokyo: University of Tokyo Press, 1983); Kazuo Yagami, *Konoe Fumimaro and the Failure of Peace in Japan, 1937–1941: A Critical Appraisal of the Three-Time Prime Minister* (Jefferson: McFarland & Company, 2006), esp. 41–74.

[43] Samuels, *Securing Japan*, 27.

of the Mukden incident. Professionally, Matsouka believed strongly in the value of cooperation with Britain and the United States, but he also saw control of Manchuria as vital to Japanese security. At the same time, throughout his career, he had a fatalistic vision of Japan's mission and national honor.[44]

The decision by the (first) Konoe cabinet and the Army General Staff to escalate a skirmish between Japanese and Chinese troops near Beijing in July 1937 into a full-scale war to topple the KMT regime of Chiang Kai-shek and consolidate control over central China proved to be a turning point.[45] The Army General Staff estimated that three months, three divisions, and ¥100 million would be sufficient to defeat the KMT.[46] However, the war soon became a quagmire for the Imperial Japanese Army, imposing tremendous strain on the Japanese economy and increasing Tokyo's short-term dependence on the United States, Britain, and the Netherlands for oil, tin, steel, rubber, and other raw materials. Defense spending rose from 6 percent of net domestic product in 1936 to 19.3 percent in 1939. The Japanese economy reached full capacity in 1937 and the dramatic increase in defense spending created inflationary pressures. To meet the army's demand, the government imposed draconian reductions on raw materials allocations to the civilian section. Military and civilian officials had hoped to extract raw materials from China. The war, however, ravaged the Chinese economy, destroyed one-fourth of the country's cultivated land, and made industrial development virtually impossible. At the same time, Japan's imports of oil, scrap, iron, rubber, and other materials needed to sustain the war effort increased until they made up more than 40 percent of total imports from the United States.[47]

The Sino-Japanese War (or "China Incident") cast an adversarial shadow over Tokyo's relations with Washington, given the Roosevelt administration's commitment to the Open Door in China and support for Chiang's regime.[48] The "Rape of Nanking" (or Nanjing Massacre)

---

[44] David John Lu, *Agony of Choice: Matsuoka Yōsuke and the Rise and Fall of the Japanese Empire, 1880–1946, Studies of Modern Japan* (Lanham: Lexington Books, 2002), 77.

[45] Konoe Fumimaro served as Japanese prime minister three times: June 4, 1937–January 5, 1939; July 22, 1940–June 18, 1941; and July 18, 1941–October 18, 1941.

[46] Barnhart, *Japan Prepares for Total War*, 91; Ikuhiko Hata, "The Marco Polo Bridge Incident, 1937," in *The China Quagmire: Japan's Expansion on the Asian Continent, 1933–1941*, ed. James W. Morley (New York: Columbia University Press, 1983), 254–68.

[47] In 1938, the civilian sector's allotment of steel fell from 5 million to 3.5 million tons. The imported fuel quota fell from ¥556 million to ¥510 million. Factories had to reduce their fuel consumption by 37 percent and their shipping by 10–15 percent. See Barnhart, *Japan Prepares for Total War*, 109–10.

[48] See Memo by the Secretary of State (Cordell Hull), July 13, 1937 and The Japanese Foreign Minister (Hirota Koki) to the American Ambassador in Japan (Joseph Grew),

and the sinking by Japanese aircraft of the American gunboat *Panay* on the Yangtze River in December 1937 increased anti-Japanese sentiment in the United States.[49] The United States, on whom Japan depended for 70 percent of its oil supply, openly supported Chiang. The Roosevelt administration protested Japan's expansionist policies by gradually imposing economic sanctions, thus threatening the Japanese war effort.[50] This began with a ban on aircraft sales to Japan in mid-1938. In July 1939, Secretary of State Cordell Hull informed the Japanese government that Washington would abrogate the 1911 Japanese-American Treaty of Commerce and Navigation in six months' time.[51] However, rather than seek a negotiated peace with Chiang or unilaterally withdraw Japanese troops from central China, the first Konoe cabinet and the Japanese army leadership continued to escalate their commitment to the war to recover sunk costs.[52] After Konoe's (first) resignation as prime minister in January 1939, this pattern of devoting additional blood and treasure to the China war continued during the short-lived tenures of the Hiranuma, Abe, and Yonai cabinets.

The defeat of the KMT and the consolidation of Japanese dominance in China quickly became an integral component of the expectation level or objective from which the Konoe cabinet (and its successors) and the military chiefs of staff evaluated outcomes. That expectation was the creation of a New Order in East Asia – an empire and trading bloc consisting of the Japanese home islands, the existing colonies in Korea, Formosa (Taiwan), and south Sakhalin, and more recent territorial acquisitions in Manchuria (the puppet state of "Manchukuo" from 1932) and northern and central China proper. The creation of this sphere would give Japan unrestricted access to raw materials (including oil) and export markets, as well as strategic depth for an eventual war with the Soviet Union, which many army planners saw as "inevitable."[53]

August 31, 1937, in US Department of State, *Foreign Relations of the United States: Japan, 1931–1941*, vol. 1 (Washington, DC: GPO, 1943), 318–21, 358.

[49] Ambassador in Japan to the Secretary of State, December, 12, 1937, Press Release by the Department of State, January 28, 1937, American ambassador in Japan to the Japanese Foreign Minister (Hirota), February 4, 1938, Japanese Foreign Minister to the American Ambassador in Japan, February 12, 1938 in US Department of State, *Foreign Relations of the United States: Japan*, 570–73, 578–82.

[50] For the actual figures, see Paul Kennedy, *The Rise and Fall of the Great Powers* (New York: Random House, 1988), chapter 6.

[51] Secretary of State Cordell Hull to the Japanese Ambassador (Horinouchi Kensuke), July 26, 1939, in US Department of State, *The Foreign Relations of the United States, 1939*, vol. 3 (Washington, DC: GPO, 1955), 558–59.

[52] Taliaferro, *Balancing Risks*, 101–03.

[53] Edward J. Drea, *Japan's Imperial Army: Its Rise and Fall, 1853–1945, Modern War Studies* (Lawrence: University Press of Kansas, 2009), 207–09.

By summer 1940, Japanese leaders had essentially two options: (1) they could extricate the army from the Sino-Japanese War and accept continued vulnerability to a possible embargo in raw materials; or (2) they could pursue a southward advance into French Indochina and the Dutch East Indies in a bid to cut off the flow of arms to the KMT and secure the raw materials they needed to win the war in China. Although Japan had the military capabilities to execute this southward advance, doing so would risk an open rupture with Washington and London. The second and the third Konoe cabinets and the military chiefs of staff not only devoted resources to an unwinnable war against the KMT and the Chinese Communists but also undertook a number of high-risk gambles in other areas as means to perpetuate that war effort. These included the previously mentioned southward advance into French Indochina and the Dutch East Indies, the signing of the Tripartite Pact with Germany and Italy in September 1940 as a means to deter the United States from further interference in China, and the conclusion of a five-year neutrality treaty with the Soviet Union in April 1941 to secure the Japanese Empire's northern flank. After the imposition of the oil embargo and failed efforts to reach a negotiated settlement with Washington, the liaison conference between the Tōjō Hideki cabinet and the chiefs of staff ultimately decided to wage war on the United States in late November 1941, knowing to a person that Japan could not win a prolonged conflict and that any US-Japanese war would likely last several years.[54]

In other venues, I undertake a detailed examination of the liaison conferences between the Konoe and Tōjō cabinets and the chiefs of staff from June 1940 to December 1941 that made each of the key decisions just mentioned.[55] Instead of recapitulating that analysis here, I will offer four observations about patterns of Japanese grand strategic adjustment and the reactions of the United States, Britain, and other great powers to Japan in the 1930s and early 1940s.

First, the aversion of senior Japanese officials to perceived losses in their country's relative power and international standing and their tendency to escalate commitment to recover the "sunk costs" of prior investments in the second Sino-Japanese War led them to undertake increasingly risky diplomatic and military initiatives, culminating in the decision to launch a preventive war against the United States, an adversary with roughly eight times the potential power of the entire Japanese Empire. The expectation or goal of the Japanese leaders of creating a New Order

[54] Tsunoda Jun, "The Decision for War," in *The Final Confrontation: Japan's Negotiations with the United States, 1941*, ed. James W. Morley (New York: Columbia University Press, 1994), 230–48.
[55] Taliaferro, *Balancing Risks*, 102–31.

in East Asia primarily stemmed from their deep-seated fear of relative decline and future predation at the hands of other great powers.

Second, Japanese grand strategy in the 1930s, especially after the outbreak of the second Sino-Japanese War in 1937, was unquestionably self-defeating. With the possible exception of the April 1941 neutrality treaty with the Soviet Union – prompted by the Soviet Far Eastern Army's decisive defeat of the Kwantung Army in the summer 1939 Nomonhan Incident and the 1939 Soviet-German Nonaggression Pact; the treaty remained in effect until August 1945 – senior Japanese leaders were remarkably impervious to negative systemic feedback to their previous diplomatic and military initiatives.[56]

Three, while the increasingly factionalized nature of Japanese politics, incessant interservice rivalry, and the absence of strong coordination mechanisms within the foreign policy executive made the actual process of strategic adjustment difficult, the ultimate driver of Japanese grand strategy was what senior officials perceived as the increasingly threatening strategic environment in East Asia.

Fourth, and perhaps more importantly, at no time during the 1930s, and especially after 1937, were the United States and Great Britain prepared to acquiesce to Japan's territorial conquests in Manchuria, let alone in China proper. Japanese leaders' stated grand strategic aim of creating a New Order in East Asia threatened the strategic and economic interests of the United States and Britain, as well as those of France, the Netherlands, and the Soviet Union. In the late 1930s, however, neither Britain nor the United States had the military forces in the region – or anywhere – to credibly deter further Japanese expansion in China and, later, South East Asia.

Conclusion

This chapter began by posing two questions: Did the United States, and to a lesser extent Great Britain, France, and the Netherlands, lose a window of opportunity to peacefully accommodate a rising Japan in the

---

[56] On the origins of the USSR–Japan Neutrality Pact, see Timothy M. Crawford, "Powers of Division: From the Anti-Comintern to the Nazi-Soviet and Japanese-Soviet Pacts, 1936–1941," in *The Challenge of Grand Strategy: The Great Powers and the Broken Balance between the World Wars*, eds. Jeffrey W. Taliaferro, Norrin M. Ripsman, and Steven E. Lobell (Cambridge: Cambridge University Press, 2012), 273–76; Hosoya Chihiro, "The Japanese-Soviet Neutrality Pact," in *The Fateful Choice: Japan's Advance into Southeast Asia, 1939–1941*, ed. James W. Morley (New York: Columbia University, 1980), 13–115.

1930s? Alternatively, was Japan simply beyond the point of accommodation without major territorial adjustments that the United States, Britain, and other established powers were not prepared to offer?

Drawing upon neoclassical realism, I argued that fear of perceived losses in Japan's relative power and international status drove much of the grand strategic thinking in Tokyo. By the mid-1930s, and certainly after the outbreak of the second Sino-Japanese War in July 1937, Japan was beyond the point of accommodation by the other great powers. The United States, Britain, and other established powers had no intention of recognizing Japan's claim of an informal sphere of influence in northern China during WWI and the immediate postwar period. If a window for the peaceful accommodation of Japan's territorial and security concerns existed, then that window closed in the 1920s. The Great Depression led to a "hardening" of Japanese elites' conception of their basic security requirements: instead of an informal sphere of influence on the continent, henceforth Japan would have to pursue autarkic economic policies at home and a measured strategy of expansion in China. The creation of this New Order in East Asia would give the Japanese Empire unrestricted access to raw materials (especially oil) and export markets, as well as the strategic depth for an eventual war with the Soviet Union, a conflict that the Army General Staff had long seen as "inevitable." Japan's efforts to establish this New Order in East Asia were simply antithetical to the strategic and economic interests of the United States, Britain, and France.

At the same time, I argued that the record of Japanese expansion in the 1930s, culminating in the 1940–41 crises between the United States and Japan and the latter's initiation of a preventive war, does not fit neatly into the rising challenger versus status quo hegemon framework. In the 1930s, civilian and military leaders in Tokyo did not perceive Japan as a rising challenger. Instead, they saw Japan as being on the precipice of deep relative decline and confronting an increasingly threatening strategic environment in East Asia. Chief among their security concerns were the resurgence of Soviet military presence in Siberia; the continuing political turmoil in China, which might have prompted the Soviet Union or the Western great powers to try to exploit the power vacuum on the Asian mainland; and the growing fear that, since future wars would likely be attritional struggles like WWI, Japan was increasingly vulnerable to embargo by its main suppliers of raw materials, the United States, Britain, France, and the Netherlands. Based upon their subjective assessments of that environment, Japanese leaders concluded that autarkic economic development through territorial expansion in China and, later, South East Asia was the only viable strategy for Japan to achieve security.

What lessons for the accommodation of rising powers in the twenty-first century can we draw from this analysis of the non-accommodation of Japan in the mid-twentieth century? Japan's territorial expansion in East Asia and the failure of the United States and Britain to either accommodate or deter Japan before WWII, just like the case of Britain's failed effort to accommodate or deter Germany before WWI and WWII,[57] constitute an extreme case of non-accommodation. It is extremely improbable that any rising power (China, Brazil, or India) or an existing major power thoroughly dissatisfied with the international status quo (Russia) would engage in the magnitude of territorial revision that Germany and Japan pursued in the first part of the twentieth century. Nonetheless, there are some parallels between the grand strategy Japan pursued in the 1930s and early 1940s and the grand strategy of present-day Russia.[58]

In the 1920s and 1930s, Japan confronted a power vacuum in China and the resurgence of Soviet military power in the Far East. The Japanese economy was completely dependent on foreign sources of raw materials. Similarly, President Vladimir Putin and his advisors perceive Russia as under siege from the United States and the European Union. Unlike prewar Japan, Russia is a nuclear-armed former superpower and a major exporter of oil and natural gas. Yet, just as the WWI victors had no intention of recognizing Japan's claim to a sphere of influence in northern China in the 1920s, the Cold War's victor (the United States) had no intention of recognizing Russia's desire for a sphere of influence over the former Soviet republics in the 1990s.

The Russian war against Georgia in August 2008, the annexation of Crimea in March 2014 following the ouster of Ukrainian President Viktor Yanukovych, and military support for pro-Russian separatists in the Donetsk and Luhansk regions of eastern Ukraine are arguably efforts by Putin to forestall the realignment of these former Soviet republics toward the West and to reassert Russia's international standing.[59] Similar to Japan's pursuit of the "New Order in East Asia," Russia's strategy appears to be driven by the fear of losing relative power, influence, and status.

There are two other sobering parallels. First, just as the United States, Britain, and others lacked the military forces to deter Tokyo or to coerce the withdrawal of Japanese forces from China, the United States and

---

[57] See Chapter 8.   [58] See Chapter 13.

[59] For the debate over the deep causes of the Ukraine crisis, see John J. Mearsheimer, "Why the Ukraine Crisis is the West's Fault: The Liberal Delusions that Provoked Putin," *Foreign Affairs* 93, no. 5 (September/October 2014), 77–89; Michael McFaul, Stephen Sestanovich, and John J. Mearsheimer, "Faulty Powers: Who Started the Ukraine Crisis," *Foreign Affairs* 93, no. 6 (November/December 2014), 167–78.

its North Atlantic Treaty Organization (NATO) allies have been unable and unwilling to deter or coerce Russia with respect to Ukraine. Both periods saw a marked disparity between the overall balance of power and the balance of interests regarding the contested territories. Second, the imposition of economic sanctions by the United States, Britain, and the Netherlands did not prompt Japan to abandon the goal of creating a New Order in East Asia and withdraw forces from China. On the contrary, Japanese leaders redoubled efforts to secure victory in the China Incident, despite the ruinous impact of sanctions on the Japanese economy. Similarly, the United States and EU member states imposed economic sanctions on Russia following the Crimea annexation and outbreak of hostilities between the Ukrainian army and Russian-backed separatists in the Donetsk and Luhansk regions. Yet, despite the crippling impact of sanctions (and lower oil and natural gas prices) on the Russian economy, the Putin government has, so far, shown little sign of changing course in eastern Ukraine.

Part III

Contemporary cases

10 China's bargaining strategies for a peaceful accommodation after the Cold War

Kai He

China's rise is a defining political event in world politics in the twenty-first century. As David Shambaugh, a leading China scholar, puts it, "the rise of China is *the big story* of our era."[1] Scholars and pundits heatedly debate over the implications of China's rise in international politics. Pessimists, mainly realists of different stripes, suggest an inevitable conflict between a rising China and the United States – the existing hegemon – in the international system. Optimists, largely from liberal and constructivist schools, argue that China can be either integrated into the exiting liberal order or socialized by the prevailing universal norms.[2] Challenging these two arguments, this chapter suggests that China's rise is a bargaining process between China and the outside world, especially the United States. Neither the optimistic nor the pessimistic view is warranted, since the final episode in the drama of China's rise is still unwritten. Depending on how China bargains with the outside world and how the outside world reacts, China's rise may lead to either a peaceful accommodation or a violent conflict.

From a rising power's perspective, bargaining for a peaceful accommodation is the Pareto-optimal outcome, since war or conflict is less efficient.[3] From an existing but declining hegemon's view, accommodating a rising power is also a rational decision, if the benefit of accommodation outweighs the cost. However, as T.V. Paul wisely suggests in Chapter 1, "non-violent accommodation is a rare event, as rising powers are often not peacefully integrated by established powers." Building on rationalism and constructivism, and borrowing insights from bargaining theory's framework, this chapter explores different strategies that a

---

[1] David Shambaugh, *China Goes Global: The Partial Power* (Oxford: Oxford University Press, 2013), ix. Emphasis in original.
[2] For an excellent review of optimistic versus pessimistic views on China's rise, see Aaron Friedberg, "The Future of US-China Relations: Is Conflict Inevitable?" *International Security* 30, no. 2 (Fall 2005), 7–45.
[3] For war as a less efficient outcome, see James D. Fearon, "Rationalist Explanations for War," *International Organization* 49, no. 3 (Summer 1995), 379–414.

rising power can use to achieve a possible peaceful accommodation to the outside world. Although a rising power's strategy is by no means the only determinant, I suggest that how a rising power behaves is one of the most important factors in shaping the final outcome of the power transition process in the international system.

This chapter has three sections. First, I discuss two types of accommodation and four strategies a rising power can adopt in bargaining for peaceful accommodation. Second, I explore how China employed these four strategies to reach bargaining deals regarding the Taiwan issue, territorial disputes in the South China Sea, arms control regimes, and anti-separatist movements in Xinjiang after the Cold War. In conclusion, I discuss the challenges for China's future bargaining with the United States in light of the post-2008 "assertive turn" in China's diplomacy. I suggest that the United States needs to take China's bargaining efforts seriously and consider how to accommodate China peacefully.

Four bargaining strategies for peaceful accommodation

If we treat China's rise as a bargaining process between China and the outside world then China is, by definition, a revisionist state, simply because it initiates a bargaining process, especially with the United States, the existing hegemon. In a material sense, China wants to negotiate for higher levels of security, more areas of influence, and fundamentally more power. Within an ideational frame, China wants to bargain for more respect, higher prestige, and eventually better and more important status in the international society.[4] One popular question in the study of China's rise is "What does China want?" or "What will China want?"[5] Although it is truly important to know what is on China's "wish list," the key issue is *how much* the outside world, especially the existing hegemon, is willing to give, or accommodate, what China wants. The answer to this question does not actually depend on *what* China wants, but *how* China bargains with the hegemon.

There are two types of accommodation from an existing hegemon's perspective. One is "accommodation for interests," which is when the hegemon chooses to accommodate the rising power's demands due to

---

[4] For an excellent work on rising powers and status, see T.V. Paul, Deborah Welch Larson, and William C. Wohlforth, eds., *Status in World Politics* (Cambridge: Cambridge University Press, 2014).

[5] See "What China Wants," The Economist (August 23, 2014). Available at: www.economist.com/news/leaders/21613263-after-bad-couple-centuries-china-itching-regain-its-place-world-how-should; Jeffrey W. Legro, "What China Will Want: The Future Intentions of a Rising Power," *Perspectives on Politics* 5, no. 3 (September 2007), 515–34.

the daunting consequences that it would face otherwise. This type of accommodation follows a rationalist logic of consequentialism, in which the benefit of accommodation must be larger than the cost. The other kind is "accommodation for identity," which refers to the situation when the hegemon believes that the rising power should get what it bargains for. In other words, the rising power's demands are appropriate for who it is; that is, for the rising power's identity. This type of accommodation is rooted in the logic of appropriateness in constructivism.[6]

Given the anarchic nature of the international system, competition for security and power is a constant feature of international politics. Since all states are self-interested in nature when it comes to survival, it is less likely that a hegemon will voluntarily accommodate a rising power's demands. Even when the hegemon believes that the rising power really deserves what it wants, it may not initiate the accommodation process if the rising power does not bargain hard enough. Therefore, whether the hegemon chooses to accommodate or not largely depends on the rising power's bargaining strategies.

Seeking accommodation for interests: costly signaling and self-restraining

In seeking an accommodation for interests, a rising power needs to show the hegemon what it really wants (its demands) as well as how seriously it wants them (its resolve). In addition, the rising power needs to convince the hegemon that its intentions and ambitions behind this negotiation are limited in scope.

First, the rising power can use a "costly signaling" strategy to strengthen the credibility of what it wants.[7] Signaling is the use of actions to reflect intentions. Since a costless signal may not be taken seriously by others, states need to add two types of cost to increase the weights of their signaling actions. One is the "audience cost," and the other is the "sunk

---

[6] For the logics of consequentialism versus appropriateness, see Thomas Risse, "Constructivism and International Institutions: Toward Conversations across Paradigms," in *Political Science: The State of the Discipline*, eds., Ira Katznelson and Helen V. Milner (New York: American Political Science Association, 2002), 597–623.

[7] See James D. Fearon, "Signaling Foreign Policy Interests: Tying Hands Versus Sinking Cost," *The Journal of Conflict Resolution* 41, no. 1 (February 1997), 68–90. Some scholars suggest that cheap talk also sometimes matters for bargaining. However, as Morrow points out, cheap talk only matters in resolving the coordination problem, not the collaboration problem, in cooperation. See James D. Morrow, "Modeling the Forms of International Cooperation: Distribution versus Information," *International Organization* 48, no. 2 (Summer 1994), 387–423; Robert Trager, "Diplomatic Calculus in Anarchy: How Communication Matters," *American Political Science Review* 104, no. 2 (May 2010), 347–68.

cost." The audience cost refers to the political costs that a political leader has to pay if he or she backs down from either a promise or a threat made to an adversary.[8] The sunk cost, in comparison, refers to the *ex ante* cost that has already been experienced and cannot be recovered. Because the sunk cost cannot be recovered, it can signal a party's credible resolve to others.[9]

Second, the rising power needs to convince the hegemon of its limited goals so that the hegemon can consider accommodation rather than conflict. This is not an easy job, however, because a declining hegemon can be likely to wage a preventive war to stop a rising power.[10] One strategy the rising power can use to address this commitment problem is to adopt a "self-restraining" policy. Self-restraining can refer to both capability and the maneuverability of capability. On the one hand, a rising power can choose to develop defensive weapons instead of offensive ones if the offense–defense advantage is distinguishable. For example, Steven Lobell suggests that Beijing should restrain the development of its naval power, an offensive capability, in order to alleviate US threat perceptions regarding China's rise.[11] Through constraining its offensive capabilities, the rising power can strengthen its non-aggressive commitment to the outside world.[12] On the other hand, a rising power can lock itself in through multilateral institutions and use the rules and norms of the institutions to constrain its own behavior.[13] For example, after signing a non-proliferation treaty, a country's freedom to develop nuclear weapons will be constrained. Although the terms of "lock-in" may not

---

[8] For the domestic-level audience costs, see Fearon, "Signaling Foreign Policy Interests." Some scholars expand the application of audience costs to the international level. See James D. Morrow, "The Strategic Setting of Choices: Signaling, Commitment, and Negotiation in International Politics," in *Strategic Choice and International Relations*, eds., David A. Lake and Robert Powell (Princeton: Princeton University Press, 1999), 77–114. In addition, some scholars argue that leaders in autocracies also face the pressure of audience costs. See Jessica Weeks, "Autocratic Audience Costs: Regime Type and Signaling Resolve," *International Organization* 62, no. 4 (January 2008), 35–64. For critiques on audience costs theory, see Jack Snyder and Erica D. Borghard, "The Cost of Empty Threats: A Penny, Not a Pound," *American Political Science Review* 105, no. 3 (August 2011), 437–56; Marc Trachtenberg, "Audience Costs: An Historical Analysis," *Security Studies* 21, no. 1 (2012), 3–42.

[9] See Fearon, "Signaling Foreign Policy Interests."

[10] Dale C. Copeland, *The Origins of Major War: Hegemonic Rivalry and the Fear of Decline* (Ithaca: Cornell University Press, 2000).

[11] See Chapter 3.

[12] See Charles Glaser, "Political Consequences of Military Strategy: Extending and Refining the Spiral Model," *World Politics* 44, no. 4 (July 1992), 497–538; Andrew Kydd, "Sheep in Sheep's Clothing: Why Security Seekers Do Not Fight Each Other," *Security Studies* 7, no. 1 (Autumn 1997), 114–55.

[13] The "lock-in" term is borrowed from Ikenberry's argument that the hegemon can use institutions to lock other states in the system. See G. John. Ikenberry, *After Victory: Institutions, Strategic Restraint, and the Rebuilding of Order after Major Wars* (Princeton: Princeton University Press, 2001).

actually stop a state from going against its promises covertly, the state will face a "reputation cost" if it is caught cheating.[14]

Seeking accommodation for identity: socialization and legitimation

In order to seek an accommodation for identity, a rising power can rely on two strategies to persuade a hegemon that it deserves what it asks for. First, the rising power can use a socialization strategy to change its own identity. "Socialization" normally refers to a process of interaction between individuals and a society in which the individuals start to learn "skills, knowledge, values, motives, and roles appropriate to their position in a group or society."[15] Here, I suggest that socialization can also be a strategy for a rising power to integrate itself into the existing international system. However, this does not mean that the rising power must follow all the rules and norms in the existing system. Instead, the rising power needs to figure out how to live with these rules and norms. Rules and norms are by no means static in nature: a rising power can modify the rules and even invent new norms.[16] But all these changes and innovations should be based on the fact that the rising power has been socialized and accepted by the existing system. Therefore, it is critical for the rising power strategically to socialize itself into the existing system. Compared to the passive or top-down approach of a state's traditional socialization by another agent, a bottom-up socialization strategy is an active, selective, strategic way for a rising power to join the existing system.[17]

Another approach a rising power can use to seek an accommodation for identity from a hegemon is "legitimation," through which the rising power can legitimize what it asks for. Legitimacy refers to "the normative belief by an actor that a rule or institution ought to be obeyed."[18] In other words, legitimacy means voluntary acceptance by others. In order to make its demands legitimate in the eyes of others, the rising power needs to influence discourses and use prevailing rules and norms to support its demands. Stacie Goddard suggests that a rising power can

---

[14] Barry Nalebuff, "Rational Deterrence in an Imperfect World," *World Politics* 43, no. 3 (April 1991), 313–35.

[15] H. Andrew Michener and John Delamater, *Social Psychology*, 4 edn. (Fort Worth: Harcourt College Publishers, 1999), 46.

[16] For mutual socialization between rising powers and existing international norms, see Maximilian Terhalle, "Reciprocal Socialization: Rising Powers and the West," *International Studies Perspectives* 12, no. 4 (November 2011), 341–61; Xiaoyu Pu, "Socialization as a Two-Way Process: Emerging Powers and the Diffusion of International Norms," *The Chinese Journal of International Politics* 5 (2012), 341–67.

[17] See Cameron Thies, *The United States, Israel, and the Search for International Order: Socializing States* (New York: Routledge, 2013).

[18] Ian Hurd, "Legitimacy and Authority in International Politics," *International Organization* 53, no. 2 (Spring 1999), 381.

set a "rhetorical trap" by using the opposing states' own words to justify its policies. For example, from 1864 to 1871, Prussia mounted a series of wars that fundamentally altered the balance of power in Europe. Yet, no balancing coalition emerged to check Prussia's rise. Goddard argues that the reason for this "underbalancing" is that "as Prussia expanded, it appealed to shared rules and norms, strategically choosing rhetoric that would resonate with each of the great powers."[19] To be sure, it is not an easy job for the rising power to legitimize its demands or set a "rhetorical trap" for the hegemon, because the hegemon will try to dominate or at least compete for the discursive power in the system. Compared with the socialization strategy, the legitimation strategy will be more difficult, because the goal of legitimation is to change others' perceptions, instead of affirming the rising power's self-identity assigned by others.

China's successful bargaining after the Cold War

In order to illustrate the different utilities of these four strategies, I examine the successes of China's bargaining for a peaceful accommodation after the Cold War. As a rising power, China has been in the center of the debate over a possible power transition ever since. Given its different political system and the stunning trajectory of its power ascent, China is the current best candidate to challenge US hegemony.[20] However, China's rise has not triggered containment efforts similar to those the United States used to deal with the Soviet threat during the Cold War. Even when the United States proclaimed its "pivot toward Asia" in recent years, it still publicly declared that China was not its target. People may question the real intention of the pivot, especially the Chinese leaders, but it is clear that the United States still intends to avoid direct and public conflicts with China. From a Chinese perspective, this may be the best that it can expect: a peaceful accommodation from the hegemon.

Costly signaling on the Taiwan issue

The Taiwan issue is one of the most difficult, if not the only, political obstacles between China and the United States.[21] After the Cold War,

---

[19] Stacie Goddard, "When Right Makes Might: How Prussia Overturned the European Balance of Power," *International Security* 33, no. 3 (Winter 2009), 110–42.

[20] For example, see Denny Roy, "Hegemon on the Horizon? China's Threat to East Asian Security," *International Security* 19, no. 1 (Summer 1994), 149–68; Richard Bernstein and Ross H. Munro, *The Coming Conflict with China* (New York: A.A. Knopf, 1997).

[21] For a similar argument to that presented in this section, see Kai He and Huiyun Feng, "Debating China's Assertiveness: Taking China's Power and Interests Seriously," *International Politics* 49, no. 5 (2012), 633–44; Kai He and Huiyun Feng, "China's Bargaining Strategies for a Peaceful Rise: Successes and Challenges," *Asian Security* 10, no. 2 (2014), 168–87.

the Taiwan issue gradually became a major irritant in bilateral relations. In 1992, President George H.W. Bush authorized the sale of 150 F-16 fighters to Taiwan, due to electoral needs in Texas, where the fighters were manufactured.[22] China protested, but did nothing concrete to retaliate. In 1995, the Clinton administration issued a visa to the then Taiwanese President Lee Teng-hui, so he could visit Cornell University for an alumni reunion. In the eyes of Chinese leaders, this reflected a sea change in US policy toward Taiwan, for two reasons. First, Lee was the first Taiwanese leader who had ever visited the mainland of the United States. This broke a diplomatic protocol between China and the United States, which was not to allow any incumbent officials of Taiwan to visit. Second, Lee was seen as a pro-independence leader, due to his active "money diplomacy" and "vacation diplomacy" in the early 1990s, which he used to expand Taiwan's international space.[23] From the Chinese perspective, Lee intended to pursue an independent Taiwan through international recognition. Therefore, Beijing was furious over the US decision to allow Lee to visit Cornell, and even deliver a pro-independence speech on Taiwan's democracy. China conducted a series of missile tests and military exercises across the Taiwan Strait between July 1995 and March 1996.[24] Given the fact that Taiwan's first democratic election was held in early 1996 and Lee was a popular presidential candidate, Beijing's military threats were widely interpreted as putting political pressure on Taiwanese voters to stay away from Lee. The 1995–96 Taiwan crisis ended after the United States dispatched two aircraft carriers to the region.

China's military intimidation seems counterproductive, in that Lee won the election in Taiwan despite the military pressures. Many factors may have played a role in shaping Chinese behavior during the crisis, including civil–military relations, domestic challenges to the party, and even nationalism. However, from a bargaining perspective, Beijing's military exercises and missile tests served as a "costly signal" to Washington.

---

[22] Jean Garrison, *Making China Policy: From Nixon to G.W. Bush* (Boulder and London: Lynne Rienner, 2005); Nancy Tucker, ed., *China Confidential: American Diplomats and Sino-American Relations (1945–1996)* (New York: Columbia University Press, 2001).

[23] See Robert Suettinger, *Beyond Tiananmen: The Politics of US-China Relations 1989–2000* (Washington, DC: Brookings Institution Press 2003); James Mann, *About Face: A History of America's Curious Relationship with China, From Nixon to Clinton* (New York: Alfred Knopf, 1999).

[24] For details on the 1995–96 Taiwan crisis, see John Garver, *Face Off: China, the United States, and Taiwan's Democratization* (Seattle: University of Washington Press, 1997); Andrew Scobell, "Show of Force: Chinese Soldiers, Statesmen, and the 1995–1996 Taiwan Strait Crisis," *Political Science Quarterly* 115, no. 2 (Summer 2000), 227–46; Robert Ross, "Navigating the Taiwan Strait: Deterrence, Escalation Dominance, and US-China Relations," *International Security* 27, no. 2 (Fall 2002), 48–85.

China was deeply concerned over the US "strategic ambiguity" policy toward Taiwan, which it interpreted as silent support for Taiwan's pro-independence forces. Therefore, Beijing intended to bargain for a new deal on the Taiwan issue with the United States. Lee's visit provided an opportunity for China to show its true resolve. The series of military exercises and missile tests can be seen as the "sunk costs" that China invested before the negotiation. Missile tests and military exercises are very costly in terms of economic expenditures and military preparations. More importantly, these costs cannot be recovered. Therefore, the "sunk costs" associated with China's missile tests and military exercises helped Beijing deliver a costly signal to Washington regarding how seriously it took the Taiwan issue.

Washington clearly received Beijing's costly signaling during the crisis. After China conducted its first round of military exercises and missile tests in March 1995, the United States sent high-ranking diplomats there to reassure the Chinese that the United States would not change its "one China" policy and would not support Taiwan's membership in the United Nations.[25] As former Chinese Foreign Minister Qian Qichen recalls in his memoir, President Clinton also delivered a personal letter to President Jiang at the end of July 1995 through his Secretary of State, Warren Christopher. President Clinton intended to assure Jiang that the United States had not changed its "one China" policy.[26] However, compared to China's costly signaling using sinking costs from missile tests and military exercises, Clinton's private letter seemed a "costless signal," with limited credibility. Therefore, China continued its missile tests and military exercises until March 1996.

The later dispatch of two aircraft carriers to the Taiwan area by the United States can also be seen as a "costly signal" from Washington to Beijing about its resolve on the Taiwan issue, since this was the largest display of American military might in Asia since the Vietnam War.[27] It was clearly the United States' intention to send a signal to China that it would not stay idle in case of a possible military invasion of Taiwan. Apparently, Beijing got the message, and it ended its military exercises soon after the Taiwan election.

Both countries adopted costly signaling strategies to send credible messages about their bottom-line positions on the Taiwan issue. China and

[25] David Lampton, *Same Bed, Different Dreams: Managing US-China Relations 1989–2000* (Berkeley: University of California Press, 2001).
[26] Qian Qichen, *Ten Episodes in China's Diplomacy* (New York: HarperCollins, 2006), 248–9.
[27] See "Taiwan Flashpoint: US Role," BBC News. Available at: news.bbc.co.uk/2/shared/spl/hi/asia_pac/04/taiwan_flashpoint/html/us_role.stm.

the United States eventually reached a new equilibrium on the Taiwan issue in this bargaining game. The United States reduced its "ambiguity," while China modified its military intimidation toward Taiwan. After the 1995–96 Taiwan crisis, bilateral relations were quickly restored through summit meetings. During Clinton's 1998 visit to Beijing, he publicly stated the so-called "three no's" policy toward Taiwan: the United States did not support efforts to create "two Chinas or one China, one Taiwan," did not support Taiwan independence, and did not support Taiwan's admission to the United Nations.[28] Compared to his previous private letter, Clinton's public statement entailed more credibility for Chinese leaders. China changed its military coercion to political pressure toward Taiwan, even after Chen Shui-bian, a pro-independence leader from the Democratic Progressive Party, was elected as the Taiwanese president in 2000. Since 2000, the US government has unofficially coordinated with China to curb the pro-independence movement in Taiwan.[29]

It should be noted that the Taiwan issue remains unsettled between China and the United States. The temporary deal based on the costly signaling efforts in the 1995–96 crisis may be challenged by both parties in the future, especially when China's military power reaches a level comparable with that of the United States. Therefore, a new round of negotiations may open in the future.

Self-restraining on territorial disputes

One of the major concerns over China's rise lies in China's unsettled territorial disputes with its neighboring states. As Aaron Friedberg suggests, the "ripe for rivalry in Asia" thesis will come true when China is ready to use force to settle these disputes.[30] Therefore, one major challenge for China's peaceful rise is how to assure its neighbors that it will not wage territorial wars, even after it becomes stronger militarily and economically.

Since the 1990s, China has settled all land-based territorial disputes with its neighboring states, except for India.[31] Over the years, it has yielded 1.3 million square miles of claims to its neighbors in these

---

[28] Richard Halloran, "China Crows over Clinton's New Policy toward Taiwan," *International Herald Tribune*, July 22, 1998.

[29] See Michael D. Swaine, "Trouble in Taiwan," *Foreign Affairs* 83, no. 2 (March/April 2004), 39–9. On China–United States cooperation to maintain the status quo in Taiwan, see Kai He and Huiyun Feng, "Leadership, Regime Security, and China's Policy toward Taiwan: Prospect Theory and Taiwan Crises," *Pacific Review* 22, no. 4 (2009), 501–22.

[30] Aaron L. Friedberg, "Ripe for Rivalry: Prospects for Peace in a Multipolar Asia," *International Security* 18, no. 3 (Winter 1993–94), 5–33.

[31] See Fu Ying, "China and Asia in a New Era," *China: An International Journal* 1, no. 2 (2003), 304–12.

demarcation settlements.[32] Through June 2013, China and India have conducted sixteen rounds of consultations on their border dispute.[33] M. Taylor Fravel believes that "regime insecurity" can explain why the Chinese government compromised with other countries in these cases. However, it is difficult to deny that China's compromises also reflected its peaceful intentions. Given its power trajectory, China's continuous willingness to settle territorial disputes with other nations also serves as a credible signal of its peaceful rise. After examining China's engagement with its neighboring states, David Shambaugh concludes that "China need not be feared or opposed... China's interests and regional preferences may well coincide with those of its neighbors and the United States, providing opportunities for collaboration."[34]

The unsettled territorial disputes between China and its neighbors are maritime disputes, especially with Japan in the East China Sea and with four Association of Southeast Asian Nations (ASEAN) countries in the South China Sea. The main obstacles to maritime demarcations are different understandings of history and divergent interpretations of the UN Convention on the Law of the Sea (UNCLOS). China's general policy on settling maritime disputes is to "shelve disputes and carry out joint development."[35] However, after China's military actions in the 1988 Sino-Vietnam naval clash over the South China Sea and the 1995 Mischief incident[36] with the Philippines, South East Asian countries have grown more vigilant toward China, especially over its possible future use of force in resolving the territorial disputes in the South China Sea.

In order to reassure its neighbors, China adopted a self-restraining strategy through participation in multilateral institutions. In 1994, China joined the ASEAN Regional Forum (ARF), the only security dialogue mechanism in the Asia Pacific that included all the major powers in the world. The ARF was originally designed to constrain China's behavior through cooperative security norms and rules; therefore, China's participation in the ARF signaled a self-restraining commitment, as well as

---

[32] M. Taylor Fravel, *Strong Borders, Secure Nation: Cooperation and Conflict in China's Territorial Disputes* (Princeton: Princeton University Press, 2008).

[33] Yang Lina, "China, India Hold 16th Round of Border Talks," *Xinhuanet* (June 28, 2013). Available at: news.xinhuanet.com/english/china/2013-06/28/c_132496108.htm.

[34] David Shambaugh, "China Engages Asia: Reshaping the Regional Order," *International Security* 29, no. 3 (Winter 2004/05), 99.

[35] The Chinese Ministry of Foreign Affairs, "Basic Stance and Policy of the Chinese Government in Solving the South China Sea Issue." Available at: www.fmprc.gov.cn/eng/topics/3754/t19230.htm.

[36] The Philippines discovered that Chinese naval forces had seized the unoccupied Mischief Reef in the Spratly Islands, located about 130 miles off the coast of the Philippine island of Palawan. Mischief Reef is also claimed by the Philippines. It was the first time China had taken a disputed island from an ASEAN state.

peaceful intention toward the South East Asian countries. After the Mischief incident, China faced collective pressure from the ASEAN states within the ARF. For example, ASEAN issued a strong joint statement to support the Philippines' appeal to prohibit the occupation of additional islands in the Spratly in March 1995. During the security dialogue between ASEAN and China in April 1995, ASEAN showed its solidarity again over the South China Sea issue. Reportedly, ASEAN's unity was a big surprise to China and led directly to China's concessions at the second ARF meeting in August 1995. China, for the first time, agreed to conduct multilateral discussions of the South China Sea disputes with ASEAN states.[37] Moreover, China also indicated its consent to discuss relevant disputes on the basis of recognized principles of international law, including the 1982 Law of the Sea.

In 1999, China started to discuss with ASEAN the possibility of signing a code of conduct over the South China Sea disputes at informal multilateral settings. After three years of negotiations, China and ASEAN finally signed a Declaration on the Conduct (DOC) of Parties in the South China Sea in 2002, in which both parties promised to "resolve their territorial and jurisdictional disputes by peaceful means" and "exercise self-restraint in the conduct of activities that would complicate or escalate disputes."[38] In 2003, China also signed the Treaty of Amity and Cooperation (TAC) to further alleviate ASEAN's suspicions and strengthen its commitment to peacefully resolving the South China Sea disputes. China is the first outside country to sign the TAC. Since the TAC is a non-aggressive treaty among ASEAN countries, China's signing of the TAC means that China is legally committed to forgoing the use of force in resolving territorial disputes with the South East Asian countries.

However, this is not to suggest that China will never break its peaceful commitment in the South China Sea. Instead, I argue that China will bear high costs for cheating on its commitment. First, China will need to pay high "reputation costs" in international society, since other countries may condemn and criticize its reneging behavior. It will not only influence China's relations with ASEAN states but also damage China's economic and political ties with other nations. Second, China's use of force in the South China Sea may jeopardize its economic and political cooperation

---

[37] See "ARF: ASEAN Regional Forum Ends with Bold Statement," *Kyodo News* (August 1, 1995); Rosemary Foot, "China in the ASEAN Regional Forum: Organizational Processes and Domestic Modes of Thought," *Asian Survey* 38, no. 5 (May 1998), 425–40.

[38] ASEAN, "Declaration on the Conduct of Parties in the South China Sea." Available at: www.asean.org/asean/external-relations/china/item/declaration-on-the-conduct-of-parties-in-the-south-china-sea.

with ASEAN in other relevant institutions, such as the ASEAN Plus Three and China-ASEAN free trade agreements. Given this impact of issue-linkage and the shadow of the future, China will need to seriously consider whether it is worthwhile breaking its peaceful commitment with ASEAN on the South China Sea issue.

So far, the negotiation or bargaining between China and ASEAN over the South China Sea is only temporarily settled. If the 1995 Mischief incident was China's first assertive move in the South China Sea, the collective reaction from ASEAN set China back to its previous "shelving disputes" position. For the South East Asian countries, China's participation in the ARF, signing of the DOC, and assent to the TAC indicated its commitment to the peaceful settlement of disputes. However, there is still no agreed resolution on the disputes. In other words, keeping the status quo in the South China Sea became the equilibrium of bargaining between the two parties.

Since 2009, China has been involved in several maritime disputes with ASEAN states in the South China Sea, especially the Scarborough Shoal standoff with the Philippines in 2012 and the "oil rig dispute" with Vietnam in 2014. This suggests that it might now be time to renegotiate a deal over the South China Sea, as the previous DOC agreement can no longer guarantee the status quo equilibrium accepted ten years ago. In 2013, China's new Foreign Minister, Wang Yi, stated that China was willing to negotiate a legally binding Code of Conduct (COC) with ASEAN to alleviate tensions in the South China Sea. He also warned that any provocation from other claimants would face the serious consequences of China's retaliation.[39] A new bargaining deal in the form of the COC between China and ASEAN may help cover up the South China Sea disputes for some time. However, until a final settlement is reached, China's commitment will face continuous challenges in the future.

Socializing in arms control regimes

During the Cold War, ideological antagonism and Mao's revolutionary policy kept China out of the international system. China was uneasy with security institutions dominated by the two superpowers. In the 1950s, China fought the United Nations' forces, led by the United States, in Korea. In the 1960s, both the East and the West camps isolated China. After resuming its UN seat in 1971, China's participation in international

---

[39] "Chinese FM: Confrontation not Conducive to Solving South China Sea Issues," *Xinhuanet* (June 27, 2013). Available at: news.xinhuanet.com/english/china/2013-06/27/c_132492885.htm.

organizations, both intergovernmental and non-governmental, remained limited to the UN-affiliated institutions. Even within the United Nations, China was still seen as a "system challenger" that "denounced the international system as unequal and unfair, often refused to participate in voting as a kind of protest, and advocated reform so as to increase the role and voice of developing countries."[40]

After Mao's Cultural Revolution, Deng Xiaoping started economic reform and opening up in 1979. China tried to change its "system challenger" identity and to learn how to integrate into international society. In other words, China, as a novice in the West-dominated system, started to socialize itself. Participating in multilateral institutions became the best way to learn how to interact with other members and "survive" in the system. Since 1979, China has gradually embraced multilateral institutions by joining major economic and political organizations, such as the International Monetary Fund (IMF), the World Bank (WB), and international human rights regimes. With Deng's market-oriented economic reforms, China needed to embrace economic institutions, for obvious economic reasons. Thus, we see that China became the largest recipient of loans and aids from the WB by the end of 2009.[41]

China also actively participated in security-oriented multilateral institutions, especially arms control regimes. Since the mid 1980s, it has accelerated its integration into arms control regimes, signing a series of non-proliferation treaties, including the Biological Weapons Convention in 1984, the Non-Proliferation Treaty in 1992, the Chemical Weapons Convention in 1993, and the Comprehensive Test Ban Treaty in 1996. Although some scholars suggest that US pressure may also explain China's participation in these institutions, there is no apparent material reward or punishment for its joining or not joining regimes such as the Conference of Disarmament (CD) and the Comprehensive Test Ban Treaty (CTBT).[42]

Johnston provides a socialization argument in which both mimicking and social influence, two microprocesses of socialization, played a decisive role in shaping China's pro-social behavior in arms control regimes. In particular, Chinese diplomats and experts were socialized by norms and rules of the arms control regimes through attending various training

---

[40] Shambaugh, *China Goes Global*, 133.
[41] Chinese Ministry of Foreign Affairs, *China's Foreign Affairs*, 2010, 318. Cited by Shambaugh, *China Goes Global*, 134.
[42] For the US pressure argument, see Evan Medeiros, *Reluctant Restraint: The Evolution of China's Nonproliferation Policies and Practices, 1980–2004* (Stanford: Stanford University Press, 2007). For a non-materialism argument, see Alastair I. Johnston, *Social States: China in International Institutions, 1980–2000* (Princeton: Princeton University Press, 2008).

programs and conferences. Through social interactions, these diplomats and experts began to believe that abiding by the rules and norms of the regimes was an appropriate behavior for China.[43] Johnston's argument is persuasive in that it opens the "black box" of Chinese decision-making processes through the eyes of participants of arms control negotiations. However, one unanswered question is why Chinese leaders allowed or decided to send these experts and diplomats to attend the activities of these institutions in the first place.[44]

The leadership-oriented socialization argument suggests that Chinese leaders purposefully joined arms control regimes because they wanted to socialize China into the existing international system. In other words, China intended to change its "system challenger" identity to become a real member of the system through participation in the arms control regimes. This analysis does not challenge the microprocess-based socialization argument; instead, it complements it.

The major goal of the arms control regimes is to maintain the stability of the system. If China wants to socialize and integrate into the system, the first thing it needs to do is to support its stability. It should be noted that under Mao, China refused all international restrictions on proliferation of missiles, nuclear weapons, and other weapons of mass destruction because "such restrictions aimed only to consolidate the two superpowers' hegemony."[45] However, after Deng came to power and started economic reforms in 1979, China gradually realized the benefits from system stability. In opposition to Mao's revolutionary or radical view on upcoming world wars between the East and the West, Deng believed that "peace and development are the two overriding issues in the world." More importantly, China's economic reform cannot succeed without a peaceful international environment. Logically, China needs to become a maintainer, rather than a challenger, of the current international system.

Joining global arms control regimes, therefore, became China's first effort in maintaining the stability of the existing international system. In 1979, Deng sent a delegation to the CD. China then officially joined the CD, its first major arms control regime, in 1980. Through participating in the CD, China sent a signal to the outside world that it wanted to become a member of the system instead of a challenger or an outlier. In other words, China started to learn how to socialize itself into the existing system after the economic reform in 1979.

---

[43] See Johnston, *Social States*, chapters 2 and 3.

[44] Johnston also admits that "it is not clear why China's leaders specifically decided to join the CD when they did." See Johnston, *Social States*, 52.

[45] See Andrew Nathan and Andrew Scobell, *China's Search for Security* (New York: Columbia University Press, 2014), 274.

The major purpose of the leadership-oriented socialization strategy is to change China's identity from a novice to an accepted member in the society. One thing China needs to learn is to take up responsibility, or the role that is comparable to its status. This means that, being a permanent member of the UN Security Council and a recognized nuclear power, China needs to do more to support arms control regimes. Therefore, it is not difficult to understand China's proactive diplomacy in various non-proliferation regimes in the 1990s, despite its tough negotiations over timing and provisions. As Shambaugh points out, "by signing these treaties and joining these [arms control] regimes, China took tangible steps to indicate it was a 'status quo' power and system-maintaining power."[46]

From a bargaining perspective, China's socialization strategy facilitates its pursuit of an accommodation for identity with the United States. For example, the United States started to encourage China to become a "responsible stakeholder" in 2005.[47] Although this can be interpreted as putting pressure on China to play a more active and responsible role in international affairs, such as the genocide in Darfur, the North Korean nuclear crisis, and the climate change issue, the stakeholder concept also means that the United States and the West-dominated system have treated China as an important member of the society and expect China to be more responsible in maintaining the system. In other words, China's new identity as a maintainer of the system has been accepted by the United States, though China still needs to do more to retain it.

Notably, socialization is not a one-way street. China can socialize into the society, and it can also transform the society in the future. In other words, China can be both rule-taker and rule-maker in the system. For example, China strived to raise its voting power in the IMF and to internationalize its currency after the 2008 economic crisis. These actions definitely challenge existing features of the system. However, since China has been accepted by or socialized into the system, its challenges are more likely to be accommodated by others, including the United States.

Legitimizing anti-separatist movements in Xinjiang

Although Chinese economic and military power rose dramatically after the Cold War, China remains one of the most vulnerable countries in terms of security. When discussing China's external security

---

[46] Shambaugh, *China Goes Global*, 134–35.
[47] Robert Zoellick, "Whither China: From Membership to Responsibility?" Speech, National Committee on US–China Relations, New York, September 21, 2005. Available at: www.ncuscr.org/files/2005Gala_RobertZoellick_Whither_China1.pdf.

environment, Andrew Nathan and Andrew Scobell point out, "China is the most penetrated of the big countries, with an unparalleled number of foreign actors trying to influence its political, economic, and cultural evolution, often in ways that the political regime considers detrimental to its own survival."[48]

In addition to the external threats, China also faces daunting internal challenges from separatist movements in Tibet and Xinjiang (Taiwan is also included in this category by the Chinese government). Tibet and Xijiang account for almost one-third of China's territory, and ethnic- and religion-based conflicts there between ethnic minorities and the central government (dominated by ethnic Hans) threaten the integrity of the nation. While Lamaist Buddhism is the dominant religion in Tibet, the ethnic minority Uyghurs in Xinjiang, who advocate "self-determination," are Muslims. Beijing is also concerned about possible penetrations and subversions by foreign countries in collaboration with local separatists in these areas.

China set up two autonomous regions in Tibet and Xinjiang, designed to give governing power to the local ethnic minorities. However, in order to ensure their loyalty to the central government, Beijing sent ethnic Han officials to co-administrate the local government, and sometimes these officials had the real control. Militarily, Beijing stationed a large number of troops and People's Armed Police (PAP) forces in both regions to deal with both external threats and internal uprisings. In addition, Beijing systematically dispatched large groups of Han migrants to support local economic development. In the eyes of local minorities, Beijing's Han-dominated modernization efforts were aimed at colonizing and assimilating the local minorities, as well as destroying local culture and religion.[49]

There are separatist movements in both Tibet and Xinjiang, but the methods of resistance are quite different in the two regions. First, while the Dalai Lama leads the Tibetan separatist movement as an internationally well-known spiritual leader, there is as yet no spiritual or political figure who guides the Xinjiang separatists. Although Beijing portrays Rebiya Kadeer, a Uyghur activist, as a powerful outside instigator, Kadeer's influence is very much limited even within her own ethnic group. Second, since the 1980s, the Dalai Lama has advocated a non-violent resistance strategy for Tibetan autonomous rights, and the Tibetan issue has been internationalized through his speeches and talks around the

---

[48] Nathan and Scobell, *China's Search for Security*, 4.
[49] See Melvyn Goldstein, *Tibet, China, and the United States: Reflections on the Tibet Question* (Washington, DC: Atlantic Council, 1995); James Millward, ed., *Xinjiang: China's Muslim Borderland* (Armonk: M.E. Sharpe, 2004).

world. Although there have been violent incidents such as the 1989 and 2008 riots and self-immolations of over a hundred monks in protest of Chinese rule, the Dalai Lama denies personal involvement in any violent events. The Dalai Lama was awarded the Nobel Peace Prize in 1989 for his peaceful resistance strategy against the Chinese government. In contrast, the Xinjiang separatist movements are much more violent in nature. Demonstrations, riots, terrorist bombings, and assassinations have frequently occurred in Xinjiang since the 1980s. In the July 2009 Urumqi riots, the ethnic conflicts between Uyghurs and Hans caused 197 deaths and 1721 injures.[50]

The Chinese government's strategy is to crack down on any antigovernment unrest and cut off any international support for separatist movements in these regions. On the Tibet issue, the Chinese government refuses to negotiate with the Dalai Lama and depicts him as a "separatist," trying to split the nation. China has also pressured foreign countries to cut their supports for the Dalai Lama. Consequently, many countries changed their policies toward Tibet. For example, India restricted Tibetan demonstrations against the Beijing Olympics in 2008. France officially announced that it refused to support "any form of Tibet independence" in 2009.[51] In Xinjiang, China claims that Uyghur separatists are terrorists with connections to al-Qaeda. Through the Shanghai Cooperation Organization (SCO), China has cracked down on the so-called "three evil forces" of terrorism, separatism, and religious extremism, with cooperation from Kazakhstan, Kyrgyzstan, and Tajikistan.[52]

The US attitude toward both Tibet and Xinjiang is ambivalent. On the one hand, the United States officially recognizes both Tibet and Xinjiang as China's territories. On the other hand, many US politicians are sympathetic about human rights situations in both areas. Since the Cold War, all US presidents have met with the Dalai Lama, publicly or privately, to display their concerns over human rights in Tibet. China always lodges strong protests against US intervention in its internal affairs. In response, the United States has not changed its position.

In Xinjiang, after the September 11 terrorist attacks, China began to bargain for a "legitimation-based" accommodation from the United States. China presented a report entitled "Terrorist Activities Perpetrated

[50] Yan Hao, Geng Ruibin, and Yuan Ye, "Xinjiang Riot Hits Regional Anti-Terror Nerve," *Chinaview* (July 18, 2009). Available at: news.xinhuanet.com/english/2009-07/18/content_11727782.htm. These numbers are based on the Chinese official report. The unofficial figures are much higher, according to Uyghur exile groups.
[51] "China Appreciates France's Commitment on Tibet," *Chinaview* (April 2, 2009). Available at: news.xinhuanet.com/english/2009-04/02/content_11121058.htm.
[52] For an excellent review of China's challenges and responses on the Tibet and Xinjiang issues, see Nathan and Scobell, *China's Search for Security*, 198–208.

by 'Eastern Turkistan' Organizations and Their Links with Osama bin Laden and the Taliban" to the UN Security Council on November 29, 2001,[53] in which it listed the terrorist attacks of the "Eastern Turkestan Islamic Movement" (ETIM) in Xinjiang after 1990, as well as its financial, personal, and training linkages with bin Laden and al-Qaeda. In February 2002, China's Information Office of the State Council published a White Paper entitled "'East Turkistan' Terrorist Forces Cannot Get Away With Impunity," which also listed terrorist activities of the ETIM in Xinjiang.[54]

The timing of these two official documents indicates that China may have attempted to legitimize its crackdowns on the Uyghur separatist movements by linking the ETIM with Islamic extremism and terrorism. Although some scholars question the real link between the ETIM and al-Qaeda and term it "imaginary terrorism,"[55] China's legitimation strategy succeeded internationally. In September 2002, US Executive Order 13224 and UN Security Council Resolutions 1267 and 1390 recognized the ETIM as a "terrorist organization," subjecting it to international sanctions.

Compared to the previously vague US attitude toward Uyghur separatist activities, this was a dramatic policy change, and it can be seen as a policy accommodation to China's anti-separatist campaign in Xinjiang. As mentioned earlier, the key to a legitimization strategy is to set a "rhetoric trap," through which a state can use its opponent's own rules and norms to justify its behavior. Here, China appealed to shared values and norms of anti-terrorism after the September 11 terrorist attacks, and used this rhetoric to justify its anti-separatism policy against Uyghurs in Xinjiang. Although details of the negotiation between China and the United States are still unknown to the public, we can imagine that it would have been difficult for the United States to say "no" to China's anti-terrorist efforts when its own campaign against terrorism was just under way.

Some may suggest that this was just an interest-based bargain between the United States and China, in which the United States abandoned the Uyghurs in return for China's support of its global war on terror.

[53] Available at: www.china-un.org/eng/zt/fk/t28937.htm.
[54] Available at: www.china.org.cn/english/2002/Jan/25582.htm.
[55] This chapter does not make any value-based judgment on either the ETIM or China's claim. Instead, it focuses on the effectiveness of China's legitimation strategy. For an argument against China's claim, see Sean Roberts, "Imaginary Terrorism? The Global War on Terror and the Narrative of the Uyghur Terrorist Threat," PONARS Eurasia Working Paper (Washington, DC: George Washington University, March 2012). For an argument supporting China's position, see J. Todd Reed and Diana Raschke, *ETIM: China's Islamic Militants and the Global Terrorist Threat* (Santa Barbara: Praeger, 2010).

That may be the case. However, the question is why the United States accommodated China only on the Xinjiang issue, and not on Tibet or other issues. It seems that without the legitimation efforts linking the ETIM to al-Qaeda, China would not easily have reached a deal with the United States.

Conclusion

It is worth noting that this chapter mainly focuses on exploring China's policy options for seeking accommodation from the United States. Why, and when, China picks certain strategies is beyond the analytical domain of this study. By the same token, this study does not explain how or why the United States chose to accommodate China, because the decision-making process in both China and the United States is more driven by domestic factors than by mere strategic considerations. However, it is also crucial to know what possible strategies China can use to bargain for a peaceful accommodation with the United States, because, as mentioned before, China is the one that will make the first move in this bargaining game. In other words, whether a peaceful accommodation will be successful or not depends on whether China makes the right strategic choice in the first place.

This chapter suggests four strategies – costly signaling, self-restraining, socialization, and legitimation – which China has used to bargain for a peaceful accommodation with the United States since the end of the Cold War. In particular, it discusses how China used these four strategies to signal its resolve on the Taiwan issue, strengthen its commitment on the South China Sea disputes, socialize itself into arms control regimes, and legitimize its crackdown of the Xinjiang separatist movements. However, there is no guarantee that these same bargaining strategies for a peaceful accommodation will continue to succeed in the future.

Since 2008, Chinese assertive diplomacy has been under harsh criticism.[56] Considering the US high-profile "pivot to Asia" in 2010, it seems that a new Cold War between China and the United States

---

[56] For an excellent review of the perceptions of China's assertiveness, see Michael Swaine, "Perceptions of an Assertive China," *China Leadership Monitor* 32 (2010); Michael Swaine, "China's Assertive Behavior – Part One: Core Interests," *China Leadership Monitor* 34 (2011); Michael Swaine and M. Taylor Fravel, "China's Assertive Behavior – Part Two: The Maritime Periphery," *China Leadership Monitor* 35 (2011). For China's assertiveness in the South China Sea, see Jane Perlez, "Beijing's Exhibiting New Assertiveness in South China Sea," *The New York Times* (May 31, 2012). For an excellent evaluation of China's assertiveness discourse, see Alastair Iain Johnston, "How New and Assertive is China's New Assertiveness?" *International Security* 37, no. 4 (Spring 2013), 7–48.

is on the horizon. From a bargaining and accommodation perspective, however, I suggest that it is still too early to predict a tragic outcome for China's rise if we treat the current turbulence in US-Chinese relations as a new bargaining process between the two. With its economic and military power increases, it is rational for China to bargain for a new accommodation with the United States. Although it is by no means easy, it is still possible for both to avoid conflict and achieve a new bargaining equilibrium if they adopt the right bargaining strategies.

For China, the first challenge is to make its new demands credible in the negotiation. It needs to send a costly signal about what it wants, just like it did during the 1995–96 Taiwan crisis. China launched its "core interests" diplomacy in 2009, identifying Taiwan, Xinjiang, and Tibet as its core interests and asking other countries, especially the United States, to respect them. The "core interests" diplomacy can be seen as a signaling strategy to inform the outside world about China's new demands. From the United States, China wanted a new accommodation policy on Taiwan. However, the United States did not easily give in to China's terms in the negotiation. Instead, it put China's resolve to the test. In January 2010, Obama authorized a new round of arms sales to Taiwan. Although China was furious and threatened to retaliate, it did not do anything meaningful. To a certain extent, China failed the credibility test for its "core interests" diplomacy.

To seek an accommodation for identity will be more difficult and challenging for China. Right now, the major obstacle to its acceptance in the international society is not its external behavior per se, but the nature of its regime. Democracy has gradually become the most accepted norm of governance in the world. In 2006, 121 of the 194 countries in the world are some type of democracy.[57] To use President Clinton's words in Beijing in 1998, China still "remains on the wrong side of history." In order for other powers to accept its rising status and possible leadership in the future, China may need to become a country like them. Therefore, how to transform its domestic identity and bargain for a peaceful accommodation is the fundamental challenge for Chinese leaders in the future.

It is not easy for the United States to accommodate or to accept China's rise. This is a rational and normal reaction of the hegemon toward the rising power. However, denying the new reality and refusing to negotiate with China cannot stop China's rise. A vivid example of this is the recent development of the Asian Infrastructure Investment Bank (AIIB). In 2013, China initiated to establish the AIIB in order to facilitate and

---

[57] Larry Diamond, *The Spirit of Democracy* (New York: Times Books, 2008).

finance infrastructure projects in the Asia Pacific. The United States strongly opposed the AIIB from the beginning, because it would challenge United States-led financial institutions such as the WB and the IMF, as well as the Japan-led Asian Development Bank. It is no secret that the United States lobbied its Asian allies, including Japan, South Korea, and Australia, to stay away from the AIIB. However, US financial "containment" against the AIIB started to collapse in early March 2015, when Great Britain announced its intention to join the AIIB as a founding member. Three more European countries, France, Germany, and Italy, soon followed suit. So did Australia and South Korea, two US allies in the Asia Pacific. By the end of March, a total of 46 countries had formally applied for membership of the AIIB, though the United State still said no to this China-led financial institution.[58]

This can be seen as a typical non-accommodation case, in which the risting power – China – established a new institution to challenge the existing liberal order, led by the United States. The outcome of the AIIB reflects a diplomatic failure of the non-accommodation policy of the United States toward China. As former Secretary of State Madeleine Albright later pointed out, "We (the United States) should not have done it this way."[59] It will be wise for US policymakers to take China's bargaining efforts seriously and consider reaching a bargaining deal to both accommodate China's rise and protect the United States' vital national interests.[60] Through tough negotiations, the United States should consider how to shape China's demands, enforce China's commitments, and transform China's identity. If accommodating China can eventually contribute to stability and prosperity in the international system, the United States will still be an indispensable nation, even if it may no longer be the hegemon.

---

[58] Jane Perlez, "Stampede to Join China's Development Bank Stuns Even Its Founder," *The New York Times* (April 2, 2015). Available at: www.nytimes.com/2015/04/03/world/asia/china-asian-infrastructure-investment-bank.html?smid=tw-share&_r=1.

[59] David R. Sands, "Democratic Titans Say Obama 'Screwed up' and Gave Rise to China's New Bank," *The Washington Times* (April 1, 2015). Available at: www.washingtontimes.com/news/2015/apr/1/efforts-to-head-off-china-development-bank-called-/.

[60] For arguments for accommodating China's rise, see Charles Glaser, "Will China's Rise Lead to War? Why Realism Does Not Mean Pessimism," *Foreign Affairs* 90, no. 2 (March/April 2011), 80–91; Hugh White, *The China Choice: Why America Should Share Power* (Collingwood: Black Inc., 2012); Amitai Etzioni, "Accommodating China," *Survival* 55, no. 2 (April–May 2013), 45–60.

11 Partial accommodation without conflict

India as a rising link power

Aseema Sinha

India's behavior at the global level has changed dramatically from that of a "reclusive porcupine"[1] to that of a rising power that wants a greater role in international organizations, negotiates strongly at the World Trade Organization (WTO), and seeks a permanent membership in the UN Security Council. It not only wants a stronger individual presence in global organizations but hopes to change the rules of the game (International Monetary Fund (IMF) reform, for example), which will also benefit the rise of similar nations. Its policymakers strongly pursue trade and global economic integration. Recent estimates suggest that India may become the fastest growing economy by 2016, overtaking China.[2] By measures of hard power, such as GDP, population, defense spending, and technological innovations, India held about 8 percent of global power in 2010, after the United States, the European Union, and China.[3] India currently spends about 1.98 percent of its GDP on defense, and it has enhanced its military capabilities in the past decade.[4] These changes, together, have led to a closer relationship with United States, as demonstrated by the passage of the United States–India nuclear deal. India claims its place as an Asian power no longer hemmed in by South Asian regional shackles.[5]

I thank Alexandra Vreeman, Janice Han, and Mira Liu for research assistance. Comments by Miles Kahler at an ISA panel were very useful, as were the comments by three anonymous referees. Special thanks to T.V. Paul for comments on the chapter. I also thank all the participants at the workshop, "Rising Powers: Is Peaceful Accommodation Possible?" held on November 2, 2013 in Montreal.

[1] C. Raja Mohan, *Crossing the Rubicon: The Shaping of India's New Foreign Policy* (Delhi: Penguin, 2003).

[2] The IMF predicts this in a recent speech. See Christine Lagarde, "Seizing India's Moment," International Monetary Fund, March 16, 2015. Available at: www.imf.org/external/np/speeches/2015/031615.htm.

[3] Gregory F. Trevorton and Seth G. Jones, *Measuring National Power* (National Security Research Division, RAND Corporation, 2005); Satish Kumar, ed., *India's National Security: Annual Review 2010* (New Delhi: Rutledge, 2011).

[4] Kumar, *India's National Security*, 1.

[5] Narasimha Rao, India's prime minister from 1991 to 1995, distilled this initial interest into a formal foreign policy orientation and visited South East Asian countries in 1993, though the term "Look East" wasn't first used until 1996, in a government publication

Many analysts recognize India and China as two strong nations that will reorder the shape of global power. While other scholars are more cautious about India's rising global influence, most agree that India could play a major role in the emerging multipolar global system.

This chapter asks an important question relevant to the shape of the emerging international system: What will be India's impact on the possibilities of peaceful accommodation or conflict in the international system?[6] Will India's strategic behavior create uncertainty, conflict, crisis, or peaceful accommodation? Will we see flashpoints of conflict between India and China, as the two rising powers compete for global prominence and scarce economic resources? Will India assume "meaningful international roles"[7] within the international system? This question is similar to that of whether India will become a "responsible stakeholder" in the international system.[8] This chapter addresses these related questions by analyzing India's preferences and strategies of global engagement and the strategies of accommodation adopted by the United States and the international system.

Most analysts of India's rising power treat the concept of "rising power" in a one-dimensional way. I disentangle an analysis of India's power into its preferences, strategies, and capabilities, which allows me to give theoretical space to the role of domestic politics and non-state actors in shaping India's global and regional ambitions. India's pursuit of its global ambitions will depend upon its ability to address its varied internal challenges. India's rising global influence cannot be understood by the traditional power transition approaches, which privilege a clear linear move from hard power to conflict and global transitions. In contrast to the predictions of the power transition approach, India may better be seen as a bridge or link power than as a rising power. Indian leaders prefer to find a seat at the table, not to initiate any conflict. Importantly, India's capacities to transform its goals into effective strategies are still limited, though the gap between goals and capabilities has been reduced with higher growth rates, nuclear tests in 1998, and higher defense

---

(Thongkholal Haokip, "India's Look East Policy: Its Evolution and Approach," *South Asian Survey* 18 (2011), 239–57). Vajpayee and Manmohan Singh continued this policy during their terms as prime minister.

[6] T.V. Paul defines accommodation as "mutual adaptation and acceptance by established and rising powers, and the elimination or substantial reduction of hostility between them." He notes that accommodation is more than an absence of war and also includes consideration of the other as a legitimate stakeholder in the regional and global system. See Chapter 1.

[7] See Chapter 1.

[8] Aseema Sinha and Jon P. Dorschner, "India: Rising Power or a Mere Revolution of Rising Expectations?" *Polity* 42, no. 1 (January 2010), 74–100.

expenditures.[9] I argue that non-state actors, such as business groups, the middle class, students, and professionals, are as important to the story of India's rise as Indian rulers and policymakers. In fact, governmental articulation of India's rising power has been somewhat ineffective. We cannot understand India's incorporation into the global system without focusing on non-state actors and Track II diplomacy (diplomacy that parallels official channels), which has afforded India a larger role than its hard power requires.

This chapter is divided into four sections. The first proposes an analytical framework and argues that India is a different kind of power, given its democratic roots. The sources of its rise lie in a form of geo-economic and soft power, and India is better described as a bridge or link power, rather than a major power. The second section analyzes India's changing negotiating behavior toward bilateral powers and global organizations. The third looks at India from an external perspective, showing how it has been partially accommodated in the global system. In line with the concepts developed in this book, I focus on symbolic, military, and institutional accommodation of India. The final section examines the possibility of a conflict between India and China. I argue that despite tensions between India and China, war is unlikely.

Concepts, analytical framework, and argument

India's accommodation in the global system must be analyzed as a combined function of its preferences and strategies, but also its capability to translate preferences into strategies. Preferences relate to the strategic vision of the foreign policymaking elites and may be a function of domestic public opinion and support for foreign policies. What do the Indian leaders want to achieve in the regional and global system? Do they see China as a threat and the United States as a partner? The ideas and preferences of non-state elites, such as businesses, the media, and students, must also be factored into an analysis of India's accommodation into the global system. Strategies refer to the menu of tactical and strategic instruments that a country adopts to achieve its stated goals. How does India negotiate with different parties in diverse global forums? Track II strategies, rather than official grand strategies, have been important to India's entry into global forums and to its forging of new relationships. Capabilities refer to the ability of a country to translate goals into strategies, especially in the long term, and to do so across issue-areas.

---

[9] Teresita C. Schaffer, "Partnering with India: Regional Power, Global Hopes," in *Strategic Asia, 2008–2009: Challenges and Choices*, eds. Ashley Tellis, Mercy Kuo and Andrew Marble (Washington, DC and Seattle: Asian Bureau of Asian Research, 2008), 201.

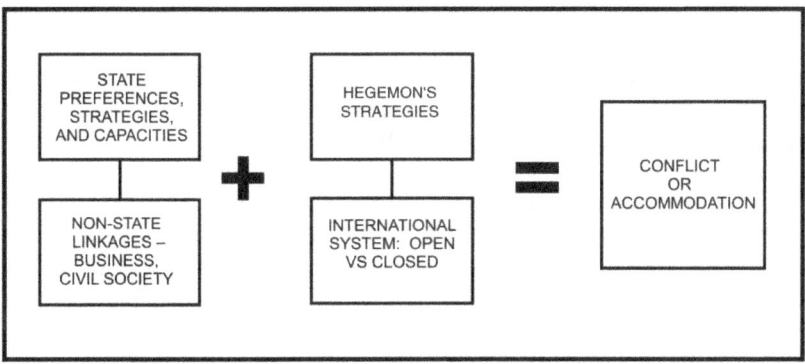

Figure 11.1 Analytical framework for understanding a rising power's accommodation

For India, ensuring long-term economic growth and building a sustainable economic basis that includes all sections of Indian society remains salient. Military modernization and refurbishment are also a very important part of a rising power's capabilities. Capacities of international influence must analyze the cognitive capacity within the country; this refers to the ability to generate debate about India's strategies or provide intellectual resources for different strategic options. Research universities and think tanks are examples of institutions that serve this purpose. In addition, the ability of a country to pursue its strategic goals is a direct product of the institutional structure of foreign policymaking. Is the structure of decision-making coherent and organized? Who are the powerful actors in the making of foreign policy? A reform of the institutional bases of foreign policies may be necessary for translating preferences into effective and long-term strategies.

Even if a country has peaceful strategies, its rise may yield undesirable outcomes if the established hegemons adopt resistant postures or if the international system is relatively closed. A country's immediate security environment will also shape the prospects of its accommodation. Thus, an analysis of the impact of such strategies must also explore the ways in which India is accommodated by dominant powers and global organizations. We must not conflate strategies with the ultimate outcomes, which are a result not only of strategies but also of how the international system reacts. This analytical framework, by disaggregating a country's responses into preferences, strategies, and capacities, gives a finer sense of what is responsible for the country's ability or inability to be accommodated in the global system. Figure 11.1 outlines the framework central to analyzing the rise of powers such as India.

The argument

I argue that Indian rulers seek incorporation in the global system, not military power or conflict. They aspire to a seat at the table, not a disruption of the international system. On the other side, accommodation implies mutual convergent interests or alignment with the United States, which Indians are wary of. They hope for engagement and recognition, not accommodation by the dominant powers. India is a *status quo power* and not a challenger to the global system in the way Germany or Japan were before World War II (WWII). India may better be seen as a *bridging or mediating power*, rather than as a major power seeking to defeat other powers. India also resists bandwagoning against the United States, seeking incorporation within global alliances and organizations. The United States and global organizations would need to evolve a different model of accommodation in keeping with "India's concept of sovereignty": one that recognizes the nuances of India's strategic goals and the emerging geopolitical realities.[10] A cautionary note must be heeded. India is a hesitant power partly because of its democratic roots, but also because the economic basis of its power is not totally stable. Thus, India's ambitions and claims must be seen in the context of its cognitive, economic, and institutional capabilities. Indian actors and rulers have done little to strengthen the institutional bases of translating preferences into capabilities, which will hold back India's quest for power.

While IR theory privileges hard power measures of rising powers, the sources of India's power lie in three distinct non-military mechanisms, which shape the kind of accommodation Indian rulers seek: (1) geo-economic and economic growth, (2) public expectations and people-to-people contacts, and (3) expansion and demand side effects. Rising economic growth increases the revenues that can be devoted to security infrastructure, including military expenditure. This may increase the capacity of the state to respond in an activist way in international or regional conflicts. It is not clear if these actions would lead to increase in conflict or cooperation. On the one hand, states may feel the need to adopt more aggressive strategies (Japan's militarism before WWII may be an example), but on the other, economic liberalization and global interdependence will also create pressures to adopt cooperative avenues of conflict resolution. In a similar vein, Kahler suggests that economic growth and liberal economic policies can create support for cooperative international strategies as countries try to bolster trade and

---

[10] Schaffer, "Partnering with India," 199.

economic interactions.[11] If this is true, India would and should respond with greater cooperative strategies within international regimes. The demand-based mechanism that fuels trade expansion at the international economic realm has been in evidence. A higher economic growth leads to new and expanding needs for energy and raw materials, creating an impetus for forays into new regions of the world (Africa) and new competition for energy resources.[12] This will create some competition between India and China, but conflict may be moderated by the expanding trade between them. The expectations mechanism works by increasing domestic support for shifting foreign policy. In India, growing support for closeness with the United States and a pro-Western tilt has resonated across India's masses, as well as the elites.[13]

What accounts for this pursuit of power strategies? First, India's nascent aspirations are a result of a historic cautiousness in power-seeking strategies. This arises because India is a hesitant power that has never sought to project its ideals abroad. Any theory of accommodating strategies adopted by these rising powers must think about how the democratic regime affects their larger strategies. Brazil and India are likely to pursue strong but peaceful strategies in their quest for incorporation into the global system. Second, India is not rising alone but both in concert and in competition with other powers, such as Brazil, China, and South Africa. The nature of the emergent multipolar order, with a number of competing powers, dictates a more cautious strategy for both the hegemonic and the rising powers. Each of the emerging powers faces a regional rival; in India's case, it is China. Indian actors do not want to escalate conflict with China, despite some structural tensions. Third, India lacks the domestic capacities that might translate its newfound power into real effective participation at the global level. Importantly, India's aspirations lack a coherent purpose and strategic vision. India also lacks institutions that can translate aspirations into achievements.

At a theoretical level, I posit three important modifications to the conventional theoretical frameworks reviewed in Chapters 1 and 2. First, I suggest that we must go beyond the conventional power transition approaches to understand India's insertion into the global system. India is a very different kind of power, given its democratic roots – the exact

---

[11] Miles Kahler, "Liberalization and Foreign Policy," *in Liberalization and Foreign Policy*, ed. Miles Kahler (New York: Columbia University Press, 1997), 16–7.

[12] John Lee and Charles Cull, "China and India's Growing Energy Rivalry," *Businessweek* (December 16, 2010). Available at: www.businessweek.com/globalbiz/content/dec2010/gb20101215_795065.htm.

[13] C. Raja Mohan, "India's Foreign Policy Transformation," *Asia Policy* 14 (July 2012), 108–10.

sources of its rise being economic prowess rather than military might – and the huge gap between its desires and its capabilities. India's rise will be peaceful, though India will not be an easy country for dominant hegemons to accommodate. India could become a rule-maker and status quo power without becoming an ally of the European Union or the United States. India's rise and entry into the global system challenges the conventional binary framework that poses only two alternative routes: power-seeking, such as by prewar Germany and Japan, and now China; versus peaceful accommodation, as represented by the United Kingdom's incorporation into the United States-led alliances after WWII. India will neither be an assertive military power nor allied with the United States. Framed another way, India will not create conflict, but will not align with the established powers, despite its natural affinity as a democratic power to the United States and the European Union. It will rather strengthen space for multipolar powers, but do so with some hesitancy, variability, and ineffectiveness. The approach I develop in this chapter takes seriously the concept of multipolar and geo-economic power represented by India and the other emerging powers. The source of India's power is geo-economic and economic growth, a divided demographic, and a large middle class, which drives India's global ambitions. Moreover, Indian policymakers are likely to use soft power to augment its strength. Importantly, India does not seek power for itself in a zero-sum manner (by inciting conflict), but looks to augment the power of like-minded nations.

The United States has sought to engage and accommodate India in global institutions and alliances. India has responded positively, but with some ambivalence, indicating that India will not become a tame ally of the United States. In the language of the concepts proposed by T.V. Paul,[14] India has been partially accommodated with symbolic and institutional accommodation more than military integration. The global system has less to worry about with India, because it can be harnessed as a bridge or link power that will uphold the liberal values of the international system but will not seek adjustment through military means.

Second, the nature of the international system faced by countries like India is very different than the one around WWII, when other rising powers flexed their muscles. In response, India, Brazil, China, South Africa, and others construct their global power not in a zero-sum but in a positive-sum way that enhances their combined powers. India, similar to Brazil and China, does not seek a purely distributive strategy of more power for itself, but wants power for a new coalition of emerging

---

[14] See Chapter 1.

states.[15] However, competition among the emerging powers also complicates issues. India and China, for example, compete with each other for global resources and have flashpoints of conflicts. If conflict is likely, it will be between India and China (or Pakistan), rather than India and the United States. Third, the rise of India reveals the role of non-state actors in shaping global power transitions. While Indian state actors and institutions have been less effective in global power strategy, societal interactions between the people and businesses across countries have created far more positive-sum integration than expected.

Historical legacies of Indian preferences over foreign policies

After independence, India was politically active at the international level but "retreated from world markets,"[16] pursuing a nationalist policy. Jawaharlal Nehru, India's first prime minister, was the main architect of nonalignment. He viewed it as a moral transformative method in terms of rejection of power politics in the international arena as well as a strategic tool to bargain effectively with the great powers.[17] Practically, this meant that from 1947 until the early 1990s India opposed hegemonic powers such as the United States. India aimed to stay away from the two great powers and to adopt equidistance in the Cold War. Yet, for Nehru, equidistance did not mean neutrality or non-participation in the global system, but non-participation in military blocs.[18] National state autonomy became one of the guiding principles of foreign policy, and India eschewed direct military alliances with great powers even as it collaborated with some of these same countries. All Indian leaders – Nehru, Shastri, Indira Gandhi – espoused a strong belief in this policy, even though they differed in their interpretation of the practice of non-alignment.[19] The state departments that dealt with foreign policy became strongly imbued with this orientation. Thus, non-alignment was a common thread across actors and institutions of foreign policy.

While non-alignment demanded political activism in international organizations where India took a leadership role in the developing world,

---

[15] Amrita Narlikar and Diana Tussie, "The G-20 at the Cancun Ministerial: Developing Countries and their Evolving Coalitions in the WTO," *The World Economy* 27, no. 7 (July 2004), 947–66.

[16] T. Roy, "The Textile Industry," in *The Structure of Indian Industry*, eds. Subir Gokarn, Anindya Sen, and Rajendra R. Vaidya (New Delhi: Oxford University Press, 2004).

[17] Baldev Nayar and T.V. Paul, *India in the World Order: Searching for Major-Power Status* (Cambridge: Cambridge University Press, 2002; Raju G.C. Thomas, *Indian Security Policy* (Princeton: Princeton University Press, 1986).

[18] Thomas, *Indian Security Policy*, 5.   [19] Ibid., 10.

India's economic policy tended toward self-reliance. To prevent dependence on external resources and support, policies favored import substitution industrialization and a suspicion of international trade. Indians called it "export pessimism." Import-substitution industrialization was implemented through a restrictive trade regime characterized by import licensing, quantitative restrictions, and high import tariffs. India's share of world markets declined from 2.42 percent in 1948 to 0.41 percent in 1979, at a time when the newly industrializing countries in East Asia (Japan and South Korea) were increasing their world market penetration.[20] Indian leaders supported state-led development and defended the cause of poor nations in international forums. Until the early 1990s, India was a closed economy; average tariffs exceeded 100 percent, quantitative restrictions on imports were extensive, and there were stringent restrictions on foreign investment. Many scholars and policymakers would concur with Joseph Grieco, who said of 1960s and 1970s India: "India possesses one of the world's most restrictive, cumbersome, and 'assertive' regimes regulating foreign direct investments."[21] Dennis Encarnation documented India's assertive strategy against multinational corporations, as India successfully undermined the market share of many foreign companies during the 1960s and 1970s.[22] These foreign economic choices led to low growth but a diversified, self-reliant economy with diffident actions at the global levels. As a result, global actors mostly ignored India.

How did these larger principles of foreign policy translate into India's bilateral relationships and global presence? Non-alignment irritated the United States, and a focus on state-led development created an ideological distance between it and India. Contempt for Indian leaders by US leaders, such as Henry Kissinger, was mirrored by Indian leaders' self-righteous tone. India's minister of defense under Nehru, V.K. Krishna Menon, adopted anti-Western foreign policies through much of the 1950s and 1960s. Yet, economic cooperation between the two was still possible. In the 1960s, the United States provided economic food aid, as well as support for India's green revolution. Such cooperation was short-lived, however. The United States stopped its food assistance in the late 1960s, alienating India. The Cold War distorted foreign relations and inhibited the economic impulses of trade and cooperation. The United States moved closer to Pakistan and India moved closer to the Soviet Union.

---

[20] Martin Wolf, *India's Exports* (New York: Oxford University Press, 1982).
[21] Joseph Grieco, *Between Dependency and Autonomy: India's Experience with the International Computer Industry* (Berkeley: University of California Press, 1984).
[22] Dennis Encarnation, *Dislodging Multinationals: India's Strategy in Comparative Perspective* (Ithaca: Cornell University Press, 1989).

In the 1970s, under Indira Gandhi, the Soviet Union became the main supplier of arms to India and trade between India and the Soviet Union expanded. In 1971, Indira Gandhi signed a treaty with the Soviet Union, as external security and economic relationships were moving in tandem. In multilateral organizations such as the General Agreement on Trade and Tariffs (GATT) and the United Nations, India became well known for its ability to say no. India was hemmed in by regional concerns and its difficult relationship with Pakistan. It did maintain good relations with some countries in the Middle East, but its relations with the rest of Asia were tenuous and distant. Focusing internally and regionally meant that India was largely ignored by other powers and was indifferent to larger global trends and alliances.

Mapping changes in India's preferences and strategies, 1990–present

In the 1990s, as the world changed around them, the Indian elite found themselves faced with a new global order. Simultaneously, India's foreign strategies changed dramatically both in terms of principles and vis-à-vis a wide range of bilateral relationships. Mohan notes, "The core concepts that defined India's political and economic development before this period – economic self-reliance, socialism, secularism, nonalignment, and third worldism – would be recast or come under great stress in the years that followed."[23] After some reversals, domestic liberalization was formally initiated in 1991, when Manmohan Singh, then the finance minister, was forced to take an IMF loan. He used this crisis as a reason to initiate widespread regulatory reforms at the domestic level. India reduced its peak applied tariff rate of 355 percent in 1990 to about 87 percent. Average tariff rates sank to 40 percent in 2000 and then 12 percent by 2007.[24] Quantitative restrictions were abolished on April 1, 2001, after India lost a WTO case.[25] Importantly, domestic economic orientations and international compulsions (both economic and geopolitical) came to reinforce each other, and security policy changes were as dramatic as the transformations in India's economic predispositions.

While the historical legacy of non-alignment continues to shape the ideational basis of India's foreign postures (the notion of strategic

---

[23] Mohan, "India's Foreign Policy Transformation," 108–10.

[24] See P. Chidambaram, "Budget 2005–2006: Speech of Minister of Finance," February 28, 2005. Available at: indiabudget.nic.in/ub2005-06/bs/speecha.htm.

[25] The India-QR case is the US challenge of Indian use of quantitative measures on balance of payments grounds. See Appellate Body Report, India, *Quantitative Restrictions on Imports of Agricultural, Textile and Industrial Products*, WT/DS/AB/R (adopted September 22, 1999).

autonomy, for example) and a non-activist attitude toward democracy promotion abroad, India's economic stances vis-à-vis states and international organizations have undergone significant changes. Some even argue that the new Modi government has eschewed non-alignment and embraced closer ties with the United States.[26] Bilateral economic and political relations with many countries have been radically transformed. Relations with Israel, the United States, China, Japan, and Asia more generally have seen significant changes. India has moved closer to the United States and embarked on new open policies with East Asia and South East Asia under the banner of its "Look East" approach. India's performance in multilateral regimes and diplomacy has improved and its negotiations have become more skillful and effective.[27]

India's capabilities to translate its rising power ambitions into reality

Many scholars have opined that India lacks the internal institutional capacity to sustain its changing foreign policy priorities and global ambitions. Its institutional structure is fragmented with numerous veto points. Foreign policies emanate from four different state agencies: the Prime Minister's Office, the Ministry of External Affairs, the Ministry of Defense, and, when trade policies are at issue, the Ministry of Commerce. The Ministry of External Affairs is the key foreign ministry and has within it regional departments related to broad regions of the world. The prime minister and his office always play crucial roles and should be considered agenda-setters in most foreign policies. The national security advisor, a member of the National Security Council formed in 1998, advises the prime minister on matters of global importance. For example, the national security advisor played a major role in India's negotiations on the United States–India nuclear deal. The Ministry of Defense and the army high command, constituted by the three military chiefs, also played a role in foreign policy-making. The Ministry of Commerce has been designated as the nodal ministry for negotiation with international trade organizations, including those related to bilateral trade discussions. This patchwork institutional structure creates issues of coherence and

---

[26] Harsh V. Pant, "Out with Non-Alignment, In with a 'Modi Doctrine,'" *The Diplomat* (November 13, 2014). Available at: thediplomat.com/2014/11/out-with-non-alignment-in-with-a-modi-doctrine/; Harsh V. Pant, "Under Modi, India Challenges Old Assumptions," *Yale Global Online* (March 12, 2015). Available at: yaleglobal.yale .edu/content/under-modi-india-challenges-old-assumptions.

[27] David M. Malone, *Does the Elephant Dance? Contemporary Indian Foreign Policy* (Oxford: Oxford University Press, 2011); Aseema Sinha, *Globalization and the Rise of India* (Cambridge: Cambridge University Press, Forthcoming).

coordination,[28] but a more serious problem is simply one of size and lack of capacity-building in new areas, such as economic diplomacy. The Indian Foreign Service, for example, is woefully small and is ill equipped to integrate economic, security, and cultural analysis.[29] Many observers have noted the lack of a cognitive infrastructure of the Indian state and the lack of think tanks to provide supportive policy advice and input.[30]

On the other hand, some positive developments deserve notice. India's trade ministry, the Ministry of Commerce, has revived itself, and puts pressure on other ministries to accommodate trade-related issues as they deal with the external world.[31] Institutions and trade policy processes, especially as they relate to multilateral negotiations, have undergone a massive change since 1998.[32] The Ministry of Commerce has gained in size, status, and intellectual power since it started to interact with businesses and think tanks. Such enhancements of state capacity are quite anomalous within India's insular bureaucratic culture. The Trade Ministry has initiated regular consultation and coordination and taken responsibility for negotiating at the multilateral level. Interestingly, new institutions have been created in the areas of intellectual property rights implementation, tariffs, and anti-dumping. Importantly, India's stances in global trade negotiations on services discussions, intellectual property, and industrial tariffs have undergone a change, catalyzed by the WTO and its institutional structure. Thus, while India's foreign policy capacity is weak at a general level, in certain areas, and within specific agencies, significant change and reform are evident.

Accommodation of India: soft, imagined, and partial

India's accommodation into the global system has outpaced its material and military capabilities as a major power. The United States seeks to evolve a new relationship that enhances India's rise in the hope that India will support US interests and counter China's rise. India has been imagined as a rising power by the United States and by an open global order ushered in after the decline of the Soviet Union and the emergence

[28] Frank O'Donnell and Harsh V. Pant, "Managing Indian Defense Policy: The Missing Grand Strategy Connection," *Orbis* 59, no. 2 (February 2015), 199–214.

[29] Kishan Rana, *Inside Diplomacy* (New Delhi: Manas Publications, 2002); Kishan Rana, *Asian Diplomacy* (Baltimore: Johns Hopkins Press, 2008).

[30] Daniel Markey, "Developing India's Foreign Policy 'Software,'" *Asia Policy* 8 (July 2009), 73–96.

[31] Interviews with the author.

[32] I document this transformation in Aseema Sinha, "Global Linkages and Domestic Politics: Trade Reform and Institution Building in India in Comparative Perspective," *Comparative Political Studies* 40, no. 10 (October 2007), 1183–211.

of global multipolarity. The international system has been more benign to India in the post 2005 period coinciding with its rising growth rates.[33] Most countries do not see India as a threatening power. As Singapore's foreign minister, George Yeo, put it in an interview with *The Hindu* newspaper in January 2007, "We see India's presence as being a beneficial and beneficent one to all of us in Southeast Asia." John Lee, a news editor, noted, "political and strategic elites increasingly see India as a predictable, stabilizing, cooperative, and attractive rising power."[34] A constructivist view of India is more valid than a realist view, as India has pursued power hesitantly. However, its rise has been promoted by the United States and other actors. Essentially, India has been given larger roles than those indicated by its hard power capabilities.

In line with the concepts developed by Chapter 1, I discuss the question of India's accommodation into the international system in terms of security, institutional, and symbolic engagement. India has been accommodated partially, with some significant symbolic and institutional accommodations, but only partial military accommodation. In addition, though, we must think about soft integration, which I define as societal integration between non-state sectors. Non-state actors have played a major role in bringing Indian concerns to the Western and global arenas.

Security accommodation with the United States

India's rising economic prosperity and the rise of China on the global stage have brought India and the United States closer, but the two countries still need to "develop a new partnership model, more selective in its foreign policy ramifications than existing US alliances and more in tune with India's concept of sovereignty."[35] Starting from a hostile and disengaged relationship with the United States, India has now begun regular but limited military cooperation. Three elements deserve study: (1) bilateral military exercises, which serve a symbolic purpose more than a military one, as well as naval cooperation, which began with the Malabar exercises in 1992 but has expanded since 2005, (2) arms and technology transfer to India, and (3) a trilateral partnership among the United States, Japan, and India. These do not transform India into a

---

[33] Manmohan Singh, India's prime minister, has clearly articulated this position: "An open economy empowers India at the international level." Manmohan Singh, "Open Democracy and Open Economy," *The Indian Express* (North American edition) (August 26, 2005), 8.

[34] John Lee, "India's Edge Over China: Soft Power," *Businessweek* (June 17, 2010). Available at: www.businessweek.com/globalbiz/content/jun2010/gb20100617_150774.htm.

[35] Schaffer, "Partnering with India," 199.

strategic ally of the United States but demonstrate that India and the United States are unlikely to be in conflict with each other. Naval cooperation is quite significant, as it signals a nascent United States–India partnership with respect to China. In fact, China sees the United States–Japan–India meetings as being about encircling China. If this is true, a de facto alliance between India and the United States is in the making.

Joint military exercises, arms sales, and naval cooperation

After September 11, 2001, India and the United States began some joint military exercises, which signaled a shift away from an alliance with Pakistan and toward one with India. In 2013, military exercises were conducted on US soil, involving 400 American and 400 Indian soldiers.[36] Air force joint exercises have also been regularized between the United States and India. Lt. Gen. Francis J. Wiercinski, the commanding general of the US Army Pacific in Hawaii, called it a "budding relationship."[37] Naval cooperation between India and the United States is more significant. In 2013, the two countries conducted the fifteenth joint naval exercise, titled Operation Malabar, since 1992. Naval cooperation accelerated after the signing of the New Framework for the US-India Defense Relationship and the Indo-US Framework for Maritime Security Cooperation of 2006. These frameworks outlined specific cooperation goals, including preventing transnational crime, maritime proliferation, and keeping naval routes open in the Indian Ocean.

US Deputy Secretary of Defense Ashton B. Carter, on a visit to India in 2012, stressed that Washington wanted to be New Delhi's "highest quality and most trusted long-term supplier of technology." According to Carter, "India had emerged as the second-largest FMS (foreign military sales) customer of the US in 2011, with imports worth $4.5 billion."[38] While some observers have noted the rise of arms sales from the United States to India as indicating that India is becoming dependent on the United States,[39] one needs to look at the evidence more carefully. Arms sales have increased to US$1.9 billion per year but do

---

[36] "India, US to Hold Joint Military Exercise at Fort Bragg in 2013," *The Times of India* (November 1, 2013). Available at: timesofindia.indiatimes.com/india/India-US-to-hold-joint-military-exercise-at-Fort-Bragg-in-2013/articleshow/17044407.cms.

[37] Ibid.

[38] Ashton B. Carter, Speech, "Towards a Joint Vision for US-India Defense Cooperation," CII, July 23, 2012, New Delhi, India. Available at: http://mumbai.usconsulate.gov/ot230712.html.

[39] Brahma Chellaney, "Arming India Into Dependency," *The Hindu* (January 14, 2014). Available at: www.thehindu.com/opinion/lead/arming-india-into-dependency/article5574316.ece.

not represent a significant sharing of military technology. As Bruce Riedel notes, "India has bought a considerable amount of military equipment from the United States in the last decade, but very few of its purchases were combat-weapons systems. Instead, India bought trainers, amphibious ships, maritime-patrol aircraft and especially transport aircraft – ten huge C-17 transport aircraft worth $4.8 billion, for example, and six C-130s worth almost another billion."[40] India and the United States have a historical distrust of each other and do not wish to share military secrets. US transfer of weapons implies export licenses, where India is required to guarantee that it will use the weapons for self-defense. Each sale has to be notified to the US Congress, which can block it.[41] India has been hesitant to accept such conditions, which are required by US law. On the Indian side, India still considers the United States to be an unreliable partner. In a military exercise conducted in 2008, India did not want to reveal the full strength of its aircraft technology and operated its radars in "training mode."[42] While US business interests have put some pressure on India to buy more arms from the United States, a careful analysis of such arms sales reveals the limited nature of such cooperation. The United States is unlikely to sell the latest and most advanced weapons to India. Two significant exceptions – the sale of twenty-two Apache attack helicopters, a purely combat aircraft,[43] and of a number of P-8 anti-submarine surveillance radar airplanes, which may involve the transfer of sensitive and secret technology – are not part of the historical equation between the two countries. Clearly, there has been some movement toward serious military cooperation between India and the United States, but it is important to take into account the details of such cooperation. The aggregate data on arms sales of US$8 billion hide more than they reveal.

United States–Japan–India strategic dialogue

A new dialogue and partnership has emerged among India, the United States, and Japan, which seeks to counter China and ensure some

[40] Bruce Riedel, "A Breakthrough in US-Indian Relations?" *The National Interest* (August 29, 2012). Available at: nationalinterest.org/commentary/breakthrough-us-indian-relations-7392.

[41] Richard Grimmett, "Arms Sales: Congressional Review Process," February 1, 2012, Congressional Research Service. Available at: www.fas.org/sgp/crs/weapons/RL31675.pdf. See also: www.dsca.mil/major-arms-sales/india-support-direct-commercial-sale-ah-64d-block-iii-apache-helicopters.

[42] Terrence Fornof, "Red Flag 2008–4: Lecture by USAF Col. Terrence Fornof," November 4, 2008. Available at: www.youtube.com/watch?v=WKEa-R37PeU.

[43] "India, US Set to Ink $1.4bn Deal for 22 Apache Helicopters," *The Times of India* (August 21, 2012). Available at: timesofindia.indiatimes.com/india/India-US-set-to-ink-1-4bn-deal-for-22-Apache-helicopters/articleshow/15578021.cms.

cooperation among the three countries. While underplayed by the participants, it is one of the most significant ways in which India is being accommodated and is playing a role in shaping the new security alignments.[44] It encompasses both security issues, such as the maritime security of India and the United States, and economic links across South and South East Asia. There is particular emphasis on the importance of protecting international sea lanes for international trade and energy security, but other economic issues are also important. As an example, "India is organizing a meeting of stakeholders from all three countries to start infrastructure projects in the northeast states that could be continued through Myanmar, Thailand and beyond. The idea is to build east-west connectivity to counter China's north-south links in south-east Asia."[45] Combined with official meetings between the three countries, many parallel forums have emerged that bring them together, including government-to-government multilateral meetings involving the three countries, starting in 2011.[46] As of June 2015, seven trilateral dialogues have been held to "exchange views on a broad range of regional and global issues of mutual interest."[47] Patrick Cronin, senior director of the Asia-Pacific Security Program at the Center for a New American Security (CNAS), notes, "The growing cooperation with India and Japan is driven by China's rise, there's no doubt about that. That doesn't mean it's directly aimed at China. They are all trying to respond to China's rise but not antagonize China. From China's perspective, any cooperation is encirclement."[48] Ten Track II strategic dialogues have taken place, organized by think tanks in the United States, Indian business groups, and Japanese companies. Another strategic dialogue was started in 2011, organized by three different institutions and co-hosted by Japan's Okazaki Institute and the Japan Institute of International Affairs, the United Service Institute of India, and the Vanderbilt University US-Japan Center. Three such dialogues have been held: "The first was in Delhi in November 2011, the second in Washington in October 2012, and the third time in Tokyo in March 2013, and it has been confirmed that this strategic

[44] Geoff Hiscock, "India, Japan Snuggle Closer as China Power Grows," *CNN* (January 25, 2014). Available at: www.cnn.com/2014/01/25/world/asia/india-japan-relations-hiscock.

[45] Indirani Bagchi, "India-Japan-US Trilateral Talks on a Higher Plane," *The Times of India* (April 27, 2014). Available at: timesofindia.indiatimes.com/india/India-Japan-US-trilateral-talks-on-a-higher-plane/articleshow/34265657.cms.

[46] US Department of State, "US-Japan-India Trilateral: Media Note," December 19, 2011. Available at: www.state.gov/r/pa/prs/ps/2011/12/179172.htm.

[47] US Department of State, "Media Note," June 27, 2015. Available at: www.state.gov/r/pa/prs/ps/2015/06/244441.htm.

[48] Josh Rogin, "Inside the First Ever US-Japan-India Trilateral Meeting," *Foreign Policy* (December 23, 2011). Available at: thecable.foreignpolicy.com/posts/2011/12/23/inside_the_first_ever_us_japan_india_trilateral_meeting.

dialogue will continue into the future."[49] These dialogues and meetings among India, the United States, and Japan are a significant indicator of India's accommodation into emerging security and economic alliances.

Symbolic accommodation

There has been a huge change in perceptions about India. The United States, especially after 2005, signaled that it would like to see India rise as a great power. Formerly disengaged and estranged democracies,[50] the United States and India have seen their relations make a remarkable turnaround. In recent times, assessments have ranged from the euphoric metaphor of "natural allies" to a more balanced sense of being "strategic allies." William Burns' comments in 2012 outline how the United States sees India at this time: "First, as India's recent economic rise has expanded its role and deepened its stake in shaping the international system, we are counting on India's rise as a truly global power – one that looks east and west, a strategic partner for economic growth, security, and the provision of public goods."[51] This is quite a striking change in attitudes and perceptions, though it has not been followed by real economic or military cooperation. Similarly, other powers in Asia (except for China) see India as a benevolent power. Observers note that India is regarded as the "preferred political partner" for regional groupings like the Association of Southeast Asian Nations (ASEAN), BRICS (Brazil, Russia, India, China, and South Africa), and the Shanghai Cooperation Organization (SCO).[52]

Improvements began during Bill Clinton's second term. Clinton categorized India as an emerging market and target for US investment. The 1998 nuclear tests by India created serious tensions; however, after Pakistan's incursion into India (known as the Kargil conflict) in 1999, Clinton supported India. This signaled a shift in US policy away from Pakistan for the first time since the United States first formed an alliance with it in 1954. In 2000, Clinton visited India, the first visit by a US president in twenty-two years. In 2005, the Bush administration initiated

---

[49] Center for Strategic and International Studies, "US-Japan-India Track Two Strategic Dialogue May 2013, Tokyo, Japan," May 29, 2013. Available at: csis.org/publication/us-japan-india-track-two-strategic-dialogue-may-2013.

[50] Dennis Kux, *India and The United States: Estranged Democracies 1941–1991* (Washington, DC: National Defense University Press, 1993).

[51] William J. Burns, "The United States and India: A Vital Partnership in a Changing World." Speech, Center for American Progress, Washington, DC, October 26, 2012. Available at: www.state.gov/s/d/former/burns/remarks/2012/199801.htm.

[52] C. Raja Mohan, "India and the Balance of Power," *Foreign Affairs* 85, no. 4 (July/August 2006), 18.

the India–United States nuclear deal, which allowed for civilian technology exports to India, overturning decades-old restrictions.[53] In March 2006, George W. Bush visited India, and Barack Obama followed in 2010, and then again in January 2015. Even as specific improvements have lagged, the shift in the symbolic recognition given to India should not be underestimated.

Institutional accommodation and integration

Historically, India has been effective at resisting any mandated requirements of international organizations, especially global trade, and it has usually voted independently on UN Security Council resolutions. Assuming the leadership of the "third world" and building a coalition of developing countries against Western powers have been the key means through which India has pursued "strategic autonomy."[54] India was a founding member of the Non-Alignment Movement (NAM) and a vocal proponent of the New International Economic Order (NIEO), as well as an important leader of the Group of 77 countries. In the late 1990s, these roles and positions were slowly reconfigured, and new coalitions and alliances within a smaller subset of emerging powers took shape. At face value, these coalitions look similar to earlier ones, but in substance they are very different. India has become part of a different set of cross-regional groupings, which has increased its global status. India joined Brazil, China, Mexico, and South Africa as a "dialogue partner" of the G8 group of advanced industrial countries. It was invited to join the "Five Interested Parties" talks within the WTO, which included the United States, the European Union, Brazil, and Australia. Brazil, Russia, India, and China began meeting regularly in 2004 and attempting to coordinate positions on financial policies, after Goldman Sachs proposed the notion that the BRICs constitute a set of countries with similar economic potential.[55] India is also part of a separate third grouping that includes the democratic emerging markets: the IBSA, comprising India, Brazil, and South Africa.[56] Indian participation in the larger G20

---

[53] Dinshaw Mistry, "Diplomacy, Domestic Politics and US-India Nuclear Agreement." *Asian Survey* 46, no. 5 (September/October 2006), 675–98; Harsh Pant, *The US-India Nuclear Pact: Policy, Process, and Great Power Politics* (New Delhi: Oxford University Press, 2011).

[54] Strategic autonomy seems to be the strategic goal of Indian rulers at this time.

[55] Dominic Wilson and Roopa Purushothaman, "Dreaming with BRICs: The Path to 2050," Goldman Sachs Global Economics Paper 99 (October 2003), 1–22. In 2012, South Africa was added to the group, making it "BRICS."

[56] Chris Alden and Marco A. Vieira, "The New Diplomacy of the South Africa, Brazil, India and Trilateralism," *Third World Quarterly* 26, no. 7 (August 2005), 1077–95.

is another illustration of a smaller cross-regional, yet more global, alliance formation. These overlapping groupings do not seek an alliance of developing countries but rather would like to negotiate with the great powers and change the rules of the game within international organizations.

In addition to changes in polices, Indian political leaders began to enmesh their policies within various regional and global institutional networks, such as the WTO, ASEAN, and the trilateral partnership of Japan, the United States, and India. Each of these relationships has both security and economic goals. Manjeet Pardesi documents these dynamics in South East Asia:

> In 1992 India became a "sectoral dialogue partner" of ASEAN and by 1995 had become a full dialogue partner. In 1996 India became a member of the ASEAN regional forum (ARF), the most important security grouping in the Asia-Pacific... India was granted the status of a "Summit level" partner of ASEAN in 2002. In 2003 India signed ASEAN's treaty of Amity and Cooperation. The same year India also agreed to establish a Free Trade Agreement with ASEAN within a decade. In 2005, India also became one of the founding members of the East Asia Summit (EAS).[57]

Soft and societal integration

Non-state actors have played a key, but largely invisible, role in shaping India's economic interaction with the Western economies. While the demise of the Soviet Union brought India and the United States closer, the Indian diaspora and business interests generated the key momentum. Though the Soviet Union collapsed in 1990, India–United States relations only began improving after 1999–2000, when a whole range of domestic and US actors began initiatives to improve them. Going against the domestic consensus in their respective time, specific political leaders, most notably Bill Clinton and George W. Bush, undertook foreign policy initiatives to cement the economic ties between the two countries. Atal Bihari Vajpayee's government was a major initiator of change, starting in 2000. During the United States–India nuclear negotiations in 2006–07, Manmohan Singh was willing to resign for the cause of saving the deal when faced with domestic opposition. Yet, domestic interests in both countries have also played a major role, lending support to society-based explanations. Manmohan Singh himself noted in 2005, "I sincerely believe that in the modern world the relationship between Governments is increasingly mediated through and influenced

---

[57] Manjeet S. Pardesi, "Southeast Asia in Indian Foreign Policy: Positioning India as a Major Power in Asia," in *India's Foreign Policy*, ed. Sumit Ganguly (New Delhi: Oxford University Press, 2010), 120–21.

by the relationship between civil society and the business community. It is on the foundation of people-to-people and business-to-business relations that we in Government try to build State-to-State relations."[58] Slowly, after 1991, business began to play a role in integrating into the global community.[59] Business organizations from India and the Indian-American community worked to change foreign policy relations during the nuclear test crisis in 1998[60] and the nuclear deal negotiations between 2005 and 2008,[61] respectively. American business interests in India (the United States India Business Council (USIBC), for example) played pivotal roles in changing the domestic debate on the nuclear deal in the United States. Without the work of such specific actors with leverage in their respective domestic contexts, United States–India foreign relations would have faced many more obstacles and delays. India's business association – the Confederation of Indian Industry (CII) – played a role in shaping India's Look East policy.[62] Increasing interaction between the Indian middle classes and American society also ensured that there was a huge support for pro-United States policies in India. For example, the United States received approximately 56 000 students from India for the year 2014, which is 9.5 percent of all foreign students in the United States, the second largest number after China.[63] Also, Indian tourist flow to the United States has increased from 378 039 in 2005 to 808 287 in 2014. Interestingly, business interests may have slowed India's integration into Asia, playing a negative rather than a positive role. Indian business interests attempted to slow India's growing trade with Asia and ASEAN. Domestic businesses were wary of being overwhelmed by goods from China or other Asian competitors. Similarly, Indian businesses resisted the entry of Wal-Mart, the US retail giant, into India.

Will there be conflict between India and China?

Contrary to the predictions of the power transition theory, there is reason to expect that conflict among rising powers is more likely than

---

[58] Manmohan Singh, "Sixth India-EU Business Summit," New Delhi, September 7, 2005.
[59] One of few authors to focus on this theme is Sanjaya Baru, "The Influence of Business and Media on Indian Foreign Policy," *India Review* 8, no. 3 (July/September, 2009), 266–85; see also Aseema Sinha, "Understanding the Rise and Transformation of Business Collective Action in India," *Business and Politics* 7, no. 2 (August 2005), 1–35.
[60] Sinha, "Business Collective Action in India," 8.
[61] Jason A. Kirk, "Indian-Americans and the US-India Nuclear Agreement: Consolidation of an Ethnic Lobby?" *Foreign Policy Analysis* 4, no. 3 (July 2008), 275–300.
[62] Baru, "The Influence of Business and Media," 270.
[63] Data from the US Visa Office for non-immigrant visas. See US Bureau of Consular Affairs, "Report of the Visa Office 2014." Available at: travel.state.gov/content/visas/english/law-and-policy/statistics/annual-reports/report-of-the-visa-office-2014.html.

conflict between emerging and hegemonic powers. If that is true, will India be forced into a power transition conflict involving China? The scholarly consensus seems to support the likelihood of war or conflict between China and India, given the prickly tensions that permeate the relationship.[64] I predict that, while competition and tensions will continue between India and China, both countries will avoid a war by design to augment their power in the international system. Mutual interdependence and global interdependence of the two rising powers is the countervailing force that might prevent war as a means of gaining power.

Historical tensions are augmented by the assertive actions of a rising and powerful China and a rising India. Historically, India's relations with China have followed a pattern of initial optimism, then a sense of betrayal, followed by mutual distrust on account of the 1962 war. Security and geopolitics have dominated the relationship, though there were some signs of an emerging trading relationship between the two in the mid to late 2000s. In the 1950s, India felt kinship with China, but this disappeared with the 1962 Indo-China war. India–China relations went into a "cold peace" period between 1963 and 1987, as India developed a more realist approach to China, shaped by power politics.[65] Indira Gandhi insisted that the border issue (loss of Indian territory during the 1962 war) was important and should be the test case for the normalization of relations.[66] Rajiv Gandhi, her son, became India's prime minister in 1985 and embarked upon a different policy toward China. In 1988, he decided to expand cooperation without solving the border issue. Rajiv Gandhi's visit to China in 1988 marked a significant change in the way India viewed China. The 1990s saw the relationship move forward with a series of high-level exchanges, as well as regular discussion on the border issue. In keeping with the predictions of the model proposed in this chapter, the absence of non-state actors within the domestic politics of India and China could also prevent further cooperation. Indian business is wary of China, despite increasing trade between the two countries.

Beneath the surface, competition and rivalry have continued to fester as a rising China grapples with the consequences of its own rise. India justified its nuclear tests in 1998 with the Chinese challenge to India, and the Chinese "punished India for its Anti-China stance in various international fora."[67] As late as 2005–07, China tried to prevent the United States–India nuclear deal within the Nuclear Suppliers Group and the

---

[64] Sumit Ganguly and Manjeet Pardesi, "Can China and India Rise Peacefully?" *Orbis* 56, no. 3 (Summer 2012), 470–85.

[65] John W. Garver, "Evolution of India's China Policy," in *India's Foreign Policy: Retrospect and Prospect*, ed. Sumit Ganguly (New Delhi: Oxford University Press, 2010).

[66] Ibid., 93.   [67] Ibid., 100.

International Atomic Energy Agency (IAEA). China's new (2013) proposal of a "Silk Road Economic Belt" to initiate a new infrastructure development across the various overland routes from China to Russia to Northern Europe and Venice has been taken up by Xi Jinping to create a Silk Road Fund of US$40 billion.[68] India is ambivalent about this new proposal, seeing a new threat to its north and east and a Chinese attempt to dominate the Asian region. Between 1998 and 2002, Indian negotiators, most notably Jashwant Singh, the Indian foreign minister between 1999 and 2004, were able to convince the US administration of China's hostility toward India.[69] US fears of China as a rising power, combined with effective diplomacy by India, led to the emergence of India as a counterpoint to China.

Despite such rivalry, there is some evidence of an emerging cooperation in the 2000s, which began to incorporate economic issues as trade between the two countries expanded. In 2005, India and China started a "strategic dialogue for peace and prosperity."[70] China allowed India observer status on the SCO. In November 2006, Hu Jintao visited India and promised not to block India's entry into the UN Security Council. Bilateral trade reached US$70 billion in 2013.[71] Despite these improvements, competition for energy resources across the world, as well as specific Indian and Chinese attitudes, has slowed the pace of possible cooperation and interchange. More recently, new hostilities ensued when China reacted negatively to visits by the Indian president and prime minister to Arunachal Pradesh. China has also opposed an Indian project in the Asian Development Bank and created tensions around the stapling of visas from India. Such incidents seem to have derailed the prospects of a peaceful relationship.

I suggest that India and China's troubled relationship must be evaluated in both a multilateral and a bilateral framework. While many bilateral tensions remain, multilateral cooperation and collaboration also mark the relationship. India and China have cooperated effectively in the WTO negotiations, even though China challenged India in the nuclear

---

[68] "Where All Silk Roads Lead," *The Economist* (April 11, 2015). Available at: www.economist.com/news/china/21648039-through-fog-hazy-slogans-contours-chinas-vision-asia-emerge-where-all-silk-roads.

[69] Ibid.

[70] Joint Statement of the Republic of India and the People's Republic of China, April 11, 2005. Available at: www.mea.gov.in/bilateral-documents.htm?dtl/6577/Joint+Statement+of+the+Republic+of+India+and+the+Peoples+Republic+of+China.

[71] See, Jason Burke, "India and China Announce Trade Deals during XI visit to Delhi," *The Guardian* (September 18, 2014). Available at: www.theguardian.com/world/2014/sep/18/india-china-trade-deals-xi-delhi; Jeff M. Smith, *Cold Peace: China-India Rivalry in the Twenty-First Century* (Lanham: Lexington Books, 2014).

suppliers group. In July 2014, India, together with China, Brazil, Russia, and South Africa, set up a "New Development Bank," with equal shares in its governance structure. While there has been competition over the new regional bank set up by China, it seems likely that India will join the new Asian Infrastructure Investment Bank (AIIB) started by China.[72] There is some evidence to suggest that some Chinese policymakers do not regard India as an enemy but rather "as an independent international power that is unlikely to be part of any US designs in which it will be used as a counterweight against China."[73] I would concur with the conclusions of Jeff Smith, who argues that it is not a rivalry of equals. He notes: "Thirteen years into the new century, the strategic gap between China and India is as large, or larger, than the gap between China and the United States... China's official military budget of $119 billion was over three times larger than India's $38 billion defense budget in 2013."[74] This inequality will prevent a real war between the two countries, though competition will be pervasive.

Conclusion

What picture of India emerges from this chapter? India adopts assertive and changing foreign policy postures but is unlikely to initiate war or conflict with either the hegemonic powers or China. India's preferences are to be incorporated and respected as a great power, without using those power achievements to initiate conflict. India should be regarded as a bridge power, which will not act in threatening ways to established powers. China does perceive some of India's actions to be threatening, especially in its partnership with Japan and the United States. India has tried to frame that partnership in subtle ways and has retreated from some actions, such as joint military exercises with Japan.[75] India will not initiate conflict, though there is some possibility of a war by accident between India and China.

India has been partially incorporated into global institutions and alliances. While India does not see its interests as convergent with the

---

[72] Prasanta Sahu, "India Considering Joining New Regional Infrastructure Bank," *The Wall Street Journal* (August 27, 2014). Available at: www.wsj.com/articles/india-considering-joining-new-regional-infrastructure-bank-1409149842.

[73] G. Venkat Raman, "India in China's Foreign Policy," *China: An International Journal* 9, no. 2 (September 2011), 350.

[74] Jeff Smith, *Cold Peace: China–India Rivalry in the Twenty-First Century* (New York: Lexington Books, 2013).

[75] In 2007, when Japan joined the joint military exercises with India and the United States, China protested and India retreated, at least for a few years. More recently, India has resumed joint and trilateral dialogues with Japan and the United States.

United States or the European Union, it is closer to the hegemonic powers than China or Russia. India has also adopted key leadership roles in some multilateral forums and enjoys the respect of developing countries. These developments ensure that India will serve as a link or bridging power that has been partially accommodated in the global system. Non-state actors, such as Indian businesses, American businesses, and the Indian diaspora, have played a large role in the integration of India into global networks. Thus, the linkages for India's peaceful rise lie in its own preferences and strategies, its weak capacity for military conflict, and the benign and open character of the international system.

12 Brazil
Revising the status quo with soft power?

David R. Mares

International politics are in flux, as the "unipolar moment" seems to be slipping away in the Chinese economic and military surge of the past decade and the Russian desire to contest US leadership along its periphery. Into this context, some of the larger developing nations (e.g., India, Brazil, South Africa, Indonesia, and Turkey) are increasingly clamoring for a greater role in global politics and demanding that the governance structures of the international system take more account of their own interests as those structures seek to accommodate new international realities. These developing nations are seeking more recognition of their economic importance and of what they perceive as their appropriate political clout, as well as a cohesive and greater role in the international organizations that make up the global governance structure in economics, politics, the environment, and security. Recognition and acceptance into the global governing structures would constitute "emergence." A leadership role in a multilateral institution that has little impact on the behavior of the major players in the international order (e.g., G77) is not an indication of emergence.

In this chapter, I argue that Brazil is attempting to emerge not for the sake of overthrowing the existing international order but in order to reform its structures and revise its foundational myths. Brazil believes that if the current world order is to survive, it must incorporate more perspectives from the South, and that Brazil can represent those perspectives.

Historical constants in Brazilian aspirations allow us to proceed without paying a great deal of attention to the variations in domestic politics.

This chapter was supported by funds from a Department of Defense Minerva grant, PR# 0010352431 ARO Proposal No. 61900-LS-MRI "The Military-Industrial-Scientific Complex and the Rise of New Powers: Conceptual, Theoretical and Methodological Contributions and the Brazilian Case." I want to thank Rodrigo da Costa Serran for his research assistance, Harold Trinkunas for long discussions on the nature of Brazil's efforts to emerge, and T.V. Paul and the participants in the McGill workshop for stimulating comments. All responsibility is mine.

This does not mean that the country is a black box internally; domestic politics play a role, but their influence has been on the margins of foreign policy, not challenging its central thrust. A vivid illustration is found in the unexpected shock of June 2013, when Brazilians protested across the country against the expense of preparations for the upcoming Olympics and World Cup. Despite these significant domestic challenges, President Dilma Rousseff still opened the General Debate of the UN General Assembly a few months later with a major international offensive against the United States' abrogation to itself of the right to use the Internet to spy on the governments and citizens of countries posing no threat to US national security.[1]

Brazil has aspired to great power status for a century, permitting analysts to evaluate how reception by great powers of Brazil's efforts to use hard and soft power to emerge has affected both its ability to rise and its behavior. Brazil has always sought full accommodation by the liberal status quo during its ascendant periods, and has been on the winning side (World War I (WWI), World War II (WWII), the Cold War) in the major confrontations against the global order. It does not need to be "co-opted" or "socialized" into a liberal world order. But it has also articulated the need to reform that order to more adequately reflect the interests of developing nations. Those interests were best advanced using soft power, and Brazil tried to develop and use soft power strategies. Brazil's revisionist interests, nevertheless, posed challenges to great power views along a number of dimensions. Since the aspects of great power preferences that Brazil sought to challenge were not critical to liberal security, political, economic, and social principles, they might have been accommodated without overthrowing the global order. Yet Brazilian preferences were opposed at virtually each stage. Such opposition influenced Brazilian behavior as it began emerging; the combination of opposition by great powers and Brazil's own behavior accounts for its failure to emerge in the past and its difficulties in emerging today.

Brazil is an important case for analyses of soft power. According to the Soft Power Index developed by the Institute for Government and *Monocle Magazine* in 2012, Brazil ranked 17 in potential influence, ahead of Turkey at 20, South Africa at 34, and India at 36; China came in at 22. Until 2014, Brazil avoided the common pitfalls by which "many states routinely undermine their own soft power with poorly-conceived policies, short-sighted spending decisions, domestic actions, or clumsy

---

[1] Julian Borger, "Brazilian President: US Surveillance a 'Breach of International Law,'" *The Guardian* (September 24, 2013). Available at: www.theguardian.com/world/2013/sep/24/brazil-president-un-speech-nsa-surveillance.

messaging."[2] The current economic slowdown and corruption scandals, however, undermine Brazil's ability to attract followers from the South.

In the next section, I lay out the argument. The section after that examines Brazilian strategies for emergence in light of these propositions, demonstrating the country's revisionist goals and its emphasis on soft power but awareness of the benefits to be achieved through developing its hard power. The subsequent section evaluates Brazil's successes in reforming and revising some of the major structures of the international order. The conclusion addresses Brazil's likely successes and failures in the future, as well as drawing out some lessons from the case concerning soft power.

The argument

Scholars have long recognized the power of leading states of the international order to bend the rules in their favor. For example, John Ruggie's discussion of "embedded liberalism"[3] helped us understand why the use of non-tariff barriers or outright protection of their own agricultural sectors could be perceived as legitimate by the United States, Western Europe, and Japan even as they were pressuring developing countries to open their markets to international competition. The insights of Robert Putnam's "two-level game" paradigm[4] have been used to legitimate the ability of great power states' domestic politics to influence the implementation of international rules and norms, but do not preclude judgments that Southern countries need to reform their domestic politics in order to promote international "cooperation." Similarly, David Lake claims legitimacy for unilateral punishment by the provider of order in the international hierarchy.[5]

Brazil contests the legitimacy of great power exceptions to the norms and rules. In the current international order, great power myths include

---

[2] Jonathan McClory, *The New Persuaders III: A 2012 Global Ranking of Soft Power* (London: Institute for Government, 2012), 11. The index is based upon "a broad set of statistical metrics and subjective data (50 metrics in total), comparing countries according to the quality of their government; diplomatic infrastructure; cultural output; capacity for education; and their appeal to business. The data is normalised, grouped into sub-indices, and calculated using our composite index formula to arrive at a single score for each country included in the study."

[3] John Gerard Ruggie, "International Regimes, Transactions, and Change: Embedded Liberalism in the Postwar Economic Order," *International Organization* 36, no. 2 (Spring 1982), 379–415.

[4] Robert D. Putnam, "Diplomacy and Domestic Politics: the Logic of Two-Level Games," *International Organization* 42, no. 3 (Summer 1988), 427–60.

[5] David A. Lake, *Hierarchy in International Relations* (Ithaca: Cornell University Press, 2009), 28–30.

an emphasis on "letting the market work" while not ensuring its competitiveness or the provision of sufficient information to permit all actors to make informed choices;[6] an insistence on extending controls of the nuclear non-proliferation regime over non-nuclear powers without making progress on its nuclear disarmament provisions; and a demand that "democracy" means not just the will of the majority, but a protection of minority views, even as the most powerful democratic government is developing capabilities to intercept private and personal communications among people across the globe, and mine and archive them for broadly defined national security purposes.

The varying combinations of hard and soft power[7] that emerging states will use to gain influence are a function of their predominant value to the existing leaders of the international order. An emphasis on hard power will be attractive for emerging states whose characteristics contain traditional strategic assets of concern to the leading powers. India, for example, borders US rivals China and Pakistan, an Islamic nuclear-armed country that is a major focus of US security concerns about international terrorism. Turkey might be another example of a potentially hard-power emerging state, since it has been reluctant to engage in widespread use of its soft power in the Islamic world, but projects hard power on its borders with the unstable Syria and Pakistan.

Emerging powers without such traditional security assets will find it necessary to convince existing great powers that their emergence will be stabilizing for the international order because they represent the restless unrepresented. Hard power is thus less relevant, since these emerging powers do not expect to fight their way to leadership; soft power will be key to realizing their aspirations. *But the soft power will be directed to the unrepresented that the emerging power claims to represent, not to the leading great powers.* That is because the value of an emerging power to a great power stems from the emerging power's ability to maintain or develop support among countries of the South for global governance structures. While the great powers may find these emerging powers credible members of the global institutions because of their democratic political

---

[6] Most advocates of "letting the market work" forget that the theory of capitalism that justifies this principle assumes competitive markets and informed choice by consumers, conditions not required by the promoters of markets in public policy.

[7] Joseph S. Nye, *Soft Power: The Means to Success in World Politics* (New York: Public Affairs, 2004). Brazilian military elites define soft power (*poder brando*) in ways distinct from the civilian leadership, which follows the accepted version offered by Nye. For the Brazilian military, soft power means the power to dissuade, but not in an intimidating manner. See article by the Army Chief of Staff, in Joaquim Silva e Luna, "Saudação aos novos oficiais-generais do Exército," May 8, 2012. Available at: www.eb.mil.br/c/document_library/get_file?uuid=5c0de301-28d9-406a-b7dc-ccbda9ffa551&groupId=16541.

systems or mixed capitalism economic structures, it is the expectation that they speak for the South that will give them influence. South Africa and Brazil are examples of these soft power emerging powers.

Soft power will be preferred by these latter emerging countries because it generates less resistance from leaders of the international order than pursuing military equivalence, and because they value avoiding militarized competition in their geopolitically marginalized area. But having sufficient military power to keep great powers respectful and cautious about their behavior toward one's goals and behavior is nonetheless important. This view is captured in the Brazilian view on nuclear capabilities: Brazil wants, as Japan and Germany do, to have the capability to produce nuclear weapons, though they promise never to develop them in normal circumstances (Brazil's constitution prohibits it, but constitutions can be amended or even replaced – Brazil has had six).

Brazilian strategies for emergence

Since the end of the Brazilian Empire in 1889, governments have understood the importance of being active participants in the governance structures of international affairs. In 1899, the new Brazilian government responded to the invitation to take part in the First International Peace Conference with a reasoned declaration that it was not yet ready to assume a major role in the governance of world affairs, nor did it have an interest in the military balance on the European continent[8] – thus, it did not want to be a mere attendee, its presence contributing to legitimize results on which it had no bearing. Brazil attended the Second International Peace Conference in The Hague in 1907 and was instrumental in defending the principle of the legal equality of states. Since then, participation with voice in multilateral institutions and fora in which Brazilian interests are affected has been an important component of Brazilian foreign policy.

Brazil believes that it belongs in global leadership councils because of its geographic, demographic, and economic size, as well as its international behavior: Brazil has not instigated any major international tensions, preferring to pursue diplomatic avenues for the resolution of conflict.[9]

---

[8] "Relatorio apresentado ao presidente da República dos Estados Unidos do Brazil pelo ministro de estado das relaçoes exteriors, 1899, annex 1, p. 74," in *The Hague Conventions and Declarations of 1899 and 1907 accompanied by Tables of Signatures, Ratifications and Adhesions of the Various Powers, and Texts of Reservations*, ed. James Brown Scott (New York: Oxford University Press, 1915).

[9] Celso Lafer, "Brasil: dilemas e desafios da política externa," *Estudos Avançados* 14, no. 38, (2000), 260–67.

One of its national heroes is the Baron Rio Branco, who used international juridical procedures to win territory the size of France from neighbors without firing a single shot.

Brazil accepts its systemic constraints, even when they present obstacles to the achievement of its international goals. In 1926, the League of Nations granted Germany, the defeated country in WWI, a permanent seat at its Council, but not Brazil, a belligerent on the winning side. Brazil withdrew from the organization in protest but did not seek to demonstrate its power through an aggressive foreign policy. In the creation of the United Nations, Brazil, whose troops participated in the Allied victory in Italy, aspired to a permanent seat on the Security Council, but was vetoed by the Soviet Union and the United Kingdom. Brazil did not protest this time, but accepted recognition of its status as an important international player, embodied in its right to be the first country to speak at the annual General Debates of the UN General Assembly. Brazil is tied with Japan for the most times elected to the UN Security Council, winning ten elections.[10]

Brazil champions international institutions, but expresses a preference for structures based on one vote per member. Brazil believes in the primacy of national sovereignty for everyone, not just great powers. By "the primacy of national sovereignty," Brazil means that states are bound by international agreements only if they accept those constraints at each point that they actually come into play, not simply because they have made a promise to follow certain behaviors in a hypothetical situation that may or may not come to pass. Brazilian foreign policy consistently defends the norm that states should give each other the benefit of the doubt when international commitments have been made, rather than design means by which institutions can force compliance with commitments. Brazil takes an active role in the multilateral institutions of which it is a member. Attaining leadership positions in these institutions is perceived as enhancing its soft power with other developing countries, and thereby providing support for its demand that current great powers recognize its emergence.

Brazilian leaders are well versed in soft power and articulate the country's focus on it. Minister of Culture Marta Suplicy has noted that hosting the 2014 World Cup contributed to Brazil's soft power,[11] former Minister of Foreign Affairs Celso Lafer has written about the use of influence

---

[10] United Nations Security Council, "Countries Elected Members of the Security Council." Available at: www.un.org/en/sc/members/elected.asp.

[11] Blog Acesso, "Marta Suplicy – Diplomacia Cultural," May 2014. Available at: www.blogacesso.com.br/?p=7305.

in multilateral institutions,[12] and Celso Amorin, former ministry of foreign affairs and twice minister of defense, has stressed the importance of cooperation between Brazil and other countries as a tool of soft power. Amorin also claims that because of the Brazilian "way" in regard to foreign policy, Brazilians now lead major international organizations (the UN Food and Agriculture Organization (FAO) and the World Trade Organization (WTO)).[13]

Brazil has advocated pharmaceutical patent reforms in the case of diseases that decimate poor developing nations and has made its own pharmaceuticals and vaccinations available at little or no cost. Its public health programs to prevent the spread of AIDS, its anti-tobacco efforts, and its family support programs, which promote education, are considered to demonstrate the country's responsible behavior vis-à-vis the challenges facing developing countries.[14] Brazil also sees itself as a leader on environmental issues,[15] where it is an active participant in global discussions. It hosted the Earth Summit in Rio de Janeiro in 1992, out of which came three major UN conventions: the Framework Convention on Climate Change, the Convention to Combat Desertification, and the Convention on Biodiversity. Brazil also hosted the UN Conference on Sustainable Development in 2012, (Rio + 20). With South Africa, India, and China, it forms the BASIC coalition, which collaborates on positions in international negotiations on climate change. Despite participation in these discussions, Brazil has always rejected the notion that international concerns over the environment should have any influence on how Brazil chooses to develop and safeguard different parts of the Amazon. The country views it as its sovereign right to expand settlements, agriculture, and energy projects into the Amazon.

Brazilians see their soft power strengths as based on their successes in democracy, economic growth, and social inclusion. But a focus on soft power does not mean that Brazil sees no place for hard power. While it has no major territorial disputes with its neighbors, Brazilian governments

---

[12] Lafer, "Brasil: dilemas e desafios da política externa."

[13] Celso Amorim, "Hardening Brazil's Soft Power," *Project Syndicate* (July 16, 2013). Available at: www.project-syndicate.org/commentary/a-more-robust-defense-policy-for-brazil-by-celso-amorim.

[14] See Kelley Lee, Luiz Carlos Chagas, and Thomas E. Novotny, "Brazil and the Framework Convention on Tobacco Control: Global Health Diplomacy as Soft Power," *PLoS Med* 7, no. 4 (2010), 1–4; Ministério das Relações Exteriores, "Ata da Sexta Reunião da Comissão Mista de Cooperação Política, Econômica, Científica, Tecnológica e Cultural Brasil-Índia," Brasília, October 15, 2013. Available at: www.itamaraty.gov .br/index.php?option=com_content&view=article&id=3418:ata-da-sexta-reuniao-da-comissao-mista-de-coope.

[15] *"Perspectivas sobre as negociações de mudança climática e seus impactos na política brasileira,"* *Comunicados do Ipea* 45 (April 22, 2010).

have been concerned to keep costs high for anyone contemplating either seizing the Amazon in the name of preserving biodiversity or safeguarding the environment, or, now, defending the pre-salt hydrocarbon basins in the Brazilian Atlantic Ocean.[16]

The country also believes that the respect and reputation that provide influence, even in international arbitrations, are significantly affected by having a modern and capable military capacity. Rear Admiral Guilherme Mattos de Abreu told attendees at the VII Academic Congress on National Defense that well-equipped, trained, and credible armed forces are essential for a country's positive image and for the exercise of soft power.[17] Defense Minister Amorim puts it most succinctly:

Yet no country can rely on soft power alone to defend its interests. Indeed, in an unpredictable world, where old threats are compounded by new challenges, policymakers cannot disregard hard power. By deterring threats to national sovereignty, military power supports peace; and, in Brazil's case, it underpins our country's constructive role in the pursuit of global stability. That role is more necessary than ever. Over the past two decades, unilateral actions in disregard of the UN Security Council's primary responsibility in matters of war and peace have led to greater uncertainty and instability. Likewise, little progress toward nuclear disarmament has been made, in disregard of the Nuclear Non-Proliferation Treaty. Brazil's abundance of energy, food, water, and biodiversity increases its stake in a security environment characterized by rising competition for access to, or control of, natural resources. In order to meet the challenges of this complex reality, Brazil's peaceful foreign policy must be supported by a robust defense policy.[18]

Brazil's defense sector and its academic allies recognize its weakness in science and technology and have been arguing for a national effort to overcome this problem.[19] The 2008 National Defense Strategy calls for increased strength in three areas of "strategic importance": aerospace,

---

[16] Brazil Ministry of Defense, *Estrategía Nacional de Defesa* (Brasilia: Ministry of Defense, 2008). Available at: www.infodefensa.com/wp-content/uploads/Estrategia NacionalDefensa_Brasil1.pdf.

[17] Guilherme Mattos de Abreu, "Defesa e Democracia," in *Revista Villegagnon* 5, supplement (2010), 144–59. Available at: www.mar.mil.br/en/REVISTA_VILLEGAGNON_ 2010_Suplemento_Ano_V.pdf.

[18] Amorim, "Hardening Brazil's Soft Power."

[19] Roberto Resende Simiueli, "A política nacional de informática e o nacionalismo militar," *Revista de Estudos Estratégicos* 3 (January/June 2008), 42; Peterson Ferreira da Silva, "ST&I and National Defense: New Directions for the Brazilian Debate," *Revista Brasileira de Ciência, Tecnologia e Sociedade* 2, no. 1 (January/June 2011), 239–51; regarding ST&I as a strategic conception, see Brazilian Government, *Concepção Estratégica: Ciência, Tecnologia e Inovação de Interesse da Defesa Nacional* (Brasilia: Ministério da Defesa & Ministério da Ciência e Tecnologia, 2003). Available at: ftp.mct.gov.br/ Biblioteca/890-Concepcao_estrategica_CTI_defasa_nacional.pdf.

cybernetics, and nuclear. Minister Amorim also favors building an aircraft carrier, through a 15-year process in which technology would be transferred from the foreign partner to national industry, refurbishing an existing carrier along the way. In addition, the government finally decided in 2013 on the purchase of thirty-six jet fighters in a US$4.5 billion deal that will transfer technology with Saab AB. Brazil has purchased fifty helicopters from European Aeronautic, Defence & Space Co. for US$2.6 billion, and has a contract with France's DCNS SA and Brazil's Construtora Norberto Odebrecht SA to build five submarines, including a nuclear-powered one. As President Dilma Rousseff declared in 2013, "We are indeed a peaceful country, but no way will we be a defenseless country."[20]

Brazil has historically and repeatedly signaled its willingness to be a part of a Western and capitalist international order. It has participated with military force once major wars broke out, and it is a major contributor to international peace-keeping forces, leading two efforts (Dominican Republic in 1965 and Haiti from 2004 to the present). The Brazilian military government that came to power in 1964 initially increased military capability and commitment to the United States in the Cold War as a strategy for emerging as a major player on the world stage. It willingly accepted US Secretary of State Henry Kissinger's scheme to decrease the cost to the United States of "protecting" the Free World by depending upon regional powers to keep order in their neighborhoods. Brazil built up a state-subsidized arms industry and became an important exporter of military arms and equipment. It promoted national development of leading technologies, such as computers and software. It also promoted economic growth through labor repression and state subsidies, which rejuvenated import-substitution industrialization policies pursued since the 1950s, thereby extending the "Brazilian Miracle" of 1968–79 (GDP growth averaged more than 10 percent from 1968 to 1973, then 6.5 percent until 1979). With economic growth and a restrained left, the government began a long process of returning the country to democracy. International relations analysts responded to these events by considering Brazil a rising power,[21] and Brazilians agreed.

Contemporary Brazil is committed to a politically democratic and basically capitalist world. Its vision of capitalism, however, falls more along the lines of Europe's social democratic approach, rather than a

---

[20] Raymond Colitt, "Brazil Plans to Build Aircraft Carrier, Defense Minister Says," *Bloomberg* (March 11, 2014). Available at: www.bloomberg.com/news/articles/2014-03-11/brazil-plans-to-build-aircraft-carrier-defense-minister-says.

[21] See Ronald M. Schneider, *Brazil: Foreign Policy of a Future World Power* (Boulder: Westview, 1976).

US "free hand to capitalists" one. Brazil also considers interstate relations to be an arena in which each state should have one vote in deciding on community strategies, and in which national sovereignty must remain paramount – points on which the United States disagrees. Indeed, international responsibility for the United Nations' founding principle of sovereign equality among nations and soft power are the two key bases for Brazil's rise as an emerging power.

The empirical record: has Brazil been able to shape the preferences of others?

Brazil's history of failed emergence makes it important to understand whether its growing capabilities will lead it to do more this time to reshape international regimes to match its preferences. In this section, I examine Brazilian behavior in the geographic region where it is de facto the great power (South America) and its views in five policy arenas (the UN Security Council, non-proliferation, human rights, the trading system, and the financial system) to gain insights into the answers.

Brazil as a regional hegemon

The vision from the United States and Europe is that Brazil has emerged as a potential regional stabilizer in Latin America, thereby linking Brazil's external recognition as an emerging power to its position in Latin America. Brazil, therefore, has to tread carefully within the region, facilitating dialogue among parties and leading multilateral mitigation initiatives that represent minimal risk of failure and do not create bilateral problems for itself.[22] Especially given its soft power focus (which was not the basis for the rise of Britain), if it cannot use its soft power to attract its neighbors or "manage" a neighborhood in which it is by far the dominant hard power, its strategy to rise as a representative of the South is seriously undermined. Increasing threats to democracy and significant economic challenges in the region, however, will provide Brazil with a regional management challenge.

Brazil enhances its soft power with a longstanding professional diplomatic corps at the foreign ministry (a.k.a. Itamaraty), insightful presidential intervention at key moments (e.g., amid the tension created by Bolivia's nationalization of Petrobras assets), public and private

---

[22] Andrés Malamud, "A Leader without Followers? The Growing Divergence between the Regional and Global Performance of Brazilian Foreign Policy," *Latin American Politics and Society* 53, no. 3 (Fall 2011), 1–24.

investment and aid for the region, and a new willingness to develop solidarity with Latin America. Brazil articulates a regional vision of cooperation, with economic integration, political alliance, and shared values (social justice, democracy, and human rights) forming the basis for peaceful relations. Brazil's view of conflict management is ultimately to build confidence in order to avoid tensions; it believes this is best accomplished through institutions that emphasize national sovereignty. Ironically, however, the primacy of national sovereignty makes regional institutions weak.[23]

Articulating this vision of cooperative interstate relations in the midst of weak governing institutions is not only a Brazilian soft power strategy, but reflects its domestic and foreign policy interests as well. Brazil has rejected the right of the Inter-American Commission on Human Rights to rule on how the country decides to build dams in the Amazon, and the 2008 National Strategy of Defense rejects the legitimacy of Brazilian citizens working with foreign NGOs in challenging government decisions for the Amazon region. Brazil itself has not proved immune to using its military power to influence relations with neighbors. For example, then President of Paraguay Fernando Lugo complained to the Organization of American States (OAS) that Brazilian military maneuvers on its border during renegotiation of the bilateral treaty regarding the Itaipú hydroelectric complex were intended to pressure Paraguay.[24]

Brazil also has competitors for regional leadership. While Hugo Chávez was alive, he used petrodollars and personality to call for grandiose schemes (e.g., an oil pipeline across the Amazon south to Argentina, a Bank of the South, and an alliance of countries dedicated to the "Socialism of the Twentieth Century") that exceeded Brazil's vision. Brazil was a driving force behind the Common Market of the South (Mercosur), with hopes that it would encompass all of South America in a trading bloc that would offset the influence of the United States. But Mercosur is stymied, and Chile, Peru, and Colombia have free trade agreements with the United States. The creation of the Union of South American Nations (UNASUR) in 2008 essentially ceded Central America and Mexico to the US orbit. Even in this reduced universe, Argentina has played a major role in the organization, with former Argentine President Nestor Kirchner becoming its president and Argentina pushing Brazil to

[23] Andrés Serbín, "Regionalismo y soberanía nacional en América Latina: los nuevos desafíos," *Nueva Sociedad* 15 (August 2010), 1–30; David R. Mares, "Constructing Real Peace and Security in Latin America: Minimizing the 'Moral Hazard' Character of Security Institutions," *Pensamiento Propio* 36/37 (July–December 2012).

[24] Raúl Zibechi, "Is Brazil Creating Its Own 'Backyard'?" Zibechi Report No 12, February 3, 2009. Available at: www.cipamericas.org/archives/1621.

support suspension of Paraguay's membership after the Legislature's rushed impeachment of its president. Although Brazilians today hold the leadership positions in the FAO and the WTO, a Colombian beat out a Brazilian for the leadership of the Inter-American Development Bank in 2005, a Uruguayan attracted more votes than the Brazilian candidate in the previous WTO selection process, and, in the recent election, a Mexican competed against the Brazilian. Even in the G20, Brazil does not stand out as the leader of Latin America, since both Mexico and Argentina are members. As Tokatlian aptly puts it, "Latin America wants a leadership committee, not one leader."[25]

UN Security Council

Brazil's disappointing experience with the League of Nations did not deter it from participating in the United Nations after WWII. Brazilian president and dictator, Getulio Vargas, was pleased when US President Franklin Delano Roosevelt (FDR) proposed Brazil for permanent member status in the Security Council. But FDR's untimely death, British and Soviet opposition, and new President Harry S. Truman's lack of interest in Brazilian membership meant that Brazil needed to content itself with the ceremonial honor of being first nation to speak at the General Assembly and repeated rotations as a non-permanent member of the Security Council.

Reforming the United Nations is a broad agenda, and Brazil has expressed itself on many issues. Security Council membership issues (total number and geographic representation, permanent status, and the veto) seem to matter most to Brazil. The country makes no secret of its desire to attain permanent member status, though current President Dilma Rousseff has taken a lower profile on this than her predecessor, Lula.[26] Brazil has the support of Great Britain, France, and Russia for permanent status, as well as of Germany and Japan, which seek similar

[25] Juan Gabriel Tokatlian, "Cuán poderoso es Brasil?" *Foreign Affairs Latinoamérica* 13, no. 1 (2013), 25–31.
[26] Vitor Sion, "Brasil muda estratégia por vaga permanente no Conselho de Segurança da ONU," *Opera Mundi* (July 7, 2013). Available at: operamundi.uol.com.br/conteudo/noticias/30071/brasil+muda+estrategia+por+vaga+permanente+no+conselho+de+seguranca+da+onu.shtml; Altamiro Silva Júnior, "Dilma cobra reforma do Conselho de Segurança da ONU," *Agência Estado* (September 24, 2013). Available at: politica.estadao.com.br/noticias/geral,dilma-cobra-reforma-do-conselho-de-seguranca-da-onu, 1078240. For a comparison with the strategies of Lula's predecessors Fernando Henrique Cardoso and Itamar Franco, see Eveline Vieira Brigido, "O Brasil e reforma do Conselho de Segurança da ONU: estratégias da diplomacia brasileira para a obtenção de um assento permanente," PhD dissertation, Universidade Federal do Rio Grande do Sul, January 2010.

status.[27] A 1965 reform increased the number of non-permanent seats on the Security Council from six to ten, in recognition that decolonization had changed the world. In 1992, UN Secretary General Boutros Boutros-Ghali called for further reforms to reflect new international realities, and Japan, Germany, India, and Brazil began caucusing for permanent member status as the G4 group. The aspirants were opposed by the Uniting for Consensus group (which includes Argentina, Mexico, and Colombia), which called for no new permanent members but an expansion of non-permanent seats; China supported this proposal, and 120 member nations attended its meetings in 2011.

Two issues block Brazil's aspirations to permanent membership. Security Council reforms can be vetoed by a permanent member, and though President Barak Obama has publically supported India's accession to such status, the United States does not support Brazil. Brazilian soft power is not sufficient to unite the South behind its candidacy, either.[28]

There are other UN issues that Brazil has attempted to influence. The United States secured adoption of the position that member states may undertake humanitarian interventions even in the absence of a Security Council resolution. Responsibility to Protect (R2P) creates a moral imperative for UN member states to use military force to protect civilian populations from government-directed or -inspired violence. Brazil's concerns about national sovereignty have always made it reluctant to sanction outside intervention, and it has seized upon some poor behavior by UN peacekeeping forces to articulate a "Responsibility while Protecting" standard to be followed by any intervening forces, making it more difficult to secure agreement to intervene.[29] This initiative, however, was stymied in the face of opposition from the United States, Brazil's inability to attract committed followers, and perhaps a sense that the United States and the North Atlantic Treaty Organization (NATO) have become reluctant to pay the costs of military intervention for humanitarian purposes.

---

[27] Wilder A. Sanchez, "Building Support for Brazil's Bid at the UNSC," *Atlantic-Community.org* (April 4, 2013). Available at: www.atlantic-community.org/-/building-support-for-brazil-s-bid-at-the-unsc; "G-4 Pushes for UNSC Reforms," *The Hindu* (September 26, 2012). Available at: www.thehindu.com/news/international/g4-pushes-for-unsc-reforms/article3939240.ece.

[28] Yehuda Z. Blum, "Proposals for UN Security Council Reform" *The American Journal of International Law* 99, no. 3 (July 2005), 632–49; Zachary Laub, "The UN Security Council," December 6, 2013. Available at: www.cfr.org/international-organizations-and-alliances/un-security-council/p31649.

[29] Richard Fontaine and Daniel M. Kliman, "International Order and Global Swing States," *The Washington Quarterly* 36, no. 1 (Winter 2013), 98–99.

Non-proliferation

In the absence of overt efforts to develop nuclear weapons, Brazil's position is that states should be trusted not to develop such weapons if that is their declared policy. Brazil also seeks to develop an international context that convinces states that they do not need such weapons.

Brazil is a late signatory to the Nuclear Non-Proliferation Treaty (NPT) – the military government pursued a secret nuclear weapons program, and the democratic government does not perceive that it "consented" to be governed by it; rather, it was confronted by a series of costs imposed by bilateral pressures and international rules that it could not modify in its preferred direction and acceded to the unequal treaty (unequal because nuclear weapons states face no pressure or sanctions to eliminate their nuclear arsenals). It is not that Brazil believes it has been forced to forego nuclear weapons – the Constitution of 1988 forbids them, it has a bilateral treaty with Argentina forbidding them, and no credible political figure has argued for them. Rather, Brazilians resent that their word is not trusted by nuclear weapons states, which hypocritically pledged to work toward nuclear disarmament when they developed the NPT.

Brazilian leaders are also aware that Israel developed nuclear weapons capabilities without being sanctioned by the United States. In addition, Brazilians believe that India's nuclear weapons (combined with its geostrategic location) have led the US government to accept India as the leading candidate among developing countries for potential inclusion as a permanent member of a revamped UN Security Council.

Among the changes Brazil would like to see in the NPT regime is pressure to move the original nuclear powers toward the elimination of nuclear weapons to which they committed when the NPT was developed. Brazil participates actively in the New Agenda Coalition, created in 1998, to pressure for more insistence on nuclear disarmament. It chaired the 2000 Conference on Disarmament, as well as the 2005 NPT Review Conference, and a Brazilian nuclear expert (José Goldemberg) co-chaired the International Panel on Fissile Materials for a number of years. The country is also a member of the Nuclear Suppliers Group and the Missile Technology Control Regime.[30]

Despite US insistence that the Additional Protocol to the NPT is a fundamental part of the NPT regime, Brazil refuses to sign it. Brazil wants alternatives to the Additional Protocol that are less intrusive than the

---

[30] Bernard Aronson, "Can Brazil Stop Iran?" *The New York Times* (April 3, 2012). Available at: www.nytimes.com/2012/04/04/opinion/can-brazil-stop-iran.html?_r=0.

US-favored means. Brazil is one of the few countries to have mastered the complete nuclear fuel cycle and to be able to export significant nuclear technologies; it also defends all states' rights to enrich uranium for peaceful purposes.[31] Brazil continues to develop its understanding of nuclear power as a national priority.[32] In 2003–04, the Navy's Technological Center, which was working on the nuclear submarine project, refused to permit inspectors from the International Atomic Energy Agency (IAEA) to see the interconnected centrifuges that enriched uranium, limiting the inspectors to evaluation of the uranium entering and the enriched material extracted from the hidden process.[33] Although the United States fears the "enrichment loophole" embodied in this right, Brazil seeks alternative means to non-proliferation. Part of the controversy over the Brazilian-French nuclear submarine project lies in US fears that without the safeguards of the Additional Protocol, knowledge, if not actual material, may become available for at least progress toward a theoretical understanding of achieving weapons-grade enrichment.

Brazil has attempted to convince Iran to forego nuclear weapons, and North Korea to renounce such weapons, by engaging with their governments. Not only did Brazil join with Turkey in a controversial offer to negotiate with Iran, but it has hosted Iranian leaders' visits, supported inclusion of Iran in talks regarding Middle Eastern security issues, and opened an embassy in North Korea, expanding trade with it. Luiz Inacio "Lula" da Silva (2002–10) visited Tehran in 2010, and trade relations expanded (much of it indirectly via Dubai) and Brazilians invested in the Iranian oil sector.[34] Relations cooled over human rights issues during the administration of Mahmoud Ahmadinejad under Brazilian President Rousseff, but she sent her foreign minister to Tehran in August 2013 for the swearing-in of Iranian President-Elect Hassan Rohani, and the minister noted that Brazil continued to consider cooperative relations with Iran important.[35]

---

[31] Maria Rost Rublee, "The Nuclear Threshold States: Challenges and Opportunities Posed by Brazil and Japan," *Nonproliferation Review* 17, no. 1 (March 2010), 49–70.

[32] Ministerio de Defensa, *Estrategia Nacional de Defensa 2009*. Available at: www.defesa .gov.br/projetosweb/estrategia/arquivos/estrategia_defesa_nacional_espanhol.pdf.

[33] João Roberto Martins Filho, citing "Lula marca visita a instalações da Marinha," in "The Brazilian Nuclear Submarine Project," *O Estado de São Paulo* 33, no. 2 (July–December 2011), 277–314.

[34] Eduardo J. Gómez, "Why Iran-Brazil Friendship has Gone Cold," *CNN* (April 5, 2012). Available at: www.cnn.com/2012/04/05/opinion/gomez-iran-brazil-chill/; Anna Mahjar-Barducci, "Brazil Moves Away from Iran," Gatestone Institute International Policy Council, February 3, 2012. Available at: www.gatestoneinstitute.org/2815/brazil-iran.

[35] "Iran, Brazil FMs Discuss Bilateral Relations," *PressTV* (August 3, 2013). Available at: www.presstv.com/detail/2013/08/03/317045/iran-brazil-discuss-bilateral-relations/.

These efforts are not pursued as means to pressure Iran and North Korea, but to convince them of the opportunities that they could enjoy were they to credibly forego nuclear weapons state status. Thus, they reflect Brazil's use of soft power in the nuclear weapons arena. The impact of Brazilian overtures in this direction is probably significantly reduced by US strategies that emphasize threats and costs.

To date, there is no indication that Brazil is affecting the manner in which the United States deals with Iran and North Korea, the development of an alternative to Additional Protocol to the NPT, or the legitimacy of the Additional Protocol itself. Although the NPT is widely criticized as an unequal treaty in the South, Brazil's principled stand does not attract many followers. Whether it is because non-pariah Southern states fear the sanctioning power of the North or the proliferation of the weapons themselves, Brazil's stand on the Additional Protocol costs it in terms of influence with the North, while not bringing soft power benefits from the South.

Human rights

Brazil advocates the defense of human rights, but subject to limitations imposed by its views regarding the primacy of national sovereignty. On the one hand, this can be an attractive position vis-à-vis governments in the South. Those governments respecting human rights can see in Brazil an ally, while those governments repressing basic human rights can appreciate the benefits of Brazil's approach, emphasizing dialogue rather than sanctions. On the other hand, at the level of civil society, this Brazilian position cannot seem very attractive. In the current political chaos in Venezuela, where the government has been detaining opposition leaders, the reluctance of Brazil, and of UNASUR, to pressure for respect of human and civil rights illustrates the limits of this approach.

We can see how this plays out by examining Brazilian behavior regarding Iranian human rights issues. During the Brazilian military rule, current President Dilma Rousseff was detained for three years and tortured; as president, she cooled bilateral relations with Iran over its human rights record. At the United Nations, Rousseff's government supported the organization's documentation of evidence revealing the human rights situation in Iran.[36] But Brazil has consistently, even under Rousseff,

---

[36] Camila Lissa Asano and Hadi Ghaemi, "Time for Brazil to Change its UN Vote on Iran," *O Estado de São Paulo* (November 25, 2012). Available at: internacional.estadao .com.br/noticias/geral,hora-de-o-brasil-mudar-seu-voto-sobre-o-ira-imp-,964760.

abstained in the UN General Assembly vote criticizing Iran's human rights record.[37]

Another example of the collision of human rights and Brazilian policy favoring national sovereignty arises in the case of the Belo Monte project, which will create the world's third largest hydropower complex and help drive economic growth. Brazil is a member of the Inter-American Commission on Human Rights. NGOs and indigenous communities in the Amazon appealed to the Commission, claiming that indigenous interests in blocking the development of Belo Monte were inappropriately discarded by the government. The Commission initially ruled that licenses for the project needed to be blocked until the indigenous were given a full and appropriate hearing, but the Brazilian government rejected the ruling, suspended its payments to the Commission, and threatened to withdraw. The Commission subsequently modified its ruling to simply require government protection of the indigenous and the environment, and agreed to let the project proceed.[38]

Brazil and the trading system

Brazil accepts the infant industry argument regarding the disadvantages of late development and thus favors a greater state role in regulating trade – for example, Mercosur is a customs union, not a free trade agreement. The country has played a lead role in promoting this view at the regional level, creating Mercosur as an answer to the US promotion of a bilateral free trade agreement with Mexico. Brazil was also instrumental in creating the G20 in 2003 as a developing nation counterweight to the United States and the European Union. Together with India and South Africa, Brazil argued that the developed world continued to protect their less competitive sectors and distort trade in multiple ways even while demanding that the developing nations open their markets. In addition, it ignored its own decision that the Doha round was intended to be a "development round." Amorim, foreign minister at the time, noted that prior to Cancun and the Brazilian-led development of the G20, the majority of humankind had to accept whatever the major powers decided in the WTO; now, they have a voice.[39]

---

[37] United Nations, "General Assembly Strongly Condemns Widespread, Systematic Human Rights Violations in Syria, as it Adopts 56 Resolutions Recommended by Third Committee," 67th General Assembly Plenary, 60th Meeting (AM), December 20, 2012. Available at: www.un.org/News/Press/docs/2012/ga11331.doc.htm.

[38] Amazon Watch, "Brazil's Belo Monte Dam: Sacrificing the Amazon and its Peoples for Dirty Energy." Available at: amazonwatch.org/work/belo-monte-dam#ilegal.

[39] Marcelo Passini Mariano, Haroldo Ramanzini Júnior, and Rafael A.R. de Almeida, "O Brasil na OMC: as lições do contencioso do algodão e da participação no G-203,"

Although Brazil joined the WTO in 1995, it only assumed an active role in 2003, when it served as midwife to the G20. Brazil now ranks among the top users of the WTO Dispute Settlement Mechanism, and its foreign ministry offers a course to other Latin American countries on how to develop and present cases.[40] Brazil has also pushed for the WTO to devote more attention to the relationship between trade and exchange rates.[41] With global negotiations stymied, Brazil undertook a major effort to attain the WTO's director generalship in 2013. Despite not being the preferred candidate of the United States, Britain, or Japan, Roberto Azevedo won, demonstrating the pull of Brazil's soft power in this arena.[42]

Brazil's role in the WTO, however, is more complex than just representing the South. Brazil was able to coalesce the interests of large export-oriented agribusiness, as found in Brazil and Argentina, and subsistence agriculture, as found in India and China. This combination thrust Brazil into the nucleus of decision-making at the WTO. Previously, China and India had not acted in concert with Brazil, but Brazil made the compromises to bring them together. As a result, India, China, and South Africa were able to keep a protected domestic agricultural market for developing countries. Brazil moved toward India's position on food security, but with the proviso that special protections were merited as long as they were part of a process designed to eventually stimulate liberalization of markets and reduction of tariffs. In 2008, Brazil had not accepted the position offered by India, China, and Indonesia in this regard. It appears that domestic politics pushed Brazil to abandon the G20 position in hopes of reaching a compromise conclusion to the Doha round.

Brazil's behavior at the WTO is criticized by Northern analysts, who argue that, given Brazil's protected market, its active role is not commensurate with its participation in international trade.[43] From the South, Brazil's abandonment of the Indian-led position at Doha is seen as the

Encontro Nacional ABRI 2011. Available at: www.proceedings.scielo.br/scielo.php?
pid=MSC0000000122011000200020&script=sci_arttext.

[40] Ministry of Foreign Affairs, "Itamaraty realiza debate sobre solução de controvérsias da OMC," October 10, 2013. Available at: www.brasil.gov.br/governo/2013/10/o-brasil-e-o-sistema-de-solucao-de-controversias-da-omc.

[41] "Report of the Working Group on Trade, Debt and Finance (2013) to the General Council," World Trade Organization, WT/WGTDF/12, October 9, 2013. Available at: https://mc9.wto.org/system/files/documents/12.pdf.

[42] Nicolas Bourcier, "Roberto Azevedo's WTO Appointment Gives Brazil a Seat at the Top Table," *The Guardian Weekly* (May 21, 2013). Available at: www.theguardian.com/world/2013/may/21/azevedo-head-world-trade-organisation.

[43] Jamil Chade, "Liderança do Brasil na OMC ganha admiradores e críticos," *O Estado de São Paulo* (July 30, 2007). Available at: economia.estadao.com.br/noticias/geral, lideranca-do-brasil-na-omc-ganha-adm.

reason for the failure to end the round.[44] China has opposed Brazil's efforts to link exchange rates and trade at the WTO. There is also the suspicion that Brazil's use of the institution's norms to gain benefits for itself winds up legitimizing those institutional norms and socializing Brazil into the system, without commensurate gains for the South. Brazil's soft power in the trading system thus has to play a delicate balancing game.

Brazil and the international financial system

Brazil has become an active player in the international financial system, both on its own and in the multilateral institutions. The country's development bank Banco Nacional do Desenvolvimento (BNDES) has increased its lending in the South to the extent that Brazil is now one of the largest aid providers to poor countries.[45] Brazil is a founding member of the BRICS (Brazil, Russia, India, China, and South Africa) Bank, which will, if implemented, provide alternative financing opportunities for Southern countries. Brazil also joined with the Paris Club to forgive debts to the Congo.[46] In total, President Rousseff forgave US$740 million in debts to Brazil from African countries – but while the Africans celebrated, within Brazil there were charges that the debt forgiveness was so that Brazilian contractor, mining, and agricultural companies with ties to the president could obtain BNDES financing for investments in Africa.[47]

Brazil succeeded in getting the WTO to ask the International Monetary Fund (IMF) to develop "surveillance reports" to track the relationship between exchange rates and trade. Brazil has criticized both the United States and China for monetary policies that seek domestic advantages while negatively impacting the currencies of other nations. Brazil is a major supporter of reform in the IMF, especially regarding its increased lending ability, distribution of votes, and position on regulating international flows of capital. As part of the reform effort, Brazil offered to increase its contribution by up to US$10 billion.[48]

---

[44] Fontaine and Kliman, "International Order," 98–99.   [45] Ibid.

[46] "The Paris Club agrees to provide 100% debt relief to the Republic of Congo," Club de Paris, March 18, 2010. Available at: www.clubdeparis.org/sections/communication/archives-2010/congo2270/switchLanguage/en.

[47] Otávio Cabral, "Dilma perdoou dívida de países africanos de olho em 2014," *Veja* (May 31, 2013). Available at: veja.abril.com.br/noticia/brasil/dilma-perdoou-divida-de-paises-africanos-de-olho-em-2014.

[48] Altamiro Silva Júnior, "Brasil eleva participação em cotas do FMI para 2,3%," *O Estado do São Paulo* (July 23, 2013). Available at: economia.estadao.com.br/noticias/geral, brasil-eleva-participacao-em-cotas-d; Fontaine and Kliman, "International Order," 98–99.

Brazilian governments recognize that capital flows can stimulate economic growth, but have insisted upon regulatory safeguards (including capital controls) to limit the ability of investors to shift the risks profit generation to others. From a Brazilian perspective, governments have the responsibility to design regulations to limit the ability of private actors to distort markets by withholding or distorting information, and fleeing the country with large profits while the country suffers from the market adjustment. Brazil was a leader in getting the IMF to consider a new framework to guide the use of capital controls, but dissented from the resulting reforms, arguing that the recommendations continue to emphasize the benefits of the flows and reflect a bias against controlling them.[49]

Brazil is one of the leaders in supporting change in the voting structure at the IMF, from one in which the weight of a country is determined by the degree of openness of its economy to a system that favors size more. Although the change has not been accepted, a reform did shift some voting power, lowering that of the United States slightly and increasing Brazil's from 2.2 to 2.3 percent of the vote total. The US Congress has been blocking reforms that would eliminate the US veto power over major reforms at the IMF and would double its lending ability, but even Great Britain has argued that Brazil and other developing nations need to have a greater voice in the institution. The G20, propelled by Brazil and Russia, is pushing the IMF to proceed even without US approval.[50]

Conclusion

Brazil wants to be at the table to articulate its views and needs as a developing country, which it believes are representative of most

[49] International Monetary Fund, "IMF Develops Framework to Manage Capital Inflows," April 5, 2011. Available at: www.imf.org/external/pubs/ft/survey/so/2011/NEW040511B.htm; Quentin Peel, "Brazil Calls for Currency System Overhaul," *Financial Times* (February 19, 2011). Available at: www.ft.com/cms/s/0/61d3afea-3bc7-11e0-a96d-00144feabdc0.html#axzz3WYpfgYOQ; Sandrine Rastello, "IMF Officially Endorses Capital Controls in Reversal," *Bloomberg* (December 3, 2012). Available at: www.bloomberg.com/news/articles/2012-12-03/imf-officially-endorses-capital-controls-in-reversal.

[50] Nicholas Winning, "UK Urges US Congress To Ratify IMF Reforms," *The Wall Street Journal* (April 7, 2014). Available at: www.wsj.com/articles/SB10001424052702304819004579487412135256386; Patrice Hill, "IMF Eyes 'Plan B' for Reforming Itself Without US," *The Washington Times* (April 10, 2014). Available at: www.washingtontimes.com/news/2014/apr/10/imf-eyes-plan-b-reforming-itself-without-us/; Jeanna Smialek and Sandrine Rastello, "IMF Quota Impasse Hurts US Reputation, Australian Treasurer Says," *Bloomberg* (April 10, 2014). Available at: www.bloomberg.com/news/articles/2014-04-09/u-s-s-imf-quota-impasse-hurts-global-reputation-hockey-says; Sandrine Rastello, "Brazil's Mantega Calls for Alternatives to US Approval on IMF," *Bloomberg* (April 12, 2014). Available at: www.bloomberg.com/news/articles/2014-04-12/brazil-s-mantega-calls-for-alternatives-to-u-s-approval-on-imf.

developing countries and not reflective of the advantages beneficial to developed countries. Brazil shares many US goals – international stability, democracy, growth – but contests the manner in which the rules are implemented. Brazil takes a normative approach, appealing to the principle of sovereign equality to decide which rules to adopt and how they should be implemented. The United States, in turn, draws on its historical experience to determine what an appropriate rule is, and on its "special rights" as guarantor of the system to determine how those rules should be implemented.

The two strategies are destined to produce friction. In addition to the cases mentioned in this chapter, the United States has defined access to communications within the Internet as a fundamental component of its national security strategy. Net neutrality, and limiting the ability of powerful states to monitor the communications of private citizens and even the governments of allies, was a major element in President Rousseff's 2013 UN speech. These ideas clearly resonated with citizens in democratic and authoritarian countries, as well as many democratic governments, around the world. They also represent a challenge to the US perspective on its "legitimate" rights to violate principles and norms it articulates for others in the name of its own national security and economic interests (e.g., it is a stretch to justify spying on Brazil's national oil company Petrobras for purposes of national security). But the two countries' agreement on goals and Brazil's relative weakness in both hard and soft power suggest that friction is not likely to develop into open confrontation.

Brazil's experiences suggest that soft power may be easier and faster to lose than hard power. Current difficulties with corruption, domestic stability, slowing economic growth, and the development of an inefficient domestic manufacturing and service sector reduce Brazil's attractiveness as a model for Southern countries to emulate and follow. If the "first source of Brazil's attractiveness is the dynamism and performance of its economic model,"[51] Brazil's rise could be in serious trouble. Its economic model depends heavily on high commodity prices, since its manufacturing and service sectors are not competitive in global markets.

There are contradictions in Brazil's strategy for emergence, but they are not peculiar to Brazil. Rather, they reflect the reality that the international system is anarchic, not hierarchical, and that governments look out for their own interests. The governments that are most successful are aware

---

[51] Lourdes Casanova and Julian Kassum, "From Soft to Hard Power: In Search of Brazil's Winning Blend," INSEAD Business School Faculty and Research Working Paper, draft, June 5, 2013, 5.

of systemic constraints, can work within them if they cannot overthrow them, and make changes on the margin to advance their specific interests.

In the post-Cold War international context up to the Syrian civil war and the Russian seizure of the Crimea in 2014, nations might have been successful pursuing either hard or soft power paths to emergence. India represents the hard power/geopolitical importance route and Brazil the soft power path to achieving acceptance in leadership positions of the international order. However, as Joseph Nye notes about soft power, international context matters.[52] The failure of the contemporary international governance structures to constrain China in the South China Sea, mold the outcomes of the Arab Spring, produce regime change in Syria, and prevent overt Russian military intervention in Georgia and Ukraine lead me to hypothesize that we are entering an era in which hard power (overt military power, deterrence strategies, and economic sanctions) pushes aside soft power.

[52] Nye, *Soft Power*, 2.

13 Prospects for the accommodation of a resurgent Russia

Nicola Contessi

The substantial fusion between the American political system and the rules-based international system has always generated special rents for the United States and its allies in terms of privileges, prerogatives, and authority.[1] However, the tenability of an international order whose benefits are so unevenly distributed is being called into question, not only by a resurgent Russia, but also by the broader coalition of rising powers.

The US National Intelligence Council (NIC) acknowledges that the relative decline of the West, and the growing fortunes of the emerging powers, will pose a challenge as to how to accompany these transformations.[2] Up until now, the United States has viewed this challenge in terms not so much of negotiating peaceful decline, but of preserving its position as the system-forming power and obtaining the acquiescence and cooperation of rising powers in addressing problems affecting its interests.

While there are perplexities about the long-term sustainability of the emerging economies, and differing assessments as to how the United States should react to the ongoing transformations,[3] these perplexities

---

[1] Sevasti-Eleni Vezirgiannidou, "The United States and Rising Powers in a Post-Hegemonic Global Order," *International Affairs* 89, no. 3 (May 2013), 637; G. John Ikenberry, "The Future of the Liberal World Order: Internationalism After America," *Foreign Affairs* (May/June 2011), 72; Carla Norloff, *America's Global Advantage: US Hegemony and International Cooperation* (Cambridge: Cambridge University Press, 2010); Marc A. Levy, Oran Young, and Micheal Zürn, "The Study of International Regimes," *European Journal of International Relations* 1, no. 3 (September 1995), 276; John G. Ruggie, "Multilateralism: The Anatomy of an Institution," *International Organization* 46, no. 3 (Summer 1992), 593.

[2] National Intelligence Council, *Global Trends 2030: Alternative Worlds*. Available at: www.dni.gov/index.php/about/organization/national-intelligence-council-global-trends.

[3] Christopher Layne, "This Time It's Real: The End of Unipolarity and the Pax Americana," *International Studies Quarterly* 56, no. 1 (March 2012), 203–13; Michael Cox, "Power Shift and the Death of the West? Not Yet!" *European Political Science* 10, no. 3 (September 2011), 416–24; Gideon Rachman, "Think Again: American Decline: This Time it's for Real," *Foreign Policy* (January 3, 2011). Available at: foreignpolicy.com/2011/01/03/think-again-american-decline/; Joseph S. Nye Jr., "The Future of American Power. Dominance and Decline in Perspective," *Foreign Affairs* 89, no. 6 (November/

turn to skepticism in the case of Russia.[4] According to the NIC, the country is sapped by overdependence on energy revenues, slow progress on modernization, and a rapidly aging workforce.[5] Western academic and policy communities seem to question even Moscow's status as a rising power.[6] Moreover, further to the fall in oil prices and imposition of international sanctions, Russia entered a recession in December 2014.

As in the case of other rising states, Washington's preferred approach to Russia boils down to the question of how to make the country a responsible stakeholder in a US-led international order.[7] The report of the 2009 Commission on US Policy Toward Russia illustrates with some clarity how this was the rationale for the Obama administration's Reset policy.[8] A wait-and-see persuasion prevails as to the utility of more far-reaching accommodation, which appears to have given way to status denial, as underlying frictions have come into the open. Nonetheless, US leaders also realize that without Russia's participation, they cannot address some of the crucial challenges of the twenty-first century, including drug trafficking, energy, European security, Islamic fundamentalism and international terrorism, strategic arms reduction and non-proliferation, Afghanistan, Iran, North Korea, and China.[9]

December 2010), 2–12; Fareed Zakaria, *The Post-American World* (London: Allen Lane, 2008), 234; Robert Singh, "The Exceptional Empire: Why the United States Will Not Decline – Again," *International Politics* 45, no. 5 (2008), 571–93; Stephen Brooks, G. John Ikenberry, and William Wohlforth, "Don't Come Home America: The Case Against Retrenchment," *International Security* 37, no. 3 (Winter 2012/13), 7–51.

[4] Ayse Zarakol, "Russia in a Sea of Rising Powers: The View from Washington, DC," PONARS Eurasia Policy Memo No. 263, 2013, 3; Robert Weitz, *Can We Manage a Declining Russia* (Washington, DC: Hudson Institute, 2011); Andrew Swift, "Dueling Analysis: 'Rising Russia' a False Narrative," *Foreign Policy Association Features* (October 22, 2009).

[5] NIC, *Global Trends 2030*, 74.

[6] Recent special issues on rising powers either tacitly excluded Russia – Amrita Narlikar, ed., "Special Issue: Negotiating the Rise of New Powers," *International Affairs* 89, no. 3 (May 2013), iii–ix, 561–792 – or explicitly ruled out its inclusion – Andrew F. Cooper and Daniel Flemes, eds., "Special Issue: Foreign Policy Strategies of Emerging Powers in a Multipolar World," *Third World Quarterly* 34, no. 6 (2013), 943–1144.

[7] Vezirgiannidou, "The United States and Rising Powers", 635; Suzanne Nossel and David Shorr, "A Stake in the System: Redefining American Leadership," in *Powers and Principles: International Leadership in a Shrinking World*, eds. Michael Schiffer and David Shorr (Lanham: Lexington, 2009), 11–44; Andrew Kuchins and Richard Weitz, "Russia's Place in an Unsettled Order: Calculations in the Kremlin," in *Powers and Principles: International Leadership in a Shrinking World*, eds. Michael Schiffer and David Shorr (Lanham: Lexington, 2009), 165–88.

[8] A Report from the Commission on US Policy toward Russia, "The Right Direction for US Policy toward Russia," Washington, DC: The Commission on US Policy toward China, March 2009.

[9] Rose Gottemoeller, "Russia and the West: Moving the Reset Forward," Assistant Secretary, Bureau of Arms Control, Verification and Compliance Remarks at the Atlantic

Although Russia partly builds its strength on the broader emerging powers movement, it also needs to ensure it is not left out in the ongoing renegotiation of power. Therefore, the general frame of the responsible stakeholder approach preferred in Washington was bound to disappoint Moscow, for which the key phrase is instead "equal partnership."[10] Russia's increasing assertiveness, its willingness to stand up to the United States and the West, and the end of the Reset underscore Moscow's frustration with Washington's reluctance to acknowledge Russia, and a new determination to play by its own rules.

Notwithstanding the turn that Russo-Western relations have taken following the Ukraine crisis of 2014 and the calls for a new phase of confrontation, this chapter examines ways to cope with the Kremlin's distinctive preferences for international order and Russia's role within it.[11] To better understand what is at stake, the next section outlines the issues underlying great power rank and explores the options available to rising and established powers. The second section establishes a correspondence between Russia's stated preferences and these strategic issues. The third illustrates Russia's moves to raise the costs of non-accommodation, and the fourth evaluates whether Russia's substantive demands are amenable to accommodation through the four main strategies presented in Chapter 1. The chapter concludes by evaluating the challenges and opportunities of accommodating Russia.

Oligarchy, unipolarity, and the accommodation of rising powers

With limited access and distinctive benefits, the great power club represents a separate and unequal tier of international society.[12] Its members vaunt exclusive prerogatives that allow them to override the autonomy and independence of weaker players. First is the recognition of special

Council, Washington, DC, September 9, 2011; Hillary Rodham Clinton, "Remarks With Russian Foreign Minister Sergei Lavrov," Secretary of State, Geneva, Switzerland, March 6, 2009.

[10] Dimitri Trenin, "Dimitri Trenin's Reaction," in *Powers and Principles: International Leadership in a Shrinking World*, eds. Michael Schiffer and David Shorr (Lanham: Lexington, 2009), 190.

[11] While indubitably taking things to another level, the Ukraine crisis is really a symptom of deeper differences between the sides.

[12] Thomas J. Volgy, Renato Corbetta, Keith A. Grant, and Ryan G. Baird, "Major Power Status Attribution: Conceptual and Methodological Issues," in *Major Powers and the Quest for Status in International: Global and Regional Perspectives*, eds. Thomas J. Volgy, Renato Corbetta, Keith A. Grant, and Ryan C. Baird (New York: Palgrave Macmillan, 2011), 1–26.

droits de regard or spheres of influence.[13] Second is what Nick Bisley terms "great power managerialism," whether limited to a sphere of influence or extending to the broader international system. Exercised in the name of "special responsibilities,"[14] great powers use managerialism and the associated provision of public goods to shape political and economic order. In return, this exonerates them from some of the "moral, legal, and political constraints experienced by the members of international society."[15] Third are the great power privileges that are built into international institutions.[16]

In its pure form, such a club, which confers its members the special quality of system "poles," qualifies as an oligarchic structure. However, its current 1 + 4 configuration enshrines a skewed hierarchy that is now under challenge, due to the widening disconnect between the distribution of power and the distribution of benefits, making such an arrangement unstable.

Insiders like China and Russia oppose US exceptionalism, thanks to which the United States claims the right to ultimately override even fellow members' decisions. Outsiders like Brazil, India, and others deplore their exclusion. As these actors increase their relative weight and ability to influence system-level outcomes, they will require a cut of the private goods of great powerhood, even as they continue to take a free ride on the public goods that have allowed them to thrive.

Accommodation involves varying degrees of mutual adaptation and acceptance between established and rising powers as legitimate stakeholders.[17] Implicit in the question is a distributional bargain between revisionist and incumbent powers over access to private goods. Thus, membership is the result of the strategies pursued by these two types of actor in the renegotiation of their roles in the international system,[18] respectively pursued through rank competition[19] and recognition.[20]

[13] Deborah Welch Larson, T.V. Paul, and William C. Wohlforth, "Status and World Order," in *Status in World Politics*, eds. T.V. Paul, Deborah Welch Larson, and William C. Wohlforth (Cambridge: Cambridge University Press, 2014), 17.

[14] Mlada Bukovansky, Ian Clark, Robyn Eckersley, Richard Price, Christian Reus-Smit, and Nicholas J. Wheeler, *Special Responsibilities: Global Problems and American Power* (Cambridge: Cambridge University Press, 2012).

[15] Nick Bisley, *Great Powers in the Changing International Order* (Boulder: Lynne Rienner, 2012), 4–5, 9; Hedley Bull, *The Anarchical Society: A Study of Order in World Politics* (New York: Columbia University Press, 2002), 202.

[16] Larson, Paul, and Wohlforth, "Status and World Order," 3–32.   [17] See Chapter 1.

[18] Miles Kahler, "Rising Powers and Global Governance: Negotiating Change in a Resilient Status Quo," *International Affairs* 89, no. 3 (May 2013), 712; Amrita Narlikar, "Introduction: Negotiating the Rise of New Powers," *International Affairs* 89, no. 3 (May 2013), 561–77; see Chapter 11.

[19] Larson, Paul, and Wohlforth, "Status and World Order," 14.

[20] Kahler, "Rising Powers and Global Governance."

The revisionist state's rank competition strategy can draw from various mixes of sticks and carrots to raise the costs of exclusion and prospect the benefits of inclusion.[21] On the other end, the incumbents will aim to preserve the international order and privileges today and to avoid more sweeping challenges in the future. Power accommodation also has implications for system polarity: full accommodation could sanction the open transition to a multipolar system; no accommodation would instead preserve a unipolar configuration.

Although by most accounts the likelihood of great power warfare in current circumstances is negligible,[22] failure to accommodate is likely to result in varying degrees of systemic conflict as rivals entrench their respective positions and opt for increasingly coercive bargaining strategies, including arms racing, delegitimization, and proxy wars.

The next section examines how Russia has pitched its bid to great power statehood and defined its interests vis-à-vis the West and the international system more broadly. After that, the chapter evaluates four strategies for the accommodation of a resurgent Russia.

Russia's red lines

The Putin doctrine aims to restore Russia's great power status and the country's tradition of independent action in international affairs,[23] defined precisely in terms of special responsibilities for the maintenance of global order, consultation in the management of international processes, and spheres of influence.

As then President Dmitry Medvedev stated in 2008, "Russia has truly gained strength and is capable of assuming a *greater responsibility* for solving regional and global problems." Foreign Minister Sergey Lavrov strengthened the point, indicating that "we need new forms of collective leadership based on mutual recognition of interests and of *responsibility* for the fate of the world," and that "Russia has come back to the international arena as a *responsible state*."[24]

---

[21] In this respect, there are parallels with the concepts of "social competition" and "social creativity." See Deborah Welch Larson and Alexei Shevchenko, "Managing Rising Powers: The Role of Status Concerns," in *Status in World Politics*, eds. T.V. Paul, Deborah Welch Larson, and William C. Wohlforth (Cambridge: Cambridge University Press, 2014), 49–51.

[22] Norrin M. Ripsman and T.V. Paul, *Globalization and the National Security State* (New York: Oxford University Press, 2010); Robert Jervis, "Theories of War in an Era of Leading Power Peace," *American Political Science Review* 96, no. 1 (March 2002), 1–14.

[23] Tatiana Shakleina, "Russia in the New Distribution of Power," in *Emerging Powers in a Comparative Perspective: The Political and Economic Rise of BRIC Countries*, eds. Vidya Nadkarni and Norma C. Noonan (New York: Bloomsbury, 2013), 178.

[24] Quoted in Marcin Kaczmarski, *Russia's Revisionism towards the West*, OSW Studies 33 (Warsaw: Centre for Eastern Studies, December 2009), 63–64. Emphasis added.

On the other hand, President Vladimir Putin's watershed 2005 State of the Nation address revealed the other idea behind Russia's bid to redress its purview on international outcomes. Although some observers erroneously read his words as Soviet nostalgia, the real point being made was that: "in those days one party was afraid to make an extra step *without consulting the other.*" Underscoring the historical basis for Russia's managerial role, Lavrov successively noted that "for 300 years Russia has already borne *a good deal of the burden of sustaining the balance* in European and world politics; when it abstained from this role . . . the result was unhealthy European politics," and that therefore in today's world "truly collective decisions . . . are unthinkable without the *equal participation* of Russia."[25]

Lastly, in 2008, then President Medvedev made waves by proclaiming Russia's "spheres of privileged interests."[26] Exposing the Russian version of the Monroe doctrine, he explained that there are certain areas of the world where Moscow expects to have a final say, though not necessarily a monopoly.

Russian leaders esteem the fact that they now have the sheer ability to flex their muscles. Although Russia entered a recession in 2014, it did so after becoming the eighth largest economy by GDP in 2012, compared to nineteenth in 2000. Its GDP reached US$2.015 trillion, from just over US$200 billion, showing a 1000 percent growth in that same period. Per capita income had reached US$14 037 in 2012, from US$1775 in 2000.[27] Russia has used this wealth to repay its debt to international lenders, expand its foreign reserves,[28] and pursue aggressive corporate shopping through its state companies, especially in the energy sector. Moscow has also converted this economic growth into increased military spending, with a budget swelling from US$6 billion in 2000 to US$90.7 billion in 2012, at 4.4 percent of GDP, a symbolic tie with the United States.[29]

---

[25] Quoted in Kaczmarski, *Russia's Revisionism*, respectively at 60, 59, and 63. Emphasis added.

[26] Charles Clover, "Russia Announces 'Spheres of Interest,'" *Financial Times* (August 31, 2008). Available at: www.ft.com/cms/s/0/e9469744-7784-11dd-be24-0000779fd18c .html#axzz3VzIBU7Ib; "Medvedev on Russia's Interests," *The Economist* (September 1, 2008). Available at: www.economist.com/blogs/certainideasofeurope/2008/09/ medvedev_on_russias_interests.

[27] World Bank, 2013; International Monetary Fund, "Nominal 2012 GDP for the world and the European Union (EU)," World Economic Outlook Database, April 2013.

[28] As of December 2014, Russia was the twelfth largest single holder of American debt, down from ninth in June 2013. Department of the Treasury, "Major Foreign Holders of Treasury Securities," Federal Reserve Board, March 16, 2015. Available at: www .treasury.gov/resource-center/data-chart-center/tic/Documents/mfh.txt.

[29] Stockholm International Peace Research Institute, *SIPRI Yearbook 2013* (Oxford: Oxford University Press, 2013).

Russian leaders further believe that the current configuration of international order has already cost Russia disproportionately in terms of its core interests. As they see it, Russia has suffered severe setbacks from the North Atlantic Treaty Organization's (NATO) enlargement, including membership proposals for Georgia and the Ukraine, the bombing of Serbia and Kosovo's successive independence, plans for ballistic missile defense at its doorsteps, the so-called Color Revolutions, and Western-led military interventions in the Middle East. They charge that, since the end of the Cold War, the United States has used its position to its advantage, acting in an egoistic rather than a responsible manner, striving to reshape the international system in its image.[30] Therefore, actively partaking in the US-led post-Cold War international order has been detrimental to Russia's interests.[31]

Although until the mid-2000s Russian elites were still committed to joining the West,[32] a broad national consensus has emerged on the necessity of engaging the United States on Moscow's own terms.[33] This came largely in response to America's reluctance to respect Russia's "red lines" – that is, those circumstances affecting its core national security interests or the international legal order – and the ensuing warning that over such issues, "Russia does not bargain and this is what our international partners should understand."[34] This consensus found ideological coherence in the idea of "sovereign democracy" and tied together domestic state-building, national security, and foreign policy in a single triad guiding the pursuit of military, industrial, and technological rebuilding, the reconstitution of Russia's sphere of influence, and the promotion of Russian values.[35]

---

[30] Kuchins and Weitz, "Russia's Place."

[31] Konstantin Kosachev, "Russia and the West: Where the Differences Lie," *Russia In Global Affairs* 5, no. 4 (October/December 2007). Available at: eng.globalaffairs.ru/number/n_9777.

[32] Anne L. Clunan, *The Social Construction of Russia's Resurgence: Aspirations, Identity and Security Interests* (Baltimore: Johns Hopkins University Press, 2009), 61, 88; Jeffrey Mankoff, *Russian Foreign Policy: The Return of Great Power Politics* (New York: Rowman & Littlefield, 2009), 24; Jeffrey Mankoff, "Russia and the West: Taking the Long View," *The Washington Quarterly* 30, no. 2 (Spring 2007), 124; Roger Kanet, "Introduction: The Consolidation of Russia's Role in World Affairs," in *Russia: Re-emerging Great Power*, ed. Roger E. Kanet (Houndmills: Palgrave Macmillan, 2007), 2. In this regard, the reader will recall that until 2001–02, Russia's possible NATO membership was on the agenda.

[33] Pavel Felgenhauer, "Russia is Building an 'Iron Fist' to Deter the West: A National Consensus in Moscow on Pursuing a Revisionist Strategy," *Eurasia Daily Monitor* 13, no. 19 (September 17, 2012); Lilia Shevtsova, *Lonely Power: Why Russia Has Failed to Become the West and the West is Weary of Russia* (Washington, DC: Carnegie Endowment for International Peace, 2010), 114.

[34] Lavrov, 2007, quoted in Kaczmarski, *Russia's Revisionism*, 71.

[35] This was developed by former Presidential Deputy Chief of Staff Vladislav Sukarov, who first aired it at a meeting of the Moscow Business Club in mid-2005. Graeme P.

These strategic goals are complemented with a vision for a new international order rooted in a comprehensive analysis of ongoing global transformations. Hence, the promotion of an international order based on international law, multilateralism, the principles of equality, mutual respect, and non-interference. The United Nations and the Security Council should be its centerpiece, exerting a coordinating function in a world made up of different regions embodying a multipolar distribution of power. Moreover, Moscow militates for the equal representation of cultural and civilizational values in international society.

Nonetheless, the Russians have a fundamentally hierarchical view of the world, premised on the "collective leadership of the major states of the world," with the Permanent Five in apical position. Russia sees itself as the indispensable midwife of such a world, which it deems better suited to the evolving nature of the international system. While this vision is neither radical nor revolutionary, it does imply a move away from the structural inequalities that have been built into international order since the end of the Cold War.

The costs of non-accommodation

Other than underscoring a renewed confidence, its revisionism suggests Russia has fine-tuned the political and bureaucratic skills needed to master diverse policy tools that will enable it to advance its interests. Moscow has adopted a sophisticated policy mix encompassing three main facets. First, a strategy of limited hard balancing to hedge US interests and power in various theaters. For example, Moscow has concluded economic and military ties with countries in the western hemisphere and the Middle East, extended its alliance with China to the Pacific as a response to America's Asian Pivot and as a prelude to its own 'pivot',[36] resumed nuclear strategic bomber patrols,[37] and even sailed a nuclear submarine to the Gulf of Mexico.[38] It has also begun to push back on a

Herd, "Russia's Sovereign Democracy: Instrumentalization, Interests and Identity," in *A Resurgent Russia and the West: The European Union, NATO and Beyond*, ed. Roger E. Kanet (Dordrecht: Republic of Letters, 2009), 3–28.

[36] Mu Chunshan, "China-Russia Ties Deepen," *The Diplomat* (September 3, 2013). Available at: thediplomat.com/2013/09/china-russia-ties-deepen-2/; "Russia's Asia Play Mustn't be Ignored," *The Diplomat* (May 17, 2011). Available at: thediplomat.com/2012/05/russia-asia-play-mustnt-be-ignored/.

[37] "Russia Resumes Nuke Bomber Sorties," *CNN* (August 9, 2007). Available at: www.cnn.com/2007/WORLD/europe/08/09/russia.sorties.reut/index.html?iref=newssearch. In a symbolic provocation, two Tu-95 Bear H bombers entered the 200-mile zone off the US Pacific coast on July 4, 2012. See Billy Gertz, "Putin's July 4th Message," *Washington Free Beacon* (July 6, 2012). Available at: freebeacon.com/national-security/putins-july-4th-message/.

[38] Lisa Karpova, "Russian Submarine Sailed Incognito along the Coast of the US," *Pravda* (July 21, 2012). Available at: english.pravda.ru/russia/politics/21-08-2012/

number of regional issues upsetting its interests. Thus, after supporting American military bases in Central Asia in the wake of 9/11, Moscow made various attempts to have them shut down, with the last base in Kyrgyzstan closing in 2014. On the other hand, the 2007 withdrawal from the Treaty on Conventional Forces in Europe and the successive European Security Initiative proposal in 2008 aimed to hijack the European security architecture. Moreover, though the exact dynamics of the Russo-Georgian war of August 2008 remain unclear, observers suggest that a hidden goal was to block Georgia's admission to NATO, which was promised at the alliance's 2008 summit in Bucharest.[39] Similarly, Russia's intervention in Ukraine and the annexation of Crimea, however misguided, responded to a similar rationale of the defense of core Russian interests.[40]

Second, the Kremlin has resorted to soft and negative balancing.[41] Instances of soft balancing include vetoing Western plans in the Middle East and boycotting the Organization for Security and Co-operation in Europe (OSCE), under the belief that the organization militates against Russia's interests and has shifted its emphasis disproportionately on the human dimension. Negative balancing includes anti-American rhetoric to undermine the United States and unite non-Western constituencies.[42] Stressing values and civilizational differences, Russia distanced itself from America's longstanding promotion of human rights and liberal democracy. Russia is also one of the main proponents of an alternative

121931-russian_sub-0/; Billy Gertz, "Silent Running," *Washington Free Beacon* (August 14, 2012). Available at: freebeacon.com/national-security/silent-running/; "Russia Probes US Military Defenses: Submarine in the Gulf," *IJReview* (August 14, 2012). Available at: dev4.ijreview.com/2012/08/13023-russia-probes-us-military-defenses-submarine-in-the-gulf/.

39 Daniel W. Drezner, "American Foreign Policy toward Russia: Is a U-Turn, or Any Turn, Possible?" in *The Policy World Meets Academia: Designing US Policy toward Russia*, eds. Timothy Colton, Timothy Frye, and Robert Legvold (Cambridge: American Academy of Arts and Sciences, 2010), 98; Roy Allison, "Russia Resurgent? Moscow's Campaign to 'Coerce Georgia to Peace,'" *International Affairs* 84, no. 6 (November 2008), 1165.

40 See John J. Mearsheimer, "Why the Ukraine Crisis Is the West's Fault: The Liberal Delusions that Provoked Putin," *Foreign Affairs* 93, no. 5 (September/October 2014), 77–89.

41 T.V. Paul, "Soft Balancing in the Age of US Primacy," *International Security* 30, no. 1 (Summer 2005), 46–71; Kai He, "Undermining Adversaries: Unipolarity, Threat Perception, and Negative Balancing Strategies after the Cold War," *Security Studies* 21, no. 2 (2012), 154–91.

42 David Satter, "Russia's Anti-American Foreign Policy," *The Wall Street Journal* (September 22, 2013). Available at: www.wsj.com/articles/SB10001424127887323308504579086894029063458; Nikolai Zlobin, "Russia Has Not Yet Created an Attractive Identity Model," *Valdai Discussion Club* (September 11, 2013). Available at: valdaiclub.com/politics/62080.html.

reserve currency and has encouraged the BRICS (Brazil, Russia, India, China, and South Africa) to lessen dependence on the dollar in their transactions.[43] Russia regards the BRICS as a geopolitical umbrella for some of its positions and strives to transform the grouping into a "full-scale strategic cooperation mechanism that will allow [her] to look for solutions to key issues of global politics."[44]

Third, Moscow has strived to divide the United States from its European allies by capitalizing on existing policy differences between the two sides and creating wedge areas to undercut American dominance.[45] Energy and pipeline politics are a key tool in this respect, though Russia has paid a price in terms of credibility as a reliable supplier.[46]

As all this suggests, while remaining committed to a non-confrontational foreign policy, Russia has proven keen on using disruptive methods to protect its interests. While this does not fail to trigger piqued responses in the West, it is not isolated from Western aversion to offering some minimum geopolitical and status recognition to Russia in the first place – most notably in the repeated infringements of Russia's former sphere of influence, attempts to isolate it from its allies, and denial of the security dilemmas generated by the West's own actions. This in turn causes retaliations that the West construes as hostility.

Thus, in one way or another, the key challenge for the United States and the West is to respond to Russia's search for a major role in a "post-post-Cold War world" in line with its historical great power tradition[47] and to engage it in terms that are acceptable to Moscow.[48] This raises the question of whether Russia's demands are amenable to accommodation, urging us to think about ways to mitigate international bellicosity.

---

[43] Pronina Lyubov, "Medvedev Shows Off Sample Coin of New 'World Currency' at G-8," *Bloomberg* (July 10, 2009). Available at: www.bloomberg.com/apps/news?pid= newsarchive&sid=aeFVNYQpByU4; "BRICS Agree to Local Currency Credits to Ease Dollar Dependency," *RT* (March 29, 2012). Available at: rt.com/business/brics-currencies-credit-deal-755/.

[44] Richard Pomeranz, "Why Russia Needs the BRICS," *CNN Global Public Square* (September 3, 2013). Available at: globalpublicsquare.blogs.cnn.com/2013/09/03/why-russia-needs-the-brics/.

[45] Janusz Bugajski, *Expanding Eurasia: Russia's European Ambitions* (Washington, DC: Center for Strategic and International Studies, 2008), 43.

[46] Andrew E. Kramer, "Russia Gas Pipeline Heightens East Europe's Fears," *The New York Times* (October 12, 2009). Available at: www.nytimes.com/2009/10/13/world/europe/13pipes.html?_r=0.

[47] George Friedman, "The Western View of Russia," *Stratfor* (August 31, 2009). Available at: https://www.stratfor.com/weekly/20090831_western_view_russia.

[48] Andrew S. Weiss, "Winter Has Come," *Democracy: A Journal of Ideas* 30 (Winter 2013). Available at: www.democracyjournal.org/pdf/30/winter_has_come.pdf.

Options for the peaceful accommodation of Russia

In recent years, Russia has put forward an increasingly articulate set of claims and constructive proposals for international and regional order. Chapter 1 presented four main accommodation strategies that speak to some of the key status benchmarks.

Territorial accommodation Russia has made efforts in recent years to reconstitute a sphere of influence in the former Soviet Union. In this respect, status intersects with survival objectives, as Russia has historically linked the ability to defend its vast territory to the maintenance of buffer areas. This objective is further connected to Russia's vision for a multipolar international system premised on various regions, each under the leadership of one great power as a pole.

For this reason, Russia has witnessed with apprehension the color revolutions of 2004–05 and the European Union's and especially NATO's eastward enlargements, as both groupings now include three former Soviet republics. The 2014 Russo-Western confrontation over Ukraine is a case in point. Although what actually led to the regime change in Kiev remains clouded in the fog of Moscow's and Washington's respective propagandas, President Barack Obama's warnings about consequences for Russia's status in the world and his dismissal of Moscow as only a *regional* power underscores that the struggle for Ukraine is a struggle over status accommodation.[49]

The Russians charge that, according to Ukraine's constitutional procedures for the impeachment of a sitting president, the regime change that followed the defection of some of the Ukraine's parties to the February 21 power-sharing agreement was technically a coup.[50] Various facts led Moscow's leadership to perceive that Western interests were involved in backing the ousting of President Viktor Yanukovych, his replacement with Oleksandr Turchynov as acting president and prime minister, and the chain of events that followed.[51] Consequently, Russia treated the

---

[49] Michael O'Brien, "Obama: Allies Agree Russia Broke International Law," *CNBC* (March 3, 2014). Available at: www.nbcnews.com/storyline/ukraine-crisis/obama-allies-agree-russia-broke-international-law-n43326; Aaron Blake, "Obama says Russia is Just a 'Regional Power.' The American People Disagree," *Washington Post* (March 25, 2014). Available at: www.washingtonpost.com/blogs/the-fix/wp/2014/03/25/obama-says-russia-is-just-a-regional-power-the-american-people-disagree/.

[50] Daisy Sindelar, "Was Yanukovych's Ouster Constitutional?" *RFE/RFL* (February 5, 2015). Available at: www.rferl.org/content/was-yanukovychs-ouster-constitutional/25274346.html.

[51] "Ukraine Crisis: Transcript of Leaked Nuland-Pyatt Call," *BBC* (February 7, 2014). Available at: www.bbc.com/news/world-europe-26079957. Moreover, President Obama's later statement in a televised interview appeared to confirm

events as foreign interference in its sphere of privileged interests,[52] and a breach of its asserted red lines. However misguided, disproportionate, and illegal, its response – with the eventual annexation of Crimea and support for separatist groups in eastern Ukraine – was not unsurprising. As Ukraine, and Georgia before it, stands to prove, territorial accommodation is of the greatest importance for Russia, and is an area where it is willing to follow through on its red lines.

On the other hand, if future historiography confirms a covert US role following the Obama administration's initial reset, it seems that the conflict of wills between Russia and the West may be destined to have long-term destabilizing effects. It is possible that history will repeat itself, absent an acknowledgment of Russia's role in the post-Soviet space, as great powers today "only resort to military means when they feel threatened."[53]

Institutional accommodation From an institutional point of view, the channels for Russia's peaceful accommodation were largely put in place between the 1990s and early 2000s, in order to incorporate a declining Russia into the American-led post-Cold War international order.

Besides inheriting the Soviet seat on the UN Security Council and in other organizations, Russia was brought into the G7 (subsequently renamed the G8) in 1997, though it was suspended on March 24, 2014, and in 2012 it was admitted to the World Trade Organization (WTO). In the Euro-Atlantic space, the NATO-Russia Council was created in 2002 (replacing the Permanent Joint Council that had facilitated cooperation since 1997); in 1995, the OSCE was formed to reconcile the Western and former Soviet states in a common security arrangement. Therefore, the main problem for Russia today would seem to be not so much the institutional architecture as the informal governance concealed in between the lines of treaty provisions and the outside prerogatives that some

---

some kind of American involvement in regime change. "Pres Obama on Fareed Zakaria GPS," *CNN* (February 1, 2015). Available at: cnnpressroom.blogs.cnn .com/2015/02/01/pres-obama-on-fareed-zakaria-gps-cnn-exclusive/. See also Charles Clover, "Clinton Vows to Thwart New Soviet Union," *Financial Times* (December 6, 2012). Available at: www.ft.com/cms/s/0/a5b15b14-3fcf-11e2-9f71-00144feabdc0 .html#axzz3Wvn7LOHw.

[52] See also Mearsheimer, "Why the Ukraine Crisis is the West's Fault," 77–89.

[53] See also Jeremy Shapiro, "Defending the Defensible: The Value of Spheres of Influence in US Foreign Policy," *Brookings* (March 11, 2015). Available at: www.brookings.edu/ blogs/order-from-chaos/posts/2015/03/11-defending-indefensible-spheres-of-influence-us-foreign-policy-shapiro.

member states reserve for themselves.[54] Russia charges that the United States has gradually altered the multilateral bargain that held together postwar institutions to pursue unilateral advantages, in breach of its obligations under those very same treaties.

So far, the West has avoided seriously rediscussing the assumptions underlying existing global and regional institutions. At both levels, Russia's asserted commitment to international law suggests that institutional accommodation would not require the redesign of the relevant regimes, but rather the renegotiation of the practices that have guided decisions, policies, and programs within them since the Cold War.

In the context of NATO, post-Cold War interaction on issues like eastward enlargement, military intervention, and the anti-ballistic missile shield have spurred Moscow's mistrust, highlighting its perceived lack of influence in the NATO-Russia Council,[55] not least due to historic American readiness to shift venues to the North Atlantic Council in order to sideline Russia when this suited US interests. Moreover, though this body has facilitated peaceful dispute resolution, it remains hampered by misunderstandings that work against Moscow.[56] Yet, Russian policymakers assert they are prepared to work with NATO provided that Russian interests are recognized on an equal footing.[57]

On the other hand, while Moscow considers the OSCE the bearer of a vision for continental security to which it originally contributed, it perceives the Western capture of the organization as having brought about an unbalanced emphasis on human rights and unwelcome "meddling" in the frozen conflicts of the South Caucasus. To ensure better alignment of the organization's activities with its own interests, Moscow militates for curtailing delegation and restoring the policymaking supremacy of its consensus-based ministerial council.[58]

---

[54] Randall W. Stone, *Controlling Institutions: International Organizations and the Global Economy* (Cambridge: Cambridge University Press, 2011).

[55] Richard Sakwa, "'New Cold War' or Twenty Years' Crisis? Russia and International Politics," *International Affairs* 84, no. 2 (March 2008), 257.

[56] Vincent Pouliot, *International Security in Practice: The Politics of NATO-Russia Diplomacy* (Cambridge: Cambridge University Press, 2010), 97, 107, 223.

[57] The Ministry of Foreign Affairs of the Russia Federation, "Concept of the Foreign Policy of the Russian Federation," February 18, 2013. Available at: www.mid.ru/brp_4 .nsf/0/76389FEC168189ED44257B2E0039B16D.

[58] The Kremlin considers supranational delegation as contrary to Russia's interests and to those of its allies. More than that, President Putin has come to believe that the OSCE is an obstacle to Russia's new aspirations. As a result, Russia has increasingly been obstructing the organization's activities in the human dimension. In 2008, it succeeded in bringing the OSCE mission in Georgia to an end. See also Terrence Hopmann, "Intergovernmental Organisations and Non-State Actors, Russia and Eurasia: The OSCE," in *Key Players and Regional Dynamics in Eurasia: The Return of the "Great Game,"* eds.

Although Russia's 2008 proposal for European order was couched in terms of a new "treaty," it says little about new institutions.[59] Instead, its exclusive focus on "hard" military security, consultations (especially within an "extraordinary conference of state parties"), and the notion that no state or international organization can claim an exclusive role in European peace and security[60] suggests that at stake is an overarching new "bargain" on the rules of the game of European security. The proposal echoes much of the language and the spirit of preexisting documents, such as the UN Charter, the Helsinki Final Act, and the 1990 Charter of Paris for a New Europe. Russian elites see the return to the spirit of these texts as a guarantee against what they regard as a Western bias in the current Euro-Atlantic framework.[61]

Although the renegotiation may require some changes to decision-making procedures, it could be achieved within the existing institutional paradigm. Moreover, this may restore credibility to the OSCE and ease cooperation with NATO on a range of issues. However, Russia's accommodation in the Euro-Atlantic space has made very little progress. Following initial diplomatic openings, the European security proposal received little attention. Although a more supple approach initially replaced the George W. Bush-era ballistic missile defense plans, this has received new impulse following the Ukraine spat. On the other hand, Russia's project for a Eurasian Union met strong American opposition, given that it would curtail the reach of Euro-Atlantic institutions. Because institutional accommodation in this region intersects with Russia's claim of spheres of influence, which Washington firmly opposes, the status quo is likely to remain unchanged. Lastly, though NATO enlargement to former Soviet states has been shelved in all but words, the granting of an EU association agreement to Ukraine in 2014 and negotiations with Georgia and Moldova reflect a similar strategy, only in civilian clothes. The resumption of discussions on Georgia's accession to NATO is likely to add a further wedge.

Maria Raquel Freire and Roger E. Kanet (Basingstoke: Palgrave Macmillan, 2010), 239, 242.

[59] Ministry of Foreign Affairs of the Russian Federation, Draft European Security Treaty, November 29, 2009. Available at: www.mid.ru/en/diverse/-/asset_publisher/8bWtTfQKqtaS/content/id/661555.

[60] Pàl Dunay and Graeme P. Herd, "Redesigning Europe? The Pitfalls and the Promises of the European Security Treaty Initiative," in *OSCE Yearbook 2009* (Baden-Baden: Nomos Verlag, 2009), 77–100.

[61] Significantly, the Soviet Union contributed 16.38 percent of the identifiable language in the Decalogue and Basket I (on security and confidence-building measures) of the Helsinki Final Act. Terrence Hopmann, "Asymmetrical Bargaining in the Conference on Security and Cooperation in Europe," *International Organization* 32, no. 1 (Winter 1978), 168.

At the global level, Russia's steadfast defense of the UN Security Council indicates support for existing institutional arrangements. What Moscow disputes is the West's inclination to sideline the body's exclusive right to authorize military interventions in the absence of Permanent 5 (P5) consensus.[62] The Russians want the United States and the other Western members of the body to accept their decisions and views as the pronouncements of a peer in the exercise of its prerogatives in full responsibility. Here, accommodation would entail a return to the traditional policy of strategic restraint and a recommitment to multilateralism. While this would restrict American exceptionalism, such a step may be necessary to sustain the relevance of this institution and the rules-based international order it embodies in the face of its eroding legitimacy. The Russo-American standoff over Syria highlighted the growing difficulties for the United States in rallying support for military campaigns in the name of humanitarian principles, and Russia's ability to appeal to international law to reinstate the primacy of the body as a board in which great power interests are concerted. Syria may foreshadow what a new institutional bargain with a greater role for Russia would look like. While this successively unlocked new negotiations on the Iran nuclear issue, it is uncertain whether it can also provide a template for other negotiations. The solution of such issues, nonetheless, may hinge on a comparable deal with Russia, allowing for compensations and tradeoffs of diverging interests.

In sum, though the requisite institutional venues have been in place for two decades, their full potential for the management of discord has not been fully seized in the post-Cold War world. The socialization approach privileged so far is now surpassed, as a stronger Russia voices disagreement over the altered multilateral bargain and the informal governance these institutions have come to embody. To the extent that opportunities for joint gains can stem from the consolidation of regional and global security governance in areas like European security, Afghanistan, Iran, North Korea, and arms control, a new bargain could unlock such potential. Conversely, failure to reach one might engender protracted institutional paralysis, irrelevance, or delegitimization. Such an option, however, would grant Russia expanded prerogatives, when in fact uncertainties remain over its ability to consolidate and maintain its new strength. Hence, the risk is not only of giving Moscow new prerogatives that could backfire, but also of its losing the means to exercise its special responsibilities, as it did at the collapse of the Soviet Union.

[62] See also Roy Allison, *Russia, the West, and Military Intervention* (New York: Oxford University Press, 2013).

Economic accommodation Although Russia's economy has grown exponentially, this growth has been driven by natural resources exports. In 2009, 70 percent of its total exports were in the oil and gas sector,[63] and in 2011, 61 percent of foreign direct investments in its manufacturing sector were concentrated in the coke, refined petroleum, and basic metal sectors.[64] Hence, economic integration between Russia and the West is overly dependent on a single sector.[65]

The fact of supplying roughly 22 percent of the European Union's natural gas imports gives Russia a certain political leverage,[66] but it is also a rent that discourages its economic modernization. Therefore, one of the primary goals of Russian leaders has been to modernize and diversify by increasing the country's integration in the global economy.[67] The expansion of trade and the attraction of foreign capitals are fundamental to these goals, and the 2012 WTO accession was sought to create new opportunities. Furthermore, though following the annexation of Crimea the OECD postponed all activities related to Russia's future membership, the bid was meant to help Russia seize those new opportunities through standardization of economic and business policies.

Although Charles Kupchan argues that economic ties follow from significant diplomatic breakthroughs rather than enabling them,[68] Russia's further integration into the global economy structured around its need for investments and capacities in the technology sector could represent a viable way to accommodate Moscow's growing ambitions that is acceptable to the West. Economic accommodation could improve the overall climate of the relationship by addressing Russian goals to improve economic performance and domestic prosperity, while at the same time creating opportunities for Western business and for Russia's opening up.[69]

---

[63] Rusimpex, Export of Russia of Basis Commodities, 2009. Available at: www.rusimpex .ru/index1.htm?varurl=Content_e/Economics/index.htm.

[64] Federal State Statistics Service, Foreign Investments in the Economy of Russia, 2011. Available at: www.independent.co.uk/voices/editorials/leading-article-dependence-on-russian-energy-places-europe-at-risk-1229945.html.

[65] Although the European Union accounted for roughly 50 percent of Russia's trade turnover in 2009, a large portion of this consisted of natural resources. On the other hand, at 3.9 percent of its total, trade with the United States is negligible.

[66] "Dependence on Russian Energy Places Europe at Risk," *The Independent* (January 7, 2009). Available at: www.independent.co.uk/voices/editorials/leading-article-dependence-on-russian-energy-places-europe-at-risk-1229945.html.

[67] Ministry of Foreign Affairs of the Russia Federation, "Concept of the Foreign Policy."

[68] Charles A. Kupchan, "Enemies into Friends: How the United States Can Court Its Adversaries," *Foreign Affairs* 89, no. 2 (March/April 2010), 120–34.

[69] Samuel Charap, "Principled Integration: A US Policy Response to the Economic Challenge Posed by Russia," in *The Policy World Meets Academia: Designing US Policy toward*

Meanwhile, the country's enmeshment in a web of vulnerabilities and sensitivities could mitigate Russia's opportunities for disruption[70] and help incorporate its economic interests into system-wide concerns. The more the allocation of productive factors and the generation of domestic product are determined outside of Russia, the more the country's destiny will be tied to that of the world economy, and vice versa.

Economic payoffs also present a tangible incentive for pro-norm behavior, with convergence in the economic sphere susceptible to spilling over to the broader societal level.[71] Aside from the reforms Russia has already adopted toward accession, an important consequence of WTO membership is the changes to domestic regulations Moscow will have to adopt in compliance with WTO rulings. The country's domestic market practices in the automotive sector have already become the object of a pile-on complaint initiated by the European Union.[72] On top of that, OECD membership would require the thorough review of public policies in accordance with OECD standards.[73] Assisting Russia's push for integration can therefore ensure the country's deeper involvement in the international economic order.

Moreover, interdependence could add a transnational dimension by increasing the number of stakeholders with a vested interest in smooth bilateral ties between Russia and the West.[74] The Ukraine crisis has demonstrated how corporate interests have constrained some of Russia's more blunt political decisions. However, in addition to rooting Russia's society in more secure foundations, stronger economic performance would also strengthen Russia, which could be detrimental should Moscow remain committed to revisionism even after these concessions.

Ideological/normative accommodation Russia differs strongly with the post-Cold War designation of (liberal) democracy and human rights

Russia, eds. Timothy Colton, Timothy Frye, and Robert Legvold (Cambridge: American Academy of Arts and Sciences, 2010), 60.

[70] Robert O. Keohane and Joseph S. Nye, *Power and Interdependence* (Boston: Little Brown, 1977).

[71] Ernst B. Haas, *The Uniting of Europe: Political, Social, and Economic Forces, 1950–1957* (Stanford: Stanford University Press, 1958); Ben Rosamond, *Theories of European Integration* (Basingstoke: Palgrave Macmillan, 2000).

[72] William Mauldin, "US to Join WTO's Complaint against Russia," *The Wall Street Journal* (July 18, 2013). Available at: www.wsj.com/articles/SB10001424127887324263404578613740584992574.

[73] "Integration of Russia into Global Economic Institutions: Accession to the OECD," Remarks by Angel Gurría, OECD Secretary General, Saint Petersburg International Economic Forum 2013, Saint Petersburg, Russian Federation, June 20, 2013. Available at: www.oecd.org/about/secretary-general/integration-russia-global-economic-institutions-oecd-accession.htm.

[74] Charap, "Principled Integration," 61.

as implicit necessary conditions for "full membership in good standing in the international order,"[75] which it regards as an undue and destabilizing political interference in the internal affairs of sovereign states. The corollary is that the practice of military intervention that has emerged from this orientation rests on "arbitrary and politically motivated interpretations of international law."[76]

Russia defends each state's prerogative to set its own domestic course, and sees itself as the protector of the world's "diversity and variety" in the face of the West's value universalism.[77] Charging that the latter is responsible for the resurgence of civilizational dynamics in international politics,[78] Russia emphasizes the need for "a common moral denominator" that can reconcile "different value systems and development models within the framework of universal democratic and market economy principles,"[79] whether a liberal, social, or sovereign democracy.

A recent report encouraged Washington to increase emphasis on values in its engagement of Russia.[80] However, this recommendation underestimates the fact that Russia's current position on values in the international system is integral to its evolving national identity. It may therefore be futile to seek to socialize Russia at this stage, given the consensus that its present foreign policy posture enjoys among its elites. Moreover, Russia's views are shared by other non-Western powers, most notably China, and the other BRICS are, to varying degrees, sympathetic to this agenda. Because they are so deeply ingrained in Western identity, it may be hard to compromise on human rights and liberal democracy, but going forward, the West may have to adjust its transformational diplomacy to the diminished appetite for domestic reforms and humanitarian intervention, not only in Russia, but across the non-Western world. In this sense,

---

[75] Nossel and Shorr, "A Stake in the System," 23.

[76] Ministry of Foreign Affairs of the Russia Federation, "Concept of the Foreign Policy," §20; The Foreign Policy Concept of the Russian Federation, July 12, 2008. Available at: archive.kremlin.ru/eng/text/docs/2008/07/204750.shtml.

[77] Ministry of Foreign Affairs of the Russia Federation, "Concept of the Foreign Policy," §§19–20; The Foreign Policy Concept of the Russian Federation, 2008. As Foreign Minister Lavrov affirmed in a speech on June 24, 2008, the world has the opportunity to choose between "Western values and become the Big West" or "another approach which we promote." Lavrov, quoted in Shevtsova, Lonely Power, 58.

[78] Critics argue that the invocation of cultural and civilizational differences helps to both justify Russia's marginality and support the importance of its participation, while at the same time opposing scrutiny of and claiming legitimacy for its increasingly authoritarian domestic governance. See Shevtsova, Lonely Power, 182.

[79] Ministry of Foreign Affairs of the Russia Federation, "Concept of the Foreign Policy," §4g, 21, §39b; The Foreign Policy Concept of the Russian Federation, 2008.

[80] John Edwards and Jack Kemp, Russia's Wrong Direction: What the United States Can and Should Do, Independent Task Force Report no. 57 (New York: Council on Foreign Relations, 2006).

the "rise of the rest" could bring about a stripped-down version of liberal internationalism, bereft of some of its substantive aspects, in order to preserve its procedural hallmarks, which, according to one leading theorist, are "openness and rule-based relations enshrined in institutions such as the United Nations and norms such as multilateralism."[81]

Although abstract, the notion of a "moral common denominator" may turn out to be a valid proposal for building common ground toward extended liberal internationalism.[82] In this more pluralistic framework, the West would obviously retain the opportunity to advance liberal values, though perhaps not as the exclusive standard of civilization.

Ideological/normative accommodation could thus give representation to different value systems and philosophies, as has occurred in Western countries domestically. This could not only appease Russia's self-image as a cultural hub between East and West, but equally represent an antidote against those social movements, radical groups, and other non-state actors around the world that see in the American-led international order their utter enemy. The Dialogue Among Civilizations and Alliance of Civilizations initiatives could offer a useful model for achieving common ground on values. However, as value relativism would replace the primacy of liberal values, the West would probably lose the ability to invoke human rights to justify campaigns against deviant states. On the other hand, Russia may be more willing to accept Western values if the West acknowledges some of its own.

Conclusion

The fundamental challenge with peaceful accommodation is to square the tradeoff between the costs and benefits of accommodation and non-accommodation in a way that doesn't dilute the incumbent's privileges or alter the existing international order excessively, while at the same time allocating new roles to the claimant(s). Hence, while they are conceptually distinct approaches, these four strategies can also be used as complements to assign limited concessions in one area but not in others, or partial concessions within all areas, or other combinations. Furthermore, accommodation, whether selective or otherwise, can be mixed with realist strategies like containment and balancing to hedge a claimant's status competition strategy.

---

[81] Ikenberry, "The Future of the Liberal World Order."

[82] G. John Ikenberry, "Liberal Internationalism 3.0: America and the Dilemmas of Liberal World Order," *Perspectives on Politics* 7, no. 1 (March 2009), 71–87.

At the same time, the four strategies are not perfectly substitutable, and the evolution of Russo-Western relations in the wake of the Ukraine crisis stands to prove this. For Russia, preservation of its historical sphere of influence represents not only the highest status goal, but also a core national interest. Furthermore, events demonstrate Russia is prepared to bear costs to secure this, including in terms of accommodation in other areas and severe systemic disruption. At any rate, the United States will continue to exercise the gatekeeping role that belongs to the incumbent in a 1 + 4 international system. Thus, it will continue to evaluate the expediency of peaceful accommodation on the basis of its national priorities, as well as broader systemic interests. Both objective and subjective factors are likely to come into play in such a decision: primarily capabilities as a measure of GDP and military means,[83] as well as the degree of homogeneity with the prevailing "standards of civilization."[84]

Although Russia can boast a stunning economic growth, it is not anticipated to represent a serious challenge in terms of capabilities. Looming questions remain over its uncompetitive technology and innovation sectors, and the sustainability of the very sources of its newly found wealth, which are intimately tied to the world prices of commodities. Moreover, its share of world GDP is expected to reach only 3.5 percent by 2020, and that in absence of an intervening recession. The United States remains by far the strongest economy, with a 2013 GDP of US$16.77 trillion and the largest military budget of US$682 billion, or 39 percent of the world's total military expenditures for 2012 (relative to Russia's 5.2 percent and China's 9.5 percent).[85]

In terms of attitudes, US officials have tended to regard Russian revisionism since the mid-2000s through the prism of its domestic regime, increasingly devoted to authoritarianism and "militant methods of self-affirmation."[86] Russian methods, particularly since the third and more autocratic Putin presidency, reveal a notable dose of militancy, including the rediscovery of Orthodoxy, the invocation of *Russkiy Mir*, and growing anti-Americanism. Moreover, Moscow's annexation of Crimea played into lingering Cold War cognitive frames particularly well.

---

[83] Bukovansky *et al.*, *Special Responsibilities*, 1; Volgy *et al.*, "Major Power Status Attribution," 12; Kenneth N. Waltz, *Theory of International Politics* (New York: McGraw Hill, 1979), 130.

[84] Larson, Paul, and Wohlforth, "Status and World Order"; Gerrit W. Gong, *The Standard of "Civilisation" in International Society* (Oxford: Oxford University Press, 1984). See also Raymond Aron, *Peace and War: A Theory of International Relations* (New York: Doubleday, 1966).

[85] Kuchins and Weitz, "Russia's Place."

[86] Shevtsova, *Lonely Power*, 182; Friedman, "The Western View."

Russia has a history as a great power, and this contributes to shaping elite preferences and role identities. Thus, in contrast to India's caution,[87] Russia has proved eager to resume its erstwhile great power status. This approach also contrasts with China's, for which the key challenge is to manage the commitment problem of reassuring other states of its limited goals[88] – and this without shying away from occasionally flexing its military muscle. For Russia, the main test is instead that of signaling resolve, precisely because of its vulnerabilities, and because, as analysts now admit, the West's handling of post-Soviet Russia "has been just about as insensitive as it could have been."[89] Russian leaders and society today resent as a national humiliation the past twenty years of Western paternalism, aimed at domestic transformation and international integration. The fact is that "the United States has behaved, and until its power is brought into a semblance of balance, will continue to behave in ways that annoy and frighten others."[90]

However, with its actions in Ukraine, Russia has greatly complicated its prospects for accommodation: in a world where territorial integrity is a fundamental norm,[91] the unilateral alteration of the territorial status quo is taken as demonstration of the failure to act responsibly. Whereas prior to the Ukraine crisis opinion on both sides of the Pacific desired a "new Reset," if still amidst overall lack of enthusiasm for full-fledged status accommodation, if anything the mood in Washington now actually favors status "demotion."

The West has already taken a number of initiatives targeting Russia on three key status markers. From an institutional point of view, Russia was suspended from the G8 indefinitely, and its bid to join the OECDE is on ice. From an economic point of view, sanctions were introduced, investment and technology transfer projects were put on hold, and plans to reorient Europe's gas supplies away from Russia were revived. From a territorial point of view, Ukraine's association agreement with the European Union was fast-tracked and concluded, and talks on NATO membership for Georgia were resuscitated.

Yet, all things considered, it seems that what Moscow really wants today – perhaps its "minimum acceptable offer" – is, paradoxically, a "dial back" to the spirit of the New Thinking, which underpins some of its main proposals and its renewed commitment to a constructive

---

[87] See Chapter 11.   [88] See Chapter 10.
[89] Angus Roxburgh, *The Strongman: Vladimir Putin and the Struggle for Russia* (London: I.B. Tauris, 2013).
[90] Kenneth N. Waltz, "America as a Model for the World? A Foreign Policy Perspective," *PS: Political Science and Politics* 24, no. 4 (December 1991), 69.
[91] See Chapter 1.

role in international affairs. In this sense, its goals may actually be more limited than advertised; not far from Brazil's "status quo revisionism."[92] This being said, no one can vouch for Russia's future intentions, as states have a tendency to update their interests as their power grows, and domestic nationalism and authoritarian consolidation are both on the rise. Moreover, analysts have warned that accommodating Russia may encourage further expansionist behavior.[93] Yet, past history has shown a Russia intent on joining rather than subverting, and Moscow has proved a constructive player when it can have an active role in global governance.

In this sense, the challenge has not necessarily changed: it remains that of engaging Russia in a mutually beneficial way, through a mix of policy tools that can encourage it to abandon militancy in its ongoing search for a post-Soviet identity. Nonetheless, as opposed to the more sweeping challenge posed by China, Russia awakens comparatively tougher responses and attitudes. While Russia often provokes this with its belligerent language and unnecessarily confrontational posture and actions, there is also a dose of self-fulfilling prophecy in the current state of relations, which partly reflects reciprocal misunderstandings rooted in centuries of Russo-Western interactions.[94]

[92] See Chapter 12.
[93] Pouliot, *International Security*, 238; John G. Mearsheimer, "The Gathering Storm: China's Challenge to US Power in Asia," *The Chinese Journal of International Politics* 3, no. 4 (Winter 2010), 388.
[94] Iver B. Neumann and Vincent Pouliot, "Untimely Russia: Hysteresis in Russian-Western Relations Over the Past Millennium," *Security Studies* 20, no. 1 (March 2011), 105–37.

Part IV

Conclusions

14 Great power accommodation and the processes of international politics

Theodore McLauchlin

On March 18, 2014, close to 100 years after it began, World War I (WWI) claimed two more lives when long-buried munitions exploded on a farm near Ypres.[1] The echoes of failure to achieve peaceful change in international politics are still with us. They remind us of the urgent need to get the current and future problems of international change right.

Rising powers pose about as big a question as there is in IR theory, and the answers usually offered are big too. They focus on the structural features of international politics: its great power hierarchies and its grand institutional orders. From one point of view, changes to global power hierarchies lead inexorably to clashes between the hegemon and the most powerful rising state. From another, the institutions, norms, and rules established under American primacy, whether because they serve the common interest or because rising powers have been socialized to accept them, might be robust enough to persist into a multipolar world.

In contrast to both grand stories, this book focuses on the processes and strategies of international politics. It locates the drivers of accommodation and conflict among specific conflicts of interest that emerge among multiple powers, the dilemmas and challenges of bargaining to resolve these conflicts of interest, and states' capacities to overcome these challenges.

On a theoretical level, then, this book focuses our attention on the processes and strategies of international politics. As T.V. Paul argues in Chapter 1, "major states do have maneuverability within the limits of the semi-anarchic structure [of world politics], and . . . can avert cataclysmic wars by devising effective grand strategies of change."

The book's arguments affect the precepts of each of the three theoretical traditions outlined by Chapter 1. Realist accounts of power changes should not work from structure alone, but should discuss instead how

---

[1] "Ypres: World War One Weapon Explodes, Killing Two," *BBC News* (March 19, 2014). Available at: www.bbc.com/news/world-europe-26654314.

states mediate structural changes in international politics through specific military threats and bargaining processes. Liberal approaches, long focused on the comparative statics of liberal orders, could fruitfully investigate the problem of how to negotiate over changes to existing rules. That is, if we accept that liberal rules help in the peaceful mediation of state behavior, how then can challenges to those rules themselves be resolved peacefully? This volume explores the institutional flexibility and broader engagement necessary to resolve this paradox. Finally, constructivist accounts can be quite productive in moving past top-down, system-to-state socialization processes. They can instead usefully highlight the differences in normative underpinnings of world politics across different states and groupings of states, and explore the mechanisms by which accommodation among these normative approaches might take place. This volume suggests a few such mechanisms.

This book finds that the problem of rising powers is not reducible to a bilateral clash of a leading power and a single rising power, but instead involves multiple powers and multiple possible substantive areas of conflict. With this in mind, the book explores several different areas where conflict and accommodation could take place: in territory, in institutions and economics, and in normative claims. The book identifies quite serious challenges to accommodation in each of these areas. It emerges that these challenges tend to involve mutually irreconcilable understandings of the situations that states find themselves in. Rising and established powers must therefore allow themselves to be influenced by each other in their outlook and understanding, and not just in their behavior. This chapter proceeds through each of these arguments in turn, and concludes with a set of accommodative practices.

Understanding rising powers: multipolarity and components of power

Must a rising power confront a leading power? Structural approaches to power transitions posit a clear picture of the structure of the system: most often, a leading power and a single rising power in confrontation.[2] The clearer the structure of the system, the more determinate the predictions a structural approach can make. Such an analysis rests on the usefulness of general, overall power rankings, and hence on the fungibility of power. In contrast, this volume argues that the emerging structure of world

---

[2] Robert Gilpin, *War and Change in World Politics* (Cambridge: Cambridge University Press, 1981); A.F.K. Organski and Jacek Kugler, *The War Ledger* (Chicago: University of Chicago Press, 1980).

politics is far from clear. Moreover, it challenges the analytical usefulness of aggregate power rankings for understanding rising powers, arguing that power is not as fungible as is often claimed. The result is this: we cannot read confrontation off of the structure of the system. Instead, if we want to know where the risks of confrontation and the necessity of accommodation lie, we need to pay close attention to the specific claims, interests, and bargaining processes at issue.

We do not actually know what power distribution the world is heading toward. How many other great powers will there be, aside from the United States? Not only are there several candidates, but how far and how fast they will rise is not entirely certain.[3] China, Russia, Brazil, and India face enough structural economic problems that there is room for doubt. With several candidate rising powers, there are many different axes along which conflict could occur; we cannot easily know which pair of powers will confront each other.

Indeed, the four historical case studies that this book explores demonstrate that the problems of rising powers are, first, problems of multipolarity. In the two cases of successful accommodation, the leading power had to deal with other great powers posing more immediate threats in their own eyes. As Ali Zeren and John Hall argue in Chapter 6, Britain could do little about the power rising furthest and fastest in structural terms, the United States. In any case, first Russia and later Germany posed the greater threat to interests London regarded as vital. Additionally, in Chapter 7, Lorenz Lüthi makes clear that the United States accommodated China during the 1970s with a view to its potential future power as a counterweight to the Soviet Union. Accordingly, this accommodation was not smooth, but quite sensitive to the ups and downs of America's détente-era relationship with Moscow.

Russia again looms large in the two case studies of confrontation, in a different way. As elaborated by Martin Claar and Norrin Ripsman in Chapter 8 and by Jeffrey Taliaferro in Chapter 9, both Imperial Germany and Imperial Japan believed themselves to be not rising powers, but powers in decline, encircled by hostile states and notably fearful of a rising Russia (and, later, Soviet Union). This does not mean that the "fault" for these confrontations lies with Germany's or Japan's adversaries. German and Japanese domestic politics were central to the feeling of encirclement and to how they reacted to it. However, the German and Japanese sense of encirclement was in any case a problem for the system. And it was Russia's rise, and not just British or American dominance, that set the stage at the

---

[3] See, e.g., Michael Beckley, "China's Century? Why America's Edge Will Endure," *International Security* 36, no. 3 (January 2012), 41–78.

system level for this sense of encirclement. That is, encirclement arose not just from the leading state, but from *another rising state*. The strategic problem for the leading state was therefore not just the problem of one rising state, but of several, and of how they reacted to one another. In short, accommodating rising powers has historically been a problem of multipolarity.

In this multipolar context, the specific components of power that a state possesses and the specific threats that it can pose assume particularly high importance. In Chapter 2, Steven Lobell reminds us that power is not necessarily very fungible. Instead, it disaggregates into multiple components, each of which is useful in some circumstances but not others. Rather than considering power shifts in terms of a hierarchy of relative power, then, it is necessary to examine how one state may threaten another's more specific interests. Hence, analysts looking for the origins of conflict must be specific. This book's historical case studies reflect this point as well. They turn to the specific character of the threats and power resources at the disposal of the great powers in question. The Russian threat to India and the weight that the British put on this colony played a role in Britain's focus on Russia rather than on the United States or Germany, until naval competition with the latter pushed its attention back to Europe. The ability of the United States to threaten Japan's interests in a wide variety of ways sealed Japan's bid for war. The immense and unrealized potential of the Chinese economy and its clashes with the Soviet Union made it an excellent candidate for the United States to court as a counterweight in the 1970s.

These points are deeply important for understanding our own time. As the world becomes increasingly concerned about a coming confrontation between the United States and China,[4] there remain Russia, India, Brazil, Japan, and the European Union as major players in global politics and economics. Rising powers, in this context, raise similar issues of uncertainty about where conflict might lie. If we do not actually know who will confront whom, the management of great power relations becomes all the more about the management of specific problems.

Indeed, one remarkable feature of the problem of international systems change is that such a consummately macro-level process devolves to a series of smaller problems. Russia and the West, having so far failed to get Ukraine right, have deepened their mutual mistrust and set the stage for future crises. The risk may be repeated for China, Japan, the Association

---

[4] Edward Luttwak, *The Rise of China vs. the Logic of Strategy* (Cambridge: Belknap Press, 2012); John J. Mearsheimer, *The Tragedy of Great Power Politics*, updated edn. (New York: W.W. Norton, 2014).

of Southeast Asian Nations (ASEAN) states, and the United States in the maritime disputes in the East and South China Seas, and for India and China in their long-running territorial disputes. Structural change thus creates the possibility of conflict but does not determine it, and says still less about who will confront whom. In this kind of world, more specific process variables can say more about the origins and management of the specific problems that could lead to great power confrontation.

In what follows, then, I discuss the four areas of accommodation identified by Paul in Chapter 1: territorial, institutional, economic, and normative. Each of these areas entails dilemmas and challenges that may make accommodation harder to achieve. In the territorial disputes that, today, have the potential to erupt into armed conflict, this book demonstrates that the classic challenges of treating threats as more serious than they are, and of effectively signaling intentions, are alive and well and very important to understanding how conflict and accommodation will proceed. In institutional and economic accommodation, which I treat together here, tensions and difficulties may arise from the double-edged nature of international institutions. They are meant to preserve a favorable order for the leading powers by limiting their freedom of action. In this context, this book uncovers the problem that a demand for a change in the rules by a rising power may be regarded by that power as a contribution to making the rules more generally acceptable, but seen by the leading powers as a challenge to their entrenched leadership. Finally, the problem of normative accommodation is, essentially, that the stronger the normative claims made by a state, the harder it is to see past these claims to understand the other side's, whether this is about the rules of the game or about status in world politics. Ultimately, therefore, the challenges of accommodation in each of these areas are challenges of mutual understanding.

Territorial accommodation: bargaining, mistrust, and crises

The problem of disputes over territory and spheres of influence looms large on the international agenda, particularly with Russia and China. Given that territorial disputes are often a step on the road to armed conflict, the international system will need to grapple with this issue long past 2016. On the basis of this book's arguments, it is inappropriate to treat territorial challenges as tests of overall American power, and in fact it would be dangerous to do so. Instead, they should be treated as bargaining processes about specific claims. As bargaining processes, they come with the classic challenges of signaling intentions effectively.

Specific, not general, challenges

As already noted, this book argues that the challenge of rising powers reduces to specific issues and confrontations. This analytical point has a practical consequence: policymakers may often be prone to overestimate the severity of a particular challenge when they lose sight of the specific matter in dispute and instead obsess over overall power rankings.[5] As Paul argues in Chapter 1, some mixture of deterrence and more pacific strategies is likely to be best for managing disputes, but the choice will depend on context-specific factors rather than the broader circumstances of global power shifts. A great power would therefore err if it saw a specific problem or crisis as indicative of the whole character of a relationship with another great power.

To illustrate, I argue that in the present Ukraine crisis, Russia's territorial gains do not indicate that the West is in a *generally* weak position.[6] The North Atlantic Treaty Organization's (NATO) "giving up" Crimea does not imply conceding on eastern Ukraine, let alone western Ukraine, the Baltic States, or Poland. While the takeover of Crimea was a rapid fait accompli about which Kiev could do little, Russia's move against eastern Ukraine has dragged it into a costly Ukrainian civil war while driving the remainder of Ukraine to clear and stable majority support for greater economic and military integration into Western institutions. It would perhaps have been better for Russia if Ukraine had remained a united but weak buffer state. Its escalation in eastern Ukraine was, I think, a mistake in a way that its move against Crimea was not. The two situations are, in principle, separable. In the same vein, there is a stronger Western interest in maintaining the credibility of its security guarantees as regards NATO allies, such as Poland, Estonia, Latvia, and Lithuania. NATO's flexible response as of this writing – tacitly accepting the Russian annexation of Crimea, issuing major economic sanctions against Russia for its attack on eastern Ukraine, and bolstering its defense of the Baltic members of the alliance – differentiates among quite different geographic settings: it cannot do much about the first, it can do something more about the second, and the third is crucial to its raison d'être as an alliance. As such, it appears an appropriately measured policy.

In consequence, Russia's seizure of Crimea – and even its war in eastern Ukraine – does not put it in the driver's seat in Europe, running rings around the United States. If power were fully fungible, NATO's failure

---

[5] See also Daryl G. Press, *Calculating Credibility: How Leaders Evaluate Military Threats* (Ithaca: Cornell University Press, 2005).

[6] Note, for context – and possibly by way of apology – that this chapter was drafted in mid-May 2014 and revised in March 2015.

to prevent Russia from taking Crimea might be seen as clear evidence of Russia's strength and NATO's weakness. But power is not fully fungible. Russia is certainly stronger than it was in 1991 when it lost control of Crimea in the secession of Ukraine, but it has not yet gained the power needed to do much more than annex Crimea and interfere in eastern Ukraine at substantial cost. Nor does the concession on Crimea have a causal effect, reducing the West's bargaining power over other territories. Thomas Schelling argues that "[i]t might be hard to persuade the Soviets, if the United States yielded on Cuba and then on Puerto Rico, that it would go to war over Key West."[7] Showing resolve now means avoiding future challenges. But empirical research suggests that there just is not much evidence for the general existence of reputation, built up during one crisis and transferable to a different one, whether for psychological or power-political reasons.[8]

It would therefore be a major mistake for Russia, Europe, or the United States to regard the successful annexation of Crimea, and even the successful slicing off of a large part of eastern Ukraine, as evidence of the West's weakness and as transferable to other pieces of territory. There is greater danger, indeed, in states mistakenly inflating specific issues – believing that resolve now can help them avoid getting a reputation for laxity and help forestall the next crisis, for example, or else inflating vivid actions as indicators of general intentions in foreign policy.[9] And the dangers of unwanted escalation through security dilemmas and spirals of mistrust are well-known enough that reputation for resolve seems a poor reason to run such risks.[10] As rising powers make territorial claims, then, the danger is that they (through hubris) or the leading powers (through fear of their own decline) mistake specific concessions and settlements for defeat in some abstract power game.

---

[7] Thomas C. Schelling, *Arms and Influence* (New Haven: Yale University Press, 1966), 124.

[8] James D. Fearon, "Signaling Versus the Balance of Power and Interests: An Empirical Test of a Crisis Bargaining Model," *Journal of Conflict Resolution* 38, no. 2 (June 1994), 236–69; Jonathan Mercer, *Reputation and International Politics* (Ithaca: Cornell University Press, 1996); Press, *Calculating Credibility*.

[9] Press, *Calculating Credibility*; Keren Yarhi-Milo, *Knowing the Adversary: Leaders, Intelligence, and Assessment of Intentions in International Relations* (Princeton: Princeton University Press, 2014).

[10] John H. Herz, "Idealist Internationalism and the Security Dilemma," *World Politics* 2, no. 2 (January 1950), 157–80; Robert Jervis, "Cooperation under the Security Dilemma," *World Politics* 30, no. 2 (January 1978), 167–214; Charles L. Glaser, "Realists as Optimists: Cooperation as Self-Help," *International Security* 19, no. 3 (Winter 1994/95), 50–90; Andrew H. Kydd, *Trust and Mistrust in International Relations* (Princeton: Princeton University Press, 2005).

Bargaining dilemmas

States and analysts should therefore generally treat different bargaining situations as separate from each other, rather than fungible parts of a broader challenge to general American hegemony. However, even treated separately, each bargaining scenario generates further dilemmas for leading and rising powers alike. The rise of great powers may produce tensions in light of both of James Fearon's two canonical bargaining problems.[11] First, Fearon and Robert Powell interpret rising power conflict as a commitment problem: rising powers cannot credibly commit to keeping the agreements they make now, since in the future they will have more power to force a renegotiation. If a power rises fast enough, compared to the likely damage of conflict, it may be better for the leading state in relative decline to fight now rather than later.[12] The aim of such a conflict, as Alex Weisiger clarifies, is to prevent another state from rising at all; and so these wars are immensely destructive.[13] Second, an era of multiple changes in the power of different states is rife with uncertainty;[14] in this context, states' intentions, given incentives to keep them close to the chest, may be very difficult to discern.

Thus, the bargaining model of conflict highlights further challenges and dangers in territorial accommodation. These dangers need attentive management from both rising powers and leading powers. Importantly, de-escalating confrontation requires that states signal and bind themselves to their benign intentions (when they have them), but also that they signal that they are willing to fight when they are. Kai He finds in Chapter 10 that China has pursued both strategies to translate its increasing capability into new international advantages without provoking a major confrontation. It has engaged with ASEAN as a way of tying its hands by making aggressive behavior in the East and South China Seas more costly. But it has also signaled its willingness to fight over Taiwan, helping Washington to avoid miscalculation. For Nicola Contessi in Chapter 13, Russia faces the very distinct challenge of inducing the United States to take it seriously as a peer; specifically, to make clear how strongly it values its own sphere of influence. The wars in Georgia

---

[11] James D. Fearon, "Rationalist Explanations for War," *International Organization* 49, no. 3 (Summer 1995), 379–414.

[12] Fearon, "Rationalist Explanations for War"; Robert Powell, "War as a Commitment Problem," *International Organization* 60, no. 1 (January 2006), 169–203.

[13] Alex Weisiger, *Logics of War: Explanations for Limited and Unlimited Conflicts* (Ithaca: Cornell University Press, 2013).

[14] See Charles F. Doran, "Economics, Philosophy of History, and the 'Single Dynamic' of Power Cycle Theory: Expectations, Competition, and Statecraft," *International Political Science Review* 24, no. 1 (January 1, 2003), 37.

in 2008 and Ukraine since 2014 may be taken not only in their local context, but also as indications of a Russian willingness to fight to dominate that sphere of influence.

How serious is the possibility of conflict from the commitment problem – that is, a war to prevent the rise of another power? Weisiger argues that, in the United States–China case that excites the most concern, it is not very likely: "it is entirely unclear how, having started such a war, the United States might plausibly expect to be able to end it."[15] This is in line with Powell's clarification of the commitment problem: for a preventive war to occur, a state must anticipate that it will decline very quickly compared to the costs of conflict, and the costs of a preventive United States–China war would be monstrous. On this view, preventive war is very unlikely. But the bargaining model of war has been developed as a two-player model above all (as makes heuristic and modeling sense). If rising powers constitute a problem of multipolarity, as I have argued, this adds an important dimension to the commitment problem. If a perception of relative decline comes from a fear of encirclement by *multiple* actors, then problems of understanding multiply. Great powers would have to grasp how their peers might respond not only to their own acts (which is hard enough), but also to the acts of third parties, in order to understand whether a preventive war is imaginable.

The dilemmas of signals, for their part, are well known. They are difficult and dangerous, and take considerable skill to accomplish well. As Fearon argues, while displays of force can be useful to reveal information, they come at serious risk of escalation.[16] There is no guarantee that a signal will be correctly interpreted. If Russia is indeed attempting to assert a sphere of influence in its near abroad, with little interest in further expansion, signals that include sponsoring rebellions in its neighbors run a considerable risk of convincing Western observers of implacable Russian expansionism. They are, after all, the "vivid" signals of intention that may often decisively influence decision-makers' analyses.[17] In addition, signals occur in the context of a history of interactions that sustain trust or mistrust.[18] For instance, in Chapter 8, Claar and Ripsman highlight the history of conflict and accommodation among great powers as a reason why Britain remained quite concerned about Russia and France during Germany's long rise. Similarly, as Contessi argues in Chapter 13, in contrast to China, "Russia awakens comparatively tougher responses and attitudes. While Russia often provokes this with its belligerent

---

[15] Weisiger, *Logics of War*, 215.   [16] Fearon, "Rationalist Explanations for War," 397.
[17] Yarhi-Milo, *Knowing the Adversary*.
[18] Kydd, *Trust and Mistrust in International Relations*.

language and unnecessarily confrontational posture and actions, there is also a dose of self-fulfilling prophecy in the current state of relations, which partly reflects reciprocal misunderstandings rooted in centuries of Russo-Western interactions" (p. 289). Russia's own belligerent actions therefore feed into and reinforce an existing hostile set of responses.

Signaling intentions in the immediate disputes in Eastern Europe and the South China Sea is thus a paramount challenge. But this volume's contributions highlight the degree to which it is a two-way street. If Russia and China need to reassure the West of their limited aims, established powers and their allies need to be willing to take disputes one by one so that the limited challenges that do take place are not inappropriately regarded as threats to the whole territorial dispensation of each region.

Institutional and economic accommodation: inclusion on better terms?

Rising powers do not just question the existing territorial dispensation. More general questions emerge about the world's institutional order: Do rising powers accept that order, seek to modify it, or seek to destabilize and rewrite it? Optimistic arguments hold that these institutions should be able to persist despite the relative decline of the American leader that put them in place. Rising powers can recognize that global institutions reduce transaction costs for global cooperation and enable elements of international order to persist "after hegemony."[19] But different institutional orders distribute goods differently, and alternative orders might provide better prospects for rising states. However, if rising powers can be socialized to accept the existing order as legitimate and valuable,[20] then the rise of new powers may be relatively smooth, not even entailing much redefinition of existing rules. In the context of this debate, this volume raises considerable reason to suppose that rising powers will demand some change even if they accept the existing broad outlines of order. Even limited demands for change to existing institutional orders raise serious dilemmas. Demands for change to institutions are open to highly contested interpretations. They might be seen as ways of fulfilling the mandate of institutions to constrain the power of the leading states, or as efforts to replace those states. They might be seen as opportunities to stabilize rules by adjusting them to reflect new realities, or as destabilizing rules by calling into doubt their primacy.

[19] Robert O. Keohane, *After Hegemony: Cooperation and Discord in the World Political Economy* (Princeton: Princeton University Press, 1984).

[20] Alastair I. Johnston, *Social States: China in International Institutions, 1980–2000* (Princeton: Princeton University Press, 2008).

The demands of rising powers

How much do rising powers accept the world's institutional order as it stands? It certainly appears that China, Brazil, and India have acted according to the broad outlines of international order. Indeed, their emergence as rising powers owes something to this strategy, and particularly to economic liberalization. As Lüthi notes in Chapter 7, China rose following its abandonment of both the domestic and international components of Mao's radical challenge. Similarly with India: as Aseema Sinha argues in Chapter 11, its rise coincided with a willingness to abandon its import substitution strategy and integrate itself much more thoroughly in the global economic order.

But there is a major selection effect at work here. That weaker states sought to succeed on the terms which the exisiting order offered does not necessarily have much bearing on what those states might try to do once they are stronger. For Mlada Bukovansky, writing in Chapter 5, "To the extent that rising powers see themselves merely as norm-takers rather than norm-makers, their investment in any existing order could easily be more instrumental and strategic, rather than a matter of deep identification with the principles of that order" (p. 94). In this way, rising powers pose a basic analytical challenge for students of international regimes and their acceptance by smaller states. For example, did Brazil, India, and China liberalize their economies and seek accession to an existing global economic order out of conviction, or because there were few other options?

In turn, what might these rising states demand, given more power? The case studies of contemporary rising powers find that much of what they want is change within the existing institutional order. India's role as a "bridging power," according to Aseema Sinha's analysis in Chapter 11, entails looking for a seat at the existing table that reflects its rising importance. India does not seek to replace that order, but likewise it remains skeptical of aligning its foreign policy with Washington's. Similarly, as David Mares argues in Chapter 12, Brazil regards itself as a champion of developing-world interests within, and not outside, a broadly liberal economic framework. It is willing to challenge elements of that framework that harm the developing world, such as the lack of adequate space for social democracy and the persistence of unfair agricultural subsidies. As Kai He argues in Chapter 10, China, having deliberately entered international institutions in order to become socialized into the system, used its newfound role in institutions to push for adjustment, such as in International Monetary Fund (IMF) voting rights and in the currencies underpinning the global monetary and investment regimes. Even

Russia's assertion of a sphere of influence, on Contessi's view in Chapter 13, can be regarded as working within the system; Russia excoriates the American willingness to bypass the UN Security Council system as it sees fit. But it remains to be seen how willing each of these powers will be to continue to accept the broad outlines of the international institutional order if faced with resistance rather than flexibility. And, as in the case of territorial accommodation, this book identifies serious dilemmas in being flexible.

Dilemmas of responding to demands for institutional change

International institutions and the distribution of power have an ambiguous relationship. It follows that demands for changes to institutions in the context of rising power are subject to differences of interpretation too. In John Ikenberry's optimistic theory, states can entrench their power in the long run by restraining it in the short run through institutions, thereby making their primacy more acceptable.[21] In a more pessimistic view, leading states have the freedom to be hypocritical, proclaiming rules for others while retaining the freedom to break them. As Bukovansky argues in Chapter 5, it is not actually clear how liberal the order is. For David Mares in Chapter 12, the willingness of the United States to violate such important constitutive norms of world politics as territorial integrity (as in the case of the 2003 decision to invade Iraq) and liberalized trade (especially for goods with politically important groups of producers in the United States and Europe) indicates a claim to a special status, specifically the right to violate such norms as a consequence of its position as a system leader.[22] Hypocrisy may, in fact, be central to unipolarity.[23]

Both the optimistic and the pessimistic views agree that America's failure to restrain itself provokes resistance[24] and demands for greater limits on American power,[25] though they differ on whether these rule

[21] G. John Ikenberry, *After Victory: Institutions, Strategic Restraint, and the Rebuilding of Order after Major Wars* (Princeton: Princeton University Press, 2001).

[22] See Mlada Bukovansky, "Institutionalized Hypocrisy and the Politics of Agricultural Trade," in *Constructing the International Economy*, ed. Rawi Abdelal, Mark Blyth, and Craig Parsons (Ithaca: Cornell University Press, 2010), 68–89.

[23] Martha Finnemore, "Legitimacy, Hypocrisy, and the Social Structure of Unipolarity: Why Being a Unipole Isn't All It's Cracked Up to Be," *World Politics* 61, no. 1 (January 2009), 58–85.

[24] Nuno P. Monteiro, "Unrest Assured: Why Unipolarity Is Not Peaceful," *International Security* 36, no. 3 (Winter 2011/12), 9–40.

[25] Finnemore, "Legitimacy, Hypocrisy, and the Social Structure of Unipolarity"; T.V. Paul, "Soft Balancing in the Age of US Primacy," *International Security* 30, no. 1

violations are central to the institutional order or evidence of poor judgment on Washington's part. In both theories, there is a deep tension in the relationship between global institutions and the position of the leader. These institutions are formally supposed to limit the leader and restrain its power. But the rules also reinforce its leadership, whether through a constitutional bargain (in the optimistic view) or through the freedom to act hypocritically (in the pessimistic view).

Hence, from either perspective, when rising powers seek changes, there may be tremendous tension in how these changes are interpreted. Rising powers present their demands as reinforcing institutions by demanding that limits on the leading power be enforced. Contessi demonstrates in Chapter 13 that Russia sees its assertion of a sphere of influence as just a return to what the international security order was supposed to look like after 1945, following the interruption created by the end of the Cold War. Brazil's demands, according to Mares in Chapter 12, consist largely of ending certain hypocritical practices pursued by the leading states. These include maintaining barriers to developing-world agricultural goods even while proclaiming neoliberal principles and failing to hold up their end of the non-proliferation regime by disarming. In each case, the rising power sees itself as *upholding* international rules, rather than disrupting them. If rules restrained the leading power more thoroughly, it is clear how rising second-tier powers would benefit.

But by the same token, it is easy to see how the United States and Europe could see these demands as disrupting the international institutional order. At one level, they may challenge formal rules such as territorial integrity. They may also challenge informal norms, especially about who gets to dominate the world's institutions. As Bukovansky argues in Chapter 5, an institutional order may be liberal but not American-led. The Chinese proposal for an Asian Infrastructure Investment Bank (AIIB) accepts a broadly liberal framework but may pose a deep challenge to the informal norm of operating through American-led Bretton Woods organizations.

Rising and leading powers thus may well not agree about *what is going on* when a rising power demands institutional accommodation. While both India and Brazil seek to secure their place in the broad outlines of the existing institutional order, Sinha and Mares point out in Chapters 11 and 12 that neither state's aspirations are easily captured in the dichotomy of revisionist versus status quo. To the extent that leading powers see any

(Summer 2005), 46–71; Robert A. Pape, "Soft Balancing against the United States," *International Security* 30, no. 1 (Summer 2005), 7–45; G. John Ikenberry, *Liberal Leviathan: The Origins, Crisis, and Transformation of the American World Order* (Princeton: Princeton University Press, 2011).

major change in the institutional order as revisionism, rising powers' demands are unlikely to be accommodated easily.

Normative accommodation: increased conflict from normative claims

The rise of new great powers, as this book makes clear, creates new normative challenges as well. The normative challenges I discuss in this section overlap with the other areas of accommodation, for territory and international rules often have a lot of normative heft. This book identifies two major dilemmas for normative accommodation in particular. The first flows from established powers' normative claims for the existing rules of international politics. The second flows from rising powers' normative claims to new status in world politics. In each case, the challenge is similar: the stronger a normative claim made for one position or another, the harder it is to resolve tensions among great powers. Neither dilemma appears easy to handle.

Defending the rules

We like to think that the rules have a normative underpinning. The current order is often justified with references to liberal arguments.[26] Socialization requires some acceptance of the legitimacy of the content of current rules. But to the extent that actors in world politics make normative arguments forcefully and with conviction, it becomes hard to justify changing the rules. The normative defense of existing rules thus sows the seeds for further tension down the line.

An important illustration of this point is in the role of international law in the face of rising powers. In Chapter 4, Krzysztof Pelc explores how law responds to problems of peaceful change and elucidates the difficulty highlighted by E.H. Carr. If law is too rigid, for example if it is held to have a moral force that is dissociated from the balance of power that brings it into being in the first place, and which changes with the rise of a new power, there are only two options. The first is to persist with a law that dissatisfies the rising power by failing to take account of its rise. The second is to abandon the rule in question entirely as incapable of dealing with reality – as, in fact, immoral, since it seems unfair now that circumstances have changed. The value placed on the existing order, and the normative claims of those seeing to change it, thus create a problem of indivisible stakes for bargaining about institutional accommodation.

---

[26] For example, Ikenberry, *Liberal Leviathan.*

The point might be extended beyond law to any important formal or informal institution in international politics. Defending institutions as morally right, not just as the product of international negotiation, makes them harder to change. As Brazil or India proposes international economic changes, then, it ignites not only a negotiation but a clash of positions of principle, each with its adherents, who regard a concession to the other as not just part of bargaining but as a moral concession. The same happens, rather more pointedly, when Russia asserts "the right to decide unilaterally how to protect Russian speakers in countries other than Russia"; according to one commentator, this "changes the rules for at least Europe and for much of the Eurasian land mass. Borders are no longer necessarily inviolate, and the weak can fall prey to the strong."[27] Thus, for some commentators, NATO's failure to resist the annexation of Crimea is not just a loss of territory for Ukraine, but also calls into question the whole normative order of European security. In this context, accepting a negotiation away from the existing rules seems to imply accepting a normatively compromised position.

This is a big problem for contemporary international politics. When we talk about the possible need to grant Russia a sphere of influence, this probably means heavy interference by Moscow in the internal affairs of its neighbors, up to and including armed conflict. If the project of claiming certain values to be Russian and promoting them is, as Contessi argues in Chapter 13, a central component of Putin's domestic and foreign policy, then it is well to face up to the fact that these "values" are often highly problematic for liberal observers. There may not be much that can be done to prevent Russia from pursuing this course, but it will come at a moral cost for many actors and observers.

Pelc argues in Chapter 4 that international law has innovated solutions to its problem of inflexibility, permitting the law to adapt to changing circumstances and thus creating the space to find a mutually acceptable compromise. But this approach implies that we not hallow existing law as much as we might. Applied to both formal and informal international institutions more broadly, it suggests that for institutions to be effective, they need to be treated not with veneration, but as a tool for resolving disputes, useful in the short run and adaptable to change. There is a very difficult balance to strike, however. A rule needs to be binding enough to be valuable in the short run and normatively justified enough to be accepted, but flexible enough not to ignite conflict once circumstances have changed.

[27] Jeffrey Simpson, "Czar Vladimir Is Changing the Rules of the Game," *The Globe and Mail* (April 18, 2014). Available at: www.theglobeandmail.com/globe-debate/czar-putin-i-is-changing-the-rules-of-the-game/article18055930/.

Hypocrisy may be a temporizing solution in some ways. I use "hypocrisy" here to refer to a state's loudly proclaiming a rule while committing or ignoring a violation of that rule. We can treat it as a gap between the moral world one proclaims and the world one actually acts from.[28] Great powers may often use hypocrisy as a way of managing great power relations in the context of a general attachment to rules. If the United States proclaims the norm of territorial integrity in general while acquiescing to Russia's annexation of Crimea, this represents at least a mild form of hypocrisy. It suggests that one set of rules applies to great powers and another to the rest of the world. It also allows Russia to be hypocritical, as it proclaims territorial integrity in (for example) the face of Kosovo's declaration of independence. In a sense, acquiescing to Russia's annexation can be seen as an extension to Russia of the privilege of hypocrisy, which the United States already takes advantage of. While normatively highly dissatisfying, and prone to provoking similar resistance to existing order in general, hypocrisy has something to recommend it. It may in particular be preferable to some of the apparent alternatives – rule-free disorder or the rigidity that Carr feared. It would make more sense to draw the line between thoroughgoing, unabashed hypocrisy and hypocrisy as an exception to the rules in exceptional situations.

Defending status claims

Like the normative defense of existing rules, status anxiety can have the effect of making small conflicts difficult to bargain over. Contributions to this volume show that status claims can create indivisible stakes.[29] They show that status is not just about demanding certain concessions, as in a bargaining framework. Rather, it is about demanding certain reasons for action, as Mlada Bukovansky argues in Chapter 5. A rising power needs to be sure that it is being granted privileges because it is a great power – that is, because there is some normative recognition that it *deserves* those privileges – rather than just to defuse it as a threat: "If accommodation is to be a sustainable practice when the most fundamental power rankings in world politics are at stake, it must also entail a morally resonant dimension of meaning, beyond rational strategic objectives. Accommodation perceived by any side as merely strategic (or, worse, hypocritical) is not likely to create the sorts of condition where the status aspirations of the respective parties will be satisfied" (p. 141).

---

[28] Bukovansky, "Institutionalized Hypocrisy."
[29] Stacie E. Goddard, "Uncommon Ground: Indivisible Territory and the Politics of Legitimacy," *International Organization* 60, no. 1 (January 2006), 35–68.

In other words, when a rising power's demand is imbued with status anxiety, it is not just a matter of concessions, but a demand about *the reasons the other party makes concessions*. In Chapter 10, Kai He identifies a salient distinction between "accommodation for interests," done just because doing so is better for the leading power than the alternative, and "accommodation for identity," done because "the hegemon believes that the rising power should get what it bargains for," because the leading power believes that those demands are "appropriate for who it is." As Deborah Larson, T.V. Paul, and William Wohlforth argue, status "refers to higher-order beliefs about a state's relative ranking – beliefs about what others believe."[30] Wohlforth suggests that much conflict can emerge not out of the feeling of being slighted from the status that is due to one, but just out of *not knowing* what one's status is.[31] Resolving such demands thus requires a clear indicator of others' reasons for acting.

It would be nice to be able to offer some policy advice to established states here, to the effect of sending the right signals to a rising power with status concerns – as Wohlforth puts it, "to stroke the status aspirations of rising powers in the pursuit of the policy objective of the moment."[32] But one tricky consequence of this argument is that it makes it hard to incorporate the logic of status into strategy. Instead, the logic of status is meant to *bypass* strategic calculus. Merely to verbally reassure the rising power of its status may well be seen as cheap talk. A costly signal of status would have to be costly enough that a state that did *not* respect a rising power's status would not send that signal. So finding a costly signal of status does not solve the initial problem of actually needing to believe that the rising power in question deserves the status it claims. If the leading power does not believe this, it is not entirely clear what can be done in the short term.

If the short-run status dilemma does not seem easy to resolve, there is more promise in the long run. Since repeated actions may be internalized over time, the most promising avenue may be to "fake it till you make it." Leading states could accommodate for interests in the first place, knowing that, over time, such a stance may come to be seen as natural and internalized.[33] As Bukovansky argues in Chapter 5, practicing

---

[30] Deborah Welch Larson, T.V. Paul, and William C. Wohlforth, "Status and World Order," in *Status in World Politics*, eds., T.V. Paul, Deborah Welch Larson, and William C. Wohlforth (Cambridge: Cambridge University Press, 2014), 8.

[31] William C. Wohlforth, "Status Dilemmas and Interstate Conflict," in *Status in World Politics*, eds., T.V. Paul, Deborah Welch Larson, and William C. Wohlforth (Cambridge: Cambridge University Press, 2014), 115–40.

[32] Ibid., 140.

[33] Martha Finnemore and Kathryn Sikkink, "International Norm Dynamics and Political Change," *International Organization* 52, no. 4 (Autumn 1998), 887–917.

accommodation makes it easier to accommodate in the future. On the other side, if rising powers seek a particular reason for action, they should be willing to wait for it. Accommodation for interests now is actually a step toward accommodation for identity later.

Reciprocal socialization and empathy

Numerous challenges attend on accommodation in world politics. In many ways, they are challenges of mutual understanding. Bargaining over territorial accommodation will require that both sides understand that a concession on one demand does not entail general weakness, because of the fungibility of power, in addition to the well-known problems of sending and receiving signals of intentions. Institutional and economic accommodation will require that leading and rising powers each understand the concerns of the other about whether existing institutions are to be overthrown or preserved unchanged. And normative accommodation will entail clashes of rules and of status claims, in which much can be gained by seeing past one's own normative justifications for action.

For each of these problems, building mutual understanding and accepting mutual influence thus appear to be indispensable components of solutions. As Paul argues in Chapter 1, normative accommodation needs to be reciprocal in order for the future normative frameworks underpinning the international order to be accepted as legitimate. As Kai He puts it in Chapter 10, "socialization is not a one-way street" (p. 215).

Here, Philip Potter's argument in Chapter 3 for being open to influence from other states through globalization shows states a way forward. Potter reminds us that classical liberals valued trade for peace not just because it created a financial stake, but because it increased cross-cultural contact and understanding at a time when there were not many other avenues for such contact. With a vast array of such avenues in contemporary globalization, there are many more opportunities for reciprocal influence than we once had. But for Potter, globalization does not just represent a change in context that states must passively accept. Instead, he recommends that states actively open themselves up to such influence, through the model of cultural engagement. This is a vital lesson across all of the areas of conflict and accommodation highlighted in this volume. Being open to influence means being open to understanding other states' views of signals in territorial disputes, to what is going on when a state demands that a rule be changed in an international institution, and to what reasons for action are normatively acceptable in international politics.

Recognizing that interdependence has a substantial social dimension, going well beyond economic exchange, also opens up avenues for deliberation about the character that international order should take. A shift from the G7/G8 to the G20 in global economic governance is an important institutional change in this direction, taking account of the fact that – to an unprecedented extent – middle-income countries like China, India, and Brazil are some of the world's largest economies, and that they may have substantively different views of how to manage the global economy. The substantive terms of the debate should change in turn. For example, one approach toward globalization was to think that international economic flows mandated the reduction and elimination of capital controls.[34] To see the debate reemerge, with the IMF officially considering such controls useful in some circumstances, suggests a less disembedded, neoliberal approach to globalization, in line with developing-world concerns.[35] The social dimension of interdependence means the possibility of meaningful influence and persuasion in the course of that debate, rather than a clash of irreconcilable normative alternatives. It helps to give normative content to world order, while avoiding the dangerous rigidity that such content can often imply.

Conclusion

Several strategies of accommodation emerge from this volume, operating across the areas of accommodation discussed in this chapter. The first few mechanisms deal with de-escalating international disputes that carry with them the threat of war. The limits to the information that states can get from the structure of the international system suggest the importance of *treating crises piecemeal*. There is a tendency to run away with interpretations of disputes, as we have seen in Ukraine. Foreign policy elites in the United States and its NATO allies might be tempted to think that allowing Russia to take Crimea, or even the Donbas, means the abandonment of other commitments. On the flipside, Russia might have a similar temptation, to think that NATO's tacit acceptance of its aggression is proof of a general lack of resolve. This does not need to be so: the major NATO states can distinguish between Crimea and NATO members, and they have. Thus, great powers can converge around common understandings of crises that are more or less limited. I suggest that they

---

[34] John B. Goodman and Louis W. Pauly, "The Obsolescence of Capital Controls? Economic Management in an Age of Global Markets," *World Politics* 46, no. 1 (October 1993), 50–82.

[35] Daniel W. Drezner, "The System Worked: Global Economic Governance during the Great Recession," *World Politics* 66, no. 1 (January 2014), 145.

should try, more often than not, to converge around the more limited view.

The standard *bargaining strategies* should also be seen as strategies of accommodation, including costly signaling (to manage problems of private information) and self-restraint (to manage problems of credible commitments). For signals, the difficulty will lie, as usual, in interpretation. It may take some time, and several rounds of interaction, for the great powers to learn what multipolarity means.[36] In the meantime, we need to avoid accidents and demonstrate empathy. International military exchanges, even – perhaps especially – among possible future adversaries, might help to build trust. For example, NATO-Russian joint exercises should not be a long-run casualty of the Ukraine crisis. In addition, the world will call upon the skill and experience of negotiators, and on what Robert Jervis, many years ago, called their "empathy" – their ability to see what their own signal might mean to their counterparts.[37] Over the long run, repeated instances of this kind of empathy may help to produce the respect that is necessary for managing great powers' status anxiety and fear of encirclement. As Bukovansky argues in Chapter 5, the practice of accommodation makes future accommodation easier. Reinvesting in states' diplomatic services – a popular area to cut in times of austerity – might help to attract and retain personnel with the experience and talent needed to properly send and receive such signals.

Self-restraint is incumbent both on the United States and on rising powers, especially militarily powerful ones like China and Russia. Accepting institutional restraints does not mean accepting all of the institutional terms of the present order, even if it does mean accepting *some*; that is, at least those that other states consider vital. But an important difficulty is that, at the same time as institutional restraints are particularly important for the sake of credible commitments, shifting power inclines states toward violating and renegotiating previously existing international rules as they gain the strength to do so. The difficulty is to know where to draw the line between enforcement of current agreements and renegotiation. I doubt that there is any fixed formula for balancing between these aims. But, for example, the current crisis in Ukraine, which has deeply damaged the Helsinki settlement in Europe, warrants a renegotiated territorial settlement that can be more credibly enforced and put into practice. A similar territorial settlement for East Asia should be a principal diplomatic objective in the next ten years, unlikely though such an agreement appears to be for the moment.

---

[36] Kydd, *Trust and Mistrust in International Relations.*
[37] Jervis, "Cooperation under the Security Dilemma," 181.

This volume suggests several strategies for managing the "rules of the game" of international order in light of their normative, ideational character. It might be much easier if international norms and rules had no normative weight and were merely on the Pareto frontier of solutions to problems of coordination or collaboration. For many problems of international politics, the latter picture may be more or less true. But this depoliticized view does not seem safe in light of how states and their citizens actually treat institutional orders, nor satisfying from the point of view of actually trying to improve the human condition. What we may need, then, are pragmatic strategies that take account of the normative weight of international institutional orders.

The strategy of *hypocrisy* might prove to be necessary at the margins, just to take account of the realities of shifting political power. It seems better to permit a violation of the territorial integrity norm by a great power if the alternative is a confrontation with the risk of general war. But to go too far with hypocrisy is to refuse to take the normative character of international rules seriously, because it means that words and deeds have no correspondence whatsoever.[38] At a certain point, the norms in question need to be enforced or renegotiated. It is never going to be easy to know where to draw the line, unfortunately.

More satisfying, however, would be to take advantage of the transnational social links embedded in globalization to conduct dialogue about the character of international order and attempt to improve it. States can facilitate this process by making themselves receptive to such debate through the kind of *cultural engagement* that leaves them open to influence. Much of this international engagement will happen (or not) regardless of state policies, but promoting and facilitating international educational exchanges is one step states might take to facilitate global engagement that goes beyond commerce and finance. If sustained, meaningful, and respectful dialogue is a possibility, then current shifts in international power hierarchies may not just be a period that we survive, but one in which we can make matters better.

[38] Lee J. M. Seymour, "Let's Bullshit! Arguing, Bargaining and Dissembling over Darfur," *European Journal of International Relations* 20, no. 3 (September 2014), 571–95.

Index

Abkhazia, 83
accommodation
  bargaining strategies in, 204–05
    costly signaling, 203
    legitimation, 205–19
    self-restraining, 203
    socialization, 205–19
  case studies of, 20–23
  constructivist perspective on, 87–88
  containment and, 150
  definition of, 4–7
  economic, 18, 283–84
  full, 5–6
  by great powers, 293–313
    bargaining with rising powers, 300–02
    demands of rising powers and,
      303–04
    economic accommodation, 302–06
    empathy in, 310–11
    institutional accommodation, 302–06
    normative accommodation, 306–10
    reciprocal socialization in, 310–11
    rising powers and, 294–97
    territorial accommodation, 297–302
  for identity, 203, 205–19
  ideological, 17, 284–86
  ideological/normative, 17, 284–86
  institutional, 18, 93–94, 239–40,
    279–82, 302–06
  for interests, 202–03
  international relations theories on, 7
  liberalism and, 92–99
  non-accommodation and, 6
  non-violent, 7
  normative, 17, 284–86, 306–10
  partial or limited, 6
  peaceful, 91
  realism and, 99–104
  reasons for, 152–53
  region-specific, 6–7
  responsibility for, 87–107
  of rising powers, 1–32

  soft interdependencies and, 65–67
  strategies of, 16–19
  symbolic, 6, 238–39
  territorial, 17–18, 278–79, 297–99,
    300–02
  trade interdependence and, 60–61
  in twenty-first century, 178–97
  vocabulary of, 90–92
Acheson, Dean, 119, 123–24, 125–26
Adams, Brook, 118, 119
Adams, Henry, 118
Afghanistan, 101, 146, 147
Agadir Crisis of 1911, 164
aggression, 44
Ahmadinejad, Mahmoud, 260
Air-Sea Battle (ASB), 37
AJAX/TPAjax, 128
Alaska, 115
Albright, Madeline, 53, 221
Alliance of Civilizations, 286
Al-Qaeda, 217, 218
Amorim, Celso, 252, 253, 262
Angell, Norman, 55
Anglo-American rapprochement
  critique of, 118–23
  Kupchan's account of, 114–17
Anglo-American War debt agreement,
  suspension of, 75, 76–77
Anglo-German Naval Agreement, 169
Anglo-Iranian concession, 123–29
Anglo-Iranian Oil Company (AIOC), 124,
  126
Anglo-Japanese alliance in 1902, 183–84
Anglo-Russian Entente of 1907, 163
Anglo-Saxonism, 116
Annenberg, Walter, 119
anti-access and area denial (A2AD), 49
Arabian-American Oil Company
  (ARAMCO), 124
Argentina, 28
Aritomo, Yamagata, 183
ASEAN Plus Three, 212

314